The Decision Point

*Six Cases in U.S. Foreign Policy
Decision Making*

DAVID PATRICK HOUGHTON
University of Central Florida

New York   Oxford
OXFORD UNIVERSITY PRESS

Oxford University Press is a department of the University of Oxford. It furthers
the University's objective of excellence in research, scholarship, and education by publishing
worldwide.

Oxford   New York
Auckland   Cape Town   Dar es Salaam   Hong Kong   Karachi
Kuala Lumpur   Madrid   Melbourne   Mexico City   Nairobi
New Delhi   Shanghai   Taipei   Toronto

With offices in
Argentina   Austria   Brazil   Chile   Czech Republic   France   Greece
Guatemala   Hungary   Italy   Japan   Poland   Portugal   Singapore
South Korea   Switzerland   Thailand   Turkey   Ukraine   Vietnam

For titles covered by Section 112 of the US Higher Education Opportunity
Act, please visit www.oup.com/us/he for the latest information about
pricing and alternate formats.

Published by Oxford University Press.
198 Madison Avenue, New York, NY 10016
www.oup.com

Oxford is a registered trademark of Oxford University Press.

Library of Congress Cataloging-in-Publication Data
Houghton, David Patrick.
The decision point : six cases in U.S. foreign policy decision making / David Patrick Houghton.
    p. cm.
  Includes bibliographical references and index.
  ISBN 978-0-19-974352-0
  1. United States—Foreign relations—Decision making.   2. United States—Foreign
    relations—Decision making—Case studies.   I. Title.
JZ1480.H68 2012
327.73—dc23
2012010958

For My Parents

BRIEF CONTENTS

CONTENTS

PREFACE

This book is intended as a different kind of introduction to American foreign policy, one whose focus is on the decisions that people in Washington make—and, indeed, on the decision-makers themselves—rather than on broad historical accounts of the general shape that U.S. foreign policy has taken in the past, guides to contemporary issues being debated or detailed accounts of the different institutions, and government offices involved in the policymaking process. I certainly not do find fault with any of these traditions; after all, I was brought up on them as a student and they formed my daily meat as it were. I have myself taught U.S. foreign policy in a variety of ways over the years, sometimes using books that focused on major institutions like the State Department, Pentagon, and CIA, sometimes focusing on the ideas (realism versus liberalism, internationalism versus isolationism and so on) that animate debate about foreign policy in the United States, and at other times surveying the fascinating history of U.S. foreign relations with a particular focus on the Cold War era and how 9/11 has affected policymakers and policymaking. But it has always seemed to me that there is one especially glaring omission from the bookshelves right now: theoretical and case-based analyses of how real U.S. foreign policy decision-makers make real decisions, in both crisis and everyday situations. Of books currently in print, only Robert Strong's excellent *Decisions and Dilemmas* comes close to what I had in mind when I wrote this book, though the former has a more historical (and less theoretical) sweep. *Presidential Decisions for War* by Gary Hess is similarly far more focused on particular theories and cases than this one.

One does not get a sense of how people behave in crisis decisions in many introductions to American foreign policy and in the broader field of Foreign Policy Analysis (hereafter, FPA), where what few general surveys of the field exist often don't show students how to apply theories to cases. While many existing introductory textbooks devote a chapter to decision-making, it's usually very brief, and most focus on Graham Allison's justifiably famous *Essence of Decision*—rebranded in this book as what I call *Homo Bureaucraticus*—with a little bit of psychology thrown in but not a lot. In many ways this is not surprising, since you can't cover everything within the covers of a single book. But I have always believed that there is an enormous gap in the otherwise-very-crowded U.S. foreign policy literature for a book that introduces the reader to a few basic theories of decision-making and applies each of these to a range of historical cases in an understandable and student-friendly way. The basic objective of this book is therefore very simple indeed: it represents a modest attempt to fill in some of the gap. It tries to give students some sense of what it is really like to make high-level decisions, shows how far many of those decisions fall short of the exalted standards of "pure rationality," and suggests ways in which they might apply various decision-making theories to some well-known cases from the recent (and not-so-recent) conduct of U.S. foreign policy.

This, I believe, is how many textbooks originate; the potential author realizes that there is no single book that discusses all the things he wants to impart to his students, and then tries as best he can to write something that will cover the bases. In this instance, having my students purchase the original texts from which my three main models or perspectives draw has in the past also been prohibitively expensive. As the reader will find throughout this book, the three approaches I call *Homo Bureaucraticus, Homo Sociologicus,* and *Homo Psychologicus* form the backbone of everything. One way of teaching the material it covers would be to use original source materials alone—let's say, *Essence of Decision* by Graham Allison and Philip Zelikow, *Groupthink* by Irving Janis, and *Perception and Misperception in International Politics* by Robert Jervis (each of these has a strong claim to represent the so-called bible of one of these perspectives). Brilliant though each of them is, they are pitched at various different audiences and levels of accessibility, none of them was ever intended to be a textbook originally, and none of them provides a straight comparison of different decision-making theories across a range of cases. In the case of *Homo Psychologicus* in particular, there is no single theory that encapsulates the perspective as a whole, at least as it exists today, and the other two perspectives have also moved beyond the books that originally inspired them. Quite apart from those barriers, however, another problem involved in using them at the undergraduate level is the simple problem of cost. Once you factor in additional photocopying of articles and printing costs to update the original works, you have easily spent several hundred dollars. Another simple objective of this book, then, is to provide an economical introduction to decision-making as applied to U.S. foreign policy, one that levels the playing field in terms of accessibility and allows students to compare the performance of the different theories across a range of case studies about which scholars have written.

A few disclaimers can be inferred from what I have said already, but they should probably be made explicit. While the book begins by introducing students to what I consider to be the major approaches to foreign policy decision-making and later applies these to six case studies, there is no special rationale for the selection of the cases other than the fact that (a) most or all have been written about at length in the research world, giving me a literature that I can at least try to summarize for the beginning scholar, and (b) all of them, in my experience, prove interesting to students. Equally, all of them are important enough in their own right to merit study. A few years ago, a White House press secretary in a recent U.S. administration—a lady slightly younger than myself but not much—was honest enough to admit that she did not know what the Cuban missile crisis was when the topic came up in a press briefing (this case is the subject, by the way, of chap. 6). Ignorance of the past is not an isolated phenomenon, though, and many of my past students have admitted with similar candor that they were entirely unacquainted not only with the missile crisis case but also Vietnam and the Iran hostage crisis before taking my classes. Setting aside what I now know and placing myself in the shoes of the person I used to be, I can also remember a time when I knew very little about these cases too. So a final objective of this book is to help out, in my own small way, the thousands of educators who try to keep these cases alive in the minds of students who are too young to have personal memories of the events they refer to. They are relevant today for a lot of reasons, but the foremost from my perspective in this book is that they help us understand how organizations, groups, and individual psychology operate in the real world.

A number of people were kind enough to read the manuscript and help me knock it into shape. Most helpful was my then Graduate Teaching Assistant, Heather Crowe, now working at the Hudson Institute's Center for Political Military Analysis in Washington, DC. Heather diligently plowed through the manuscript almost in its entirety, helping me edit out my various gaffes and glitches with a hawk's eye, and making some very useful comments about the various chapters, many of which have been incorporated into the text. Her enthusiasm was infectious and kept me going through the whole lengthy process of generating a first draft. I also "road tested" parts of this manuscript in the fall of 2010 in my *Seminar in International Politics* class at the University of Central Florida, and particular thanks are due to the members of that class for their often very useful suggestions as to how the early chapters on Cuba, Vietnam, and Iran might be improved. Allysa Bowers, Joshua Edson, Robert Fuhrer, David Glassner, Nikki Hughes, Matt Kiernan, Michael Kyryliw, Travis Large, Ari Litwin, Nathalia Martens, Lauren Michalski, Nodwarang Niamvanichkul, Roger Powell, Jennifer Sanguilliano, Sabrina Stein, and Miguel Ubiles all gave me a great sense of how the things I'd written would play in the real world of the classroom, and I'm grateful to them all for being *The Decision Point*'s guinea pigs. (Special thanks to Matt Kiernan for the liquid inspiration he has sometimes provided since he stopped being my student.) One of my undergraduates, Matty Robin, also deserves a special mention for helping me research the Kosovo case that appears in chapter 9. I had lived through that case study from afar but was not at that time much acquainted with the details behind the decision-making. Matty's runs to the university library and trawls across the Internet guaranteed that I got off to a good start. I would like to thank the following reviewers: Joe Clare, Louisiana State University; Renato Corbetta, University of Alabama–Birmingham; Kenneth Cosgrove, Suffolk University; Jalele Erega Defa, University of Nebraska–Lincoln and Addis Ababa University;

Christopher J. Fettweis, Tulane University; V. Nicholas Galasso, University of Delaware; Laura V. Gonzalez-Murphy, State University of New York at Albany; Anna N. Gregg, Austin Peay State University; Michael D. Kanner, University of Colorado, Boulder; Douglas W. Kuberski, Texas A&M University; Stephen D. Morris, Middle Tennessee State University; Jason J. Morrissette, Marshall University; Glenn Palmer, Penn State University; Leanne C. Powner, University of Michigan; Jungkun Seo, University of North Carolina, Wilmington; Becky Steffenson, DePaul University; Brent Strathman, Dartmouth College; Adam Van Liere, University of North Carolina at Greensboro; and Kristen P. Williams, Clark University. Finally, heartfelt thanks are due to various anonymous reviewers, many of whose comments I benefited from greatly, and of course to Jennifer Carpenter, David Wharton, and Maegan Sherlock at OUP. Jennifer prodded me again and again to write this book, even when I wasn't sure that I wanted to publish another textbook. Maegan, meanwhile, shepherded me through the remainder of the process, diligently reminding me of deadlines coming up in the publication process and making sure that I stayed on the straight and narrow. Students have professors to ensure that they turn in work on time, but who makes sure that professors do the same? Often, the answer is that publishers do!

I cannot close this brief preface without paying tribute to Professor Roger Handberg, who has just retired as chairman of the Department of Political Science here at University of Central Florida. Without going into too many details, it is no exaggeration to say that this book was written during what was certainly the most difficult and personally painful period of my life. Roger was a constant source of support during this period, and he helped shepherd the department through the beginning of what was (and will continue to be) one of the most astonishing periods of change it has ever witnessed. This university has been transformed almost unrecognizably during the last eight or nine years I have been employed here, and thanks to Roger's vision and the forward-thinking of people like Dean Peter Panousis (also recently dispatched to well-earned retirement) I am now surrounded by brilliant colleagues like Mark Schafer, Tom Dolan, Peter Jacques, Nikola Mirilovic, Myunghee Kim, Paul Vasquez, Anca Turcu, Kurt Young, Quan Li, Nathan Ilderton, and Andrea Vieux, none of whom were here when I arrived for my second teaching stint in the United States back in 2003. If we can keep them, I think they will really make the Department of Political Science's new PhD program in International Security Studies work and hopefully put us on the map, if readers will forgive me the use of an old cliché. I suppose every textbook deserves at least one.

Finally, I will end with a little story about the title of this book, which the reader may find amusing, concerning a piece of information that came my way after I had signed the contract to write it. When the signing took place, I had written very little of the manuscript apart from a prospectus indicating the title, what each chapter would be about, and what the target audience was. In other words, the book itself was little more than a twinkle in my eye at the time. But I knew exactly what I was going to put into it, and the structure was set in my mind. I also had developed a very firm idea about the title itself. What should it be called? I had considered variations on the "think" part of groupthink but ruled those out as too Orwellian. Graham Allison's *Essence of Decision* had been written years ago, so that was definitely out, but something *like* that—something that would, in a sense, pay tribute to that famous work—was what I was after. *Moment of Decision* sounded corny. I then considered *Point of Decision*, but it didn't quite sound right, mostly because I have never really heard anyone talk about "points of decision" as such. In the end of course, I plumped for *The Decision Point*, which I was more than happy with and not just because it's a term I have increasingly heard other scholars use in recent years. Turning on *CNN* at some point in the summer of 2010 I heard the news that George W. Bush would be publishing his presidential memoirs. This came as no great surprise, since pretty much everyone who has occupied the Oval Office eventually puts out a memoir of his time there (whether or not he has actually written the thing himself). But my jaw dropped when I heard that the title of his book was to be *Decision Points*! "Damn," I said, or something to that effect.

As you can see from the cover of the book, though, I decided to keep the existing title. For one thing, the two titles are not identical, and the cover of this book looks nothing like the one George W. Bush chose. There is a partial overlap of the subject matter in chapter 10, where the former president's book is actually cited, but there all substantive similarity ends as well. More decisive in my mind, though—if you'll again pardon the pun—is the fact that no one remembers the titles of presidential memoirs anyway. They typically have a very short shelf-life, selling millions in the first year but then increasingly consigned to the bargain tables as another incumbent takes over and memories of his predecessor (as well as general interest in him) begins to fade. Who remembers what Jimmy Carter called the memoir he published after leaving office, for instance? Who even remembers what the one Bill Clinton authored was called? Did George H. W. Bush write one at all? Only a few people can remember, so *The Decision Point* it is. More importantly, I hope you enjoy reading the contents.

David Patrick Houghton
Orlando, March 2012

PART 1

Theories

CHAPTER 1

Introduction

This is a book about how foreign policy decisions are made at the top pinnacles of American government. The design of the book is quite straightforward; I make use of the three most prominent or best-known theoretical models in the study of foreign policy decision-making—the bureaucratic politics perspective, the groupthink approach, and the cognitive/emotional approach—and apply each of these to six prominent case studies in the history of American foreign policy: the Bay of Pigs episode in 1961, the Cuban missile crisis of 1962, the Vietnam escalations of 1965, the Iran hostage crisis of 1979–81, the Kosovo crisis of 1999, and the 2003 decision to invade Iraq. Each of these perspectives will be used to try to throw light on that rather mysterious moment of presidential choice, the *decision point* at which a leader or group of advisers decides that "we are going to do Y" or that "X is going to occur." Every U.S. president, whether he likes it or not, must eventually make some very hard decisions about intervening (or not intervening) in the rest of the world. America's rise as a global hegemon—indeed, its continued status as the world's only remaining superpower—has meant that other entities look to the United States (and in particular, to its presidents) to act when trouble spots appear around the world. An American president may come to office armed with a well-thought-out set of precepts about what he wants to do in foreign policy, as Richard Nixon did when he took the presidential oath in 1969 and as George H. W. Bush did in 1989; or he may come to the presidency hoping to put foreign policy issues on the back burner while urgent domestic problems are addressed, as did Lyndon Johnson in 1963 and Bill Clinton in 1992. But either way, he inevitably ends up making a range of decisions that impact the rest of the world, whether he wants to or not.

In a sense, of course, we can never know exactly what goes through the head of a president as he makes the fateful decision to commit troops, or launch a covert operation, or to save foreign citizens from a genocide. And we can never be 100 percent sure of the group or organizational pressures that compelled him in one direction or another (and, if they did exert an effect, *how much* of an effect). Probably only President John Kennedy knew exactly why he had decided to sponsor a CIA-led invasion at the Bay of Pigs in 1961, for instance. Only President Jimmy Carter really knows why he decided to launch an aborted rescue mission to save U.S. hostages being held in Tehran in 1980. And only President George W. Bush knows for sure why he decided to invade Iraq in 2003. Obviously, we can never acquire real certainty about these things, even in retrospect. What we can do, however, is to reconstruct the reasoning processes of top decision-makers after the fact, using documentary sources and interviews to piece together the facts. Of course, even when we do this there is always ample room for disagreement as to what those facts are, and one purpose of this book is to show you how the same decision point can be explained from several theoretical perspectives simultaneously.

THE TRADITIONS OF FOREIGN POLICY DECISION-MAKING

This book is far from being the first to ponder questions like these, and it will almost certainly not be the last. In fact, scholars of international relations have been studying foreign policy decision-making since as far back as the early 1950s, and so a birds-eye view of the main developments and trends in the field since its earliest beginnings is in order before we get into the details. The earliest literature within the study of how foreign policy is made drew upon what we term here the *Homo Psychologicus* tradition, emphasizing the subjective nature of many international political phenomena and the differing ways in which rival decision-makers perceive the world around them. Snyder, Bruck, and Sapin's work in particular (though it is sadly little read today) set the tone of what was to come. Their book *Foreign Policy Decision-Making*, which originally appeared in 1954, was and remains the formative work on this subject (Snyder, Bruck, and Sapin 1962). Much existing work within international relations at that point assumed that states made foreign policy decisions by responding quite rationally to whatever their objective national interests happened to be. The central idea of *Foreign Policy Decision-Making*— one of the first books to blend elements of psychology into the analysis of foreign policy—is the now well-known concept of the definition of the situation. As Richard Snyder notes in his introduction to the 1962 edition, "it is difficult to see how we can account for specific actions and for continuities of policies without trying to discover how their operating environments are perceived by those responsible for choices, how particular situations are structured, what values and norms are applied to certain kinds of problems, what matters are selected for attention, and how their past experience conditions present responses" (Snyder, Bruck, and Sapin 1962, 5). In other words, we do not apprehend the world "out there" directly; we always look at it subjectively, through our own very personal and sometimes rather distorted set of psychological lenses. Snyder, Bruck, and Sapin urge us to try to re-create the world of the decision-makers, not as it objectively was—assuming that we could know that—but as *they* viewed it: "The manner in which they define situations becomes another way of saying how the state oriented to action and why." The task is to reconstruct the constructions of foreign policy elites, showing how "of all the phenomena which *might* have been relevant, the actors the decision-makers finally endow only some with *significance*" (Snyder et al. 2002, 70).

Joseph de Rivera's *The Psychological Dimension of Foreign Policy* continued this tradition during the late 1960s and may be regarded as another foundational text in the history of foreign policy analysis (de Rivera 1968). He discusses the subjectivity of many phenomena in international relations: "It is difficult even to intellectually grasp the fact that we construct the reality in which we operate. We take our perception of the world for granted," de Rivera notes. "We know what is real. We live in this reality and act accordingly" (De Rivera, 1968, 21). Major contributions to this approach were also made by figures like Alexander George with his work on operational codes (George 1969), Ole Holsti on beliefs and images (Holsti 1969), and Robert Jervis on the consequences of the human tendency to seek cognitive consistency in international politics (Jervis 1976). More recently, work on schema theory and the related topic of analogical reasoning has dominated this approach (Larson 1985; Khong 1992), and today attention is increasingly focusing on the part played by emotion in decision-making. This body of theory is discussed more fully in chapter 4.

During the early 1970s another (far less psychological) tradition began to take root in foreign policy analysis. Unlike the previous approach, what I call here the *Homo Bureaucraticus* tradition draws upon organizational theory and practitioner observations about how governments really work, providing a second perspective upon which we will draw in this book. Originally developed by Graham Allison in his classic book *Essence of Decision* and by Morton Halperin in *Bureaucratic Politics and Foreign Policy*, this perspective understands foreign policy as organizational products, treating foreign policy decisions as the outcomes that result from bureaucratic bargaining and organizational routines (Allison and Zelikow 1999; Halperins 1974). The approach has become especially associated with the axiom "where you stand depends on where you sit," the view that the policy positions or beliefs of decision-makers are often shaped by their position within the government (one's vantage point, in other words, determines the side of the issue one sees). *Homo Bureaucraticus* is the subject of chapter 2.

At about the same time that the bureaucratic politics perspective became popular, Irving Janis would take foreign policy back in a psychological direction, albeit in a rather different way than previous scholars of foreign policy analysis had done. Janis was a social psychologist who became fascinated by the array of foreign policy fiascoes he had observed in postwar American foreign policy: U.S. military personnel famously failed to heed warnings that the Japanese were about to attack Pearl Harbor in 1941, for instance. Why? John Kennedy gave the go-ahead to a disastrous attempt to invade Cuba and depose its leader Fidel Castro in 1961, despite many indications available to him at the time that the plan would not work; and Lyndon Johnson decided to escalate U.S. involvement in Vietnam, despite warnings that the war there could not easily be won without enormous cost to the United States in both blood and treasure, and predictions from both civilian and military advisers that the war would be long and drawn-out. These ultimately rather prescient warnings were considered but ultimately rejected, resulting in the deaths of 58,000 Americans by the time U.S. troops were withdrawn and millions of Vietnamese. Why, Janis asked, had our foreign policy leaders so often "got it wrong"? Founding a tradition I call *Homo Sociologicus* (discussed in chap. 3), Janis traced the cause of all of these fiascoes to a process he called *groupthink* (Janis 1982). Although Janis himself did apply his theory to domestic cases, within political science it has exerted its greatest impact upon the study of foreign policy decision-making. Janis illustrated his theory with a range of examples—including the Pearl Harbor, Bay of Pigs and Vietnam cases—and contrasts this with what he calls *vigilant appraisal* in which decision-makers rigorously and thoroughly consider all possible options; he holds up the Cuban missile crisis of October 1962 as a notable instance of a case in which this kind of superior process occurred.

The work of Snyder and his colleagues, as well as James Rosenau's later "pre-theory" of foreign policy (Rosenau 1966), reflected the earnest hope that Foreign Policy Analysis (FPA) would one day derive a series of finding which would put the discipline on a scientific footing, as long as it was studied with sufficient care and rigor using the appropriate methodological techniques. This approach is loosely referred to in political science as *positivism*, and it uses the natural sciences as a model for how we should garner knowledge about the social world. This first generation was concerned that research about foreign policy decisions never seemed to accumulate, since it tended to be based on single case studies; its members therefore sought to employ more rigorous techniques instead, using quantitative (statistical) approaches instead of qualitative ones (Neack, Hey, and Haney 1995,3). There was always a tension here, however; much of mainstream political science suggested that concrete behavior should be the focus of study, not the ways in which actors described themselves or their beliefs; and yet actors' self-descriptions became a major focus of study in the new approach. Perhaps problematically, if one treats international relations (IR) as an objective science of explanation while simultaneously stressing the ways in which decision-makers have access only to subjective and often flawed beliefs, one places oneself on a higher philosophical plane than the decision-makers themselves; in this original positivist form, the approach seemed to simultaneously suggest that decision-makers lived in a *subjective reality* while political science scholars lived in an *objective* one.

Ultimately, the first-generation attempt to turn FPA into a science failed. Second-generation analysts have certainly not abandoned the search for a single, unified theory of foreign policy altogether and have certainly not abandoned the search for explanation, but their methods nowadays are a mixture of the neo-positivist and the postpositivist. Methodologically, the second generation is far more eclectic than the first, with some scholars continuing to employ advanced statistical procedures, while others have returned to the more traditional qualitative case study approach. The field today consists of a continuing proliferation of old-fashioned, context. or area-specific case studies. and often sophisticated but context or area-specific statistical analyses (Hudson 2007, 27–31).

Homo Economicus or the Rational Actor Model (RAM)

To appreciate how radical the approaches we have just briefly alluded to were at the time—and, indeed, how they remain so today—we need to detail the ways in which they question key assumptions, which have underlain a great deal of theorizing in the field of international relations. Many analysts with this field assume that states are rational, unitary actors, an approach sometimes known as *Homo Economicus* because many of these assumptions are derived from microeconomics or classical economics. It is also commonly known as the *Rational Actor Model* (RAM), because it essentially assumes that decision-making involves both an ordered and an orderly process in which the participants behave rationally (Allison and Zelikow 1999). This approach makes a number of assumptions about both state and human behavior, which are listed in figure 1.1.

In *Essence of Decision*, Graham Allison famously noted that most analysts (as well as laypeople) consciously or unconsciously make use of this approach, which he terms Model I in his book, when they seek to explain why a particular state acted as it did. When we do this, we ask ourselves what *goals* or objectives the state had in mind; in other words, we reason backwards, reconstructing the decision-making process as if the state were a single person with highly efficient reasoning capacities. This is known as the unified actor assumption. As Morton Halperin puts it:

> In trying to explain foreign policy decisions, most observers assume that decision makers are motivated by a single set of national security images and foreign policy goals. Supposedly decisions reflect these goals alone, and actions are presumed to flow directly from the decisions. Thus "explanation" consists of identifying the interests of the nation as seen by the leaders and showing they determine the decisions and actions of the government. ... This type of analysis is the pervasive form of explanation for foreign policy actions of the United States and other governments (Halperin 1974, 4).

- The state behaves as a unitary actor, acting and speaking with one voice.
- Decision-makers are comprehensively "rational" actors.
- Decision-makers are assumed to possess perfect information.
- The decision-makers generate a list of all available options, and they then weigh up the costs and benefits of various options.
- Decision-makers collectively select that alternative which delivers the greatest benefits relative to cost (maximizes "subjective utility").
- Decision-makers update their beliefs when new information becomes available.

Figure 1.1 *Homo Economicus* or the Rational Actor Model (RAM).

Under the RAM or *Homo Economicus*, the state is assumed to be act rationally in the sense that its decision-makers are assumed to share clear objectives, and that they collectively weigh up the costs and benefits of each alternative means of getting to that objective. Having done this, they (the government) then selects the "utility-maximizing choice" (a phrase from classical economics and equivalent in common English usage to "the best choice, given what your goals are"). When new information becomes available, moreover, *Homo Economicus* assumes that people simply update their beliefs accordingly; indeed, if the information in question is sufficiently earth-shattering, decision-makers may change track, altering the original decision made.

These assumptions may seem unrealistic to you, but the advocates of this approach are not fools. Some economists and devotees of the rational choice approach to political science treat this model as if it were a literal depiction of how states and policymakers behave, arguing that any psychological biases and/ or dysfunctional features of the decision-making process effectively cancel one another out. While they do not deny that human beings are fallible in some ways, in the long run at least the state tends to respond rationally and predictably when confronted with a particular situation. Others, however, use it as a set of simplifying assumptions in the full knowledge that these assumptions do not describe the ways people behave in the real world; they are, however, prepared to sacrifice a measure of accuracy in the expectation that doing so will generate powerful models and predictions. *Homo Economicus* offers a useful set of assumptions for some political scientists, and its great strength lies in the fact that it provides a way of simplifying human behavior in a way that makes it predictable. It appeals to those who want to model decision-making (and, more generally, political behavior) in a straightforward, parsimonious way. However, even some economists have begun to question the utility of simplifying reality this way (a school of thought known as behavioral economics). Indeed, what unites devotees of these theories is precisely this reaction against oversimplification. *Homo Psychologicus, Homo Sociologicus,* and *Homo Bureaucraticus* are all decidedly empirical in nature; in other words, they are concerned with describing and explaining how political agents in foreign policy *actually do* behave and not primarily with how they *ought* to. Nor are they interested in making simplifying assumptions for the sake of parsimony. Of course, doing this makes things messy; as soon as the complexity and greater realism of these other approaches is conceded, it becomes clear that much of human behavior is idiosyncratic and unpredictable. This, however, is a price most scholars of foreign policy decision-making are prepared to pay.

THREE ALTERNATIVES TO *HOMO ECONOMICUS*

In important but very different ways, each of the three models of foreign policy decision-making we shall examine and apply in this book departs markedly from the Rational Actor or *Homo Economicus* perspective. Each attacks the bundle of assumptions that collectively make up that approach from a different level of analysis, however, and summarizing these will provide a handy way of briefly introducing each approach to you. A much fuller description of each approach will be provided in chapters 2–4, but for now—and to get a flavor of what is to come—consider the following thumbnail sketches of each.

Homo Bureaucraticus

Unlike those of *Homo Economicus*, the insights of *Homo Bureaucraticus* are mainly derived from organizational theory. The latter begins from the position that the analogy between states and individuals is flawed; states are composed of multiple, competing actors, which often pursue different objectives and priorities. This fragmentation of authority and power, and the competition that often goes on inside America's foreign policy machinery, has some important consequences. The most notable of these is that our foreign policies are often not the result of any single person's intentions, nor is policymaking an entirely rational process. Instead, decisions often take one of two forms. Sometimes, they take the form of bureaucratic compromises or bargains between the competing agencies of government. The representatives of bureaucratic units are often parochial and look after their own organization's interests, seeing these as synonymous with the national interest because that is the perspective that their own perch within the government offers. What looks to an outsider like a reasoned and considered action by a head of state, though, may actually represent the outcome of bureaucratic bargaining or what Graham Allison famously described as "pulling and hauling" between agencies. This kind of decision is termed a bureaucratic *resultant* (Allison and Zelikow 1999, 294–96). Decisions can end up being the least common denominator (that thing which everyone can agree upon, but which may satisfy no one), or a collage (something pieced together from bits of what each organization wants). The possibility exists that the processes of bureaucratic bargaining and compromise may produce an outcome (or decision) that *no one* actually favors. American foreign policy can end up looking very much like a patchwork quilt, with something for everyone. Or perhaps more typically, it can reflect the preferences of the winners in the interdepartmental disputes, with the president—especially if he is disengaged from the process—becoming little more than a bystander attempting to referee a process, which he is barely able to control, from the shadows. Alternatively, a government decision may simply reflect what a particular organization, which happens to be dominant in that sphere of policymaking, can do or is accustomed to doing. Foreign policy is also sometimes the result of mindless organizational routines or standard operating procedures (SOPs). In *Essence of Decision,* this kind of decision is described as an organizational *output* (Allison and Zelikow 1999, 168–76).

Anyone who has ever been frustrated by a faceless bureaucracy knows that organizations are certainly capable of some pretty odd behaviors. They are especially adept at defensive maneuvers in the face of imminent change. The invention of motor vehicles (especially the tank) posed a profound challenge the U.S. cavalry, for instance. It is said that when this technological innovation threatened to make horses obsolete as a means of military transport, the cavalry initially reacted to mechanization by suggesting that the horses could simply be placed on the backs of trucks! Clinging to existing ways of doing things is in a sense efficient; after all, no one wants to go to the trouble of constantly reinventing the wheel. It is in some ways quite rational to keep a series of plans and procedures on the shelf, as it were, since these can simply be pulled down as and when needed. We want agencies to retain some sort of organizational memory, since the alternative (a kind of bureaucratic amnesia) is obviously undesirable. The problem comes when organizations fail to adapt to genuinely new challenges; they usually change only incrementally, and once established they can be difficult to get rid of or reorganize. Consider, for instance, the Bush administration's attempt to reform the U.S. intelligence community, a change that the 9/11 Commission had argued was essential in order to improve information sharing among agencies. The attacks of September 11 2001, the commission suggested, could have been prevented if the various agencies of American government, many of which possessed vital clues as to what the radical Islamic terrorists were planning to do, had pooled together what they knew and considered the evidence *in toto*. But while some changes did occur, organizations like the FBI and CIA successfully resisted a fundamental overhaul of their fiefdoms; the main change was arguably the introduction of the Department of Homeland Security, which a cynic might see as just another layer of bureaucracy.

Another problem arises during the competition over resources and control to which we have alluded, a consequence of the fragmentation of the executive branch and of the simple fact that many agencies hold power simultaneously. It can be damaging, moreover, when an agency which has won out in the process of pulling and hauling takes control of a bureaucratic task that another agency is far better suited to undertake. The postwar reconstruction of Iraq provides a case in point. The State Department had developed fairly elaborate reconstruction plans as contingencies should a U.S.-led invasion of Iraq take place, a series of strategies which were collectively known as the "Future of Iraq" project. These plans were resisted by the Pentagon, however, which under Secretary of Defense Donald Rumsfeld successfully lobbied to have them shelved altogether (Packer 2005; Phillips 2006). The Defense Department was working on the assumption that the occupation of Iraq would be a brief affair and that essential services within the country would not be much affected; as it happened, however, much of Iraq was derived of electricity and water for months on end as Pentagon officials struggled to cobble together ad hoc plans on the spot. An ill-considered and overzealous "de-Ba'athification" process also fuelled a Sunni insurgency, which would bedevil U.S. efforts in Iraq for a number of years.

Homo Sociologicus

There are other potential problems with the RAM as well that give rise to a second major critique, which we term *Homo Sociologicus* in this book. Despite the terminology employed here, this tradition derives not from sociology as an academic field but from social psychology (although the former has some close affinities with the latter).[1] *Homo Economicus* says relatively little about the precise conditions under which members of a decision-making group actually reason, but in general it implies that members of that group either reason individually and then come together to express their individual preferences collectively—individual preferences somehow get aggregated—or else that they reason collectively in the first place in a way that allows the free expression of all preferences and opinions. This sounds like a reasonable approach. How, then, might it be mistaken?

Briefly stated, in the real world of decision-making, *social pressures matter*: individuals do not usually make decisions on their own. For a variety of reasons, decisions are frequently made in groups, and the key point to notice here is that individuals often behave *differently* in a group context than they would when acting alone. This is the starting point for *Homo Sociologicus*. Group-derived and broader social pressures may induce the actor to behave in nonrational ways, even contrary to his or her beliefs and values. Policy alternatives may not be explored if they violate the group consensus. Decision-makers may fail to even voice their private concerns about the group's chosen course of action. Some members of a decision-making group may also take it upon themselves to police the existing consensus by knocking down any dissent from the favored course of action. Such individuals have been termed "mindguards" (Janis 1982).

The existence of powerful dynamics within groups gives *Homo Sociologicus* its distinctive character. Rather than focusing on the ways that interorganizational rivalries can distort policymaking, this second perspective stresses the role that social pressures toward conformity within a group can play in influencing individual judgment. Instead of the differences of view that rival organizational cultures can sometimes promote, interorganizational meetings can often be characterized by a drive toward agreement and consensus in a way that stifles debate. Indeed, so powerful can these group-derived forces be that they may prompt us to ignore our own beliefs and even the evidence of our own eyes. Janis was strongly influenced by the work of Solomon Asch, who had conducted some pathbreaking research in this vein. In a series of famous line experiments, Asch showed that subjects could be induced to give what they knew were blatantly wrong answers to simple questions when other group members did so as well (see fig. 1.2). In one variation of his experiment, Asch would fill a room with six individuals. One individual was a so-called naïve subject who had no idea what was going on, but the other five were actors who had been trained to give certain responses on cue. They were shown a series of cards similar to the one shown in figure 1.2, and each member of the group would be asked to state which line in Exhibit 2 was equivalent in length to the one in Exhibit 1. This is of course a simple task, and most small children can perform it successfully without much difficulty. But Asch put the cards and actors to fascinating use.

To begin with, Asch had the five actors give the correct responses to the card tasks, so that the subject could also follow along without feeling any social pressure to conform or would not suspect that anything untoward was happening. But then he did something rather tricky; he got the actors to deliberately give the

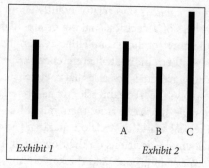

Figure 1.2 Solomon Asch's Line Experiments.

wrong answers, giving responses that were obviously incorrect. The purpose of this experiment, of course, was to see what the naïve subjects would do. Would they speak out against the majority, perhaps even denouncing their stupidity? Or would they quietly go along with it, doubting the evidence of their own eyes and/or going along with the group so as not to rock the boat? Amazingly, Asch found that many subjects did the latter. Participants in one version of this experiment provided incorrect responses on a high proportion of the questions (32 percent), while 75 percent of the participants gave an incorrect answer to at least one question.

Are elite-level decision-makers any more immune to these kind of social pressures than ordinary subjects examined in a laboratory? *Homo Sociologicus* suggests that they are not. Irving Janis showed that when placed under intense social pressure to conform to the majority view in a foreign policy setting, most individuals will cave in to this pressure much in the way that Asch's subjects did. In 1941 the U.S. naval fleet was destroyed by Japanese forces at Pearl Harbor in Hawaii. Policymakers in Washington had repeatedly warned the on-site commander, Admiral Joseph Kimmel, that the Japanese were preparing to attack. However, Kimmel and his colleagues seem to have been laboring under the misapprehension that the fleet was immune from attack, or at least that such an attack was very unlikely. What Irving Janis calls an "illusion of invulnerability" appears to have been present within the group, and he notes that this illusion is almost always a cause for concern. Groups that are highly cohesive may come to believe that they are not only invulnerable but morally superior to their adversaries, refusing to countenance outside views or warnings that disaster is imminent. The group that discounted the advice emanating from Washington seems to have exhibited just these characteristics.

As we will see in chapter 5, Arthur Schlesinger harbored strong doubts about the wisdom of the Bay of Pigs operation in 1961 but never really voiced these doubts in any forceful way. In the language of Janis's theory, he engaged in *self-censorship*. Similarly, during the decision-making within the U.S. space community about whether to launch the space shuttle *Challenger* in January 1986, a senior engineer by the name of Roger Boisjoly was among those who warned NASA officials that unusually low temperatures at Cape Canaveral on the planned launch date could cause a catastrophic accident. Given a final opportunity to object to the launch going ahead, however, Boisjoly fell silent, bowing to the social pressure to conform he undoubtedly felt all around him. Both the Bay of Pigs and *Challenger* episodes ended in disaster, largely for reasons that Schlesinger and Boijoly had foreseen.

Janis coined the term "groupthink" to describe this kind of pressure toward conformity. He defined the groupthink phenomenon as a process through which a group reaches a hasty or premature consensus and then becomes closed to outside ideas or alternative thoughts within. The effort to achieve unanimity and agreement overrides the desire to consider a full range of policy alternatives. High group cohesion or excessive *camaraderie* lies at the heart of the groupthink phenomenon and may develop where the members think too much alike or have developed powerful links of friendship or collegiality, all of which inhibit the challenging of assumptions. While Janis did not feel that groupthink was inevitable in such a situation, he maintained that this kind of group can fall victim to groupthink where members of the group come to prize "concurrence-seeking" (unanimity or agreement) over the comprehensive, rational consideration of all available courses of action.

Homo Psychologicus

Imagine that you want to make a fully rational, fully informed decision about where to eat tonight, and that you have decided to eat out rather than at home. To meet the standard of pure rationality, you would in principle have to read all the menus of all the cafes and restaurants in your town or city. You would have to taste the various dishes in each dining option that night, comparing taste and quality and price, and deciding which represented the optimal choice given your preferences. In that way, you would (as economists put it) "maximize your utility," selecting the best option relative to its cost. Of course, in the real world, human beings very rarely behave this way. The neuroscientist Antonio Damasio has suggested that practically the only individuals who actually make decisions in this laborious, time-consuming way are people who have experienced damage to the prefrontal cortex, an area of the brain located at just about eye level, that is closely associated with emotions and decision-making. In his book *Descartes' Error*, Damasio relates the story of a brain-damaged patient whom he calls "Elliot" (Damasio 1994). When asked to set up a time for his next appointment, Elliot begins an all-encompassing attempt lasting several hours to weigh up the pros and cons of every conceivable date in his diary, until his exhausted doctors ask him to stop. What psychologically normal decision-makers do instead is to process information by means of what are generally called cognitive short cuts or heuristics. These are devices for prematurely cutting short the search for information, tactics that allow us to reach a reasonable decision more quickly and expeditiously than we could if we were to replicate Elliot's approach. Such shortcuts represent the basis of the *Homo Psychologicus* approach.

Homo Psychologicus, a perspective derived primarily from cognitive science and neuroscience, treats decision-makers as "boundedly rational" actors (Simon

1957, 1983). Decision-makers are assumed to possess only imperfect information, and there are limits to our cognitive processing capabilities. As already noted, the decision-maker employs various cognitive shortcuts when generating a list of available alternatives. Not all conceivable alternatives are fully considered, and the decision-maker often selects that alternative which is 'good enough'(the actor "satisfices" instead of maximizing utility, to use Herbert Simon's phrase). Moreover, decision-makers often fail to update their beliefs in response to new information, an approach that lies in direct contradiction to *Homo Economicus*. Emotions, which are also largely ignored by the Rational Actor Model, may drive decision-making as well.

To employ but one example, decision-makers in foreign policy very often cut short the process of exhaustively considering the information at hand by falling back on the use of historical analogies (Khong 1992: Hemmer 2000; Houghton 2001). This approach emphasizes the cognitive limitations of all human beings, including top-level decision-makers. Our basic difficulty is that the human mind can handle only so much; we are often either bombarded by information or sometimes our uncertainty arises from the fact that we have too little information. Faced with this dilemma, we often unconsciously cut a path through complexity and ambiguity by resorting to cognitive shortcuts. Analogical reasoning is one such device, and when we use it we—again, often unconsciously—ask ourselves "what does this look like to me?" What, in other words, can we find in our past experiences, which might throw light upon the situation at hand? Faced with a complex situation in the Middle East in 1990, George H. W. Bush very often used the Munich or World War II analogy, frequently comparing Iraq's President Saddam Hussein to Adolf Hitler and implying that if Saddam were not stopped in his tracks, he would rampage across the Middle East much as Hitler had done in the Europe of the 1930s.

Decision-makers very often fail to update their beliefs in the way that *Homo Economicus* suggests that they do. The latter approach assumes that when new information comes along, which should cause us to revise our interpretation of the situation and evaluation of available facts, we do in fact take this new information on board and respond appropriately. However, *Homo Psychologicus* fundamentally questions this assumption, arguing that in real life people frequently cling to their existing beliefs and preconceptions, often rationalizing away the new information as insignificant or explaining it away so as to preserve their existing attitudes and mind-sets. According to the theory of cognitive consistency, inconsistencies between our beliefs, or between our beliefs and our behavior, cause us to experience an uncomfortable state of tension, at least if we are made aware of our inconsistencies. The social psychologist Leon Festinger famously referred to this condition as *cognitive dissonance*, a term that has since entered the English language (though it is not always used in precisely the way he intended). Since we generally do not like to be inconsistent, we become motivated to reduce dissonance in some way and bring things back into balance or consonance (Festinger 1957).

The Marian Keech story illustrates this tendency in an especially striking way (Festinger et al. 1956). During the 1950s, Festinger infiltrated a religious cult, whose leader "Marian Keech" was predicting the end of the world (her name was changed in Festinger's book to protect her identity). Keech specifically predicted that the world would come to an end on December 21, 1954, but she also prophesied that a flying saucer would pick up the "true believers" on December 20, thus saving them from all the death and devastation that would befall the rest of the world. Many members of the group had invested a lot in Keech's prediction; they had given up their jobs, given away their savings, and had sold their houses in preparation for the coming of the flying saucer. For Festinger, this represented a tantalizing scenario for the testing of his theories. He knew—or at least strongly suspected!—that the flying saucer would never show up, and this in fact proved to be the case.

But what fascinated Festinger was what the group members would do when their theory proved false. How would they handle the news? When the saucer failed to show, Keech had a new (and rather convenient) "vision from God" shortly before 5 a.m. on the December 21, saying that "everyone was saved." The group members then rationalized away the evidence that they had been wrong all along, and for some the saucer's non-appearance even strengthened their belief in the cult! While it would be easy to dismiss the members of the group as simply crazy, Festinger thought that this incident actually illustrates a very common and very human psychological tendency. While *Homo Economicus* suggests that we just update our beliefs when our theories are disconfirmed, Festinger argued that in reality we usually just ignore or try to somehow explain away dissonant information. We bring things back into balance, in other words, by coming up with some sort of psychologically comforting excuse. In a foreign policy context, Ole Holsti famously showed how Secretary of State John Foster Dulles preserved his uncompromising belief that Communism represented a moral evil by explaining away any indication that the Soviets were seeking *détente* with the United States as an indication of Soviet weakness (Holsti 1969). Similarly, as we shall see in chapter 10, there are some indications that Vice-President Dick Cheney and others engaged in similar rationalizations after invading U.S. forces failed to find evidence of Iraqi weapons of mass destruction (such as the highly dubious yet psychologically comforting claim that Saddam had simply moved his weapons to a neighboring state such as Syria before the war began).

LEVELS OF ANALYSIS

Conventionally, students of foreign policy analysis analyze the behavior of states and policymakers by looking at the variety of causal factors or levels of analysis which might shape that behavior (Singer 1961; Rosenau 1966). Many *system level* theories of international relations argue that we can explain a great deal by knowing a state's position (or its degree of power) within the international system. For example, superpowers behave very much like one another throughout world history, and the United States and the Soviet Union engaged in rather similar behaviors during the Cold War. Others object that we cannot really explain very much about a state's behavior without knowing what *kind* of state we are dealing with. This may seem like a far-fetched example, but suppose for a moment that Canada and the United States had been the two great powers during that same Cold War era. Would there actually have been a Cold War at all? Would there really have been that much rivalry? This may be a so-called miracle counterfactual—an outcome that is hard to imagine coming to pass—but the salient point is that states are not simply interchangeable; their identities matter too. Starting from this observation, *state level* analysts argue that we need to know a lot about the internal characteristics of a state if we're going to explain how it behaves on the world stage. What, for instance, are the state's foreign policy traditions? Is it aggressive (like Nazi Germany in the 1930s), or is it traditionally inclined toward pacifism (Switzerland and Sweden provide good examples today). Is it normally isolationist, shying away from contact with global affairs, or is it more activist and interventionist? Advocates of the democratic peace thesis, for instance, argue that democracies behave very differently than non-democracies; put simply, they suggest that democracies do not fight one another. Others argue that simply knowing that a state is a democracy tells us very little about how it will behave in the international arena; for instance, look at the disagreements between the United States and Europe over the desirability of invading Iraq in 2003. That issue inspired passionate disagreements within the democratic world, with France and Germany objecting especially strongly to the U.S.-led invasion (to the point of refusing to help with the postwar reconstruction of Iraq afterwards). Knowing how much power a state has and what type of state we are dealing with are certainly very useful facts to have if we want to explain a given state's behavior, but they don't tell us much of a specific nature about how that state is likely to behave across a range of cases.

This is the point at which advocates of the foreign policy decision-making approach come into their own. System level theorists essentially *black box* the state; in other words, they never look inside it to see what its characteristics are, mostly because they think that this is not necessary and/or confuses the issue when it comes to explaining international relations.[2] State level theorists begin the process of opening up the black box, but many scholars of decision-making argue that state level analysis does not go far enough. One thing we find when we open up a state is its *regime type*: whether it is democratic, authoritarian, and so on. But what else do we find, within government itself? One thing we discover within many states (and this is certainly true of the United States) are powerful branches of government, including a legislature and an executive branch. Most top-level decisions in the United States during crises and other major foreign policy issues are made within the executive branch, though, and so most theories of foreign policy decision-making open up that box next. Taking apart the executive branch, we find organizations like the State Department or the Pentagon, and many scholars prefer to work at this *bureaucratic* or *organizational level* of analysis. Still others prefer to open up the organizations themselves. When we do this, we find groups of decision-makers, or the *group level* of analysis; and when we look inside groups, we find human beings—influenced by their beliefs, personalities, past experiences and so on—and this is usually termed the *individual* or *psychological* level of analysis. Conceptually, you may find it useful to think of each of these levels in terms of a Russian *matryoshka* doll. This is a set of dolls of decreasing sizes placed one inside the other, and an example is shown in figure 1.3. The largest doll can be thought of as representing the international system; inside this, we find states; inside this, organizations, and so on. The choice of which level to focus on is not just a matter of whim or casual taste; when we pick a level, we are making a judgment about what we really think *causes* the behavior of states on the global stage.

This book is really about the last three dolls in the row: the bureaucratic, group, and individual levels of analysis. In the next few chapters, you are going to be presented with a more detailed outline of three approaches that work at precisely these levels, and ultimately the wider goal of this book will be to help you decide for yourself which theory you find most compelling, and more generally which level of analysis you think international relations and foreign policy decision-making really ought to be studied at. You should note that each level of analysis contains a number of different theories, though; most notably, the systemic level contains a variety of approaches—for instance, neorealism, neoliberalism, and world systems theory—whose members often disagree quite markedly about what the international system actually looks like. Similarly, state level theories highlight a variety of factors—culture, regime type, and so on—which might influence a state's behavior. Equally, the groupthink approach we are going to

Figure 1.3 Russian Matryoshka Dolls. © Robyn Mackenzie

analyze in chapter 3 is not the only theory of foreign policy decision-making that operates at the group level, nor is the bureaucratic politics perspective (in chapter 2) the only approach one can locate at that level. In chapter 4 we will draw, moreover, on a range of perspectives, which operate at the individual or psychological level. But the levels of analysis device provides us with a handy beginning; it shows us where the approaches we are going to discuss fit within the larger scheme of things, and begins to make it apparent why those theories are especially useful for explaining the concrete choices that U.S. administrations have made in foreign policy.

Another way of thinking about these issues is through what has become known as the *agent-structure debate* (Wendt 1987; Carlsnaes 1992; Hollis and Smith 1991). Looking again at the *matryoshka* dolls, we can see that—examined in one way—the structure (or surrounding force) is the system and the state is the agent (or actor). But when we move down a level, the state is the structure and the organization is the agent. Opening up the organization, the group might be seen as the agent and the organization is now the structure. And finally, the group becomes the structure and the individual the agent. As you can see, disentangling all these issues and deciding what causes what is no easy matter, to say the least. But the purpose of this book is to help you to do that, at least in some measure; my goal is to help you acquire some ideas about what really drives foreign policy behavior.

OUTLINE OF THE BOOK

Chapters 2 through 4 look in more detail at the three theories we are going to examine in this book, devoting one chapter to each model and discussing each as dispassionately as possible so as to avoid pushing a reader unfamiliar with the three perspectives in any one direction. *Homo Bureaucraticus* (chap. 2) locates the sources of foreign policy at the organizational level of analysis, contending that it is the fragmentation of government, the interplay of its competing organizations, and "the games bureaucrats play" that shape external behavior. *Homo Sociologicus* (chap. 3) understands foreign policy at the group level of analysis, treating foreign policy decisions as the result of group dynamics (some of them dysfunctional, others more beneficial to effective decision-making). Rather than treating the interaction between bureaucracies as the key to understanding decision-making, this approach prefers the greater analytical precision that moving down to the group level provides (e.g., to groups *within* a bureaucratic unit, such as the State Department). This approach stresses that people behave differently in groups than they would if acting on their own, so that examining either organizational behavior (the level above) or individual cognitions (the level below) will be inadequate on its own. Finally, *Homo Psychologicus* (chap. 4) is used here as an umbrella term for what is in reality a series of separable theories, which became increasingly popular during the 1960s and 1970s and have remained so ever since. As a general approach, however, this perspective understands foreign policy at the individual level of analysis, treating foreign policy decisions as the product of the psychological mind-sets of dominant members within a group, rather than group dynamics themselves or bureaucratic routines. Belief system/ operational code-based approaches are discussed first, followed by an analysis of other perspectives within this category, including cognitive consistency theory, attribution theory, and schema/analogical reasoning theory. Newer perspectives stressing the impact of emotion on decision-making are also discussed here. As with the previous two chapters, the aim of this one is merely to describe—again as dispassionately as possible—what the approach entails and how it differs from the other two perspectives. These three chapters break down the basic approaches that have been developed within foreign policy analysis, describing their various components in a clear, comprehensible way, and laying the groundwork for their later application to the six cases.

Chapters 5 through 10 cover the case study portion of the book, moving beyond the abstract treatment of our three theories to show the reader how each throws differing light upon a range of case studies across a number of U.S. administrations. Methodologically, this part of the book is consciously modeled after Allison's *Essence of Decision*, in which he viewed a single case study through the lens of three theories of his own. Although the case studies utilized here are far more extensive and the theories are different (reflecting the development of the field since his book first appeared in 1971), the method is similar and is intended as a conscious tribute to Allison's style, which I regard as a model for good qualitative research. As in that classic work, each case is approached from a different theoretical approach in successive "cuts." The order in which each theory is treated is deliberately varied across chapters, both to avoid falling into a predictable pattern and to highlight the cases where particular theoretical explanations have become dominant.

The Bay of Pigs is one of the most celebrated cases of defective decision-making ever studied. Irving Janis gave it pride of place in *Groupthink*, using it as a prime illustration of his theory. Chapter 5 begins by discussing his findings and his reasons for believing that group effects bedeviled Kennedy's decision-making process in 1961. The two other approaches—bureaucratic politics and the cognitive approach—have not been utilized nearly as much as Janis's in the attempt to understand the administration's decision-making, but this chapter is intended to show how these perspectives also can account for JFK's fatal decision to give the go-ahead for the invasion. Although Allison himself has never applied his approach to the Bay of Pigs case, others (such as Lucien Vandenbrouke) have done so, and I draw on this work to show how aspects of the Bay of Pigs decision-making might be explained by bureaucratic "pulling and hauling" between the CIA, the Joint Chiefs, and the State Department, for instance. Equally, the cognitive approach has much to say about the psychological mind-sets of the most prominent decision-makers in this case. *Homo Psychologicus* highlights the degree of wishful thinking and other psychological errors to which Kennedy's inner circle fell prey during the run up to the invasion. Analogical reasoning seems particularly useful in explaining the overconfidence that many in the CIA, fresh from its success in removing equally problematic foreign leaders in Guatemala in 1954 and Iran in 1953, felt in 1961, convincing its leaders that removing Fidel Castro from power would prove a straightforward exercise. Equally, JFK's own excessive deference to Eisenhower's judgments seems to have played a key role as well. This case study is the subject of chapter 5.

Chapter 6 moves on to a discussion of the Cuban missile crisis, beginning with an interpretation through the lens of *Homo Bureaucraticus*, which has provided the dominant explanation of JFK's decision-making during October 1962 ever since *Essence of Decision* first appeared. Allison argues that both U.S. and Soviet decision-making were heavily influenced by what their respective organizations both could do and were accustomed to doing. Janis, on the other hand, viewed the missile crisis as a classic example of the ways in which groupthink might be avoided. He created a counterpoint to groupthink, what he termed "vigilant appraisal," on the basis on this case study, highlighting the lessons he thought JFK had learned from the first Cuban crisis. The cognitive approach also has much to say about the ways in which fear affected the deliberations of the Executive Committee of the National Security Council (or ExCom); in many ways, this emotion sharpened the decision-making of key members of the administration. Various historical analogies, notably World War I, Munich, and Pearl Harbor, played visible roles in convincing members of the group both for and against various options that JFK was considering.

Chapter 7 begins with an examination of LBJ's Vietnam decision-making viewed through the lens of *Homo Psychologicus*. Yuen Foong Khong's *Analogies At War* is discussed, in which he argues that two historical analogies in particular—Korea and Dien Bien Phu—critically conditioned the debate about what the United States should do in Vietnam. From this general perspective, personality and leadership style may have mattered just as much; Dwight Eisenhower's decision-making style on Vietnam is contrasted with that of Lyndon Johnson under this heading, drawing on the work of Burke and Greenstein. The groupthink perspective also has a great deal to say about Johnson's decision-making process, and Janis gives this case study equal billing with the Bay of Pigs as an archetypical case of groupthink syndrome. Finally, although the U.S.-Vietnam decisions of 1965 have rarely been analyzed from a bureaucratic politics perspective, it is clear that the attitudes of many of those who worked in the Pentagon may have been colored by their bureaucratic interests, just as the White House primarily saw the Vietnam issue in terms of the domestic political ramifications of failing to act.

Chapter 8 analyzes Jimmy Carter's handling of the Iran hostage crisis from our three perspectives. From the vantage point of *Homo Bureaucraticus*, it is clear that many of Carter's advisers "stood where they sat" when the time came to consider a rescue mission. Predictably, the Defense Department advised in favor of the mission in 1980, while the State Department advised against it, arguing that diplomatic measures needed to be given more time. But there are also strong indications that groupthink may have played a role, with dissenters like Secretary of

State Cyrus Vance being excluded from the president's inner circle on this issue. Equally, it has been argued that the cognitive approach, which highlights the clashing beliefs of Vance and the National Security Adviser Zbigniew Brzezinski, as well the competing analogies that each used, can explain both the administration's persistence with a diplomatic strategy and Carter's eventual resort to the hostage rescue mission. From a *Homo Psychologicus* perspective, it has been suggested that decision-making on the Iran hostage issue was shaped by the clash between the Entebbe and *Pueblo* analogies; the former suggested that a bold, daring rescue mission can pay off in both military and political terms, while the latter suggested that a strategy of patience and persistence is the only surefire way to get hostages back alive. As in previous chapters, however, each theoretical approach will be applied evenhandedly, and no attempt will be made to suggest that any particular theory is the correct one in this instance.

Chapter 9 covers a rather less well-known but more contemporary case study, the Kosovo crisis with which the Clinton administration grappled in 1999. This brief conflict—NATO's first-ever military engagement—was fought between that organization and Serbia from March to June 1999. Following the failure of peace talks at Rambouillet over the status of the Yugoslavian province of Kosovo and the decision of Serbian President Slobodan Milosevic to step up the "ethnic cleansing" of Albanians living there, the United States and NATO began a bombing campaign against Serbia. From the *Homo Psychologicus* perspective, President Bill Clinton was reluctant to commit ground troops to Kosovo, in part because of the so-called Vietnam syndrome that had heavily influenced his thinking throughout his presidency and the shattering experience of the Somali "Black Hawk Down" incident in 1993. Secretary of State Madeleine Albright, on the other hand, frequently used the Munich analogy, which suggested—as did previous experience with the Serbian dictator—that if Milosevic was not stopped early by the use of military force, the United States would simply have to confront him later. The World War I analogy also suggested that regional conflict in the Balkans could spill over into a major conflagration (Hehir 2006). There is also evidence that the decision-makers (especially Ambassador Richard Holbrooke), may have been victims of groupthink, collectively convincing themselves that Milosevic would back down if confronted by the threat of force. Finally, the Pentagon's reluctance to intervene and concern that a quick bombing campaign would not work also provides some support for an approach based on *Homo Bureaucraticus*.

Our final chapter within this section deals with the Iraq invasion decision-making of 2003. Chapter 10 will inevitably be more speculative than the others, since there is obviously much we still do not know about the manner in which the decision to invade Iraq in 2003 was made. There are some interesting indications, however, that groupthink may have played a prominent role in that decision. Secretary of State Powell seems to have played the dissenter role in this instance. Those who argued against an invasion were soon excluded from Bush's inner circle, which became an "echo chamber" in Ron Suskind's memorable phrase. From the vantage point of bureaucratic politics, it is interesting that those who sat in the State Department (most notably Powell, his deputy Richard Armitage, and his Chief of Staff Lawrence Wilkerson) were least enthusiastic about a military invasion, arguing that sanctions, weapons inspections, and diplomatic pressures needed to be given more time, while those in the Pentagon exhibited an almost reckless can do attitude. Bureaucratic infighting between State and Defense (and between State and Vice President Cheney's office) during the postinvasion reconstruction phase has been widely reported. Finally, various cognitive and motivational errors also seem evident in the decision to go into Iraq, including misperceptions about the adversary, the "drunkard's search" (looking for data in psychologically convenient places), the use of Munich/Hitler as an analogy, the resistance of entrenched beliefs in the face of disconfirming evidence, and the impact of wishful thinking in general.

Finally, chapter 11 summarizes the arguments that have been made. It then examines the strengths and weaknesses of the three theoretical approaches across the six cases, and prompts students to answer in their own minds an array of questions. Is there any approach that emerges especially strongly from the foregoing analyses? If so, does this approach tend to work best for particular types of decision and not others? How might our three approaches be integrated? Is it possible or even desirable to integrate them? Each approach explains foreign policy decision-making at a different level of analysis. Are they really examining the same phenomena, or subtly different ones? The intent of this final chapter is to help the reader answer these questions for him- or herself. Before we begin to examine the six case studies from each of our theoretical perspectives, of course, we will need to begin by describing our three main theoretical approaches in more detail.

CHAPTER 2

Homo Bureaucraticus

THE OPENING TO CHINA 1972

In September 1969 President Richard Nixon, working through his National Security Adviser Henry Kissinger, instructed U.S. diplomatic staff in Poland to approach their Chinese counterparts with what was then a highly novel and unusual proposal. The President's objective was to begin the negotiations that he hoped would lead to the United States opening up diplomatic relations with the People's Republic of China (PRC), which the United States government had not recognized diplomatically and had deliberately sought to isolate since its takeover by the Communists in 1949. Since at that time America had no formal relations with China, there was of course no U.S. Ambassador to China. The only established channel of communication was a mechanism called the Warsaw Talks, a device used mostly in the 1950s to discuss POW issues arising from the Korean War but which had fallen into disuse by the late 1960s. The U.S. Ambassador to Poland Walter Stoessel was instructed to reopen this channel and specifically ordered to approach his Chinese counterpart in Poland, Lei Yang, in order to relay the President's message at the next available social occasion.

Like all American diplomats, Stoessel worked for the State Department. Most of us simply assume that an organization of this importance simply does as it is told, faithfully obeying the orders of the president and his close advisers. This is certainly a comforting belief, and it may indeed be true much of the time. But a surprisingly long line of American presidents have complained that this is frequently not the case. Harry Truman, for instance, is said to have quipped of his successor Dwight Eisenhower as the latter succeeded the former, "poor Ike. It won't be a bit like the Army. He'll sit here and he'll say, 'Do this, do that,' and nothing will happen." We know that Nixon and Kissinger felt something very much like this with regard to the State Department, and with some justification. Initially, the very idea of even talking to representatives of the Chinese government was anathema to Stoessel and his State Department colleagues, for whom preserving close ties with the island of Taiwan, run by the anti-Communist Chiang Kai-shek, had long been an article of faith. As Kissinger himself later put it, talking to the Chinese was "against orthodoxy." To Kissinger's great annoyance, Stoessel seems to have dragged his feet on this instruction, taking almost three months to approach the Chinese Ambassador in Warsaw (Mann 1999, 22). Indeed, the National Security Adviser had to recall the Ambassador to Washington to meet with Nixon in person, simply to convince Stoessel that this was a presidential *order* and part of a larger scheme of "triangular diplomacy," which Nixon hoped would preserve global peace and order. The President hoped that by opening relations with China, he could exploit the growing gap in the Communist world between China and the Soviet Union, playing one off against the other and thereby creating a new "structure of peace" (see Kissinger 1994, 703–32).

Aside from the difficulties that Nixon would inevitably face in fashioning a new relationship, there was also a problem *within* the U.S. government. Nixon's order violated the State Department's established ways of doing things, what have been termed bureaucratic routines or standard operating procedures (SOPs). "The bureaucracy and many of the professional foreign service officers thought that opening to China was extremely dangerous," Kissinger later recalled. Somewhat reluctantly, the Ambassador agreed to comply with Nixon's request but only after the president had to explain to Stoessel in person how important this was. "I brought him back and took him into the President and the President instructed him to do what I'd already asked him to do, namely to stop the highest ranking Chinese diplomat he could find at the next social occasion and tell him we wanted to talk," Kissinger remembers (Kissinger 2000).

Stoessel's approach to the Chinese was finally made in December 1969. Together with other State Department officials—and following a script carefully laid down by the White House—the Ambassador sought to reassure Chinese representatives on a number of points as a precursor to beginning some sort of dialogue between the two nations. After a further meeting, the Chinese agreed to reopen the Warsaw Talks. However, to the displeasure of both Nixon and Kissinger, Stoessel then followed the State Department's SOP, which was to widely disseminate a report on the meetings to embassies, State Department desk officers, and even foreign allies around the globe. But Nixon and his National Security Adviser wanted to keep the politically sensitive and highly controversial overture *secret* at the outset. After all, if it failed it could become a significant embarrassment to the administration and might well draw criticism from Republicans as well as Democrats. Nixon and Kissinger worried that the State Department's bureaucratic procedures could destroy the initiative before it had even begun. "We'll kill this child before it is born," Nixon complained. The President was troubled, of course, that his own government might unwittingly kill off his plans through its use of what he clearly saw as mindless organizational routines (Kissinger 1979, 190; Isaacson 1992, 337). The State Department's representatives had made it clear, moreover, that they held no enthusiasm for Nixon's idea in any case. Marshall Green, the Assistant Secretary of State for East Asia, was an especially determined opponent of Nixon's "China game," arguing that an approach to the PRC would upset not just Taiwanese leaders but American allies as far afield as Japan and Australia. He also proposed that, rather than leading to a genuine *rapprochement* in U.S.-Chinese relations, the Chinese would simply use the American approach to make the Russians uneasy. Ironically, this was exactly the kind of effect Nixon and Kissinger were trying to produce, although Green was apparently unaware of this (Kissinger 1979, 193).

From the President's perspective, a way needed to be found to cut the unenthusiastic State Department out of the decision-making on this issue. Luckily for Nixon, this would come as an unintended byproduct of his own decision-making. In 1970 Nixon undertook a highly controversial invasion of Cambodia, labeled at the time as an "incursion." This effectively killed the Warsaw channel, since the Chinese pulled out of the talks in protest at this widening of the Vietnam war. But for Kissinger this turn of events proved, as he would later put it, "providential" (Kissinger 1979, 693). With the failure of the Warsaw initiative, Kissinger had to seek out sympathetic but discreet third parties to serve as intermediaries, and by 1971 Pakistan had agreed to serve as such a go-between. When the Chinese indicated that they were happy to work with Pakistan as well, Kissinger had the secret back channel he wanted, effectively allowing the White House to bypass the State Department altogether. Nixon subsequently cut State completely out of the decision-making on this issue, failing to inform Secretary of State William Rogers (or for that matter, the rest of his Cabinet) of the overture to China until it was effectively a *fait accompli.*

After extensive and often difficult negotiations between Kissinger and the PRC in 1971, a deal was reached which would lead to something entirely unprecedented, and to many people unthinkable: the visit of a U.S. president to the People's Republic of China. As the journalist and Far Eastern expert Stanley Karnow later put it:

> The dogma, especially among right-wing Republicans like Nixon, was that Communism was a monolith. That there was somebody at a control panel in Moscow, who pressed buttons and Communists all over the world responded to that. Now he gets evidence that there is a growing split between the Russians and the Chinese, and he's going to use this as a lever. By making a move toward the Chinese, that would increase his leverage with the Russians, at the same time, he's going to maintain with relations with the Russians, as leverage against the Chinese (Karnow, 2000).

On February 21, 1972, Richard Nixon stepped off *Air Force One* and into history, beginning a process which would eventually lead to normalization of U.S. relations with China. But Nixon's visit would not prove straightforward. Apart from some attempts to scupper the deal by hard-liners within the PRC government who disliked the idea of a closer relationship within the United States, Nixon and Kissinger had to contend with their own State Department's continued objections to such a relationship. Rogers and the State Department delegation, which

Nixon could not avoid bringing with him on a diplomatic trip of such importance, continued to fear that the President would abandon Taiwan to the Communists. At one point, infighting between the two U.S. factions became so severe that Chinese Premier Zhou Enlai had to visit Rogers in person in order to reassure the secretary of state and break the impasse within the American government. Realizing that the U.S. delegation was internally divided, the politically astute Zhou Enlai managed to persuade Secretary Rogers to go along with a joint U.S.-Chinese communiqué which made no mention of American treaty commitments to Taiwan. President Nixon had eventually prevailed over his own government, though ironically he had managed to do so in part because the Chinese Premier was politically savvy enough to know when to intervene in what he regarded as America's internal affairs.

THE HAINAN ISLAND INCIDENT OF 2001

A reader who already knows something about the Nixon administration may be skeptical about the broader applicability of this example. After all, Nixon and Kissinger were known for an almost paranoid, highly compartmentalized, and secretive style of foreign policy decision-making. One of Nixon's successors, Jimmy Carter, would dismiss Kissinger's style during the 1976 presidential election campaign as the "lone ranger" approach to American foreign policy. In order to convince such a reader that this kind of bureaucratic infighting was not peculiar to the Nixon administration, then, a second example is probably in order. Many years later—on April 1, 2001, during the early days of the George W. Bush (43) administration—an incident involving an American EP-3 military aircraft and two Chinese J-8 fighters briefly brought relations between the two nations to a boiling point.[1] An in-air collision occurred sixty miles from the Chinese coast between the EP-3 and one of the J-8s, resulting in the death of a Chinese pilot. The American plane, which had apparently been gathering intelligence (spying) on Chinese military installations, a practice in which both sides commonly engage, was then forced to make an emergency landing on the PRC island of Hainan.

The United States and China define the notion of territorial airspace differently; the Chinese argued that the planes had collided in Chinese airspace, while the United States insisted that the collision took place in international airspace. It is not entirely clear today whether the American pilot buzzed the Chinese one or whether the J-8 purposely or accidentally clipped the wing of the larger American aircraft. As far as we can tell, however, the accident seems to have occurred because the pilot of the Chinese J-8 became dangerously overzealous in implementing the Chinese air force's standard strategy of intimidating aircraft that the PRC believes are violating its airspace. According to the American pilot Lt. Shane Osborn:

> He came up on us twice, and both times were really close. The second time, I could see him right out of our cockpit ... he was like ten feet away. Looking right in his face, I was like, "This isn't good." We were nervous. I'm just guarding the

autopilot, making sure we don't make any movements into him because it was that close, a couple of feet from hitting us. He dropped away once, came back. The second time I was like, "OK, he's going home for sure." Then when I heard him come the third time, I had an eerie feeling. I just knew he was going to hit us, because he wasn't stable. He was all over. The third time, you heard screams coming from the back as he came and he pitched up into us. ... The plane just shook violently and we kind of pitched up. I heard a pop, and that was his nose hitting ours. He shot off to the side and we were upside down before I knew it. [I was] trying to stop the plane from going completely inverted ... and I was pretty certain we were dead at that point. We were upside down in a large reconnaissance aircraft. I had lost my nose. I could hear the wind screaming through the plane, and I knew that number one prop was violently shaking. We were pretty much inverted. I was looking up at the ocean, so it was not a good feeling. (Osborn 2001)

After the plane was somehow able to land on what was now indisputably Chinese territory, the twenty-four U.S. crewmembers on board were detained and interrogated by the PRC authorities. However, the issue then seems to have become a pawn in the bureaucratic struggle between hard-liners and reformers within the Chinese government. For the first few days of the crisis, Secretary of State Powell was puzzled that he was getting nowhere on this issue by going through regular diplomatic channels; the response from China was simply silence. The incident, however, seems to have been largely controlled by the Chinese military during this early period. These hard-liners or conservatives thought that Premier Jiang Zemin was being too soft on the United States, moving too close to a state, which they regarded as a threatening adversary (a position that, rather ironically, echoed that of American conservatives like William Buckley who had opposed Nixon's linkage with Communist China). Moderates within the Zemin government, on the other hand, seemed anxious that this incident not jeopardize the broader strategic relationship between the two countries. Initially compelled to accept the military's version of events, the moderates may have eventually come to see that it was at least possible that the incident had occurred because of a Chinese, rather than American, pilot error.

There is also some evidence that the way in which the issue was handled by the Chinese military initially was driven by SOPs, standard practices that did not much differ from those of their American counterparts. Both the United States and China maintain a two-hundred-mile Air Defense Intercept Zone along their respective coasts, and U.S. fighter jets are sent out to intercept and escort any foreign military aircraft which enters the protected zone. As Indira Lakshmanan has argued, "there is no precise historical parallel, but numerous military historians and analysts said several cases with some similarities, as well as standard U.S. procedures, suggest that Washington would just as vehemently oppose surveillance flights sixty miles off the U.S. coast—and be just as quick to dismantle and delay returning a high-tech Chinese plane if one landed uninvited on U.S. shores or at an overseas U.S. base." Indeed, the closest parallel was perhaps the 1976 Soviet

MIG-25 incident, when a Soviet pilot defected to Japan. The CIA dismantled the aircraft, returning the plane to the Soviet Union in various pieces after more than two months had elapsed (Lakshmann 2001).

The danger, of course, was that the United States would treat standard operating procedures or the product of internal power struggles as representing the will of the Chinese government *in toto,* treating China as a unitary actor. The longer the incident dragged on, the greater the tendency in the United States would be to see this not as an unfortunate incident, but a full-fledged hostage crisis. It is, of course, hard to say with any degree of certainty what was occurring within the PRC. As in the 1972 example, though, the supporters of engagement in particular seem to have believed that the continued captivity of the EP-3 crew had to be considered in the light of internal debates going on within the Chinese government. Just as Zhou Enlai had "rescued" Nixon from his own State Department, so Secretary Powell and others seem to have performed a similar favor for Zemin with regard to his own (hard-line) Defense officials in the People's Liberation Army (PLA). Powell himself was the first to express regret for the loss of the Chinese pilot, seemingly the most attuned to the Zemin's need to cover his conservative flank, and President Bush (43) then issued a similar statement. The crew was eventually released on April 11 after the administration delivered what was in effect a letter of apology to the Chinese government. The plane itself was not returned until July, perhaps to assuage the hard-liners within Zemin's circle (although the aircraft had some obvious intelligence value in its own right). In all, the American crew spent ten days in captivity as a result of what has become known as the Hainan Island incident.

According to David Sanger, there was a clear division within the Bush 43 administration throughout the incident that reflected a much broader split within the Republican party on the issue of U.S.-Chinese relations:

> The Republican Party throughout the 1990s became bifurcated [into] two different camps. One was a very business oriented camp ... where business executives, who wanted to increase American trade with China, saw [China] as the greatest market in Asia, and perhaps the greatest market anywhere in the world. [They] wanted an American policy that was designed to be tough-minded militarily but fundamentally open to the embrace of China into a capitalist system. Now there's a second element to the Republican Party here, and that is a containment crowd, a group that believes that the portion of the administration and the Republican Party that wants closer economic ties, is naive about the growing military threat from China. This group saw in the EP-3 incident the confirmation of all that they had been saying for many years—which is, "They want to trade with us, but boy, when it gets to a real moment, an incident, their initial instinct is not to do what they should do, which was say this was an accident, and turn the crew over" (Sanger 2001).

The first group, which we might term the *engagement* faction, had been associated with Republicans like Nixon and Kissinger, and with George W. Bush's own father (who had been Ambassador to China and had himself remained comparatively silent as president during the Chinese military's crackdown on pro-democracy protestors at Tiananmen Square in 1989). Somewhat ironically, given the events related in the 1972 example, Colin Powell's State Department seems to have provided the natural base of this group within the Bush 43 administration. The second group—the *containment* faction—was based mostly in the Pentagon under Secretary of Defense Donald Rumsfeld and in Vice-President Cheney's office within the White House. According to Sanger, this group "basically wanted the president to come out and take a very tough line, to make it clear to the Chinese in their first interchange that this administration would be very tough-minded on security issues" (Sanger 2001). The first faction were essentially realists, placing the EP-3 issue in a broader strategic context, while the second faction was composed mostly of neoconservatives (a division that would surface most clearly later on in the Bush 43 administration, as the two factions clashed over the invasion of Iraq).

Bush's stance seems to have reflected a classic bureaucratic compromise in which the president sought to appease both factions simultaneously, alternating between hot and cool approaches, and using words aimed at keeping both the engagement and containment factions happy. In Sanger's words, the president simply "split the difference." Having previously condemned the holding of the U.S. plane in the strongest terms and demanded its return just two days into the crisis, Bush moderated his language thereafter and resisted military recommendations to place the aircraft carrier *Kitty Hawk* off the coast of China. During the 2000 presidential campaign, Bush had criticized the Clinton administration for being too soft on China and for failing to recognize the military threat he thought China posed, but he also used many of the same words Clinton used, arguing that an intensified trading relationship would eventually bring more openness and perhaps even democracy (Sanger and Myers 2001). Seeking perhaps to appease the neoconservatives, however, Bush then used much more belligerent language after the crew was safely back in the United States, and the administration revealed that it was considering various punitive measures against China (Wang 2009, 87).

THE ASSUMPTIONS OF *HOMO BUREAUCRATICUS*

The two Chinese examples illustrate a number of important things from the perspective of what I call the *Homo Bureaucraticus* model in this book. First of all, states are not *unitary* actors; in reality, they are composed of a number of (often discordant) organizations, which frequently like to go their own way. The bureaucratic politics approach was originally developed by Graham Allison in his classic book *Essence of Decision* and by Morton Halperin in *Bureaucratic Politics and Foreign Policy* (Allison 1971; Allison and Zelikow 1999; Halperin 1974). If you think again of the nested Russian dolls we encountered in chapter 1, the *Homo Bureaucraticus* approach considers foreign policy at the organizational or bureaucratic level of analysis; it thinks of American foreign policy largely as the *output* or *resultant*, which are the end-product bureaucratic bargaining, infighting, and the routine ways that organizations like to do things. In *Essence of Decision*, Graham

Allison famously noted that most analysts (as well as laypeople) consciously or unconsciously make use of the *Rational Actor Model* (RAM), termed *Homo Economicus* in his book, when they seek to explain why a particular state acted as it did. As we saw in chapter 1, when we employ this approach we effectively "personify" the state; in other words, we treat it as if it were a single human being (McGraw and Dolan 2007). We think of that person (state), moreover, as possessing rather efficient reasoning capacities. In attempting to reconstruct *why* the state acted in the way it did, we reason backwards; we ask ourselves what goals or objectives the state had in its mind when it did X or Y. This is a very commonplace and instinctive way of thinking about foreign policy decision-making. As Hans Morgenthau and his colleagues suggest, it is also rather satisfying since it allows us to reconstruct the reasoning of the decision-maker in a relatively simple fashion, looking "over his shoulder" (Morgenthau, Thompson, and Clinton 2005, 5). If state A had this in mind, so the reasoning goes, it is little wonder that it did X or Y.

As an example, consider Soviet decision-making during the Cuban missile crisis, a case we will examine in detail in chapter 6. In October 1962, the United States discovered that the Soviet Union had secretly placed nuclear missiles on the island of Cuba. How would we explain this from the perspective of the RAM? Allison and Zelikow consider this in *Essence of Decision*:

> The typical analyst of citizen begins by considering various aims that the Soviets might have had in mind—for example, to probe American intentions, to defend Cuba, or to improve their bargaining position. By examining the problems the Soviets faced and the character of the action they chose, the analyst eliminates some of these aims as implausible. When he is able to construct a calculation that shows how, in a particular situation, with certain objectives, he could have chosen to place missiles in Cuba, the analyst has explained the action. ... The attempt to explain international events by recounting the aims and calculations of nations or governments is the trademark of the Rational Actor Model (Allison and Zelikow 1999, 13).

But there are a number of (sometimes highly questionable) assumptions that lurk unexamined behind such an approach. Under the RAM or *Homo Economicus*, the state is assumed to act rationally in the sense that its decision-makers are assumed to share clear objectives; members of the decision-making apparatus (personified as "the state") are assumed collectively weigh up the costs and benefits of each alternative means of getting to that objective. Having done this, they then select the "utility-maximizing choice" (a phrase from classical economics and equivalent in common English usage to "the best choice, given what your goals are").

What is wrong with these assumptions from the perspective of *Homo Bureaucraticus*? The leading problem from this view is the analogy drawn in the RAM between the state and an individual decision-maker, or the assumption that the state is a unified, purpose-driven actor. As we have seen already, governments do not always behave as if they were single individuals; rather, their component parts often pull in different directions, and their decision-makers hold markedly different images of the world. Think again of the two Chinese examples just discussed. Neither the United States nor China is, from this perspective, a unitary actor, so it is not particularly useful to think of either state's foreign policies as representing the "will" of that nation's government. In the 1972 example, the divisions within the U.S. government were so obvious to Chinese moderates that it became apparent to Premier Zhou Enlai that something needed to be done to help the Nixon-Kissinger faction win the day. In 2001, Secretary of State Powell and others seem to have recognized that the continued captivity of the U.S. crew on Hainan Island was probably being driven by hard-line factions within the PRC government, especially the Chinese military. It followed that patient negotiation—eventually leading to some sort of U.S. apology or expression of regret—was the best way to smooth things over so that the moderates could win.

Second, although presidents nominally head the executive branch, they cannot always be assured of full compliance from the bureaucratic agencies that supposedly exist to do nothing but the president's bidding. Richard Neustadt argued that presidential power in the United States represents "the power to persuade." He further suggested that the U.S. system does not represent a true separation of powers, but rather "separate institutions sharing power." This fits the *Homo Bureaucraticus* approach rather well and not coincidentally; as Garry Clifford notes, Richard Neustadt and others were the intellectual forerunners behind the bureaucratic politics perspective at Harvard back in the 1950s and 1960s, exerting a critical influence on the thinking of younger scholars such as Allison (Clifford 1990). The notion of a separation of powers, Neustadt noted, implies that "'institution A does X, and institution C does Y.'" In fact, however, both A and B *share* responsibility for X, as they do for Y. While this is clearest in the case of executive-legislative relations in the United States—the Founding Fathers made Congress responsible for declaring war, while giving the president the powers of commander in chief, for instance—it is also clear that organizations represent a further check and balance within the executive branch itself.

Organizations frequently bridle under presidential control, resisting direction rather like an unruly horse straining to go its own way in spite of the rider's wishes. They often resist change in particular, even when the president expresses a clear preference for that change; they prefer to rely on their existing SOPs, which in their view represent the institutional memory or wisdom that the organization has accumulated over many years. Consequently, government policy may be less the product of deliberate, well-thought-out *choices* by politicians and more by what organizations can do and are accustomed to doing. In this sense, decisions may be thought of as the (sometimes mindless but automatic) *outputs* of large organizations. Presidential choices are limited by organizational capacities and missions, and this can lead to behavior which is less than fully rational and/or to unintended consequences, which in turn can have very harmful effects (especially when misconstrued by the other side). As the noted organizational theorists James March and Herbert Simon put it:

> Actions are chosen by recognizing a situation as being of a familiar, frequently encountered type, and matching the recognized situation to a set of rules. ... The logic of appropriateness is linked to conceptions of experience, roles, intuition and expert knowledge. It deals with calculation mainly as a means of retrieving experience preserved in the organization's files or individual memories (March and Simon 2003, 8; also quoted in Allison and Zelikow 1999, 146).

Organizations operate according to their own logic and culture once created, only partially controllable by elected politicians (the difficulty in reforming intelligence agencies after 9/11 being just one especially prominent example). They seek *incrementalism*, in other words, doing things bit by bit in slow, methodical fashion, rather than radical change. The U.S. military was geared to the fighting of conventional wars against conventional enemies, for instance, and it has often been noted that it fought the Vietnam War as a conventional exercise; the obvious problem, however, was that confronting the North Vietnamese and the Vietcong involved some highly unconventional challenges, including an enemy which often could not be seen, where friend sometimes could not be distinguished from foe, and where the adversary usually employed guerilla or insurgent tactics rather than conventional warfare. It can also be hard to get an organization to stop doing something once it has started. Allison and Zelikow give the example of the CIA's role in planning for the overthrow of the socialist Salvador Allende in 1973 as an example. Nixon and Kissinger both claimed that they ordered CIA planning for a coup in Chile "turned off," but we know that CIA assistance went ahead anyway (Allison and Zelikow 1999, 173–74). The resistance of organizations to change is perhaps even more clearly on display in the 1972 case where Secretary Rogers, Ambassador Stoessel, Assistant Secretary of State Green and the State Department in general were noticeably slow to embrace President Nixon's clear wish that his government reach out (albeit for rather Machiavellian reasons) to the PRC. State Department representatives uniformly preferred the orthodoxy and existing SOPs over radical changes to U.S. foreign policy. This seems to be true of the Chinese military as well, which may simply have been following its own SOPs when holding onto and then dismantling the U.S. EP-3 in 2001.

Third, membership of an organization often significantly colors one's views. There is a well-known axiom in American government and the study of bureaucratic politics known as "where you stand depends on where you sit," a proposition variously attributed to Arnold Miles and Don Price. In other words, the policy positions or beliefs of a given decision-maker are often at least partially shaped by the position that he or she holds within the government (one's vantage point, in other words, determines how one views an issue or problem). In the examples just discussed, where you stand on the issues does seem to be significantly affected by the organization to which you belong. The director of the CIA will tend to argue for intelligence operations, involving the use of spies and covert operations, because that is essentially what the CIA does; and people like the White House chief of staff and the vice president will tend to support whatever makes the president look good politically, because their bureaucratic interest lies in protecting the president's image. In short, everyone looks after his own bureaucratic corner. Diplomacy is what the State Department does, and its representatives are especially attuned to see that face of an issue (especially where we have some pre-existing treaty obligation to a particular country). Those occupying particular bureaucratic roles perceive "different sides of an issue" (Allison and Zelikow 1999, 299–300).

Madeleine Albright brings this out particularly clearly in her memoir of her time as United Nations Ambassador and Secretary of State under Bill Clinton. She notes that she and Anthony Lake basically viewed the world in similar ways, though Vietnam had more impact on Lake and the World War II/Munich experience more effect on Albright. But when she was UN Ambassador, she saw the difference as strongly mediated by their differing bureaucratic roles. As National Security Adviser, Lake viewed the issue of genocide in Yugoslavia from the vantage point of the White House and the president's interests. For Albright, on the other hand, "my convictions were reinforced by my perch at the UN, where I saw more foreign officials on a daily basis than any other member of our team. Bosnia was a constant preoccupation, and I felt I needed a good answer to representatives from Islamic nations who pressed me hard to halt the slaughter of their brethren" (Albright 2003, 180).

While Albright saw the moral case for action, then Chairman of the Joint Chiefs Colin Powell (a holdover in 2003 from the Bush 41 administration) not unnaturally saw the military side of the issue, and he regarded any U.S. intervention in Bosnia as fraught with peril. From Albright's perspective, Powell was being too cautious, staying America's hand and failing to utilize our massive military advantages. "Time and again," Albright relates, Powell "led us up the hill of possibilities and dropped us off on the other side with the practical equivalent of 'No can do'. After hearing this for the umpteenth time, I asked in exasperation, 'What are you saving this superb military for, Colin, if we can't use it?'" (Albright 2003, 182). In the examples discussed, moreover, Marshall Green and others in his department in 1972 uniformly opposed moving closer to the PRC, citing our existing obligation to Taiwan and concern about how our other allies would react. State Department employees were also almost uniformly concerned that a move towards the PRC carried a significant danger of antagonizing the Soviets. Llewelyn Thompson, a former U.S. Ambassador to the USSR and by then a senior diplomat in the State Department, had warned privately that the Russians would be "genuinely angry" if the United States moved closer to China (Evans and Novak 1971, 100). From their perch in the White House, however, Nixon and Kissinger were far more concerned with the bigger game of geopolitical advantage, as well as with taking the domestic political credit for a major foreign policy coup.

Fourth, the distribution of power among organizations means that the potential always exists for bureaucratic infighting to occur. Because organizations like the

State Department or the Pentagon exist within a decentralized system in which no one actor—perhaps not even the president—possesses a monopoly on power, various actors with competing goals and strategies compete for influence. In the words of Graham Allison, in many ways the founding father of the *Homo Bureaucraticus* approach, organizations engage in pulling and hauling among themselves. We see evidence of such pulling and hauling for influence within both states in both Chinese examples, with the struggle for power between hard-liners and moderates a recurrent theme. In the EP-3 or Hainan Island example, the engagement and containment factions, centered on the State and Defense Departments respectively, were clearly tussling for influence from the earliest days of the Bush administration. These divisions seem to have been mirrored within the Chinese government, where a clear division existed between the People's Liberation Army and Jiang Zemin's comparatively moderate approach.

Fifth, a state's foreign policies may end up representing *the least common denominator*, that thing which everyone can agree upon but which actually represents nobody's first choice or real preference. Decisions emerge as *resultants* in a process of bargaining. Taken to its extreme, American foreign policy may be nothing so much as a series of bureaucratic compromises and deals, or at least the outcome of a process in which power resources have decided the winners and losers, and these compromises may even end up reflecting what no one actor wanted or intended. Moreover, we cannot assume that organizations have only the national interest at heart; their goals and objectives may be self-interested, pursuing policies that maximize their own budgets or influence. In the EP-3 example in particular, the outcome seems to have been a bureaucratic compromise between the two factions in the U.S. context, with President Bush choosing language that straddled the division between those who wanted to engage China economically and those who wished to contain it militarily. Decisions can also take the form of *collages,* in which a policy emerges which has something for everyone but which is rather puzzling when taken as a whole.

Last, the competition between bureaucratic units—far from making decision-making more efficient, as competition between firms in a marketplace might—seems to make government *less* effective and coordinated, giving organizations incentives to cut one another out of the policy process, with a corresponding failure to share information and bring the strands of policymaking together. In the examples discussed here, this happened most clearly in the 1972 opening to China case, as Nixon and Kissinger deliberately removed the State Department from of the entire decision-making process on China. Although some departmental expertise was utilized selectively along the way and Secretary Rogers remained influential on other issues such as the Middle East, decision-making with regard to the China opening was highly centralized in the White House. Distrust between Nixon and the State Department was so serious that he even preferred to rely on Chinese government translators rather than the American translators! Even Henry Kissinger, a leading beneficiary of this process in the early 1970s when he was National Security Adviser, subsequently admitted that this is not how government is = supposed to work and acknowledged that it rendered the decision-making process inefficient in some ways. Indeed, when he subsequently became secretary of state himself, his new vantage point may have helped to alter his view. When one part of the government does not know what the other part is doing, the players in the game can work at cross purposes to one another. When Vice-President Spiro Agnew spoke out against an overture to China in 1971, for instance—at precisely the time that Kissinger was engaging in secret negotiations with the Chinese—Agnew had to be told to "keep his mouth closed." More seriously, when a president fails to draw on the accumulated wisdom and expertise within his own bureaucracy, he may diminish any efficiency the (admittedly laborious) governmental process within the executive branch possesses.

Collectively, these points form the core assumptions of *Homo Bureaucraticus*, and they are summarized in figure 2.2.[2] The thinking and behavior of *Homo Bureaucraticus* is heavily influenced by his membership of the organization to which he belongs: he thinks, eats, and sleeps his organization. He sees the world through the particular set of lenses that his organization provides, and he competes for influence and resources with the members of other organizations. *Homo Bureaucraticus* also tends to see the national interest as synonymous with his own organization's interests: what is good for the organization, it is often assumed, must also be good for the nation.

"WHERE YOU STAND DEPENDS ON WHERE YOU SIT"

Does where you stand really determine where you sit? In other words, do the representatives of organizations really take on the cultures or identities of the

- States are not unitary actors: they are composed of a variety of organizations, agencies, and forces, which often disagree and compete with one another. Our foreign policies are often not the result of any single person's intentions.
- Organizations often resist change, even where presidents try to "order" such change; they cling to Standard Operating Procedures (SOPs).
- Membership of an organization significantly colors one's views ("where you stand depends on where you sit"). Members of bureaucratic units are often parochial and look after their own organization's interests.
- The distribution of power among organizations means that the potential always exists for bureaucratic infighting to occur ("pulling and hauling"). Decisions are often bureaucratic compromises (*decisions as resultants*) or derive from what organizations can do (*decisions as outputs*), so policymaking is not an entirely rational process.
- A state's foreign policy may simply represent the least common denominator, or simply reflect bureaucratic winners and losers on a particular issue.
- Competition between bureaucratic units seems to make government less effective and coordinated.

Figure 2.1 *Homo Bureaucraticus* Summarized.

agencies they represent? At first sight many readers may find this proposition difficult to accept. Surely most top-level decision-makers come into their positions with sufficiently strong beliefs and personalities to resist becoming mere creatures of their organization, and many critiques of the *Homo Bureaucraticus* approach have reserved particular criticism for this claim (see for instance Krasner 1972; Art 1972; Smith 1980; Bendor and Hammond 1992; Welch 1992; Rhodes 1994). As one might perhaps expect, the "where you stand ..." proposition plays a greater role in textbook accounts of Graham Allison's work than it did in *Essence of Decision* itself or the refinements which followed it. As Allison and Halperin put it in their joint article fusing together Models II and III, the decision-maker's "perceptions and preferences stem both from his individual characteristics ... and from his position" (Allison and Halperin 1972), and Allison makes a similar point in the original work. Nevertheless, individual personality and worldview play relatively little role in the analysis that follows this remark in each major statement of the approach, and as Hollis and Smith note, Allison's bureaucratic politics model "works by the implication that position determines preferences" (Hollis and Smith 1986, 273). So even though very few analysts have argued that role alone determines policy preferences, it is not wholly unfair to attribute such a view to Allison, who has referred to individual characteristics rather dismissively as "baggage" (Allison 1971, 166).

Before dismissing this claim out of hand, though, consider a more recent example from Barack Obama's administration. Before becoming CIA director in 2009, Leon Panetta had gone on record as being firmly opposed to the Bush 43 administration's policies in the "War on Terror." Noting with some distaste that many Americans had said in opinion polls taken after 9/11 that they supported the use of torture under some circumstances, Panetta argued that American values, the Constitution, and respect for the rule of law actively prohibited this practice:

> We have preached these values to the world. We have made clear that there are certain lines Americans will not cross because we respect the dignity of every human being. That pledge was written into the oath of office given to every president, "to preserve, protect, and defend the Constitution." It's what is supposed to make our leaders different from every tyrant, dictator, or despot. We are sworn to govern by the rule of law, not by brute force. We cannot simply suspend these beliefs in the name of national security. Those who support torture may believe that we can abuse captives in certain select circumstances and still be true to our values. But that is a false compromise. We either believe in the dignity of the individual, the rule of law, and the prohibition of cruel and unusual punishment, or we don't. There is no middle ground. We cannot and we must not use torture under any circumstances. We are better than that (Panetta, 2008).

Equally, Obama's Attorney General, Eric Holder, had given indications prior to joining the administration that he was opposed to any aggressive attempt to investigate past misdeeds by intelligence officials during the Bush 43 administration. Indeed, he had on one occasion gone so far as to suggest in a *CNN* interview in 2002 that detainees at Guantanamo Bay in Cuba (or "Gitmo" as it is popularly known) were not entitled to protection under the provisions of the Geneva Convention. As the future Attorney General put it:

> One of the things we clearly want to do with these prisoners is to have an ability to interrogate them and find out what their future plans might be, where other cells are located; under the Geneva Convention that you are really limited in the amount of information that you can elicit from people. It seems to me that given the way in which they have conducted themselves, however, that they are not, in fact, people entitled to the protection of the Geneva Convention. They are not prisoners of war. If, for instance, Mohammed Atta had survived the attack on the World Trade Center, would we now be calling him a prisoner of war? I think not. Should Zacarias Moussaoui be called a prisoner of war? Again, I think not (Holder, 2002).

Although Holder also expressed criticism of the Bush administration's handling of detainees, his appointment as Attorney General in 2009 may have been particularly attractive to President Obama because he had gone on record with this kind of position. Obama made it clear once in office that he did not want to get bogged down in a large-scale investigation of the previous administration's activities. The new president was clearly fearful that such an investigation might distract congressional attention from the passage of his own agenda, a concern Holder seems to have shared, and wished to focus initially on economic policy rather than the foreign arena.

Something interesting seems to have happened to both Panetta and Holder *once in office*, however. The issue of prisoner abuse during the previous administration was debated almost as soon as President Obama took office, and by August 2009 the debate had come to a head. The discussion that took place essentially boiled down to the question of whether the Obama administration should appoint a special prosecutor to investigate detainee abuses during the George W. Bush years. Given the previous discussion, the reader might well expect Leon Panetta to come down firmly in favor of appointing a prosecutor, since he had, after all, spoken out publicly against the practice of torture; indeed, he had insisted that abusing detainees was downright "un-American." Equally, one might expect Eric Holder to resist such a move, since he had seemed to partially condone the practice of aggressive interrogation during the Bush years and was also attuned to President Obama's desire not to deflect attention away from the new administration's agenda. In fact, as internal debates within the administration leaked to the press show, the opposite proved to be true. Now director of the CIA, Panetta came out solidly *against* any investigation, sending the CIA's top lawyer to the Justice Department in order to insist that it abandon any plans to investigate possible wrongdoing. Now as Attorney General, Holder made the decision to *proceed* with an investigation and appoint a special prosecutor, arguing that the legal case presented to him by Justice officials essentially left him no option but to do so. According to one account, a terse phone call between Holder and Panetta took place in August 2009, during which the new CIA chief expressed his strong opposition to any investigation, and is even said to have sworn at the new Attorney General (Baker, Johnston, and Mazzetti 2009). In short, the two men seem to have switched their initial positions. But what had happened to them in the interim between their expression of views as private individuals and taking office as the head of a powerful organization within the U.S. government? While it is difficult to say with any degree of certainty exactly what produced this sea change, both individuals appear to have been critically influenced by the *organizational cultures* surrounding them.

ORGANIZATIONAL CULTURE: "THE WAY THINGS ARE DONE AROUND HERE"

Large, well-developed organizations like the Pentagon, the State Department, and the CIA are naturally steeped in memory and ritual. They have, over a considerable number of years, developed certain ways of doing things; they cling to such methods because they seem to work, and they are usually loathe to change their operating procedures in consequence of this. Organizations hence develop specific cultures, which embody successful solutions to problems encountered in the past. Writing from a management perspective, Edgar Schein—one of the foremost exponents of this general view—argues that cultures are shaped by leaders over time (Schein 1995). Nevertheless, organizations are slow to change and contain a number of values, beliefs, and assumptions that are simply taken for granted and may even be taboo, and new members are both socialized within and commonly take on these assumptions. Indeed, even some organizational leaders seem to come into the job committed to going along with the status quo, while others self-evidently and sometimes rather noisily attempt to turn the whole organization upside down. Deal and Kennedy rather succinctly describe organizational culture as "the way things are done around here" (Deal and Kennedy 2000).

A number of analysts of organizational culture have attempted to categorize different kinds of culture which typically develop in the corporate world, and at least some of their observations may be readily adapted to better understand the cultures of governmental organizations. Deal and Kennedy, for instance, divide cultures into four fundamental types, according to their risk-taking propensities and the extent to which they seek and/or receive rewards. The "Work Hard/Play Hard Culture" often exists in the world of high finance, as does the "Bet Your Company Culture." But for our purposes, two of their classifications seem especially relevant. In the "Process Culture" there is little or no obvious *feedback* (their term for instant rewards). This is often true in large bureaucracies, where fitting in with how things are done sometimes becomes more important than outputs or the product. This kind of organizational culture encourages cautious conservatism. But governments also contain more dynamic organizations, which are willing to take risks and see tangible rewards for their efforts. In the "Tough-Guy Macho Culture" feedback is quick and the rewards are high. Brokerage firms often fit this category, but gung-ho elements of the CIA and Pentagon also seem to meet this kind of description. Under George Tenet, for instance, the CIA seems to have developed a back-slapping, manly quality in which sports metaphors and a simple, straightforward no bullshit style predominated (Tenet's famous or infamous "slam dunk" statement about the supposedly simple task of invading Iraq being seemingly only one of numerous examples). Tenet relates in his memoirs the natural affinity he had with George W. Bush, a shared love of hard-hitting, macho sports being one thing that drew them together (Tenet 2003, 363).

The Pentagon probably best exemplifies Deal and Kennedy's conception of the Tough-Guy Macho Culture. Colin Powell, at that time Chairman of the Joint Chiefs under the Bush 41 and then Clinton, describes the gays-in-the-military issue as "the hottest social potato tossed to the Pentagon in a generation" (Powell 1995, 547). Here was an issue that directly challenged prevailing rituals, habits, and assumptions, revealing deeper taboos, which had long been dealt with at an underground level. As is now well known, the Clinton administration faced intense resistance from the uniformed military to its original intention in 1993 to allow gays to openly serve in the armed forces. While analogies were drawn between this issue and that of racial integration in the 1940s, Powell rejected that comparison at the time as "a convenient but invalid argument" (although he later accepted the idea many years after leaving the Pentagon).

More generally, the Department of Defense also provides a good example of an organization whose culture is difficult to change *per se*. More than any other Defense Secretary since Robert McNamara, Donald Rumsfeld consciously came into the job (at least in his second stint) committed to changing the organizational culture of the Pentagon (Woodward 2002, 22–24).[3] Like many of his colleagues in the Bush 43 administration, Rumsfeld believed that the Clinton administration had been too cautious in its use of military power, or at least had used America's military might for the wrong things; the organization had, he thought, become too accustomed to engaging in peacekeeping and nation building, both of which he regarded with disdain (Scarborough 2004). He also evidently believed that Defense's culture had been overly shaped by the so-called Powell Doctrine, associated with the use of overwhelming force, favoring in its place his own rival Rumsfeld Doctrine, which advocated the use of high technology and small, pared-down U.S. forces. This was especially true of the Pentagon's special operations capability, where caution had been encouraged by disasters like the failed Iran hostage rescue mission in 1980 and the "Black Hawk Down" incident of 1993 (Scarborough 2004, 14–16). In a curious way, Rumsfeld would have agreed with Madeleine Albright's assessment that the Pentagon had developed a "no can do" organizational culture, putting up military roadblocks whenever adventurous civilian ideas were broached.

Whatever one may think of the policy results of the Rumsfeld Doctrine—on display in both Afghanistan and Iraq—he was partially successful in changing the ethos of the Pentagon, at least temporarily. As Schein notes, leadership is critical in the development of an organization's culture, and a forceful leader may change the way things are done within his institution (Schein 1985, 209–43). Largely out of favor during the Reagan and Bush 41 years, Rumsfeld had spent the last twenty five years or so in the corporate world, and it is therefore not surprising that he sought to run the Pentagon on business or managerial lines. He would scatter the Defense Department with unsigned memos (known as "snowflakes") which pressured his subordinates and highlighted what he saw as gaps in the organization's thinking and practices, a technique he had developed in the Nixon administration and utilized during his corporate years. While most secretaries of defense traditionally allow their deputies to run the sprawling Pentagon bureaucracy, leaving themselves free to act as a funnel for ideas to the president, for much of Rumsfeld's time in office he reversed this practice, preferring to manage the bureaucracy while the more intellectual Paul Wolfowitz acted as the ideas man.

As Bob Woodward notes, "Rumsfeld's transformation plans met with something just short of organized resistance bordering on insubordination among a significant part of the senior uniformed officers." He viewed the military as "hidebound and outdated," a stance that led to significant friction between the civilians and officers within the Pentagon, and the Army in particular was seen as "unresponsive, unimaginative and risk averse" (Woodward 2002, 22–23; Ricks 2006, 68). One example of how Rumsfeld countered (and overcame) resistance within the established bureaucracy to how things were done, however, is provided by his desire to change the way the Pentagon engaged in manhunts, a capacity that was at best diffused within the organization. The Special Operations Command (SoCom) Chief General Charles Holland was given the task of creating a global command unit for this purpose. As Scarborough writes, "Holland was reluctant, however, to turn SoCom into a global combat command; the military traditionally ran wars with regional commanders, not global ones" (Scarborough 2004, 20). In meetings, Holland expressed an unwillingness to interfere with what commanders were doing on the ground. Rumsfeld then simply bypassed Holland by issuing his own directive, eventually getting Holland to tow the line. Those who refused to go along with this or other aspects of Rumsfeld's new design (Eric Shinseki, who argued before Congress for a Powell Doctrine–type invasion of Iraq with much larger numbers of troops, provides one especially well-known example) were dismissed from their posts or pushed into early retirement. Moreover, when Rumsfeld found the intelligence coming from both the CIA and his own DIA wanting, he simply created his own "'intelligence shop," the controversial Office of Special Plans then headed by Douglas Feith.

The purpose of this chapter has been to briefly highlight the main theoretical features of the *Homo Bureaucraticus* approach, and the empirical chapters that follow this theoretical section will show in rather more detail how each perspective works across a number of case studies. However, a final example—one which highlights the resistance of bureaucrats to change even in the face of concerted attempts by elected politicians to force through such change—may prove particularly illustrative. The 9/11 Commission, appointed to uncover the root causes of the intelligence failures that had led to the attacks on the World Trade Center and Pentagon, reported that intelligence about potential terrorist attacks was too decentralized prior to 9/11. Various agencies had failed to share information, it noted, and it faulted the FBI and CIA especially in this regard. The principal remedies it recommended were the creation of a new Department of Homeland Security and an office called the Directorate of National Intelligence (DNI). Both were eventually set up in spite of determined bureaucratic resistance from the agencies within the executive branch, which stood to lose out from reform. The purpose of creating the DNI, for instance, was to establish a single office within the government which could connect the dots, overseeing each agency's intelligence and gathering information in a centralized location. The office of the DNI, created by the Intelligence Reform Act of 2004, was intended to *outrank* that of the CIA director, since the CIA is in fact only one of sixteen intelligence agencies within the U.S. government.

These reforms hit significant roadblocks from the start. Unlike the CIA, the DNI's office lacks an established organizational culture and power base, and its staff is relatively small. Critics have frequently argued, moreover, that it merely adds a layer of bureaucracy to the existing intelligence structure rather than streamlining it. In both the Bush 43 and Obama administrations, the DNI has often clashed with CIA director, and the latter has attempted to preserve the existing power structure regardless of whether Republicans or Democrats were in office. The first-ever DNI, John Negroponte, clashed repeatedly with CIA Director Porter Goss during the George W. Bush administration and also had to contend with an expansion of the Pentagon's intelligence activities under Rumsfeld. For instance, under the terms of the 2004 Act, Congress gave the DNI authority to appoint the chief U.S. intelligence official abroad, but the CIA has always resisted this; traditionally, it has always run its intelligence operations from foreign embassies, and it jealously guards its ability to cultivate direct relations with overseas intelligence bodies this way.

Negroponte appeared to have won this battle by 2006, when Goss resigned unexpectedly and was replaced by Negroponte's own deputy, Michael Hayden (Burger and Cooper 2006). Nevertheless, the same debates and bureaucratic tussles resurfaced under President Obama. CIA Director Leon Panetta clashed with DNI Dennis Blair during the summer of 2009, telling his own organization to ignore a directive from the DNI stating that his own office would now select America's intelligence chiefs abroad. Blair was reportedly furious about this. Like the authors of the bill that was intended to overhaul America's intelligence apparatus, he believes that in some nations it would be more appropriate to appoint a head from an agency other than the CIA. For example, the National Security Agency (NSA) has a major intelligence installation in Britain, so it might be more appropriate to appoint a chief from this body; in Iraq and Afghanistan someone from the Defense Intelligence Agency (DIA) might be most useful, while in Bolivia or Columbia an official from the Drug Enforcement Administration (DEA) might be the best fit (Mazzetti 2009). After extensive bureaucratic tussles over this issue, President Obama sided with the CIA. Influential members of Congress such as Senator Diane Feinstein have publicly expressed their concern that the CIA appears to be defying the will of the legislative branch, clinging to what many see as outdated, Cold War–era procedures at a time when Congress has made clear its desire to overhaul the way intelligence is gathered and disseminated.

Interestingly, *Homo Bureaucraticus* does *not* dispense the core idea of rationality altogether. In this approach, you should notice that while the *state* is not viewed as a rational actor—recall that the bureaucratic politics approach views the analogy between governments and individuals as flawed—*Homo Bureaucraticus* never challenges the view that the agencies and institutions of the state (and the individuals that comprise them) might be rational; indeed, agencies like the CIA and the DNI's office are seen as highly rational, carefully pursuing their own bureaucratic interests and seeking to preserve and extend their own missions and budgets. Put in terms of our Russian dolls, it moves the level of analysis down to organizations and begins to pick the state apart. In that sense, *Homo Bureaucraticus* represents only a limited (but nevertheless still radical) critique of the idea that states act in a rational way. As we will see in chapters 3 and 4, *Homo Sociologicus* and *Homo Psychologicus* launch a more concerted assault on the assumptions of the Rational Actor Model.

CHAPTER 3

Homo Sociologicus

Do people make better, more rational decisions when they operate in groups? In a book called *The Wisdom of Crowds*, James Surowiecki has recently argued just this. Pushing against a long-established tradition within social psychology and sociology, he claims that what he calls "wise crowds"—groups of highly informed individuals, such as experts in the corporate or political worlds—often make better decisions than people acting alone, in part because the aggregation of information and expertise, combined with diversity of opinion within a group, frequently leads to more rational decision-making outcomes (Surowiecki 2004). But even this relatively optimistic observer concedes that there are many circumstances where the conditions necessary for group wisdom are just not present. For instance, many researchers have found that people may be more inclined to behave in risky and even reckless ways in groups as opposed to when they are acting alone. This is known in the literature as the phenomenon of *risky shift*: as we shift from an individual to a group context, our responsibility for what occurs becomes shared; some psychologists have suggested that this diffusion of blame or guilt even when things go wrong, or when the group is acting in an unethical way, may underlie our increased willingness to engage in risky behavior (see for instance Wallach, Kogan, and Bem 1964). In the summer of 2011, widespread looting in British cities may have been encouraged by the perception that "everyone was doing it." Under normal circumstances, most of us would never dream of stealing a 50-inch Plasma television from a store whose window happens to be broken, but we *might* consider reaching in and taking the TV if people all around us were already doing it, if those people were individuals we knew or felt some sort of kinship with, and of course if we thought we could get away with it.

There are plenty of examples in political decision-making of groups taking extraordinarily risky decisions, which seem well-nigh incomprehensible to us in retrospect. "What were they thinking?" we ask ourselves afterward when everything goes wrong. Why do apparently sensible individuals, sometimes with decades of government experience behind them, often gamble everything in a way that seems almost calculated to lead to disaster? It has been argued, for instance, that the Reagan administration's decision to sell arms to Iran in the 1980s—a country which had held fifty-two Americans hostage for 444 days and which President Reagan himself had designated as a terrorist state—constituted a reckless action of this group-induced kind. Key administration members not only agreed to the sale of U.S. missiles to the government of the radical cleric Ayatollah Khomeini, apparently laboring under the misconception that the missiles were going to Iranian moderates, but then used the proceeds from the arms sale to continue to fund Nicaraguan rebel groups from which Congress (exercising its constitutional "power of the purse") had cut off funding. Then, as now, it seemed to make no sense. Pursuing either or both of these policies was incredibly risky, certainly unlawful, and potentially unconstitutional. In combination, they could even have led to the President's impeachment. Were group dynamics to blame? Was what Irving Janis called *groupthink* at the root of this?

In order to try to answer these questions, we first need to know a little bit about the Cold War politics of the mid-1980s. During this period, the Reagan administration faced two (initially unrelated) foreign policy problems on opposite sides of the globe, issues that would soon collide in spectacular fashion and forever alter the historical perception of Reagan's presidency. One problem involved the fear of Communism in what is sometimes known colloquially as "Uncle Sam's Backyard"; the other was the growth of terrorism and the taking of American hostages in the Middle East. Reagan and his colleagues were especially concerned that a regime similar to that controlled by the Marxist Fidel Castro in Cuba was now emerging in Central America. In Nicaragua, Reagan was trying to destabilize the sitting Marxist Sandinista regime by arming a group of anticommunist rebels known as the Contras. The president was also confronted by a growing hostage crisis in Lebanon, where a number of American citizens had been taken hostage by kidnappers associated with radical groups such as Hezbollah and Islamic Jihad and allied with Iran. Understanding the whole episode that became known as the Iran-Contra scandal—as well as the decision-making process that led the administration to take actions which at the very least skirted the law and probably violated the spirit of the Constitution—requires an appreciation of the ways in which these two issues became connected by Reagan officials.

Although that connection probably looks more artful in retrospect than it did at the time, a rather ingenious linkage was made between the two problems, the roots of which may lie in the deep emotional commitment to both the hostages and the Contras that Reagan and many of his advisers shared. Although the president later stated in a court of law that Iran-Contra was an operation undertaken "at my behest," his exact level of knowledge about Iran-Contra will probably never be established.[1] Reagan clearly knew about and approved the arms-for-hostages deal with Iran, but it remains unclear whether he approved the subsequent diversion of funds to the Contras. Nevertheless, we do know that the president was clearly willing to try unconventional methods to resolve both problems, even if the solutions his advisers came up with skirted the law and ran counter to the expressed will of Congress. The CIA Director William Casey felt an especially deep sense of kinship with his own employee, Beirut CIA Chief William Buckley, who was one of hostages. Casey, a close friend of the president and the former head of his 1980 election campaign, also knew that Buckley was probably being tortured by his captors.[2] Casey's Director of Operations, Clair George, had an even more personal link to the issue, having previously held Buckley's job in Lebanon in an earlier posting. George was reportedly prepared to do almost anything to get Buckley back. Reagan had also seen the Iran hostage crisis (examined in depth in chap. 8) destroy the presidency of his predecessor Jimmy Carter, and sought to improve relations with moderate factions within Iran as a counter to the rise of the radical cleric Ayatollah Khomeini in the region.

Reagan felt a similar (if not even more intense) degree of emotional commitment to the Contras. The president saw them as "freedom fighters"; indeed, so great was his commitment to the Contras that he sometimes compared them to the Founding Fathers of the United States. From his perspective, there was little difference between the men who had resisted King George II of England and those who were resisting Sandinista leader Daniel Ortega. Unfortunately for Reagan, many members of Congress, which was controlled by the Democrats at the time, saw the Contras not as freedom fighters but as terrorists; numerous reports had emerged from Nicaragua of human rights atrocities committed by the rebels, and public opinion in the United States had turned against the Contras. Congress used its most formidable power in foreign policy, the power of the purse, to assert its will. In 1982 and again in 1984, it passed the Boland Amendments, which cut off economic and then military aid to the Contras. Named after their sponsor Rep. Edward Boland, the amendments—tacked onto annual budgets so that Reagan could not veto them without rejecting painstakingly negotiated economic programs in toto—effectively resolved the issue in favor of Congress. Under the Constitution all funds spent by the government need to appropriated by the Congress first, so the president's hands were effectively tied once the legislative branch "cut off the spigot," as Reagan later put it.[3] In the language of the 1984 version of the amendment:

> During fiscal year 1985, no funds available to the Central Intelligence Agency, the Department of Defense, or any other agency or entity of the United States involved in intelligence activities may be obligated or expended for the purpose or which would have the effect of supporting, directly or indirectly, military or paramilitary operations in Nicaragua by any nation, group, organization, movement, or individual.

On the hostage issue, moreover, the president was similarly constrained. He had run as a hard-liner on foreign policy during the 1980 presidential election, and had constantly taken the public position both then and afterward that there would be "no deals" made with hostage-takers during his presidency.

How was the president to navigate these constraints? While no evidence has emerged that Reagan ever expressly told his advisers to break the law, we know that he instructed them in 1984 after the second Boland Amendment passed—in Reagan's typically emotive language—to keep the Contras alive "body and soul." This phrase was used in front of the National Security Adviser Robert McFarlane, George H. W. Bush (then vice president), and the Treasury Secretary James Baker (Draper 1991, 33). Reagan's typical management style was to make forceful but vague statements, which made it clear what he wanted to achieve, but then leave it to his advisers to decide *how* this general objective should be attained in an operational sense. The "body and soul" comment seems to have been consistent, then, with Reagan's standard practice. The president also made it clear that he wanted his advisers to get the hostages in Lebanon back, and again does not seem to have been overly concerned with how this was to be done.

One way that the administration found to raise funds for the Contras was by effectively privatizing American foreign policy: it asked third-party states, such as Saudi Arabia, to replace the funding lost to the Boland Amendments. Private individuals within the United States were also approached and asked to contribute to the cause. If this were the full extent of what occurred, the administration might have emerged relatively unscathed; while both of these actions certainly skirted the law, they were not *unambiguously* unconstitutional. At a June 25, 1984, meeting of the National Security Planning Group, attended by various high-level officials, including Reagan, Bush, Secretary of State George Shultz, Defense Secretary Caspar Weinberger, CIA Director William Casey, Chairman of the Joint Chiefs Gen. John Vessey, Attorney General Edwin Meese, Robert McFarlane and McFarlane's then deputy, John Poindexter, Secretary Shultz (citing the views of then White House Chief of Staff James Baker, not present that day) suggested that seeking funds for the Contras through third parties could lead to the President's impeachment, while Bush, Weinberger, and Casey took a contrary view:

> SECRETARY SHULTZ: Several points: (1) everyone agrees with the Contra program but there is no way to get a vote this week. If we leave it attached to the bill, we will lose the money we need for El Salvador. (2) We have had a vote on the anti-Sandinista program and the Democrats voted it down. It already is on the record and the Democrats are on the record. (3) I would like to get money for the Contras also, but another lawyer, Jim Baker, said that if we go out and try to get money from third countries, it is an impeachable offense.
>
> MR. CASEY: I am entitled to complete the record. Jim Baker said that if we tried to get money from third countries without notifying the oversight committees, it could be a problem and he was informed that the finding does provide for the participation and cooperation of third countries. Once he learned that the finding does encourage cooperation from third countries, Jim Baker immediately dropped his view that this could be an "impeachable offense," and you heard him say that, George.
>
> SECRETARY SHULTZ: Jim Baker's argument is that the U.S. government may raise and spend funds only through an appropriation of the Congress.

SECRETARY WEINBERGER: I am another lawyer who isn't practicing law, but Jim Baker should realize that the United States would not be spending the money for the anti-Sandinista program; it is merely helping the anti-Sandinistas obtain the money from other sources. Therefore, the United States is not, as a government, spending money obtained from other sources.

The meeting ended with the following (rather remarkable) exchange:

VICE PRESIDENT BUSH: How can anyone object to the U.S. encouraging third parties to provide help to the anti-Sandinistas under the finding? The only problem that might come up is if the United States were to promise to give these third parties something in return so that some people could interpret this as some kind of an exchange.

MR. CASEY: Jim Baker changed his mind as soon as he saw the finding and saw the language.

MR. MCFARLANE: I propose that that there be no authority for anyone to seek third party support for the anti-Sandinistas until we have the information we need, and I certainly hope none of this discussion will be made public in any way.

PRESIDENT REAGAN: If such a story gets out, we'll all be hanging by our thumbs in front of the White House until we find out who did it.[4]

Bush's view that pursuing funds through third parties would be acceptable as long as there was no *quid pro quo* (something promised to the third parties in return) ultimately prevailed, since the attorney general subsequently did give the decision-makers "the information we need," writing a legal opinion in July 1984 that encouraging third-party funding would not be impeachable. In reality, at least some of these countries *would* receive a variety of benefits in return as the Iran-Contra project got off the ground, however, and this became an embarrassing issue to Bush when he ran for president himself in 1988. In Reagan's second term, which began in February 1985, administration officials then went much farther than seeking funds through third states or private citizens within the United States. The president's wishes were met by creating a rather ingenious linkage between the hostage and Contra problems: the United States would secretly sell arms to Iran—ostensibly to Iranian moderates, and initially using Israel as a conduit—in return for Iran exerting its influence with the hostage-takers in Lebanon. In this way, the release of Americans could be obtained through an "arms-for-hostages" deal. The administration later diverted the proceeds from the arms sales to help fund the Contras. An NSC aide, Col. Oliver North, served as the desk officer for the plan, although he was clearly acting at least partly under the direction of CIA Director Casey; indeed, Bob Woodward described Casey as "a guiding hand, almost a case officer for North" (Woodward 1987, 466).

What was wrong with this, from a constitutional and legal perspective? Most obviously, it violated the spirit of the Constitution. The executive branch had effectively tried to nullify Congress's control over funding for government operations in precisely the way that had concerned both Baker and Shultz. Congress had expressly cut off aid to the Contras, but the Reagan administration had then sought to get around this. But there were other problems as well. Ironically, the sale of arms to Iran had been rendered illegal by an executive order that Reagan himself had issued. The sale was also illegal in the sense that it violated the Nelson-Bingham Amendment of 1974, which requires congressional review of arms sales of more than $25 million. Since the arms sale was secret, reporting to Congress was not done as the law requires. The diversion of funds to the Contras was certainly illegal and probably unconstitutional also; all funds must be appropriated by Congress under the Constitution, but in this case secret funds unknown to Congress were placed in a Swiss bank account and then used to fund a policy which potentially short cut the democratic process as well. If citizens are kept in the dark as to what the government's real policies are, how are they to assess the results of those policies at the ballot box?

In terms of concrete results, Iran-Contra can only be described as a fiasco, since it proved disastrous in a number of respects ('t Hart 1990, 258). The arms sales arguably led to the release of two hostages but since these Americans were later replaced by others, the whole exercise ultimately proved fruitless. The notion of selling arms to the so-called Iranian moderates was also logically inconsistent, since those who might have influence with Hezbollah—and might therefore be in a position to get the hostages out—would by definition be more radical. The missiles sold to Iran may well have prolonged the enormously destructive and savage Iran-Iraq War. The scandal also consumed the president's political capital during his second term, and no less than four investigations took place, which sapped Reagan's energy and that of his administration: one congressional, two by the executive branch itself (first an internal investigation by Meese and then the President's Special Review Board or Tower Commission, so-named because it was chaired by the then Republican senator from Texas, John Tower), and one judicial (conducted by Independent Counsel and former Eisenhower Attorney General Lawrence Walsh). Reagan's opinion poll ratings dropped precipitously after the arms sales became public, and he never quite recovered politically.

The legal ramifications of Walsh's investigation were especially dire for the administration. Oliver North, Robert McFarlane, and John Poindexter were all tried in a court of law for crimes relating to Iran-Contra. McFarlane pled guilty to withholding information from Congress and received a token sentence. North and Poindexter were found guilty on various counts but were later acquitted on appeal because Congress had effectively granted them legal immunity. After the Reagan administration ended, Iran-Contra also led to the bizarre and unprecedented spectacle of a former president testifying at the criminal trial of his former National Security Adviser (Poindexter). Reagan's successor George H. W. Bush—himself implicated as a "loyal lieutenant" to Reagan in the decision-making process that led to Iran-Contra—later felt compelled to issue presidential pardons to former Defense Secretary Weinberger, the Assistant Secretary of State for Inter-American Affairs Elliott Abrams, Robert McFarlane, the former national security adviser, and to

Duane Clarridge, Alan Fier, and Clair George, all of whom had worked for the CIA and had helped implement various aspects of the Reagan administration's plan.

EXPLAINING THE IRAN-CONTRA FIASCO

From a decision-making perspective, the truly surprising thing is how such an experienced and politically savvy collection of decision-makers could have arrived at a set of policies which virtually *invited* the impeachment of a previously highly popular president. Like Richard Nixon in 1972, Ronald Reagan was in a politically unassailable position after his landslide victory of 1984. Reagan himself was admittedly a foreign policy novice or neophyte; like most former state governors, he possessed next to no foreign policy experience prior to arriving in the Oval Office, and had to learn the position on the job.[5] But Vice President George H. W. Bush in particular had held an array of high profile foreign policy positions, including those of CIA director, ambassador to China, and U.S. representative at the UN; CIA Director William Casey had served as an undersecretary of state from 1973 to 1974, had once been a CIA operative himself, and was considered well-versed in foreign affairs; Secretary of State George Shultz, while perhaps better versed at that time in economic policy, had served President Nixon as his treasury secretary and was familiar with the ways of Washington politics; Defense Secretary Caspar Weinberger's background was similar in some ways to Schultz's, and he had previously been Chairman of the Federal Trade Commission, Director of the Office of Management, and Secretary of Health, Education, and Welfare under Nixon and then Ford; Robert McFarlane had done two tours of duty in Vietnam and had worked for the Nixon White House in the Office of Legislative Affairs before becoming Military Assistant to Henry Kissinger from 1973 to 1976, accompanying the national security adviser on the trips to China (see chap. 2); and finally, while Admiral John Poindexter's resume was admittedly thinner, he had enjoyed a successful naval career before going to work in various capacities within Reagan's National Security Council. Graduating first in his class at Annapolis, Poindexter had later earned a doctorate in nuclear physics (Walsh 1997, 52). Why did such an esteemed and experienced collection of individuals, then, arrive at such an ill-considered approach to the Contra and hostage problems?

We know that both Shultz and Weinberger were opposed to the arms sales; the latter argued against selling weapons to Iran but had supported funding the Contras through third parties, while Shultz was the only senior member of the administration who opposed both policies. As Defense Secretary, Weinberger could not be kept entirely out of the loop since U.S.-owned missiles could hardly be transported to the CIA or the Middle East without the Pentagon's knowledge, and he later acquiesced in the implementation of the plan and was indicted by Independent Counsel Walsh for failing to turn over documents in his possession relating to Iran-Contra. In any case, both men were effectively cut out of the decision-making process once their opposition became evident. Instead of utilizing the normal advisory process, policymaking occurred within a narrow clique, centered on Casey, Poindexter, North, and perhaps Vice President Bush, a group which Theodore Draper later described as a "presidential junta" (Draper 1991). The NSC was utilized in part because it could be argued that doing so got around the language of the Boland Amendments. As quoted earlier, that language expressly forbade "the Central Intelligence Agency, the Department of Defense, or any other agency or entity of the United States involved in intelligence activities" from getting involved, but it could also be argued that the NSC was not such an entity. The resulting clique, which was small and cohesive, rather like the Tuesday Lunch Group that Lyndon Johnson used to make decisions about Vietnam (see chap. 7), does not appear to have been exposed to dissenting views once Shultz and Weinberger were eliminated from the inner circle on this issue.

Several observers have suggested that top Reagan officials may have been victims of *groupthink* ('t Hart 1990; Kowert 2001; Shafer and Crichlow 2010). This rather Orwellian-sounding term, originally invented by the social psychologist Irving Janis, is one of those pieces of social scientific terminology that has entered popular usage, where it is now used rather loosely and colloquially to refer to defective or dysfunctional group decision-making in general. The U.S. Senate Intelligence Committee concluded in 2004, for instance, that there was evidence of groupthink in the mistaken assessment that there were weapons of mass destruction (WMDs) in Iraq prior to the 2003 American invasion. The chairs of that committee were using the term to refer to a kind of generalized or collective misperception. In the study of public policy, international relations, psychology, and management, however, groupthink has a rather more precise usage. As Janis himself put it:

> I use the term "groupthink" as a quick and easy way to refer to a mode of thinking that people engage in when they are deeply involved in a cohesive group, when the members' striving for unanimity override their motivation to realistically appraise alternative courses of action. ... Groupthink refers to a deterioration of mental efficiency, reality testing and moral judgment that results from in-group pressures" (Janis 1982, 9).

Janis frequently described groupthink as a "concurrence-seeking tendency," a process in which unanimity and agreement come to seem more important to group members than the full consideration of available alternatives.

Groupthink has a number of antecedent conditions in addition to high group cohesiveness (see fig. 3.1). For instance, it is encouraged where the group is insulated from outside advice, where an aggressive or opinionated leader prevents meaningful debate, where norms requiring the use of methodical procedures are absent, where most members of the group come from a similar social and educational background and/or think alike, where the group is confronting high levels of stress, and where its members are experiencing temporarily low levels of self-esteem.

Janis also identified a number of consequences of these conditions, including symptoms that can be used to diagnose the presence or absence of groupthink.

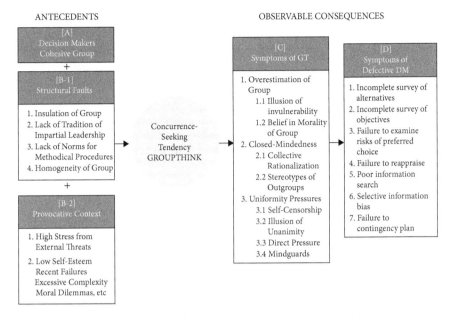

ANTECEDENTS

OBSERVABLE CONSEQUENCES

Figure 3.1 Groupthink Summarized. source: Adapted from Irving Janis, *Groupthink: Psychological Studies of Policy Decisions and Fiascoes* (Boston: Houghton Mifflin, 1982), 244.

These include the presence of an "illusion of invulnerability," a phrase Janis used to describe a kind of excessive optimism, which encourages risk taking among the group; "collective rationalization" about the risks of a chosen option, where the problems associated with that option are downplayed or ignored; a belief in the inherent morality of the group, in which members come to believe in the exclusive moral rightness of their cause; the appearance of stereotyped views of outgroups or the enemy; the exertion of direct pressure on those who dissent from the majority opinion; self-censorship, where doubters fail to express their true feelings; the false perception of unanimity, where in fact some members may harbor personal doubts about the policy option chosen; and finally the emergence of self-appointed "mindguards," members of the group who take it upon themselves to protect the group and its leader from dissenting views (guarding our minds much as a bodyguard protects our physical bodies). Perhaps the greatest strength of this approach is that it highlights the fact that groups are more than the sum total of the individuals who compose them; once policymakers form a group, the resultant body subsumes (and may overwhelm) its members. The fact that a decision is made in a social environment, Janis suggested, often makes a difference to the substance of that decision, and his greatest contribution may have been his persuasive argument that even the best and the brightest can fall prey to dysfunctional group dynamics.

High group cohesiveness, Janis argued, is a necessary but not sufficient condition for groupthink to occur. This type of camaraderie may develop, for instance, where the members have known each other for many years and/or have come think in ways that are very much alike. While such a group *can* make effective decisions—indeed, group cohesiveness is probably an essential asset to groups that rely on successful operation as a single unit, such as sports teams—it can become prey to the groupthink pathology or syndrome, whereby members of the group come to prize concurrence-seeking over the full and rational consideration of all available courses of action. In his book *Groupthink*, Janis argues that the syndrome was present in a number of cases, including the Kennedy administration's decision-making about the Bay of Pigs invasion in 1961 and the Johnson administration's deliberations about Vietnam in 1965 (see chaps. 5 and 7 respectively). Janis contrasts this with what he terms "vigilant decision-making"—in which decision-makers rigorously and thoroughly appraise all available options—and holds up the Cuban missile crisis as a notable instance of a case in which this kind of superior process occurred (see chap. 6).

While the presence of groupthink tends to be associated with policy fiascoes, Janis argued that the link is a matter of tendency rather than an absolute law. It is possible to get a good decision from a bad decision-making process, in other words, since a number of factors—among them sheer luck—can intervene. For instance, many observers consider the Persian Gulf War of 1991 a success, at least judged purely on its own merits. The objective President George H. W. Bush was seeking—the removal of Saddam Hussein from Kuwait, which he had invaded in 1990, and the reestablishment of the *status quo* in the Middle East—was quickly attained; moreover, Bush avoided the collapse of the international coalition that had sustained the war by refraining from removing Hussein from power (a move with which, as we will see in chap. 10, neoconservatives like Paul Wolfowitz profoundly disagreed). Yet despite the success of this venture when one defines policy outcomes this way, it has been argued that there were at least some elements of groupthink in Bush's decision-making process (Yetiv 2004, 104–20).

Steve Yetiv argues that pretty much all the antecedent conditions required to produce groupthink were present on the road to war with Saddam Hussein. Bush's inner circle was highly cohesive, and its members were also highly similar in an ideological sense. As Yetiv puts it, "the group was so closely knit that some meetings seemed like a convivial card game, with feet kicked up and laughs making the rounds, rather than a sober, formal review of options. Cohesiveness was also fuelled by norms of loyalty, notions on which Bush had been nursed starting at an early age, and which he proceeded to instill in others" (Yetiv 2004, 107). The president had cut off debate early on within the administration by making a strongly emotional and moral case for the war up front, and his leadership was highly "partial" in this sense. There were also a number of symptoms of groupthink present. It is worth noting that Janis always emphasized that not all of the symptoms need to be present for a diagnosis of the "concurrence seeking" tendency to be made, but Yetiv argues that a sufficient number were identifiable here. Colin Powell had expressed dissent against Bush's tough military approach outside the decision-making group: he reportedly believed that economic sanctions needed to be given more time, but in key meetings Powell seems to have mostly self-censored these doubts. When he did briefly express whether it was worth going to war over Kuwait, he seems to have been mindguarded by Dick Cheney; Cheney told Powell (who was then Chairman of the Joint Chiefs) to "just do the military options. Don't be the Secretary of State or the Secretary of Defense or the National Security Adviser" (Yetiv 2004,115–19). Although his argument was different later, as we will outline in chapter 10, Cheney also seems to have acted as a mindguard when Powell (who by that time *was* the Secretary of State) expressed reservations about George W. Bush's Iraq War.

How might the groupthink approach explain why the Reagan administration ended up pursuing such a disastrous course of action in Iran-Contra, though? The President's Special Review Board's report, the Tower Commission, is arguably consistent with a groupthink-style interpretation (*New York Times* 1987). Tower and his colleagues found that the administration's foreign policies on Iran were wholly inconsistent; the United States was seeking simultaneously to both strengthen and weaken a terrorist state, for instance, unsure whether our interest lay in supporting Iran or its neighbor Iraq. The decision-making process was flawed: key expertise was not used, the process was too informal, there was no proper legal review conducted, and the arms sales only encouraged more hostage-taking. As Colin Powell later put it, the National Security Council, which was initially intended purely as an advisory body to the president, "had become its own Defense Department, running little wars, its own State Department, carrying out its own secret diplomacy, and its own CIA, carrying out clandestine operations" (Powell 1995, 333). The consuming obsession with secrecy meant that intelligence support was inadequate or missing altogether. The report also criticized President Reagan for being too "hands off." He did not actively run the advisory system or closely monitor the activities of his subordinates, nor did he seem to appreciate the illegalities involved. Reagan's "body and soul" comment, moreover, gave implicit license to what occurred, suggesting again that anything goes.

Once Shultz and Weinberger were excluded from the decision-making process on Iran-Contra, a small circle of advisers dominated decision-making (Kowert 2001). The group was by necessity obsessively secret, and was therefore insulated from outside advice; the group neither sought nor permitted outsiders to offer their own opinions, fearful that non-members simply would not understand how necessary the Iran-Contra strategy was. According to Paul 't Hart, this group was highly cohesive in an ideological sense, and all of its members shared the same conviction that the national security of the United States hinged on preventing the spread of Communism at all costs. Many of the symptoms of groupthink were present as well ('t Hart 2000, 249–58; Schafer and Crichlow 2010, 100). The group first of all harbored an illusion of invulnerability, a feeling that they could not lose. Members also discounted warnings that their strategy ran counter to the administration's stated policies and might lead to Reagan's impeachment, failing to reconsider their core assumptions. Furthermore, members of the inner circle, including Reagan himself, seem to have engaged in collective rationalizations concerning what the Iran-Contra plan was really about. The president constantly defended himself against the charge that this was an arms-for-hostages deal by variously asserting (a) that the Iranians were not given arms but had paid for them, and (b) that the real purpose of the whole enterprise had been strategic (that is, aimed at improving relations with Iran) and was therefore largely unrelated to the hostage issue ('t Hart 1990, 251–54).

The group members also believed passionately in the moral rightness of their course. Reagan and Ollie North in particular viewed the issues of the hostages and support for the Contras in highly moralistic terms; they wanted to do what they saw as the right thing, irrespective of the legal or constitutional niceties, and they became blind to the ethical consequences of their decisions (such as the fact that the United States was placing weapons in the hands of a terrorist state and helping to prolong a war in which many thousands of civilians had already perished). According to Robert McFarlane, Reagan had a "disdain" for Congress, which seems to have sprung from his belief that they were wrong on the *Contra* issue while he, Reagan, was on the right side of history.[6] In the memorable phrase of Senators William Cohen and George Mitchell, those who formulated and implemented the Iran-Contra plan were "men of zeal" (Cohen and Mitchell 1988). The group also seems to have developed stereotyped views of out-groups, coming to regard Congress and the mass media as enemies rather than simply adversaries in a political process.

The way in which dissenters were treated is also consistent with the group-think hypothesis. Janis argues that dissenters who persist in voicing their disagreement with the policies of the inner circle frequently become neutralized or "domesticated":

> From the standpoint of reducing tension and bolstering morale within "the club", the subtle domestication process may work well, both for the dissenter and for the rest of the group. The nonconformist can feel that he is still accepted as a member in good standing. Unaware of the extent to which he is being influenced by the majority, he has the illusion that he is free to speak his mind. If on occasion he goes too far, he is warned about his deviation in an affectionate or joking way and is reminded only indirectly of his potentially precarious status by the labels others give him ("Mr. Stop-the-Bombing," "our favorite dove"). The others in the group … feel satisfied about giving full consideration to the opposing position and can even pat themselves on the back for being so democratic about tolerating open dissent (Janis 1982, 115).

Janis may have overgeneralized from the Vietnam case—the above description is drawn from his account of how two of those "domesticated dissenters," George Ball and Bill Moyers, were treated by Lyndon Johnson (see chap. 7)—and it does not quite fit the manner in which George Shultz, the leading dissenter in the Iran-Contra case, was treated. Nevertheless, Shultz would be criticized by the Tower Commission for allegedly looking the other way during Iran-Contra, a habit consistent with self-censorship. Former CIA Counsel Stanley Sporkin observed that on the issue of arms sales, Weinberger was "Dr. No" while Shultz was "Dr. I Don't Want To Know" (quoted in Cannon 2000, 565). As mentioned earlier, however, Shultz was the only senior member of the administration who consistently opposed both third party Contra funding and the arms-for-hostages deal. He was also the only senior official, as far as we know, who frequently tried to get Reagan to change course and abandon the Iran-Contra strategy. Shultz described these struggles in his memoirs as "a lonely battle" and Iran-Contra itself as "the snake that would not die" (Shultz 1993, 816–18, 841–59; Walsh 1997, 333–34).

There is also evidence that the Secretary of State came under concerted pressure from other members of the administration to tow the line, especially from Casey and Poindexter. In January 1986, after the operation had become public and had started to unravel, Casey made a determined effort to get everyone to sign on to the false claim that everyone in the administration had agreed with the premise of the Iran-Contra strategy. Not surprisingly, Shultz in particular baulked at signing publicly onto such a position.

The CIA Director Bill Casey then produced a draft statement to be released to the press. The purpose was to say that all the president's advisers were fully aware of this operation and supported it. "Everyone must support this policy", the president said. That I was *not* prepared to do. President Reagan was being ill served by advisers who were putting forth schemes for arms-for-hostages swaps—which this was—despite the refusal to call it that. I continued to ask questions about the structure of arrangements, which always came down to a trade of arms for hostages" (Shultz 1993, 814).

The evidence of direct mindguarding in this case is perhaps less clear. Did anyone take it upon themselves to protect the group and its leader from dissenting views that might challenge the group's assumed consensus? As 't Hart states, the complete exclusion of Shultz and Weinberger from the group may have obviated the need for self-appointed mindguards to exert direct pressure on them ('t Hart 1990, 257). Nevertheless, Shultz himself suggests that Casey in particular appears to have acted as a kind of thought policeman, in ways that are at least consistent with the kind of practices that Janis would have recognized. Shultz notes in his memoirs that he was under constant pressure from Casey to subject everyone in the State Department to lie detector tests, a measure Shultz steadfastly opposed. Casey's concerns were no doubt an extension of the obsession with secrecy and his worry that the Iran-Contra affair might be blown wide open by one of Shultz's employees (or, indeed, by Shultz himself). But Shultz suggests that lie detectors were also used as a mechanism of intimidation to ensure that potential dissenters were silenced. "You could keep people in line by intimidating them was the impression I got from Bill Casey and other disciples of lie detector tests. Discipline has its place in running an organization, but management by intimidation never appealed to me" (Shultz 1993, 804).

THE ASSUMPTIONS OF *HOMO SOCIOLOGICUS*

The first element or assumption of *Homo Sociologicus* is quite simply that decisions are often taken in groups rather than unilaterally. When we think about governmental decisions, we very often conjure a visual image in our heads of a single individual, such as a president or prime minister, sitting at a desk and poring over various policy alternatives. On some occasions, this image may constitute an accurate picture of reality. Although Franklin Roosevelt was famous for his strategy of playing one adviser off against one another, many other U.S. presidents (Richard Nixon, Lyndon Johnson, and Ronald Reagan come to mind in particular) were uncomfortable with witnessing their advisers slug it out with one another. Nixon reportedly preferred to work in isolation from others for this reason, hunkering down in the Oval Office away from most of his administration. Similarly, Ronald Reagan often preferred to have his advisers debate one another and generate a list of options at another level of government; only once that list of options had been drawn up did the president become involved.

For various reasons, however, even presidents with a Lone Ranger style often find it useful to rely on group-based decision-making (Gaenslen 1992). First of all, this most obviously allows a leader to draw on a broad range of opinions and expertise, exposing him or her—at least in theory—to a variety of differing and possibly dissenting views. As Yaacov Vertzberger writes:

> Decision-makers operating in a group are likely to be exposed to new information and interpretations more rapidly than if they were operating alone and to arguments they might not have been aware of as independent decision-makers; both exposure and arguments improve the quality of group members' problem solving and learning ... argumentation in the process of group decision-making clarifies ambiguities and inconsistencies by disseminating information and alternative perspectives and can illuminate weaknesses in the logical structure of accumulated knowledge and beliefs (Vertzberger 1990, 223).

Leaders may prefer to work in groups where they are not well-informed about the policy area concerned. George H. W. Bush, for instance, was comfortable with foreign policy but was less interested in domestic policy issues, while the opposite was true of Lyndon Johnson. Second, group decision-making lends greater legitimacy to a decision than its unilateral counterpart. Third, as William Casey's attempt to get Secretary Shultz to sign onto the Iran-Contra strategy suggests, group decision-making can offer political cover; if all members of an administration have publicly associated themselves with a course of action, it becomes harder for them to reject that course of action *after the fact* if it becomes unpopular or fails to produce the intended results. Fourth, group decision-making may reduce psychological strain on leaders, especially where they are uncomfortable with a given policy question. And last, making decisions in groups may actually be mandated by the legislature under some circumstances; the National Security Act of 1948, for instance, is intended to make sure that senior figures like the secretary of state and secretary of defense are consulted about major foreign policy matters (another provision of the law that one could argue was violated, at least in spirit, during Iran-Contra).

A second major assumption of *Homo Sociologicus* flows from the first but is less intuitive. That decisions are often taken in groups matters because it may affect not just *how* a decision is taken but also what that decision *is*. In short, process matters (Schafer and Crichlow 2010). There is a rich literature in social psychology which suggests that decision-making groups are not reducible to the individuals who comprise them (for a summary, see Levine 1989). Put differently, people behave differently in groups than they do when acting singly or alone; we are social animals, and we often rely on social cues as a kind of shorthand method when we make decisions. As we read at the beginning of this chapter, we may be more inclined to take risks in groups. Equally, it is often difficult to reject social pressures within a group. Most of us find it difficult to be the odd man out, the individual who bucks the trend and speaks or acts in a way different from the majority. As the well-known Asch line experiment alluded to in chapter 1 illustrates (see p. 11–12), we often fear being thought of as different, so much so that we will even deny the evidence of our own eyes or simply "go along to get along" when confronted by evidence that the majority is taking a position that is simply wrong.

Another famous example of the power of social pressure within a group was the "smoke under the door" experiment, originally conducted in the 1960s by the social psychologists John Darley and Bibb Latané (Latané and Darley 1970). Subjects were asked to sit in a room and fill out a questionnaire. The experimenters then arranged for smoke to pour into the room under the door. When the subject was alone, he or she almost always reported the incident immediately. But Darley and Latané also set up a group situation in which the naïve subject was

---

- Decisions are often made in groups, for a variety of political and psychological reasons.
- Social pressures matter: individuals often behave differently in a group than they do when acting alone. In particular, they may be more willing to make risky decisions (*risky shift*).
- Some groups induce *conformity* or a "concurrence seeking tendency" (*groupthink*); social pressures toward consensus may induce the actor to behave in nonrational ways (even contrary to his/her beliefs and values).
- There may be at least three different routes to groupthink—high group cohesion, deindividuation, and "anticipatory compliance" to leaders by group members—and at least two types of groupthink: a pessimistic variation (Type 1) and an optimistic one (Type 2).
- New administrations may be especially prone to Newgroup Syndrome.
- *Deadlock* within groups may be as much a risk as the consensus, conformity and compliance inherent in groupthink; some groups induce a stultifying variety of views and information with which a leader may not be able to cope.
- Derived primarily from social psychology and from the allied sociological tradition.

Figure 3.2 *Homo Sociologicus* Summarized.

placed in the room together with a number of actors, who had been instructed beforehand to completely ignore the smoke. Amazingly, 90 percent of the naïve subjects disregarded what was happening in the group situation, even to the point where the smoke in the air got so thick that visibility became difficult and people began to cough and choke.

A third major assumption, as we have seen already, indicates that while we often assume that groups make *better* decisions than individuals working alone, this does not necessarily follow; the potential advantages of making decisions in groups can sometimes be outweighed by other, more pathological processes, and Irving Janis's argument that some groups induce *conformity* or a concurrence-seeking tendency is only the best known example of this position. Social pressures toward consensus may induce the actor to behave in nonrational ways (even contrary to his or her beliefs and values). Policy alternatives may not be explored if they violate the group consensus. Because of group pressure, dissenters may fail to even voice their private concerns about the group's chosen course of action, and some members of a decision-making group may take it upon themselves to police the existing consensus by knocking down any dissent from the favored course of action. While Ronald Reagan does not appear to have engaged overtly in what Janis calls "aggressive, opinionated leadership" during Iran-Contra, there was clearly an absence of norms requiring the methodical consideration of options by the group, as discovered by the Tower Commission. Most of the discussion seems to have centered not on generating a full list of options or on whether the administration *should* try to get around congressional restrictions, but rather on *how* this might be done (legally or otherwise), and once Shultz and Weinberger voiced their dissent, they were simply excluded altogether as the group shrank in on itself.

In a fourth assumption, there may be at least three different routes or paths to groupthink: high group cohesion, de-individuation, and anticipatory compliance to leaders by group members, as well as at least two distinct types of groupthink: a pessimistic variation, and an optimistic one ('t Hart 1990, 197–205; see also Schafer and Crichlow 2010). These are distinctions that Janis himself never really explored, but Paul 't Hart develops these ideas in his book *Groupthink in Government*. One route to groupthink is through the mechanism of high group cohesion, which Janis did discuss and which has already been alluded to in the Iran-Contra example; a high esprit de corps within the group, as we have seen, seems to be present in many if not all cases of the groupthink syndrome. Highly congenial groups, as we saw in the example of George H. W. Bush's inner circle, may become so relaxed, familiar, and informal with one another that they fail to engage in the more formal and rigorous consideration of options. A second mechanism, 't Hart argues, takes a somewhat darker and troubling form. Groupthink can occur through de-individuation, where the individual comes to identify with the group to such an extent that he or she effectively becomes lost in that group: here one loses his sense of individual identity and comes to see himself merely as an agent of the group. This second mechanism constitutes an extreme form of social cohesion, although t'Hart argues that this form of groupthink is rare in elite decision-making groups (it may be more characteristic of religious cults, or genocidal and terrorist groups). Nevertheless, unlike Janis, 't Hart suggests that cohesion is not in fact an essential antecedent condition, since other pathways are possible. The third alternative does not require social cohesion, since under this pathway members "preemptively comply with real or perceived policy preferences of group leaders or high-status members" ('t Hart 1990, 197). This is termed the "anticipatory compliance" pathway, and it suggests that group members need only *perceive* that they are coming under pressure to favor a particular option, whether that pressure is real or not; under such conditions, group members—especially those of lower status—will tend to comply with superiors, whether a demand is real or not. According to 't Hart, especially forceful chief executives can often breed this kind of groupthink, sometimes unwittingly ('t Hart 1990, 200–201).

A further distinction has been made between types of groupthink: Type 1 or Collective Avoidance and Type 2 or Collective Overoptimism ('t Hart 1990, 202–03). Type 1 groupthink may be thought of as the pessimistic variation, while Type 2 is more optimistic. According to 't Hart, collective avoidance "rests on the following proposition: if members of a decision group perceive the issue confronting them as a problem that may result in failure rather than as an opportunity for success, they will attempt as much as possible to avoid being associated within the decision process concerning the issue" ('t Hart 1990, 202). Type 1 decision-makers are pessimistic in the sense that they expect failure, and under these conditions they seek to avoid responsibility (e.g., by registering dissent or leaving the group altogether). Conversely, in Type 2 groupthink decision-makers are collectively optimistic in the sense that they expect success and see the policy problem confronting them as an opportunity. Under these conditions, group members have a strong incentives to associate themselves with the policy.

As 't Hart suggests, it may only be under Type 2 groupthink that policymakers experience an "illusion of invulnerability." As we will see in chapters 5 and 7 respectively, the Bay of Pigs case seems to best fit Type 2, since members of the incoming Kennedy administration are said to have felt that they "had the magic touch" and "could not fail." The Vietnam case, on the other hand, seems to best fit Type 1, since most of Johnson's inner circle, including LBJ himself, appear to have been well aware that they might well be headed for failure, or at least a prolonged and costly war. Applied to the Iran-Contra case that we have used as the main vehicle of explanation in this chapter, Oliver North, Robert McFarlane, and John Poindexter may all have seen the Iran-Contra issues as an opportunity for success. Indeed, McFarlane later admitted that he viewed the Iran initiative as an opportunity to replicate the Nixon administration's overture to China, in which he had participated as an aide to Henry Kissinger.

A fifth assumption proposes that new administrations may be especially prone to what has become known as "newgroup syndrome" (Stern and Sundelius 1994; Stern 1997). Like the groupthink approach, the newgroup syndrome perspective focuses on group conformity and compliance, but it traces it to a different cause: the fact that conformity is often a feature of newly formed policy groups, which have yet to find their way. As Stern further explains, in new groups:

> A common group subculture and well-developed procedural norms tend to be lacking. This vacuum creates uncertainty among the members who are likely to be anxious, tentative, dependent, and, therefore, particularly inclined to take direction from a leader or other assertive group members within the group. These conditions create incentives for both compliance and internalization on the part of the individual member, which in turn results in a tendency toward conformity in the group as a whole. (Stern 1997, 182)

Stern stresses that while dysfunctional decision-making is not inevitable in new groups—it really all depends on the kind of norms that the group leader encourages at the outset—there is an in-built tendency toward conformity in the early stages. With this comes an unwillingness to engage in open and critical thinking. As we will see in chapter 5, he applies this approach to the Bay of Pigs case study. Briefly stated, Stern suggests that on coming to office in 1961, John Kennedy swept aside many of the formal, structured procedures preferred by Dwight Eisenhower, favoring a looser and more informal approach. The president himself had little management or executive-level experience, and his youthful advisers were not well-acquainted with one another. The new president did not seem aware that the group norm he was fostering at this stage, Stern argues, was one of deference to the experts, and his laissez-faire management style combined with this to produce an early foreign policy disaster at the Bay of Pigs.

A final assumption suggests that *deadlock* within groups may be as much a risk to the integrity and efficiency of the policymaking process as the consensus, conformity, and compliance that characterizes groupthink (Kowert 2001; 2002). A number of recent scholars have suggested that there has been too much attention devoted in research and textbooks to groupthink and to conformity within groups in general. This has prompted many scholars to look beyond groupthink, reexamining the wider literature on group behaviors within social psychology for clues as to how other theoretical frameworks might be developed ('t Hart, Stern, and Sundelius 1997). Paul Kowert has been especially prominent in this effort, seeking to redirect our attention to the way in which *divided* groups may be just as harmful to the foreign policy decision-making process. He argues that there is no perfect or ideal kind of advisory system; rather, it is the fit or interaction between a president's decision-making style and the structure of the advisory group that matters in reaching (or failing to reach) an effective policy process (Kowert 2002, 23–30). Some leaders (Jimmy Carter or Bill Clinton offer good examples) are comfortable with complexity and have a great appetite for information. Such open leaders are best served by an advisory process that is also open; in other words, they will function best in an environment that offers the free interchange of ideas and opinions. Equally, closed leaders (Reagan again provides a notable example) learn in a different way; according to Kowert, such leaders "rely primarily on their instincts and on a much smaller quantity and variety of information to make decisions"

(Kowert 2002, 17). This type of leader is best suited to a group environment, which is contained, hierarchical, and carefully managed rather than freewheeling. However, it is precisely where a mismatch occurs between a leader's style and the advisory system employed that group pathologies become most evident:

> Open leaders in closed groups will not receive the information they need (and are capable of handling), will consider fewer options than they should, and will base their decisions on a distorted and incomplete understanding of the problems they face. The result will resemble what Janis called groupthink. Closed leaders in open groups receive too much (and too challenging) information. They are more likely to suffer from a very different problem, which might be called "deadlock". In the face of conflicting advice and variety of information, they are likely to withdraw. In these circumstances, they will actually learn even less than had they been presented with fewer options and a more managed flow of advice (Kowert 2002, 23).

As we will discover in the empirical chapters that follow, Kowert's approach to the analysis of group decision-making can potentially be applied to a number of cases, as can older approaches such as that of Janis and modified groupthink perspectives like that of Paul 't Hart.

FROM *HOMO SOCIOLOGICUS* TO *HOMO PSYCHOLOGICUS*

In this chapter and in chapter 2, we have examined foreign policy decision-making from the organizational and group levels respectively. But there is a final element in the series of enclosed *matryoshka* dolls that must be examined: the one representing the individual level of analysis. It seems obvious that the personalities, values, and beliefs of decision-makers matter just as much as (if not more than) bureaucratic infighting, organizational routines, or group processes; indeed, Kowert's approach suggests that we cannot consider group dynamics apart from the decision-making style of the individuals who lead them. Reexamining the Iran-Contra example from such a perspective, we might argue that this fiasco occurred not primarily because of group dynamics per se but because President Reagan and other key decision-makers had a set of *mental images*—the domino theory, for instance, or fear of a second Cuba, and/or a repetition of the Iran hostage crisis—which led them to take extreme measures and reckless risks (Hemmer 2000). Ultimately, the real decision to proceed with the Iran-Contra venture may have been made in Reagan's head. Once we begin to make this kind of argument, we are moving into the territory of *Homo Psychologicus*, which is the subject of the next chapter.

CHAPTER 4

Homo Psychologicus

The date was May 12, 1975. Only twelve days earlier, the last helicopter had taken off from the roof of the U.S. embassy in Saigon, signifying the failure of America's long commitment to keep South Vietnam from falling to Communism. Saigon would soon be renamed after the late and much-revered leader Ho Chi Minh, as the victorious forces of the North rolled into the city and achieved their long-standing aim of uniting the nation under a single banner. And now this: neighboring Cambodia, lately under the control of the murderous pseudo-Marxist Pol Pot,[1] had seized an American ship. On the afternoon May 12, a U.S. merchant vessel, the SS *Mayaguez,* was captured by the Cambodians in international waters, some sixty miles off the mainland. The ship itself was of little value, but the capture of its crew of thirty-nine Americans was obviously more valuable. The crew was soon spirited off the ship and taken hostage on nearby Koh Tang Island. The crisis would last only three days, however, in part because President Gerald Ford and his advisers quickly decided to launch both a bold rescue attempt and a punitive strike on the Cambodian mainland. On May 14, President Ford made the decision at a meeting of his NSC principals to push ahead quickly on both these fronts.

In a complaint which calls to mind some aspects of *Homo Bureaucraticus,* the U.S. military would later grumble that there had been far too much civilian control of the *Mayaguez* raid. According to Edward Luttwak, Gerald Ford "spoke directly with Navy pilots actually over the target, to make tactical decisions in minute detail" during the rescue operation (Luttwak 1984, 86). While this is probably an exaggeration, we do know that the Acting Chairman of the Joint Chiefs, General David Jones, complained about being rushed into military action with very little planning or preparation. Jones argued at the May 14 meeting that the military needed a bit more time to conduct a rescue mission effectively, especially since intelligence on the exact whereabouts of the hostages was poor and inconsistent. "Explaining that U.S. troops were poised to take the *Mayaguez* and Koh Tang," Lucien Vandenbroucke relates, "[Jones] observed that by waiting another twenty-four hours, U.S. forces would be better prepared. Command and control would be more firmly in place, giving the mission a better chance of success" (Vandenbroucke 1993, 82). Under concerted pressure from Ford and Kissinger to launch the rescue mission right away instead of the waiting a day, Jones argued that a rescue operation would be difficult, if not impossible, to do at that stage; more time was needed to coordinate the various forces involved in a rescue bid, and many of these had not even arrived in the area yet (Head, Short, and McFarlane 1978, 118).

Nevertheless, President Gerald Ford—aided principally by Secretary of State Henry Kissinger, Defense Secretary James Schlesinger, Deputy National Security Adviser Brent Scowcroft, and the White House Chief of Staff Donald Rumsfeld[2]— decided to act swiftly; the mission could not wait and would be launched immediately. Unlike the subsequent Iran hostage crisis under President Carter or the hostage crisis in Lebanon under President Reagan, the hostages were quickly returned to U.S. control in this case; the mere threat of force seems to have been sufficient to obtain the hostages' release, so that its actual use proved largely unnecessary. Ford and his colleagues regarded the military operation as a great success, especially coming right on the heels of the departure of U.S. forces from Vietnam. "*Mayaguez* provided us with a shot in the arm as a nation when we really needed it. ... It convinced some of our adversaries we were not a paper tiger," the president later suggested (quoted in Isaacson 1992, 651). It is fair to say that Ford and Kissinger's raid on the Cambodians was also a domestic political success; the president's popularity ratings went up 12 percent in the aftermath of the operation as Americans rallied around the flag (Neustadt and May 1986, 64).

However, in almost all other respects, and certainly in a purely military sense, the *Mayaguez* operation can only be described as a fiasco. Eighteen U.S. Marines died in the rescue mission and in the subsequent punitive strike launched against the Cambodian mainland, fifty more were wounded and twenty-three members of the U.S. Air Force died in a related crash. First of all, and most critically, this means that more U.S. personnel died in the rescue mission and subsequent punitive strike than there were American hostages. Second, it was later revealed that by the time that the punitive strike on Koh Tang took place, the crew of the *Mayaguez* were *already* in the process of being released, making the loss of life unnecessary. Indeed, many of the Americans who lost their lives did so after the Cambodians had already announced that the hostages would be freed. Third, it has been suggested that the U.S. government officials came terrifyingly close to killing the hostages *themselves* during the *Mayaguez* affair. When the hostages had been deposited on the island, Brent Scowcroft—presumably acting under Ford's instructions—directed Defense Secretary Schlesinger to "sink anything coming off Koh Tang." At dawn on May 14, U.S. forces saw a fishing boat set off from the island to the mainland and immediately reported this to the Pentagon. Rather than bomb the boat as instructed, Schlesinger decided not to obey Scowcroft's order. This was fortunate indeed, since it was later discovered that the boat was carrying the American hostages (Guilmartin 1995, 55-56). As Christopher Lamb puts it, "in retrospect, the rescue of the *Mayaguez* was a hasty, risky, ill-conceived action not commensurate with publicly stated objectives" (Lamb 1984–85, 682).

Because of the many problems which beset the mission, Irving Janis suggested that the *Mayaguez* incident might be a candidate for analysis using the groupthink model, a suggestion which has so far not been taken up within the FPDM litera- ture in any serious way (Janis 1982, 178–80). Although General Jones was worried about inadequate intelligence on the whereabouts of the hostages and the nature of the resistance the enemy was able to put up, he "never voiced forceful reservations," for instance (Head, Short, and McFarlane 1978, 163). This suggests that Jones may have engaged in the kind of self-censorship derived from social pressure that we discussed in chapter 3. Certainly, there are elements of *Homo Bureaucraticus* and *Homo Sociologicus* present in this case study that might make it an interesting candidate to pursue from either or both of those perspectives. One reason that they have not been may be that there is already another explanation, which seems to account for the administration's preference for military action—and Ford and Kissinger's haste in launching a military raid—at least equally well or better than either of these approaches: the cognitive/emotional psychological perspective, for which we will employ the shorthand term *Homo Psychologicus*.

THE *MAYAGUEZ* RAID: WHY THE RUSH?

Any account of the *Mayaguez* decision-making must explain both (a) why Ford and Kissinger settled so quickly on a military rescue operation, and (b) why they were so convinced that a rescue mission and punitive strike must be implemented *immediately*. Why did they dismiss the idea of negotiating for the release of the hostages almost out of hand, and why act with such haste? The answer seems to have something to do with the historical analogies that both men had in their heads (Neustadt and May 1986, 58–66). For Ford in particular, the *Mayaguez* crisis instantly recalled a very similar incident which occurred when he was the House Minority Leader, the Pueblo hostage incident of 1968. Like many Republican crit- ics of President Lyndon Johnson's handling of that affair, Ford regarded *Pueblo* as a national humiliation and an instance of failed leadership. Unlike Ford, Johnson had been slow to contemplate using force. LBJ's own thinking had been influenced by other analogies, though, which predisposed him against the rapid use of mili- tary force.

For most of 1968, the captured U.S.S *Pueblo* and its crew were the subject of a prolonged crisis in U.S.-Korean relations. *Pueblo* was a U.S. Navy vessel sent on an intelligence mission off the coast of North Korea, part of an effort to monitor North Korean radio and electronic transmissions. On January 23, 1968, the ship was attacked by North Korean forces. One crew member was killed and four were wounded. The eighty-two surviving members of the crew were taken hostage, tor- tured, and held until December 23, 1968, a total of 335 days in captivity. After extensive consideration of various military options, President Johnson and his advisers opted for negotiation and diplomacy, in part because they feared initiating (or in this case, re-sparking) a second land war in Asia. The decision-makers also concluded that any rescue mission or retaliatory raid would probably jeopardize the lives of the hostages. As Secretary of State Dean put it, "we were faced with the fact that if you tried to use military force to rescue the men you might pick up dead bodies, but you wouldn't pick up live men" (Rusk 1969, 21).

Tom Johnson, later to become president of the satellite and cable news giant *CNN*, is one of the few people alive today who witnessed LBJ's initial reactions to the *Pueblo*'s seizure. Still a young man at the time and thrust into a highly unusual and memorable situation, Johnson (no relation to the president) has an especially crisp recollection of events during the crisis, and he remembers that it was the president who drove the initial decision-making on the night the information reached the White House. Asked to stay on in the administration by Bill Moyers after his White House internship ended in 1966, Johnson became Deputy White House Press Secretary and the note taker for many high-level secret NSC gatherings the president did not wish to record. Not only did Johnson become the note taker for the top-level meetings of the principals on the *Pueblo*, but he also happened to be on duty in the White House Situation Room the night the ship was seized:

> What I remember most is that the flash came through to the Situation Room of the White House that the North Koreans had encircled the ship and were board-ing the ship, and that brought President Johnson over to the West Wing, and there were three of us who were duty officers, junior level duty officers, one from the National Security Council staff, Richard Moose, myself from the Press Office, and a young head of the Situation Room. And we're sitting there. [Defense Secretary] McNamara is just being alerted, Rusk is being alerted, [National Security Advisor Walt] Rostow is being alerted. We're sitting with him as he's trying to decide what to do. And I know this. He did not want war, this trigger-baiting war with the North Koreans. But also, though, he was thinking about how can we rescue these men? How can we keep the ship? ... President Johnson was talking directly with the Pentagon and seeing about scrambling our jets that were all on alert in South Korea. ... And the question was why aren't they getting out over the location more quickly? And the reason, I learned later, was that those aircraft that were on alert were loaded with nuclear bombs (Johnson 2007).

Interestingly, LBJ's own decision-making, especially his hesitancy in respond-ing militarily, also seems to be been shaped by a powerful analogy, the 1964 Gulf of Tonkin incident. "We knew the ship was being seized, we knew the ship was probably going to be taken ashore, we knew we weren't able to get out over sta-tion quickly enough," Tom Johnson says, "but LBJ also wanted to *make sure* of the information he was getting." While we cannot know with absolute certainty what LBJ was thinking about that night in the White House Situation Room, Tom Johnson feels sure that he was thinking of one (superficially similar) event in par-ticular. "He did not want a repeat of the Gulf of Tonkin controversy," Johnson recalls. "President Johnson thought he was getting accurate information about the Gulf of Tonkin when our ships were being attacked by these gunboats. Then it became a real controversy as to whether or not there were gunboats and what had the radar screens picked up, and LBJ wanted to make certain that he was getting accurate information. That was his key" (Johnson 2007).

Johnson was acutely aware of what had happened the last time he responded hastily in the face of incomplete information about an intelligence-gathering ship stationed off the coast of Southeast Asia. On August 2, 1964, the destroyer USS *Maddox*, engaged on a spying mission off the coast of North Vietnam, was attacked by torpedo boats. Two days later there was supposedly a second attack, although most historians now agree that this never occurred (it seems to have been imagined by an inexperienced sonar man). The White House received conflicting and contradictory intelligence throughout the day, before the president finally went on national television late at night to request what would later become the Tonkin Gulf resolution authorizing a military response.

There was such an obvious similarity between the case of the USS *Maddox* and that of the USS *Pueblo* that it scarcely needed to be articulated in the Johnson's administration's meetings. As Mitchell Lerner notes, "both ships were conducting SIGINT [signals intelligence] operations along the coast of an Asian rival when they were unexpectedly attacked. Both missions' risks had been underestimated, and the officers and crew were thus somewhat unprepared. Both ships also suffered from problems in crucial areas such as communications and defense" (Lerner 2002, 17). Nevertheless, Johnson occasionally did draw the parallel quite explicitly, according to Tom Johnson's notes of the meetings that took place on the *Pueblo* crisis. Similarly, Nicholas Katzenbach recalls that "the one thing I think Johnson was clear about is 'I ain't gonna get myself involved in a second war in Vietnam' … and I think he was pretty firm on that line throughout" (Katzenbach 2006).

As Admiral Bobby Inman recalls, there was in any case "no liaison" in place for dealing with this precise kind of situation and "no organized process to react if something happened" (Inman 2007). Moreover, Deputy Secretary of Defense Paul Nitze notes that "by the time that we in Washington knew about the *Pueblo* seizure, there wasn't enough time to act effectively immediately. By the first time we heard that the *Pueblo* was being seized, there were very few hours left before she actually was in the port" (Nitze 1969, 9). As the President later told reporters in a behind-the-scenes briefing, "if any good thing comes out of this, it was that the Commander of the Fifth Air Force did not send U.S. planes in there. We would have had another Bay of Pigs." Similarly, the Chairman of the Joint Chiefs Earl Wheeler later concluded that "aircraft would have been of little use in aiding the *Pueblo*. Their use could have been more harmful than helpful." Soviet-made MiG aircraft would likely have engaged the U.S. F-4s, and a battle would almost certainly have ensued in which some or all of the crew might well have been killed.[3]

The obvious solution at that point, being urged by many in Congress, was to launch a daring rescue operation into North Korea. But as both Assistant Secretary of State Nicholas Katzenbach and State Department official James Leonard recall today, there were simply too many obstacles in the way. "There's no way it was taken seriously," Katzenbach remembers. "It was far too complex. I mean, you could do retaliatory actions, but a rescue mission really didn't make any sense because you couldn't get that many troops in there without starting a full-scale war, and that was something LBJ sure as hell didn't want" (Katzenbach 2006). Another problem which killed off this option was a lack of intelligence about the exact whereabouts of the hostages once they reached the mainland. Leonard recalls that "I did discuss [a rescue operation] with the Pentagon, but we had no idea where they were held. We presumed it was somewhere in Pyongyang. But there were a hundred different locations, including outside the city, where they could be. ... Our intelligence, as far as I can remember, was virtually zero" (Leonard 2006). The Joint Chiefs agreed that once the hostages had been moved to the mainland, any rescue mission would be virtually impossible. Eventually, after nearly a year of slow-moving, intense, and often frustrating negotiations, the crew was released, but not until the U.S. government was forced to issue a bizarre statement of apology, in which the U.S. negotiators were simultaneously permitted to renounce and disavow their signature on the document as meaningless.

LBJ's rejection of a rescue mission in this case was not preordained, however. History has a tendency to look more inevitable in retrospect than the events in question did at the time, a now well-known phenomenon that psychologists term "hindsight bias" (Fischhoff and Beyth 1975). Plenty of individuals who *might* have been president in 1968—including three future occupants of the Oval Office, Nixon, Ford, and Reagan—all urged LBJ to use force against North Korea anyway and might well have reacted differently. As a presidential candidate running in 1968, Nixon was fairly bellicose in his comments about the *Pueblo* incident, and like Ford he saw the whole affair—and especially the way in which it was resolved, by means of a U.S. apology—as a profound humiliation for the United States. When *Mayaguez* came along, Ford was resolved not to allow the same thing to happen again and often mentioned the lessons of the *Pueblo* affair in NSC meetings on *Mayaguez* (Head, Short, and McFarlane 1978, 108). He proved prepared to launch a military rescue operation in the full knowledge that many of the hostages might be killed in the process. He perceived the risks differently, weighed the options differently, and proved far less receptive than Johnson to a lengthy waiting game in getting the hostages back.

Ford made this point clearly in his memoirs, *A Time To Heal*:

> Back in 1968, I remembered, the North Koreans had captured the U.S. intelligence ship USS *Pueblo* in international waters and forced her and her crew into the port of Wonsan. The U.S. had not been able to respond fast enough to prevent the transfer, and as a result, *Pueblo*'s crew languished in a North Korean prison camp for nearly a year. I was determined not to allow a repetition of that incident (Ford 1979, 277).

Kissinger also frequently recalled the lessons of *Pueblo* when dealing with the *Mayaguez* case, and as Neustadt and May relate:

> That may have been because he perceived its force with the President. It may also have been partly because of his own experience. In 1968 he had been an adviser to Nelson Rockefeller, then seeking the Republican nomination, and had almost surely helped Rockefeller frame a comment on the *Pueblo*, which Rockefeller's rival, Richard Nixon, had upstaged by calling for U.S. military action against

North Korea. In addition, because of the reports of North Korean mischief, Kissinger had had reason recently to review the *Pueblo* case (Neustadt and May 1986, 302).

Similarly, Brent Scowcroft also subsequently alluded to the impact of *Pueblo* on his own thinking and on the decision-making process in general. He especially wanted to avoid more international embarrassment at a time when the United States looked especially weak around the globe:

> What we were trying to do in the *Mayaguez* was prevent that from happening; prevent the ship and especially the crew from being spirited away somewhere, where we'd certainly lose the possibility of rescuing them, and then be subject to the kind of humiliations that we were with the *Pueblo* and appear powerless (Quoted in Lamb 1984–85, 693).

The secretary of state was also driven by the lessons of at least two other analogies, this time from his years as Nixon's national security adviser and both of which were consistent with those derived from *Pueblo*: the EC-121 crisis from 1969, and the Vietnam War. In April 1969, an American EC-121 aircraft was shot down, killing all members of the crew. In Kissinger's judgment, the United States had not acted in a swift or bold manner, losing face in the eyes of our allies and appeasing our adversaries. Similarly, in Kissinger's eyes the United States had lost the Vietnam War in large part because we fought "with one hand tied behind our backs." Military force was used half-heartedly in the hope that the ethical scourge of using it could be avoided, but restraint only led to failure (Lamb 1984–85, 685).

In short, Ford, Kissinger, and Scowcroft were driven by powerful historical analogies in their heads, which predisposed them against a negotiated solution and toward bold action designed to resolve the crisis very early on, just as LBJ's earlier experiences had predisposed him in the opposite direction. In particular, Ford and his advisers drew the more precise lesson from *Pueblo* that what had made a rescue mission difficult in that case was that the enemy had been allowed to take the U.S. hostages to the mainland. Every effort had to be made, therefore, to prevent the Cambodians from doing the same thing with the crew of the *Mayaguez*. Time was of the essence, and hence Ford and Kissinger would insist on pushing David Jones into a rapid rescue attempt, whether the General liked it or not.

"BEARS TO HONEY": THE IRRESISTIBLE PULL OF ANALOGICAL REASONING

Former Secretary of State Alexander Haig once said that international politics attracts analogies the way honey attracts bears. While this may be overstating the case a bit, the use of historical analogies in foreign policy decision-making is certainly very common (Khong 1992). Cognitive scientists have long suggested that there are good reasons why this is so. Much of the existing psychological research on human problem-solving examines how people deal with familiar, routine, and recurring situations, but we know that decision-makers can also solve novel problems, which are far less familiar unfamiliar or routine. Uncertainty and ambiguity, which may be inspired by the absence of information or too much of it (information overload), put a premium on certain cognitive shortcuts that allow us to process information expeditiously. *Homo Psychologicus* assumes that there is only so much information one can process; when that information becomes too burdensome to manage, for instance, we can expect people to resort to the use of analogy and other shortcut mechanisms.

Of course, analogies may mislead as well as illuminate. Because our minds often downplay the differences between situations—we unconsciously ask ourselves what this case *resembles* from our own repertoire of experiences but may be less inclined to recognize that no analogy represents a perfect fit—we may miss critical dissimilarities between two cases. Nevertheless, as Yuen Foong Khong has argued in the case of Johnson's escalation in Vietnam (see chap. 7), analogies allow us to peer into the (likely) future, mapping out what is likely to happen before it actually does, and they serve other functions as well. Khong argues that we can think of analogies as "diagnostic devices," which assist policymakers in performing six crucial functions: they "(1) help define the nature of the situation confronting the policymaker, (2) help assess the stakes, and (3) provide prescriptions. They help evaluate alternative options by (4) predicting the chances of success, (5) evaluating their moral rightness, and (6) warning about dangers associated with the options" (Khong 1992, 10). He proposes what he calls the "AE (Analogical Explanation) Framework," essentially a shorthand term for the belief that analogies are genuine cognitive devices that perform the tasks specified above.

Khong finds that analogies played a prominent part in the reasoning processes of both those who opposed the Vietnam escalation and those who supported it. For instance, undersecretary of state George Ball argued that increased American involvement there would soon lead to a repeat of the disastrous French experience in Indochina; however, for President Johnson and many of his other advisers (such as Dean Rusk), Korea was the analogy of choice. "To be sure, Johnson was informed by many lessons of many pasts," Khong argues, "but Korea preoccupied him. ... Whatever it was that attracted Johnson to the Korean precedent, a major lesson he drew from it was that the United States made a mistake in leaving Korea in June 1949; the withdrawal emboldened the communists, forcing the United States to return to Korea one year later to save the South. Johnson was not predisposed toward repeating the same mistake in Vietnam" (Khong 1992, 110–11).

The analogical reasoning perspective often provides a richer understanding of decision-making than perspectives based on broader worldviews can. General constructs like belief systems are sometimes ill-suited to explaining particulars. Thus a belief that Communism should be contained can explain why the United States was willing to intervene under Lyndon Johnson—obviously, American decision-makers believed that Vietnam would be the first domino in a falling chain, but the Eisenhower and Kennedy administrations also shared a belief in containment. Yet Eisenhower failed to assist the French at Dien Bien Phu in 1954, and Kennedy opted for a negotiated solution over Laos in 1961. Khong explains Johnson's intervention in terms of the Korean analogy, from which LBJ had drawn the lesson that the United States—having fought one limited war in Asia—could do so again (see chap. 7).

Sometimes we *do* simply rely on our belief systems to cut short the process of considering information. For example, when a voter is confronted with two candidates about whom he knows little or nothing, he may simply use his party identification as a shortcut (Popkin 1993). Similarly, a decision-maker may fall back on his or her existing beliefs; indeed, this may be the default mechanism, and perhaps analogies are used only where our belief systems fail to provide us with precise inferences about how things are likely to turn out. There is now a considerable literature on analogical reasoning within foreign policy analysis, but there is an even larger and much older literature that deals with belief systems. An especially large body of research exists on the role of *operational codes* in foreign policy decision-making, an approach within the study of belief systems pioneered by Alexander George which remains vibrant today (George 1969, 1979; Schafer and Walker 2006a, 2006b).

The basic groundwork for this approach was created in the early 1950s, when Nathan Leites studied the political beliefs of Lenin, Trotsky, and Stalin. In a classic and much-cited 1969 article, Alexander George then took this work and reformulated

---

1. **PHILOSOPHICAL BELIEFS**
   - What is the "essential" nature of political life? Is the political universe essentially one of harmony or conflict? What is the fundamental character of one's political opponents?
   - What are the prospects for the eventual realization of one's fundamental political values and aspirations? Can one be optimistic, or must one be pessimistic on this score?
   - Is the political future predictable? In what sense and to what extent?
   - How much control or mastery can one have over historical development? What is one's role in moving and shaping history in the desired direction?
   - What is the role of "chance" in human affairs?

2. **INSTRUMENTAL BELIEFS**
   - What is the best approach for selecting goals or objectives for political action?
   - How are the goals of action pursued most effectively?
   - How are the risks of political action calculated, controlled, and accepted?
   - What is the best "timing" of action to advance one's interests?
   - What is the utility and role of different means for advancing one's interests?

Figure 4.1 The "Operational Code."

Leites's observations into two sets of questions: *philosophical* beliefs and *instrumental* beliefs. The operational code, George argued, provides a "set of general beliefs about fundamental issues of history as central questions as these bear, in turn, on the problem of action" (George 1969, 191). Its central features are listed in figure 4.1.

The first set of beliefs has to do with one's general philosophy about the nature of political life; the second deals with more practical questions such as how one goes about implementing one's chosen political objectives. As you can probably see from a brief perusal of the questions, a leader's philosophical beliefs have to do with the issues which animated classic political thinkers such as Thomas Hobbes and John Locke. While Hobbes had an exceptionally dark view of human nature, Locke held a rather more optimistic view. While Locke saw the world as a harmonious place, Hobbes held the opinion that if man were freed from the order-providing shackles of government, life would be "solitary, poor, nasty, brutish and short." Contrasting with these fundamental "*what* is the political world like?" questions, are questions having to do with "*how* should we achieve our goals?" These are our instrumental beliefs. As will see in later chapters, operational code analysis provides us with a useful way of breaking down the belief system of a leader like Lyndon Johnson or George W. Bush.

THE ASSUMPTIONS OF *HOMO PSYCHOLOGICUS*

The first proposition of *Homo Psychologicus* is quite simply that *individuals matter*. Historians, philosophers, political scientists, and journalists have long debated whether leaders make a difference to the course of events in political life: Do leaders make history, or does it make them? It may seem obvious to you that individuals matter; American culture in particular with its strong individualist tradition makes the assumption that it does, and the dialectical historical arguments of thinkers like Karl Marx and Friedrich Hegel have been far less popular in the United States than in some other places. Many of the theories we encounter in the study of political science tend to emphasize the importance of structures, context, or what might be called the nature of the times, however, rather than the analyzing the properties of actors or individuals. Put in terms of our *matryoshka* metaphor, they tend to privilege the largest, outer dolls and argue that we need open up only a limited number of them.

Marxism offers an especially stark example of this kind of structuralism. It tends to discount the role of individuals in history, ascribing to material factors a powerful causal effect, which overwhelms the significance of particular leaders. History, according to this dialectical view, follows a familiar and predictable drumbeat no matter who the actors involved happen to be at any given point in time. Within international relations theory—to give another example from a wholly different theoretical tradition—the neorealist approach argues that we can explain a great deal about how and why a state behaves as it does by looking at that nation's position within the international system. Superpowers, neorealists argue, tend to behave the same way no matter who they are, as do all middle powers and weak powers. If this is so, it follows that we need not trouble ourselves with the analysis of who is leading a particular state or what their psychological characteristics happen to be. Notice that both *Homo Bureaucraticus* and *Homo Sociologicus* tend to subsume the individual within organizations and groups respectively. The point being made here is not that the approaches examined in chapters 2 and 3 ignore individuals, since they do not; however, they do tend to see foreign policy behavior as driven by the surroundings or environment within which the individuals work, rather than the dispositions or characteristics of the individuals themselves. On the other hand, *Homo Psychologicus* unambiguously assumes that individuals do make a difference, shaping history as much as, if not more than, it shapes them; the final and smallest doll is the most critical, in other words. The personalities, beliefs, and past experiences of our leaders matter because they influence the *images* contained in the heads of decision-makers; and these images, in turn, often affect how we behave (Holsti 1967; Jervis 1976).

Second, this perspective places a great deal of weight on the importance of personality and also frequently makes use of counterfactual reasoning in order to establish the importance of individual decision-makers. First, classic work by Fred Greenstein and James David Barber in particular has argued both for the critical significance of personality and for the importance of particular personality types. Barber, for instance, classified U.S. presidents according to whether they were active or passive (a reference to how much they put into the job) as well as positive or negative (how much enjoyment they derived from the job). He contended in his book *The Presidential Character* that the best personality type to have is active positive (Barber 1992). Active negatives like Richard Nixon and Lyndon Johnson, on the other hand, are the most dangerous, driven to obtain power but deriving little or no pleasure from it.

Barber's framework has had a great deal more influence in the study of the American presidency than it has in the study of foreign policy decision-making. Later work such as the research of Thomas Preston has expanded on this kind of approach and added a great deal more subtlety to it (Preston 2000). One of the problems with Barber's framework when applied to someone like John F. Kennedy is that Kennedy's personality is judged compatible both with a foreign policy disaster (such as the Bay of Pigs episode examined in chap. 5) *and* what many regard his greatest success (the Cuban missile crisis, discussed in chap. 6). The lack of variation in the variable of personality, pretty stable over time, suggests that something other than personality may be at work in accounting for different outcomes.

Preston attempts to get around this by adding more categories, complexities, and nuances. Along one dimension is the leader's need for power and control, contrasted with his or her level of experience or policy expertise: *directors* possess both high policy experience and a high need for control of the policymaking process, while *magistrates* share the same desire for control but without the requisite policy expertise. *Administrators* have a low need for control and so are satisfied with a less centralized policymaking process, but they also have high policy experience. Finally, *delegators* have a low level of interest and expertise in foreign policy, and their need for power is low as well. Both Bill Clinton and George W. Bush seem to have been delegators with little experience of foreign policy and a willingness to devolve decision-making powers to others, while Dwight Eisenhower was more of a director and his predecessor Harry Truman something of a magistrate (Preston 2000, 16–17).

There is, however, another dimension along with presidential style or personality that might be considered, namely a leader's sensitivity to context (need for information, receptivity to colleagues opinions, and so on), contrasted with his or her cognitive complexity. *Navigators* exhibit a high degree of interest in obtaining information before making a policy decision and a strong interest in foreign policy; they also show a high degree of cognitive complexity. *Observers* exhibit the same general characteristics but are far less interested in foreign policy. On the other hand, *Sentinels* have a high level of interest in foreign policy but a low need for information and a low degree of cognitive complexity. Finally, *mavericks* have a low cognitive complexity, a low need for information, and also a limited degree of interest in foreign policy. John F. Kennedy and George H. W. Bush would be regarded as navigators, Clinton as an observer, and Johnson, Reagan, and George W. Bush all as *mavericks* (Preston finds no recent example of a foreign policy sentinel) (Preston 2000, 22–23).

Putting the two dimensions together in foreign policy, Preston derives the following characterizations of presidents since Truman:

BOX 4-1

Leadership Style Types in Foreign Policy

Truman	Magistrate-Maverick
Eisenhower	Director-Navigator
Kennedy	Director-Navigator
Johnson	Magistrate-Maverick
Reagan	Director-Maverick
G. H. W. Bush	Administrator-Navigator
Clinton	Delegator-Observer
G. W. Bush	Delegator-Maverick

Adapted from Thomas Preston, *The President and His Inner Circle* (New York: Columbia University Press, 2000), 28.

A concern with personality meshes most explicitly with counterfactual reasoning in the work of Fred Greenstein (see Greenstein, 1998). Counterfactual propositions often begin with the phrase: "what if?" or "imagine that … ," and counterfactual reasoning can be thought of as imagining something that you know *did not* happen in order to better understand what *did* (Tetlock and Belkin 1996,

Blight, Lang, and Welch 2009). We shall see a number of examples of this in the empirical chapters that follow, but one classic counterfactual involves the question "what if Kennedy had lived?" To answer this, we imagine something we know did not happen—for instance, Lee Harvey Oswald's bullets missing their target—and then imagine how the 1960s would or would not have been different. This is what is known as a *plausible counterfactual* since it involves a plausible rewrite of history (for instance, moving the fatal bullet that killed Kennedy a few inches to the left), and these are often contrasted with *miracle counterfactuals* (imagining that the two superpowers after World War II had been the United States and Canada). Some have argued that we would not have become so involved in Vietnam had JFK both lived and won the 1964 presidential election. While counterfactuals are of course difficult to prove one way or the other, advocates of this approach maintain that when carefully used, they can be just as rigorous as well-done comparisons (Lebow 2000).

Third, as we have seen already, this perspective assumes that human beings (in an information-processing sense) are inherently limited creatures who frequently rely on cognitive shortcuts. To use a word invented by Herbert Simon, we often engage in *satisficing*; in other words, instead of engaging in an exhaustive information search, we often settle for the first option that will do (Simon 1955). In the movie *Limitless*, the character Eddie Morra (played by Bradley Cooper) gains access to, and becomes hooked on, a drug which allows him to access 100 percent of his brain capacity, and the whole plot then hinges on what amazing things he might be able to do if such a drug existed. The storyline is based on the fact that human beings are normally limited, since we in fact use no more than 20 percent of our brain capacity. Consider again for a moment the *Homo Economicus* approach we discussed in chapter 1. The reader may recall that the neuroscientist Antonio Damasio had a brain-damaged patient he called "Elliot" (Damasio 1994). When Damasio asked Elliot when he would like to meet for his next appointment, the patient went painstakingly through his diary for a couple of hours, weighing the costs and benefits of each potential date with almost agonizing care. We know, of course, that most psychologically normal individuals do not do this. Instead of going through this laborious process, we employ various shorthand devices, which make it much easier to reach a quick decision. If Tuesday worked well for us as an appointment last week, for instance, we may select Tuesday for the next one as well.

How do such arguments affect how we study American foreign policy? The notion of cognitive scripts provides a handy example. This idea has played an important role in the understanding of foreign policy decision-making since the 1970s, when cognitive psychologists—and later scholars of international relations—began to explore the role of cognitive shortcuts in information processing (Schank and Abelson 1977; Abelson 1981). According to Robert Abelson, one of the leading advocates of this approach, scripts are "conceptual representations of stereotyped event sequences." Put more simply, a script may be thought of as a particular kind of schema or mental box, which provides the typical default values for an event of some kind or an act which we are accustomed to performing, such as watching a movie or eating at a restaurant. We usually experience little difficulty dining at a restaurant we have never visited before, since we simply rely on the default values stored in our memory to guide our behavior; we wait to be seated by the host or hostess, a server presents us with menus, we pick what we want to eat, we eat it when it arrives, and so on. By the same token, if a friend informs you that she went to see a movie last night, you can easily use the default values you keep in your head for typical visits to the cinema to guess how her evening probably went.

The concept of a script clearly draws itself upon the cognitive image of a movie or theatrical script in which events are played out one after the other; this concept can also be compared to a cartoon strip. This idea is consistent with the more general notion that human beings are cognitive misers, and the approach may be viewed as part of the bounded rationality tradition within political science that stresses the ways in which individuals depart from pure or comprehensive rationality. Rather than considering everything we experience sui generis, according to this view, we are usually far more economical in our information processing. We commonly fit new sensory data into established mental categories, both because it requires little effort and because it allows us to make sense of the outside world quickly and expeditiously. This is particularly the case under conditions of high uncertainty and ambiguity, where the individual is being bombarded with too much information, or where he or she possesses too little of this. As well as helping us to make sense of what has happened in the past or is happening now, scripts often play a strong predictive role in decision-making, allowing us to ascertain in advance with a reasonable degree of confidence what is likely to occur in the future (or at least what we *think* is likely to occur).

Scholars of foreign policy decision-making were quick to pick up on the political relevance of scripts in international relations (Shapiro and Bonham 1973; Larson 1985). For example, "Balkanization" and the "Trojan Horse" are two scripts often used in international relations, and scripts appear to play an especially prominent role in the analysis of strategic threats (Vertzberger 1990). In American foreign policy, the "Munich script" and the "Vietnam script" have frequently impacted the deliberations of decision-makers, both during the Cold War and since. This provides a useful political example of the ways in which rival scripts can compete for a decision-maker's attention and of the manner in which scripts are used to predict future events. The generation of policymakers who had experienced World War II were particularly attuned to the memory of British Prime Minister Neville Chamberlain after the Munich conference of 1938, where he famously waved a piece of paper upon which Adolf Hitler had agreed not to invade Poland and Western Europe in exchange for part of what was then Czechoslovakia. Chamberlain emerged from the conference promising "peace in our time." When this attempt at accommodation failed and war followed, many policymakers (especially in the United States) drew the wider lesson that any effort to appease a dictator was bound to lead to disaster. The widespread use of the domino theory by U.S. decision-makers during the Cold War, for instance, was clearly based upon the cognitive appeal of this script. From this perspective, attempts to appease an adversary inevitably lead to well-intentioned but empty negotiations; verbal or written promises are followed by betrayal, causing a nation to fight a war against an enemy it should have confronted much earlier using its military might.

During the Cuban missile crisis, John F. Kennedy appears to have had the World War I script in mind, urging his advisers to read Barbara Tuchman's book *The Guns of August*; Kennedy was determined not to allow events to spiral out of control in 1962, as they had in 1914 prior to the onset of World War I (Neustadt and May 1986; see also chap. 6). The Munich script was evoked on far more numerous occasions during the Cold War, and it was perhaps most famously utilized by President George H. W. Bush after Saddam Hussein invaded Kuwait in 1990. Bush argued that if Hussein's aggression was not confronted early on—if the Iraqi leader was appeased, in other words—events similar to those of the 1930s would play out, albeit in the Middle East rather than Europe and with Hussein as the antagonist instead of Hitler. This cognitive image remains highly potent in American political discourse today, despite the passage of (to date) more than seventy years. During the 2008 U.S. presidential election, then candidate Barack Obama was accused by Republicans of appeasement for advocating direct talks with Iran over the issues of nuclear weapons and terrorism. The Vietnam script (which remains equally potent) stresses the dangers of confrontation rather than accommodation, on the other hand. Recalling the military and political errors that cost the United States so much blood and treasure in that war, one popular interpretation of Vietnam suggests that a nation should exercise extreme caution when contemplating the use of military force. Images of body bags, getting bogged down in enemy terrain, and mass protests are all evoked by the Vietnam script, as well as the considerable human and political costs of a military intervention, which effectively destroyed Lyndon Johnson's presidency.

Fourth, the cognitive structures in our brains are remarkably resistant to change. Cognitive consistency theory, for instance, suggests that we very often fail to update our beliefs and attitudes in response to information that *ought* to lead to this (recall the Marian Keech example from chap. 1 [p. 15]). The psychologist Leon Festinger argued that when a piece of information which is incompatible with our beliefs, comes along, it creates an uncomfortable state of psychological tension which Festinger termed "cognitive dissonance" (Festinger 1957). Under such conditions, we become strongly motivated to do something about the discomfort. The obvious thing to do would be to modify our belief system, and this sometimes does occur; more commonly, though, we simply find a way to dismiss the new information as irrelevant or immaterial to the matter in hand or we add on a new belief, which allows the piece of information to become consistent with or assimilated to what we think. One example from U.S. foreign policy is provided by the reaction of President George H. W. Bush and his CIA Director Robert Gates to the policies of Mikhael Gorbachev in the late 1980s. The youthful Gorbachev had come to power in 1985, presenting himself as a new style of Soviet leader who sought to reform both the political system (*Glasnost*) and the economic one (*Perestroika*). Perhaps because of his pliant personality, Bush's predecessor Reagan had eventually come to embrace Gorbachev as "the real deal," developing a relationship with the Soviet leader which at times looked like genuine friendship (something most observers could not have predicted when Reagan came to office in 1981, describing the Soviet Union as the "Evil Empire"). On coming to the White House in 1989, George H. W. Bush maintained a much colder distance. Both Bush and Gates were wary of the notion that Gorbachev was genuinely different from previous Soviet leaders such as Leonid Brezhnev, and they were comparatively slow to accept the olive branch Gorbachev was offering. Ultimately, Reagan's intuitive feel for the situation proved a better guide to what was happening than Bush's caution, and historians will probably view Reagan's performance in U.S.-Soviet relations far more kindly than they will his mishandling of the Iran-Contra affair.

A fifth assumption has to do with the sources of error in foreign policy decision-making. According to *Homo Psychologicus*, many pathologies in decision-making result not from the operation of standard operating procedures and bureaucratic infighting (*Homo Bureaucraticus*) or from the conformity or deadlock-producing effects of social group dynamics (*Homo Sociologicus*), but from the way in which the human mind works. As the previous example suggests, the fact that we view the world with a great deal of baggage already in our heads—and because human reasoning is subject to various biases—may cause us to misperceive the nature of the situation we are facing. Due in large part to the pioneering work of Robert Jervis (especially his book *Perception and Misperception in International Politics*) the notion of misperception in foreign policy has gained acceptance within the wider political science community. Jervis saw misperception as rooted in cognitive consistency, with leaders clinging stubbornly to their existing mind-sets even as the world around them changes. We also engage in a great deal of wishful thinking, something that helps maintain consistency but which is also emotionally comforting.

Beginning with a compelling argument which strongly suggested that structural arguments were by themselves insufficient to explain the decisions that human beings reach, Jervis examined the ways political leaders commonly misinterpret the signals that other leaders intend to send. As Jervis puts it:

> This means not only that when a statesman has developed a certain image of another country he will maintain that view in the face of large amounts of discrepant information, but also that the general expectations and rules entertained by the statesman about the links between other states' situations and characteristics on the one hand and their foreign policy intentions on the other influence the images of others that we will come to hold. Thus western statesmen will be quicker to see another state as aggressive if a dictator has just come to power in it than if it is a stable democracy (Jervis 1976, 146).

Jervis provides a number of examples in which prior beliefs affected the perceptions of the actors. Prior expectations, he notes, critically affect what we see. During World War II, for example, British aircraft bombed their own battleship (the *Sheffield*) by mistake (Jervis 1976, 92). The reason was that they were expecting to be confronted by what they were looking for, the German ship *Bismarck*. Ironically, the two ships did not even resemble one another, and the flight crews were quite familiar with the British ship, but the expectation proved powerful enough to result in a disastrous misperception. The same psychological phenomenon may have underlain attacks in August 1964 on the USS *Maddox* in the Gulf of Tonkin—apparently, many of these occurred only in the imagination of a sonar operator—and is undoubtedly behind the many friendly-fire incidents witnessed during the first Persian Gulf War and in the more recent war in Iraq, where U.S. forces attacked their own allies by mistake.

Rather than viewing human beings as consistency seekers, attribution theory sees individuals as naïve scientists or problem solvers. Instead of being motivated to constantly restore balance in the own beliefs or between those beliefs and their own behavior, attribution theory suggests that human beings are mainly concerned to *uncover the causes* of their own behavior and that of others. People are constantly looking for causes and effects (i.e., "why did this happen?") albeit in a far less sophisticated manner than a scientist working in a laboratory would. They are continually looking to make sense of the world around them, and they draw upon a range of assumptions about themselves and others in doing so (Nisbett and Ross 1980). According to the theory, we sometimes attribute the causes of someone's behavior to the situation they are in, while at other times we attribute that behavior to the person's internal dispositions. Unfortunately, we frequently make quite substantial errors and mistakes when we try to do this, and decision-makers are not always very careful when they make attributions.

One particularly notable kind of error with potentially major political consequences is called the *fundamental attribution error*. When we are explaining our own actions, we very often use situational attributions, and in fact we often overestimate the extent to which our actions are the result of the situation. On the other hand, when asked to explain why someone else acted as they did, we often make the opposite kind of mistake: we underestimate the extent to which the situation mattered (and hence overestimate the importance of that person's dispositions). How might this be of interest to students of politics? As the political psychologist and expert on foreign policy decision-making Deborah Welch Larson puts it in her classic study of the birth of Cold War containment:

> Policymakers tend to infer that the actions of their own state were compelled by circumstances, even while they attribute the behavior of other states to the fundamental "character" of the nation or its leaders. Applied to the problem of explaining the change in U.S. foreign policymakers' orientation toward the Soviet Union, attribution theory would suggest that Washington officials were too willing to impute ideological, expansionist motives to Soviet actions that could just as plausibly reflect security calculations similar to those that prompted analogous policies pursued by the United States. (Larson 1985, 38)

Attribution judgments became a matter of life and death during the Cuban missile crisis (see chap. 6). "Why have the Soviets placed missiles in Cuba?"

members of the ExCom asked themselves in those first, tense meetings. "What are their intentions?" Air Force Gen. Curtis Le May attributed rather sinister dispositionist motives to the Soviet leadership, while others like Robert McNamara, Ambassador Tommy Thompson, and President Kennedy were more attuned to the possibility that Khrushchev's actions might have been compelled or encouraged by situational factors (by the force of circumstances, in other words). Officials from both the United States and the Soviet Union were cognizant of the very real risk, moreover, that situational forces might take over the process and thus spiral into war. This case shows that we are not preordained to blindly follow common attributions. Nevertheless, we may also have a special tendency to invoke dispositionist attributions in others when we have a strongly negative attitude toward them. As Yaacov Vertzberger notes, "dislike tends to evoke dispositional explanations for undesirable actions by others, while empathy biases explanations of such behavior toward situational attribution" (Vertzberger 1990, 162–63).

Supporters of attribution theory argue that two shortcuts or heuristic devices are especially important in human decision-making: the *representativeness heuristic* and the *availability heuristic*. As Samuel Popkin states, "representativeness is a heuristic, a rule of thumb, for judging the likelihood that a person will be of a particular kind by how similar he is to the stereotype of that kind of person" (Popkin 1993, 363). Perceived similarity is what matters here, but one major problem is that people usually ignore *statistical* probabilities when making these kinds of judgments. When asked to estimate the likelihood that the late North Korean leader Kim Jong-il was another Hitler, for instance, most people attempted to match apparent similarities between the two (each was a threat to neighboring states, each was repressive domestically, and so on). What most people do not do is look at what is commonly termed "base information"; in other words, we rarely consider the statistical probability that Kim Jong-il was another Hitler (as a scientist presumably would). Arguably, there have been very few genuinely Hitler-like leaders in recent history, but this is not the way most people estimate probability.

When people use the *availability heuristic*, on the other hand, they estimate the likelihood of something based on how cognitively available it is to them. Often something is available in our memories simply because it happened recently or because it constituted a very vivid experience (like the events of September 11, 2001) that we are unlikely to forget. World War II and Vietnam are especially vivid for makers of U.S. foreign policy, and new situations tend to be compared disproportionately to these two events. This too is clearly unscientific because it ignores statistical likelihood. Viewing something as likely to happen simply because something similar happened recently or you were especially influenced by some vividly memorable event is obviously a poor way of estimating probability.

Like the notion of analogies that they closely resemble, cognitive scripts can also be a major source of cognitive error. Because they contain information about things which are only *typically* true, at least in that individual's experience, there is always the potential for oversimplification of a novel stimulus. We may make assumptions based on the typical or prototypical behaviors that may be entirely misleading or false. Scripts can also compete with one another in our minds where it is unclear what is actually happening. Two or more scripts may seem relevant to the case in hand, and the decision-maker may grapple with uncertainty as to which best suits the issue in question. The prominence of the Munich and Vietnam scripts in debates about military intervention since the 1970s presents a case in point, and both illustrate the perils of overlearning the lessons from a single event. Munich in particular illustrates the dangers of overgeneralizing one set of historical events into a script, which purports to predict what will usually happen when a ruthless or expansionist leader is appeased (or, taken to its extreme, where any form of diplomacy is used).

Equally, one can argue that the Vietnam script has often led American leaders to be overly cautious in responding to genuine threats, creating a sometimes inappropriate reluctance to use military power. As a young antiwar activist, Bill Clinton had been strongly influenced by the costs of Lyndon Johnson's decision to escalate American involvement in the Vietnam War. As president, Clinton was consequently often slow to use military force, most notably when the former Yugoslavia began to break up in the early 1990s. Eventually, U.S. firepower was used against the Serbs in 1995, helping to bring the parties together at a peace conference in Dayton, Ohio, but not before hundreds of thousands had perished in the conflict. Similarly, Clinton may also have been reluctant to intervene in Rwanda when major acts of genocide erupted there in 1994 because he was relying on what might be termed the Somalia or "Black Hawk Down" script; the latter suggested that military interventions and/or attempts to nationbuild in Africa are fraught with danger, drawing on the cognitive image of the disastrous 1993 attempt by U.S. forces to capture the Somali warlord Mohammed Farah Aidid, during which eighteen American soldiers died and seventy-three were wounded (the death toll among Somalis was much higher). Although the similarities between the Somali and Rwandan cases were arguably superficial, Clinton administration officials later admitted that the dangers of committing troops to intervene in the slaughter of Tutsis by Hutus in Rwanda dominated their thoughts as a result of what had happened the previous year in Somalia.

Like the groupthink approach, psychological perspectives have not stood still in recent years, and a couple of newer theoretical perspectives have gained special popularity in the literature: poliheuristic theory (PH) and prospect theory. Briefly stated, the poliheuristic model tries to blend a recognition of the heuristics and shortcuts that decision-makers use together with some elements of *Homo Economicus*, recognizing that decision-makers do engage in the calculation of costs and benefits once they have already employed various cognitive shortcuts to rule certain options out and others in. Alex Mintz, the leading advocate of this approach, argues that decision-making is a frequently a two-step process. During the first stage, policymakers use shortcuts to eliminate options that are not acceptable, often avoiding those that seem likely to involve heavy political costs. Then, during the second stage, they become more analytical, choosing among options in a more rigorous way and often minimizing military and/or strategic costs (Mintz, Geva, Redd, and Carnes 1997; Mintz 2005).

As an alternative view under the heading of *Homo Psychologicus*, we can also consider the application of what cognitive and social psychologists call prospect theory to the Iranian case. In essence, prospect theory, developed in the late 1970s by Daniel Kahneman and Amos Tversky, suggests that the way in which we define a situation or problem can have a very decisive impact on the attractiveness of various choices available to us (Kahneman and Tversky 1979). "Prospect theory distinguishes two phases in the choice process: an early phase of editing and a subsequent phase of evaluation," the authors of the theory note. "The editing phase consists of a preliminary analysis of the offered prospects in the second phase, the edited prospects are evaluated and the prospect of highest value is chosen" (ibid., 274). The theory revolves around the distinction between *risk aversion* and *risk acceptance*, and it suggests that individuals will be risk averse (that is, will avoid risky options) when dealing with gains, but they will be risk accepting or seeking when dealing with losses. As the well-known political psychologist Robert Jervis puts it, in prospect theory "people are loss-averse in the sense that losses loom larger than the corresponding gains. Losing ten dollars, for example, annoys us more than gaining ten dollars gratifies us … more than the hope of gains, the specter of losses activates, energizes and drives actors, producing great (and often misguided) efforts that risk—and frequently lead to—greater losses" (Jervis 1992, 187).

As a simple illustration, imagine that you are playing blackjack or roulette in a casino in Las Vegas. You have had a good night, meaning that you have won a few hundred dollars (let's say $300). But it is getting late and you are tired. You are just about ready to go back to your hotel room and get some rest. As you place your last bet, you will probably not put down the whole $300 on the next hand or spin of the wheel; unless you have a sudden brainstorm or are so wealthy that you really don't care one way or another, you will hold onto what you have. Put in the terms of prospect theory, under this kind of condition you will be *risk averse*, because you are in a "domain of gains" (in other words, you are winning). Now let's assume that it's the next day. You are not doing quite so well now; in fact, you have lost all the money you won last night, plus $100 out of your own pocket. Your plane leaves Las Vegas in a couple of hours, and you had better grab a taxi to the airport very soon. Sadly, it looks like you are going to leave a loser. But it just so happens that you have a couple of hundred dollars in your pocket. You have lost the last few bets, so if Lady Luck is on your side you should be due a win, right? So you put down the whole $200 on the last hand. With one fell swoop, you could erase your losses and still leave a winner (or at least recoup what you had). Sadly, the odds are that you have just lost even more money—this is, of course, how casinos make money—but from our perspective whether you actually win is beside the point. You have become *risk acceptant* because you are operating in a "domain of losses." Notice that your behavior is totally different from that of last night; instead of being prudent as before, you have become rather reckless. Notice also that this is *not* a matter of your personality (unless you are a schizophrenic, you probably woke up this morning with the same personality you went to bed with) but instead has to do with your perception of the situation you are facing. When you saw yourself as a winner, you were content to hang onto what you had; equally, when you perceived yourself as a loser, you were prepared to act more recklessly.

Prospect theory was originally developed to address the psychology of economics, so it is easy to apply to examples like these. Nevertheless, it can also be applied to political decision-making, as Rose McDermott and others have shown. Whether an individual believes himself or herself to be operating within a situation of losses or gains is admittedly a very subjective process, and we have to reconstruct the feelings of the policymaker (not how we ourselves think he or she should be thinking or feeling) in order the use the theory. Since we cannot place ourselves directly inside the head of the decision-maker, we also need to be prepared to make some indirect inferences about how he or she feels. Under some circumstances, however, it may be relatively easy to assess what a decision-maker is subjectively experiencing. Rose McDermott provides the following rather useful example:

> [I]f an investigator wanted to know whether a decision-maker felt hot or cold and wasn't able to ask directly, he could look at a thermometer to make a best guess. If the temperature read 92 degrees, chances are the decision-maker felt hot. If the thermometer read 32 degrees, chances are the person felt cold. In a similar way, it is possible to use external indicators to determine, in general, how a president assessed his domain of action. (McDermott 1992, 240)

Finally, emotion may also have a critical impact on decision-making via its effect on judgment. Until relatively recently, many psychological approaches to the analysis of American foreign policy left emotion out of the picture. This was not uniformly true (see, for instance, important studies by Richard Cottam and Ned Lebow for notable exceptions), but "cold" cognitive processes were often assumed to be more significant in reasoning about foreign policy issues than "hot" or emotional factors (Cottam 1977; Lebow 1981). The computer metaphor inherent in Artificial Intelligence (AI) and much cognitive psychological research produced during the 1970s and 1980s left its mark on the study of foreign policy decisions; the analogical reasoning literature, for instance, has often assumed that when we draw analogies, we simply match one thing to another in a neutral way, much as a computer might pair together two similar pieces of data. But human beings do not process information in such a neutral, affectless fashion; we *feel* as well as think, and there is not always a neat distinction between thinking and feeling.

In addition to highlighting the ubiquitous role of analogical reasoning in American foreign policy, the *Mayaguez* case we examined in this chapter nicely illustrates the impact of emotion in the making of foreign policy decisions. Analogies have a strong emotional component as well as a cognitive one, and the seizure of the *Mayaguez* set off a range of emotions within Ford and his advisers. In particular, members of the Ford administration were intensely frustrated in 1975 that the Democratic Congress had used its power of the purse and cut off further military funding for Vietnam, and the humiliation of our ignominious departure from Saigon was fresh in their minds. Emotions like anger, apprehension, dismay, disillusionment, and pride may have thus been the real roots of the U.S. response. As Lamb notes, a deep sense of frustration may have been especially important in the reasoning of Henry Kissinger, who had made a personal commitment to South Vietnam across two administrations that he was now compelled to abandon (Lamb 1984–85).

Given the outcome of *Mayaguez*, this example suggests, perhaps, that emotion might be inherently damaging to a reasoned decision-making process. Wouldn't we want to avoid allowing emotions to intrude into that process? A long-established tradition in Western thinking suggests that the answer is yes, but modern cognitive neuroscience suggests that the appropriate answer ought to be "not necessarily." As we will see in chapter 6, James Blight has argued that fear, one of the most common of human emotions, had a highly beneficial impact on the reasoning processes of JFK's circle of advisers during the Cuban missile crisis. In fact, recent research within neuroscience suggests that emotion, far from being inherently damaging, may actually be *essential* to anything approaching reasonable and competent decision-making. Damasio's patient Elliot had damage to the prefrontal cortex, a part of the brain just behind the area above the eye line that plays an integral role in both emotional processing and decision-making in general. Once a brain disease damaged Elliot's prefrontal cortex, he began making bizarre life decisions; previously a rather conservative family man, he emptied the bank account

- Individuals matter, not simply the organizational and group environments in which decision-makers are embedded. Counterfactual reasoning can establish this through the use of plausible "imagined worlds."
- Human beings (in an information-processing sense) are inherently "limited" creatures who frequently rely on cognitive shortcuts (e.g., analogies, scripts, schemas, and satisficing in general).
- The cognitive structures in our brains are remarkably resistant to change (e.g., belief systems and operational codes). Many pathologies in foreign decision-making from the way in which the human mind works, and misperception of adversaries is commonplace.
- The personality of the decision-maker may exercise a crucial impact on the character of the decision made.
- Recent advances within this general approach include the POLIHEURISIC model (which ties together cognitive approaches) and prospect theory (which tries to specify the conditions under which individuals take risks).
- Emotion may have a critical impact on decision-making via its effect on judgment, and this impact may sometimes be beneficial. However, it may also be damaging (for instance, engaging in wishful thinking).
- Derived primarily from cognitive psychology and neuroscience.

Figure 4.2 *Homo Psychologicus* Summarized.

and moved in with a prostitute. Put simply, individuals with prefrontal cortex damage make bad decisions because they no longer have the capacity to care one way or another. As political scientist Jonathan Mercer relates, "people without emotion may know they should be ethical, and may know they should be influenced by norms, and may know that they should not make disastrous financial decisions, but this knowledge is abstract and inert and does not weigh on their decisions. They do not care about themselves and others, and they neither try to avoid making mistakes nor are they capable of 'learning' from their mistakes" (Mercer2005, 93). All of this is a relatively new direction within the study of foreign policy decision-making, but there is a growing recognition that we may need to alter many of our assumptions about emotion as we integrate this kind of approach into the field. As we move through the case studies in chapters 5–10, we will consider not just the cognitive forces that appear to have influenced the reasoning of particular decision-makers but their emotional or affective motivations as well (fig. 4.2).

FROM THEORIES TO CASE STUDIES

So far, we have examined our three perspectives—*Homo Bureaucraticus, Homo Sociologicus,* and *Homo Psychologicus*—largely in isolation from one another. The reader will probably have noticed that each of these perspectives is a collection of separable theories, not a single view; the bureaucratic politics approaches of Graham Allison and Morton Halperin, for instance, are not identical, and Paul 't Hart's approach to groupthink is slightly different from that of Irving Janis. Equally, *Homo Psychologicus* contains a bundle of approaches; Deborah Welch Larson's book *Origins of Containment* adopts an approach which is rather different to this one, since she accentuates the differences between varieties of cognitive theory that have been fused here for analytical convenience (Larson 1985). Nevertheless, in each case the reader will probably appreciate by now that while there are differences *within* each of the three approaches, these are minor compared to the differences *between* them. Each of the perspectives treats foreign policy behavior as springing from a different root cause. But which explains that behavior *best*? Ultimately, the only way to form a judgment on that question is to compare how each of the approaches performs across a range of case studies. That will be our next task, beginning with John F. Kennedy's disastrous attempt to invade Cuba at the Bay of Pigs.

PART 2

Case Studies

CHAPTER 5

The Bay of Pigs:
"How Could I Have Been So Stupid?"

John Kennedy and Robert Kennedy discuss what went wrong at the Bay of Pigs.
SOURCE: Getty Images

The distinguished American journalist Theodore Draper called it "one of those rare politico-military events—a perfect failure." The main architect of the venture, CIA Deputy Director for Plans Richard Bissell, viewed it as "a defeat for the United States and an unqualified victory for [Cuban leader Fidel] Castro." Richard Goodwin, one of Kennedy's advisers, called it "a preposterous, doomed fiasco." Grayston Lynch, one of the CIA's on-site commanders at the Bay of Pigs, called it "a tragedy." And Admiral Arleigh Burke, Chief of U.S. Naval Operations at the time, described it as "a complete breakdown in governmental ability to take actions in a complex situation" (Draper 1962, 59; Bissell 1996, 190; Goodwin 1988, 176; Lynch 1998, 132; Burke quoted in Bissell 1996, 198). In April 1961, the Kennedy administration launched Operation Zapata, an unambiguously disastrous attempt to invade Cuba at the Bay of Pigs (*Bahia de los Cochinos*). The result was a humiliating foreign policy and political defeat for John F. Kennedy just three months into his presidency.[1] Perhaps most significantly, the fact that Kennedy had attempted to invade Cuba and failed appears to have convinced Soviet Premier Nikita Khrushchev that the young American president would almost certainly try again (Lebow and Stein 1994, 67–93). Although Khrushchev seems to have had multiple motivations in mind when deciding to place missiles in Cuba in 1962, the Bay of Pigs operation may well have helped precipitate the Cuban missile crisis, which pushed the world to the brink of nuclear war.

On New Year's Day 1959, Fidel Castro had triumphantly rolled into Havana, the capital city of Cuba, having deposed the U.S.-backed government of Fulgencio Batista that had held power since 1952. Cuba had been a playground of wealthy Americans for many years up until this point, much prized for its wild nightlife, brothels, beaches, and casinos. Corruption had been rife under Batista, however, and most Americans never saw the dark side of life in Cuba, the grinding poverty, and heavy-handed political repression under which many inhabitants of the island lived. By 1959 the Eisenhower administration had become impatient with Batista and initially welcomed Fidel's takeover of the island. Castro even toured the United States, meeting Vice President Nixon (who, like other members of the administration, was uncertain whether Fidel was a Communist or simply "naïve," as he put it at the time). While historians continue to debate whether Eisenhower lost a golden opportunity in not extending the hand of friendship to the new Cuban leader, it is clear that by the middle of 1960 Castro had allied himself with the Soviet Union and had nationalized American-owned oil refineries, sugar mills, and utility companies. The Eisenhower administration, moreover, had already begun a series of covert sabotage operations—including the burning of sugarcane fields and the bombing of buildings—designed to undermine the new Cuban leader's hold on the island. We now know that Soviet assistance to Castro began as early as the spring of 1959 and that arms sales began in the fall of that year (Fursenko and Naftali 1997, 11–39; Allison and Zelikow 1999, 83).

President Eisenhower did not regard the sabotage operations as effective. The CIA had hoped that Castro's government would be undermined as a wave of fear spread across Cuba. In fact, it was increasingly apparent that the raids, although destructive, were nothing more than annoying inconveniences for Castro. Eisenhower instructed the CIA to develop something better. By April 1960, CIA Director Allen Dulles and Richard Bissell, deputy director of plans, had come up with just that: a plan to invade Cuba. Although the President knew that he would be leaving office in January 1961, he nevertheless gave the plan his initial approval but left it to his successor to decide whether it would actually be implemented. Jacob Esterline of the CIA and Col. Jack Hawkins, on loan to the CIA from the military, were given day-to-day control over the operational details.

How did the planners expect the invasion to work? The basic idea was to train 1,400 Cuban exiles, many of them recruited from anti-Castro groups in the Little Havana area of Miami, under cover of secrecy in Guatemala. They became known as "Brigade 2506." The CIA and the U.S. military would then assist the exiles in mounting an amphibious landing and invasion of the island, supposedly without taking part in the fighting themselves. Originally the landing site was to be at Trinidad, although this was later changed to the Bay of Pigs since Kennedy regarded the original plan as "too noisy." The invasion was expected to spark an uprising or revolt among disaffected elements within Cuba, hopefully leading also to the elimination of Castro by some means.[2] In a memorandum dated January 4, 1960, Hawkins outlined the basic idea behind the plan:

> The initial mission of the invasion force will be to seize and defend a small area, which under ideal conditions will include an airfield and access to the sea for logistic support. … The primary objective of the force will be to survive and maintain its integrity on Cuban soil. There will be no early attempt to break out of the lodgement for further offensive operations unless and until there is a general uprising against the Castro regime or overt military intervention by United States forces has taken place. It is expected that these operations will precipitate a general uprising throughout Cuba and cause the revolt of large segments of the Cuban Army and Militia. The lodgement, it is hoped, will serve as a rallying point for the thousands who are ready for overt resistance to Castro but who hesitate to act until they can feel some assurance of success. A general revolt in Cuba, if one is successfully triggered by our operations, may serve to topple the Castro regime within a period of weeks. If matters do not eventuate as predicted above, the lodgement established by our force can be used as the site for establishment of a provisional government which can be recognized by the United States, and hopefully by other American states, and given overt military assistance. The way will then be paved for United States military intervention aimed at pacification of Cuba, and this will result in the prompt overthrow of the Castro Government. (Hawkins 1961)

The hand of the United States was supposed to be hidden from view, however, and the whole thing was supposed to look like a purely Cuban operation. World War II–era American B-26 aircraft were provided to the invasion force, repainted to look like the planes of Cuban defectors, and these were to be used to destroy Castro's own planes in a series of air strikes so that they could not threaten the invading forces at the beachhead. If all went well, the invading exiles would establish a secure position at *Playa Giron*. They would then move inland, heading for Havana. From there or from the beachhead, they would set up a provisional government, which could then be recognized by the United States and given economic and military assistance. Should the invasion fail, however, there was a backup plan: the exiles could always retreat to the Escambray Mountains, a mountain range about fifty miles in length located in the south central region of the island. The worst that could happen, Kennedy was told, was that the invading force would have to regroup and mount a guerilla operation against Castro from the mountains.

Almost no part of the plan actually worked in practice. The invading force was far too small and was easily crushed by Castro's troops. Most tellingly perhaps, there was never any popular uprising, and the lone air strike mounted against Castro's planes failed to finish the job. The invading force was thus pinned down from the air and left defenseless. To make matter worse, the exiles were unable to flee to the Escambray Mountains. Castro's forces stood in the way, as did eighty miles of alligator- and mosquito-infested swampland. Apparently, Bissell had not told the President that escape would be far more difficult if the invasion site was moved from Trinidad to the *Bahia de los Cochinos*. Within seventy-two hours it was apparent that the invasion had failed, and the United States had to pay a substantial ransom to get the surviving exiles released from Castro's prisons. As a result, Castro not only outlasted Kennedy in office but eight other American presidents as well until his retirement in 2008. The planners had convinced themselves in 1961 that the young, charismatic Cuban leader was deeply unpopular on the island, but the opposite was true.

Apart from the Escambray fallback, there was also a kind of unwritten backup plan, which seems to have existed only in the minds of Dulles, Bissell, and the other CIA planners: they were operating under the mistaken assumption that Kennedy would send in the U.S. military if the exiles ran into difficulty. The President had repeatedly stressed that he would under no circumstances give such an order; he was concerned that the existing plan was already too noisy, potentially revealing the hand of the United States behind everything. But Dulles and Bissell do not seem to have believed Kennedy. When it became clear after three days that the operation would fail, the President steadfastly resisted the advice of the CIA and the Joint Chiefs to "Americanize" it by sending in the Marines and/or bombing Cuba. There was an American warship, the USS *Essex*, stationed only a few miles from shore at the Bay of Pigs. Having told his advisers that there would be no direct U.S. intervention, Kennedy called Admiral Burke and instructed him to move the ship away from that location.

Politically, this must have been immensely difficult for any president to do, and afterwards Kennedy was said to be "shattered" by the resulting defeat. Undersecretary of State Chester Bowles related that in one meeting on April 20th—after having heard his advisers shift the blame back and forth among one another—the President simply walked out of the room without saying a word. "I attended the cabinet meeting in Rusk's absence and it was about as grim as any meeting I can remember in all my experience in government," Bowles recalled.

"Here for the first time he faced a situation where his judgment had been mistaken." Kennedy is said to have wept in the days afterward, looking distracted in meetings and repeatedly muttering "how could I have been so stupid as to let them proceed?" (Blight, Lang, and Welch 2009, 335; Reeves 1993: 94–95).

A THORN OR A DAGGER?

Looking at the operation in hindsight, many commentators have expressed amazement that Kennedy gave the go ahead for the invasion, especially since the President was generally disinclined to approve military ventures. Of course, it is easy to be wise after the fact. The phenomenon known to psychologists as *hindsight bias* may be at work here to some extent, the tendency after an event has occurred to claim that "I knew it all along" (Fischoff and Beyth 1975). It is certainly true to say that relatively few of Kennedy's advisers expressed misgivings before the event as opposed to during its grim aftermath. As the President noted at a conference podium on April 21, 1961, where he accepted full responsibility for the failed operation: "[T]here's an old saying that victory has a hundred fathers and defeat is an orphan."

Nevertheless, a variety of critics have suggested that the failure of the operation should have been perfectly predicable *prior* to its launch, given the information that the decision-makers already had. Afterwards, even Kennedy himself seemed to agree. On more than one occasion after Operation Zapata failed, he asked friends and advisers how this calamity could have occurred, after countless meetings at which the CIA plan had been dissected and discussed. JFK subsequently set up the Taylor Commission, chaired by the President's trusted military adviser General Maxwell Taylor and including his brother Robert Kennedy, Admiral Burke, and Allen Dulles as members, which concluded that "the impossibility of running Zapata as a covert operation under CIA should have been recognized" as early as November 1960. This postmortem concluded that the likelihood of failure was evident as much as five months before the invasion went ahead in April of the following year. An internal audit within the CIA, lead by Lyman Kirkpatrick, reached a similar conclusion (Kornbluh 1998).

While opponents of the invasion had been few and far between, three discordant voices in particular—Chester Bowles, William Fulbright, and Arthur Schlesinger—had warned of impending disaster before the event. In a memorandum to his boss Secretary of State Dean Rusk dated March 31, 1961, Bowles found the invasion plan "profoundly disturbing." Much of his opposition, he noted, derived from "a deep personal conviction that our national interests are poorly served by a covert operation of this kind at a time when our new President is effectively appealing to world opinion on the basis of high principle. Even in our imperfect world," Bowles argued, "the differences which distinguish us from the Russians are of vital importance. This is true not only in a moral sense but in the practical effect of these differences on our capacity to rally the non-Communist world in behalf of our traditional democratic objectives" (Bowles 1961).

Bowles offered seven reasons as to why, in his view, the operation should not go ahead as planned. First of all, he argued that a U.S.-sponsored invasion would violate the treaty obligations that the United States had signed in creating the Organization of American States (OAS), which prohibit direct or indirect intervention by one state "in the internal or external affairs of any other state." Such an intervention would also violate international law more generally. Second, the operation would be too risky; the planners of the invasion had themselves admitted that the chances of success were not greater than one out of three, and Bowles considered it likely (with some prescience) that the failure of the plan would significantly enhance Castro's popularity and prestige. Third, Bowles maintained that the reaction against the United States worldwide, especially within Latin America, would be adverse and would undercut America's position everywhere. Fourth, Bowles foresaw—again with some accuracy—that if the mission failed in its early stages, the pressure on Kennedy to intervene directly with U.S. forces would be immense. The President would be left with the choice of starting a war without provocation against a tiny Third World nation, or abandoning the invasion force to a grim fate. Fifth, it was possible, Bowles argued, that Castro's fragile new regime would fall of its own accord. Sixth, even if, as seemed more likely, Castro became stronger not weaker, and if, again, the Soviet Union sought to support his revolution with military aid, a blockade could be used to cut this support off. Finally, if Castro sought to export his revolution to the surrounding area within Central America, the United States would then be justified in acting military, but not, Bowles heavily implied, at this stage. "I believe it would be a grave mistake for us to jeopardize the favorable position we have steadily developed in most of the non-Communist world by the responsible and restrained policies which are now associated with the President by embarking on a major covert adventure with such very heavy built-in risks", Bowles concluded. Kennedy never saw this memorandum, since Rusk "did not bother" to forward it on to the White House (Goodwin 1988, 177).

Senator William Fulbright, not a member of the administration but nevertheless a trusted ad hoc advisor and Chairman of the Senate Foreign Relations Committee, was also called in prior to Kennedy's decision to give the green light.[3] Asked to give his own views on the adequacy of the plan and desirability (or otherwise) of going ahead with the plan at a meeting with Kennedy and his key advisers on April 4, Fulbright came down forcefully against it. Aided by a memorandum prepared by his assistant Pat Holt, Fulbright offered a whole series of reasons why the plan should be rejected, many of them similar to those expressed by Bowles. As Holt later recalled:

> If this [invasion] happened it would succeed in overthrowing Castro only at the cost of massive and pervasive American entanglement in Cuba, the end of which could not be foreseen. Then the argument was made that even if we thought it would work, we ought not to do it because it violated a number of treaties to which the United States was a party. Indeed, to the degree that these Cuban exiles came from the United States or were supported in exile by the United States, it violated domestic laws of the United States. The point was made that one of the

things which distinguished us from the Soviet Union was respect for law and by God we ought to respect it. And then, finally, the argument was made that the threat to United States interests posed by Cuba was not great enough to warrant this kind of effort, in any event. The phrase . . . we used was that Cuba is a thorn in the flesh, it's not a dagger in the heart (Holt 1980).[4]

When Fulbright had finished presenting his case, Kennedy went around the room asking each of his advisers to vote a straight yes or no on the plan. Fulbright was the only one to vote against; the whole venture, he said, was "ill considered," and it would be impossible to disguise the role of the U.S. government (Goodwin 1988, 177). Clearly not ready to give the final go-ahead, the President suggested that they should sleep on it. "You're the only one in the room who can say, 'I told you so,'" Kennedy said to Fulbright as the meeting ended (Reeves 1993, 82).

Finally, the presidential adviser Arthur Schlesinger voiced his own doubts in a series of memoranda to Kennedy. Schlesinger's criticism of the plan was perhaps more muted than that of Bowles or Fulbright, and he always regretted not speaking up more forcefully against the plan in meetings. Nevertheless, he did make a number of points on paper prior to the invasion, which are similar to those offered by other opponents of the invasion. The key criticism he made on a number of occasions was that the role of the United States in guiding the Bay of Pigs operation would be all too evident. By invading Cuba, the new administration would be jeopardizing the support it had generated around the globe and returning to a less progressive, more backward Cold War approach. In a memorandum to JFK dated February 11, 1961, Schlesinger note that:

> However well disguised any action might be, it will be ascribed to the United States. The result would be a wave of massive protest, agitation and sabotage throughout Latin America, Europe, Asia and Africa (not to speak of Canada and of certain quarters in the United States). Worst of all, this would be your first dramatic foreign policy initiative. At one stroke, it would dissipate all the extraordinary good will which has been rising toward the new Administration in the minds of millions (Schlesinger 1961).

Like Bowles, Schlesinger occupied only a junior role within the administration, and his arguments do not appear to have been taken that seriously. Fulbright, on the other hand, had the even more formidable handicap of not being a member of the government, and many members of JFK's inner circle appear to have reacted quite defensively to his presence at the meeting. By the time he joined the meeting on April 4, moreover, it was probably too late; the juggernaut was already rolling. In the end, Castro was indeed viewed as a dagger rather than a thorn.

In some ways, it was ironic that it was JFK who decided to launch the ill-fated invasion. The operation had been planned for at least a year before by the Eisenhower administration, working under the general supervision of then Vice President Richard Nixon.. Kennedy had won the 1960 presidential election against Nixon, posing as a tough-minded, uncompromising Cold Warrior in an attempt to outdo the Republicans at their own game (although his behavior as President would later be characterized by cautious moderation and the avoidance of conflict with the Soviets). This domestic factor may well have played on Kennedy's mind once he arrived in office. Having run as a tough anti-Communist, how could he begin his presidency by canceling an operation designed to nip the expansion of Communism in the bud (a plan created, moreover, under the direction of his militarily astute and far more experienced predecessor)? Fidel Castro had set up a pro-Soviet regime, right there in Uncle Sam's backyard, and the CIA was presenting Kennedy with an opportunity to remove this potential threat. To reject this plan would smack of weakness and would seem to expose JFK as an opportunist and a hypocrite. "The fear of sounding soft on Communism was a very strong one," as Schlesinger later recalled. "A liberal Democrat like Kennedy had to be constantly concerned with this issue" (quoted in Blight and Kornbluh 1998, 65). Moreover, Kennedy had attacked Nixon during the 1960 campaign for supposedly doing too little about Cuba. To cancel the invasion plan of his predecessors once in office, then, would seem like a wholehearted reversal of the stance he had taken during the election.

Administration insiders like Schlesinger and Theodore Sorensen tend to argue the "CIA Entrapment" explanation for the Bay of Pigs, an argument compatible with the *Homo Bureaucraticus* perspective. According to this view, Dulles deliberately maneuvered the president into a situation where he thought Kennedy would be forced to go ahead with the plan. Revisionist historians and the administration's critics on both the Left and the Right, on the other hand, see what happened at the Bay of Pigs as nothing less than presidential betrayal. They argue in particular that the invasion might well have succeeded if Kennedy had not meddled in the details of the plan, placing his own political fortunes above individuals who were literally risking their lives (the President, as already noted, had cancelled the U.S. air cover for the invading forces that had originally been part of the plan, including a planned second air strike against Castro's air force). Grayston Lynch, one of the CIA commanders at the Bay of Pigs during the invasion, is a leading proponent of this view, which is also held by many of the surviving members of the Cuban invasion force today (Lynch 1998). Writing from a liberal perspective, the journalist Seymour Hersh has expressed a similar view:

> Kennedy's refusal to go forward with the essential second bombing mission—or, for that matter, simply to call off the exile invasion—was not a military but a political decision. As Kennedy had to know, his decision amounted to a death sentence for the Cuban exiles fighting on the ground. But he and Nikita Khrushchev had just agreed, after weeks of secret back-and-forth, to an early June summit meeting in Europe. A second bombing attack was sure to focus attention on American involvement; it would jeopardize Kennedy's face-to-face meeting with the Soviet premier and his chances for an early foreign-policy triumph. In terms of domestic politics, the president understood that a failure at the Bay of Pigs was preferable to the political heat he would take from Republicans and conservative Democrats if he did not go forward with the invasion. He would be considered just another liberal, like the much maligned Adlai Stevenson. Nothing—not even the death and capture of hundreds of Cuban patriots—was worth that (Hersh 1998, 212).

From the perspectives of Hersh and Lynch, what happened had less to do with bureaucratic politics than it did with a simple failure of presidential courage and a willingness to lay down his friends for his political life. It is of course impossible to resolve this still-heated political debate here, and we will not attempt to do so. What we can do, however, is to focus on those aspects of the decision-making process that have been established by general consensus as factually accurate, rather than impugning the motives of particular participants (as both sides in this debate have been all too willing to do). We know, for instance, that the CIA under Allen Dulles and Richard Bissell was very much in favor of the plan, but that the President and others were more torn about its wisdom. Why were representatives of the CIA so much more confident than the newly arrived occupants of the White House? Why did the representatives of different organizations exhibit different degrees of enthusiasm in general? Is there evidence that the plan that emerged might have been the product of compromise, for instance? And why did the mission go ahead despite the misgivings of several of those close to the president? Were group dynamics to blame for a half-baked plan being given the go-ahead? What beliefs, both general and specific, seem to have inspired the supporters of the invasion, and what historical models did they draw upon as evidence that this sort of project could succeed? Why did Dulles and Bissell operate under the assumption that Kennedy would send in the U.S. military if the exiles ran into difficulty? Compelling answers to these questions have been offered from the perspective of each of our three models of decision-making.

All three perspectives regard the Rational Actor Model (RAM; see chap. 1) as inadequate here, not least because only one alternative was given serious consideration: the invasion plan. *Homo Economicus* assumes that the decision-makers generate a list of options for addressing a problem—in this case, how to get rid of Fidel Castro—and then weigh the pros and cons of each. While the invasion plan itself was certainly discussed exhaustively at a considerable number of high-level meetings (indeed, this was one of the reasons why Kennedy was so puzzled as to why it had had failed so spectacularly), the decision-making process was faulty in a number of respects. We are now fairly sure, for instance, that no remotely comprehensive discussion of the alternatives to invasion ever took place, at least not at the highest levels of government around Kennedy. As Lucien Vandenbrouke notes, "the rational actor interpretation suffers from the fact that the president and his advisers did not carefully weigh competing alternatives and then select the invasion of Cuba as the best policy. In reality, in response to the Eisenhower administration's growing concern about Cuba, the CIA conceived a plan in the middle of 1960 to topple Castro, submitted it to the president, and received authorization to proceed with the preparations." Although Eisenhower had not yet given his ultimate approval at the time he left office in January 1961, the organizational juggernaut was already rolling when Kennedy succeeded him, so that the decision essentially became one of "do we, or don't we?" The President was therefore compelled "to decide for or against an invasion project to which considerable resources had already been committed, and that a powerful agency vigorously promoted"

- Would any president have done what President X did, as far as you can tell?
- Is there evidence that personality and beliefs of key individuals actually mattered in terms of shaping the decision reached?
- Do key individuals "stand where they sit"?
- Is there evidence of bureaucratic infighting and/or compromises being reached?
- Does anyone seem to be defending their own particular piece of 'bureaucratic turf'?
- Are the decision-makers taking risks, even acting recklessly? If so, why do you think this is happening?
- Do the decision-makers tend to agree with one another rather than disagreeing?
- Is there evidence that dissenters are excluded from the key decision-making forums?
- Do the decision-maker seems to have carefully weighed all available options, or are they dismissing some out of hand? Again, why does this seem to be happening?

Figure 5.1 What to look for.

(Vandenbrouke 1984, 473). Moreover, the alternatives that *were* examined were all alternative invasion plans, not a comprehensive examination of different means to the end being sought.

Perhaps as a direct result of this highly abbreviated process, the decision-makers failed to probe basic assumptions. As Richard Neustadt and Ernest May note:

> The Bay of Pigs affair of 1961 is perhaps *the* classic case of presumptions unexamined. The affair was marked from first to last by absence of explicitness even about "maybes," let alone about "if/thens" and "truths." Participants differed widely at least on the "maybes" and the "if/thens," but they explored neither those differences nor discrepancies between what they expected and what was occurring. They skirted doing so in extraordinary fashion. The organizers walled themselves off from colleagues who might have challenged their presumptions. The President did likewise, often inadvertently, for most of those whose comment or advice he asked were too inhibited to plumb his underlying presumptions or to spell out theirs. They were too new to him and he to them (Neustadt and May 1986, 140).

Of course, this still begs the question of how each of our approaches would explain this failure to probe presumptions or assumptions. We need to dig deeper, and that will be our next task. As we do so, the reader will find it useful to refer to figure 5.1. This provides you with a reminder as to what you should be looking for in each case study, and while the same diagram will not be reproduced in the other case studies, referring back to 5.1 should prove helpful in reminding you what each perspective is trying to show.

Homo Bureaucraticus

The reader will recall that from the perspective of *Homo Bureaucraticus*, decision-makers are best viewed as players in a kind of organizational game. Knowing what we know already about this approach, we should expect Graham Allison's bureaucratic politics model to explain the decision to go ahead as a product of both *bargaining* and *routine*: first of all, bargaining and compromise should have taken place between the players in the game, such that the end result should have been a kind of patchwork quilt of ideas that failed to capture the preferences of any one player exactly. Second, organizational routines should have propelled both the formulation and implementation of policy; what the relevant organizations could do and their preference for their own SOPs should have influenced the eventual plan as well. "Where you stand" in the debate about invasion should depend on "where you sit," and organizations should bridle under political control like an unruly horse.

Both Arthur Schlesinger and his former colleague Theodore Sorensen have suggested that the CIA tried successfully to compel the President to go along with the original invasion and then —this time unsuccessfully—to persuade him to mount a full-scale military invasion (Schlesinger 1965; Sorensen 1965). Schlesinger argues that Kennedy felt legitimately "trapped" for both strategic and domestic political reasons. Knowing this, he suggests, Allen Dulles deliberately played upon the President's political fears:

> He inherited this project from Eisenhower. When he talked to Dulles about it, Dulles kept emphasizing what he called the "disposal problem." Dulles was telling Kennedy, between the lines, that if you cancel this venture it means that the 1,200 Cubans we have been training in Guatemala will disperse around Latin America, and they'll spread the word that the U.S. government has changed its policy toward Castro. This, in turn, will be a great stimulus to the *Fidelistas* through-out Latin America. The political impact of cancellation, Dulles implied, will be very serious for the balance of force in the hemisphere. . . . For a lieutenant JG (junior grade) in the Navy in the Second World War to cancel an expedition that had been advocated, sanctioned, and supported by the general who commanded the largest successful amphibious landing in history, would have been hard to explain. I think that this was more important than anything else, that Kennedy felt trapped, having inherited the operation from Eisenhower. Kennedy's basic approach, from the moment he heard about the operation, was to try to do *some-thing*, but as little as possible. He wanted a neat little infiltration that was plausibly deniable, but which had some chance of success (Quoted in Blight and Kornbluh 1998, 64).

From this perspective, Dulles and Bissell perhaps even pushed for a mission that they *knew in advance* would fail because they thought that Kennedy would be forced to transform the limited invasion into a full-scale U.S. operation once it became clear that it would not succeed otherwise. The argument that the CIA deliberately entrapped the president is of course hard to prove or disprove either way, but it also finds some support in the account of the journalist Peter Wyden, who reconstructed the events of early 1961 during the 1970s using behind the scenes interviews with many of the participants. "If the CIA, acting out of control and independently, had not escalated its plans against Fidel Castro from a modest guerilla operation into a full-fledged invasion," Wyden argues, "President Kennedy would have suffered no humiliating, almost grotesque defeat" (Wyden 1979, 7).

This argument is quite compatible with the *Homo Bureaucraticus* approach that emphasizes the independent power of organizations and their tendency to go their own way. As Allison and Zelikow note in *Essence of Decision*, Presidents often find it difficult to stop an organization from doing something once a process has begun. "Intervention by government leaders does sometimes change the activity of an organization in an intended direction, but instances are fewer than might be expected. These machines are not just turned on or off just by pulling a switch," they argue. They give the example of CIA planning for the overthrow of Salvador Allende in Chile in 1970. Richard Nixon and Henry Kissinger found the CIA reluctant to take covert action against Chile in the first place. Later on (at least according to the memoirs of the two men) Nixon told the CIA to abandon the covert action, and this proved problematic as well. "Nixon had trouble getting the agency to do what he wanted, yet, by his and Kissinger's account, he then also had trouble getting the agency to stop doing it," Allison and Zelikow point out (Allison and Zelikow 1999, 173–74).

While most of his subordinates seem to have obeyed (albeit reluctantly) Kennedy's order not to intervene directly when it became obvious that the plan would fail, others apparently did not. Seymour Hersh argues, for instance, that when the order not to proceed with the second air strike reached the commanders of the USS *Essex,* four U.S. pilots simply ignored this and took off to bomb Castro's aircraft anyway. The pilots were members of the Alabama National Guard who had secretly trained with the exile force. No doubt they felt such a strong sense of kinship with their comrades in arms, this account suggests, that they felt obliged to ignore Kennedy's order as a matter of principle. According to Hersh's account, the Kennedys were enraged that a presidential order had been ignored. Bobby Kennedy in particular was furious, and reportedly told Bissell "those goddammed pilots better well be dead" (Hersh 1998, 215).

This story would provide quite dramatic evidence for *Homo Bureaucraticus* were it true; this does not seem to be the case, however.[5] The accounts of Wyden and Lynch, although they part company about who was to blame, both agree that the U.S. forces stationed on the *Essex*—while immensely frustrated at being forced to stand by and watch the brigade crushed—nevertheless obeyed their orders to the letter (Lynch 1998, 124; Wyden 1979, 240–45). The mission to resupply the brigade by the B-26s was in fact explicitly authorized by the president in the early hours of April 19. He also authorized the use of military jets for one hour, flying from the *Essex* to provide air cover. This was a classic bureaucratic compromise: the CIA and Joint Chiefs were pushing for a second air strike, while the State Department opposed it. The result was an agreement from the President that jets from the *Essex* could be used to help shore up the invasion. Their task was to protect the B-26s, and they were not to seek combat (although the president must have known that they might well have to shoot at Castro's planes in order to defend the brigade aircraft). Due to an error in calculating the time difference between Washington, DC and Cuba, however, Jacob Esterline mistakenly ordered the jets to fly over the Bay of Pigs one hour late. Left without air cover, the four Americans were killed, their lumbering B-26s shot down by Castro's forces.

There is still evidence, however, that both the CIA and the Joint Chiefs did violate Kennedy's orders in other ways. While Kennedy had allowed U.S. forces to be used as air cover on the morning of the 19th, he does not seem to have been aware that *American* pilots were flying the B-26s, let alone that members of the Alabama National Guard were involved. The Cuban pilots who had been flying the missions over the beachhead were disheartened and exhausted, and there were not enough of them willing to fly the mission. Under these circumstances, but acting without authorization from the White House, Richard Bissell authorized the use of American pilots for the first time during the invasion (Wyden 1979, 235). This may have been the real source of the Kennedys' anger—if indeed that part of Hersh's story is accurate—because the President had quite expressly forbidden Americans to become directly involved in the fighting. It is hard to imagine that John or Robert Kennedy would be angry at the pilots for implementing a strike, which the President himself had sanctioned, but the anger becomes explicable once one realizes that the pilots were Americans. Earlier on, as Arthur Schlesinger notes, JFK was almost certainly not aware either that "the first frogman on each beach was, in spite of Kennedy's order, [was] an American" (Schlesinger 1965:,274). According to Bissell, there was no presidential authorization for Grayston Lynch and "Rip" Robertson to accompany the invading forces onto the beaches, and Bissell claims that the CIA never authorized this either. "There not only was none received from above my level, but that's something I never authorized," Bissell later recalled, "and I am quite certain that there wasn't an authorization" (Bissell 1975).

Equally, there is strong evidence that Admiral Burke, not just Navy Chief at this time but Acting Chairman of the Joint Chiefs, greatly exceeded the President's orders during the invasion. One puzzle that remained unclear until the 1990s—given the fact that Kennedy had expressly forbidden the use of American forces—is why 2,000 U.S. Marines were aboard the *Essex* just outside the Bay of Pigs, waiting in the full expectation that they would be called in to invade Cuba. During the 1996 Musgrove Conference on the Bay of Pigs, the following rather revealing exchange between Jacob Esterline, former Eisenhower and Kennedy Cuba expert Wayne Smith, and former CIA official Samuel Halpern provided the answer:

SMITH: Kennedy . . . tells Bissell that he will not use U.S. forces. Bissell does not believe it and thinks that if he puts the brigade ashore and it starts to fail—or even that there is a possibility of failure—that Kennedy will have to change his mind. He thinks Kennedy will not let it fail. And then there are those 2,000 marines standing off the beach. Who orders those marines there? The president has said no U.S. forces are going to be used. So who gives the order for 2,000 marines to be standing offshore, ready to go in?

ESTERLINE: Well, Arleigh Burke, I think, issued that order.

HALPERN: He did that on his own authority.

> ESTERLINE: I agree. He did that on his own authority. He didn't have any authority from the president, did he, Sam?
>
> HALPERN: It's the same as during the missile crisis, when general power of SAC put out DEFCON 2 on his own, without authority from anybody. Washington didn't find out about it until hours later.
>
> SMITH: My God! It's *Burke* who issues orders to the *Essex*? There was the president saying we don't want any indication of U.S. involvement; then there is the Essex standing offshore from Playa Giron . . .(Blight and Kornbluh 1998, 96–97).

Bureaucratic routines or SOPs also played a significant role in the decision-making. Most significantly, since this was a CIA plan rather than a military one and since organizations tend not to tread on the bureaucratic turf of other agencies where they lack any interest in doing so, the Joint Chiefs did not overtly criticize the Bay of Pigs venture (Kramer 1998, 247). There is some evidence that they were not overly impressed by the plan; asked to scrutinize it by the President, they refrained from criticizing its various components, even though they judged the chances of success to be only "about one in three" overall. Organizational routines encouraged the Pentagon to stay out of it. As Robert McNamara later admitted in his book *In Retrospect*, he displayed a "deference to the CIA on what I considered an agency operation." Instead of immersing himself in its details and acting as an independent check within the process, McNamara became what he described as "a passive bystander" (McNamara 1995, 26). He later clearly felt guilty that he had failed Kennedy by not subjecting the plan to closer scrutiny.

Looked at more generally, representatives of the various organizations involved in the decision-making process seem to have indeed stood where they sat. *Homo Bureaucraticus* emphasizes the point that the representatives of different organizations tend to see different sides of a given issue. The CIA came to be an advocate of the plan, not an impartial advisor on its wisdom; it specialized in covert operations, and advocated what the agency did (Vandenbrouke 1984, 474). Its representatives were concerned purely with the success of the operation, regardless of how it might play abroad. On the other hand, representatives of the State Department, including Secretary Rusk and his subordinates Schlesinger and Bowles as well as the U.S. Ambassador to the UN Adlai Stevenson were notably preoccupied with the diplomatic side of the operation. What, they asked, would a successful invasion (or, equally, an unsuccessful one) do to our image abroad and our relations with our Allies? How would it affect our ability to conduct diplomacy effectively with other states? The State Department was, as one might expect, focused on its own bureaucratic interests.[6] The White House also stood where it sat because it was most concerned with how the invasion would look politically, both in a domestic political sense and in broader international terms. If the operation were cancelled, Kennedy would have an embarrassing disposal problem that would almost certainly hurt him domestically. If the plan did not go ahead, the exiles might be expected to roam across the United States and Latin America accusing Kennedy of lacking the courage to confront Communism.

As we saw in chapter 2, the *Homo Bureaucraticus* approach also often treats decisions as resultants, essentially the outcome of pulling and hauling. What states do may end up reflecting the least common denominator, failing to represent what any of the actors wanted but keeping everyone minimally happy. This does seem to be a fair characterization of the Bay of Pigs plan. The plan that Dulles, Bissell, and Esterline put into effect did not represent the first choice of any actor or agency; instead, it was a strange patchwork quilt of what the CIA, the White House, and the State Department wanted. While it is difficult to say exactly what Rusk's position on the Bay of Pigs was—he had a well-earned reputation for playing his cards close to his chest that frustrated many of his colleagues, the President included— but we do know that he was especially concerned with the diplomatic aspects of the plan and that State Department representatives pressured Kennedy to water it down (Lynch 1998). Equally, Adlai Stevenson, greatly embarrassed that he had unwittingly lied about American involvement in the first air strike,[7] is said to have pressured Kennedy to call off the second planned strike. The White House shared these kind of concerns and Kennedy worried about the domestic repercussions of acting or failing to act, concerned that the existing plan revealed the U.S.'s hand in too obvious a fashion and that intervention risked embroiling U.S. forces in a civil war. Conversely, the CIA had originally pushed for a noisier landing at Trinidad. The result was the bureaucratic deal that produced Operation Zapata, or the Bay of Pigs plan. As Piero Gleijeses notes, "in a clumsy compromise, the Trinidad Plan was abandoned for one in which the U.S. role would be less flagrant" (Gleijeses 1995, 19).

No overall consideration of the compromise that resulted from this process was undertaken. At Kennedy's insistence, the Joint Chiefs did indeed assess the viability of the competing invasion plans, but that was before the cancellation of the second air strike and other concessions had been made. The end result, therefore, had not been planned by anyone. This goes some way toward explaining the amazement that students and scholars still feel today when discussing the whole Bay of Pigs episode. How could Kennedy have been so stupid? How could such an intelligent, highly trained, and experienced collection of people have come up with such a plan? The answer, from the *Homo Bureaucraticus* perspective, is that *no one had*. When we consider questions like this, we typically place ourselves in the shoes of the decision-maker, assuming that states are analogous to individuals, missing the fact that governments represent a composite of various organizations, each with their own preferences, priorities and standard routines.

What, though, if group dynamics as opposed to bureaucratic infighting lay at the heart of the Kennedy administration's dysfunctional decision-making processes regarding the Bay of Pigs? Despite the impressive evidence on behalf of the bureaucratic politics approach in this case, this has not been the most popular explanation for what went wrong at the Bay of Pigs. That distinction belongs to the sociological view, by virtue of the key role that Irving Janis accorded to this case study in his book *Groupthink*. It is to this approach that we turn next.

Homo Sociologicus

The failure of Kennedy's inner circle to detect any of the false assumptions behind the Bay of Pigs invasion plan can be at least partially accounted for by the group's tendency to seek concurrence at the expense of information, critical appraisal, and debate. The concurrence-seeking tendency was manifested by shared illusions and other symptoms, all of which helped the members to maintain a sense of group solidarity. Most crucial were the symptoms that contributed to complacent overconfidence in the face of vague uncertainties and explicit warnings that should have alerted the members to the risks of the clandestine military operation—an operation so ill-conceived that among literate people all over the world, the name of the invasion site has become the very symbol of perfect failure (Janis 1982, 47).

Janis gave the Bay of Pigs case study pride of place in his book *Groupthink*, assuring his interpretation a vital role in what we have called the *Homo Sociologicus* perspective in this book. The reader will recall that groupthink is a kind of hastily arrived tendency toward premature consensus. It is a form of premature agreement, which can occur in especially cohesive groups. "The more amiability and esprit de corps there is among the members of a policy-making ingroup," Janis argues, "the greater the danger that independent critical thinking will be replaced by groupthink, which is likely to result in irrational and dehumanising actions directed against outgroups" (Janis 1982, 13). Once agreement is reached, the decision-making group then becomes closed to outside advice. Its members seek to defend the consensus at all costs, self-censoring their own doubts. Self-appointed mindguards emerge, who take it upon themselves to preserve the decision reached and knock down dissent. Dissenters who persist in voicing their disagreement are eventually excluded from the group altogether.

While the student of *Homo Bureaucraticus* looks for evidence of dissensus or disagreement—differences that can be traced to clashing organizational priorities and bureaucratic interests—the scholar of *Homo Sociologicus* looks for evidence of the opposite tendency: unquestioning consensus and agreement, derived from the powerful social pressures that can cause individual minds to close and questioning voices to fall silent. He or she looks for evidence that individuals who harbored private doubts about a policy failed to voice those doubts in a group context. This type of analyst also looks for evidence that individuals who do speak up are warned not to do so, or that such individuals are gradually pushed out of the President's inner circle. Such a scholar also sifts the evidence for instances of leadership behavior in which disagreement or the free interchange of ideas is discouraged, and/or where options are not considered because the members of the group share an unquestioned set of assumptions or beliefs derived from their similar social or political background.

In retrospect, Kennedy and his colleagues made six fundamental errors, Janis argues (Janis 1982, 19–27). First of all, they reasoned that most people would believe the CIA's cover story that this was entirely a Cuban exile operation. This seemed unlikely even at the time, since the details of the plan had not only been leaked but had even been published in the *New York Times* ahead of the invasion. Even if this had not been a CIA-sponsored invasion, it would probably have been viewed as such in Latin America anyway, given the long history of intervention by the United States within the hemisphere. Second, Kennedy and his advisers reasoned that the Cuban Air Force was too ineffective to represent a threat to the invading forces, and third that Castro's planes could be easily destroyed by the rather elderly World War II–era B-26 aircraft that the CIA had furnished to the exiles. Neither of these assumptions turned out to be accurate, not least because JFK's cancellation of the second planned air strike against the Cuban forces—largely out of a fear that another strike would make the hand of the United States far too obvious—undercut these assumptions. Fourth, the planners assumed that Castro's army was so weak that the exile brigade would be able to establish a well-protected beachhead at their landing point. They failed to envision that the exile force of just 1,400 men would likely face a much larger force of 20,000. Fifth, they assumed that morale was so high among the invading force of 1,400 Cuban exiles that they would not need the support of U.S. troops, but morale was actually so low among some of the exiles that they had rebelled against their CIA handlers in Guatemala; in fact, this had led to the imprisonment of some of the exile leaders. Finally, the president and his colleagues made the critically flawed assumption that an invasion would somehow automatically spark a popular uprising. This was perhaps the most dubious assumption of all since Castro, having gotten wind of the invasion plans, had already rounded up and imprisoned anyone he thought likely to join up with the invasion force. If a spontaneous uprising did not occur, Bissell told Kennedy, the exile forces could always retreat to the Escambray Mountains and join anti-Castro guerrillas there. Bissell failed to warn the president, however, that escape would now be virtually impossible if the plan were moved from Trinidad to the Bay of Pigs. Assuming that they could even fight their way past Castro's forces, the invaders would now have had to wade through those eighty miles of swampland, but none of JFK's advisers seem to have thought to look at a map.

Like other analysts, Janis noted that the Bay of Pigs was a huge military and political embarrassment for an administration only a few months old. He was especially surprised that this particular administration could have made errors of these colossal proportions. Kennedy's administration was filled with young, well-schooled, confident individuals, men whom JFK had deliberately selected because he wanted the very best talent in America from academia and business. The young president deliberately staffed his administration with what David Halberstam would later call "the best and the brightest," men who—while not necessarily well-versed in the ways of Washington—had nevertheless proven themselves in a variety of highly demanding fields (ibid. 1982, 16–19). Given these simple facts, Janis wonders, why did they get Cuba so wrong?

He finds the official explanations for the fiasco (including some of the points that a scholar of *Homo Bureaucraticus* would mention) only partially convincing (ibid 1982, 30–32). First of all, Janis notes that many observers have blamed the decision to go ahead on Kennedy's *political calculations*. The CIA put Kennedy under enormous pressure to act, especially Allen Dulles who emphasized the point that the President would face the aforementioned disposal problem if he failed to give the go-ahead. He was in some ways trapped by his own campaign rhetoric and wanted to look as tough as the Republicans—if not tougher—on issue of Cuba. Janis notes, however, that the political pressures cut both ways. If Kennedy had examined the plan more carefully, he would have noticed that the political risks of action were even greater than those of inaction. And if the disposal problem was uppermost in Kennedy's mind, why did he fail to explore other options, short of an outright invasion, that might have kept the exiles happy?

Janis is equally dissatisfied with a second explanation, this time based on the fact that this was *a new administration*. This argument stresses the inexperience of the President and his advisers. Most of them did not know one another person-ally and had not settled into comfortable routines or decision-making procedures, which might have headed the flawed plan off at the pass were it presented later (say, in early 1962). But Janis points out that "most of the men who participated in the decision were old hands at policy-making." How probable is it, he asks, that figures like Robert McNamara, McGeorge Bundy, Dean Rusk, Adolf Berle, and Paul Nitze would fail to express their objections "merely because they were uncer-tain about the proper way to behave?" (ibid. 1982, 33). Rusk, Berle, and Nitze had all served in the Truman administration more than a decade before, and none of them were new to the ways of Washington.

Another official explanation relates to the *excessive secrecy* that surrounded the plan. There was never a written version of the plan; it was essentially kept in the heads of Dulles and Bissell, and many agencies and organizations within the administration were excluded from the planning and/or unaware altogether of what was going on. Relevant experts who might have pointed out the flaws in the plan were simply not consulted. While this claim must certainly have contributed to the fiasco, Janis thinks, Kennedy and his advisers were sufficiently expert to ask pertinent and rather obvious questions about the assumptions that underlay the plan. The real question for Janis, then, became why they failed to do so, since the defects of the whole thing were so obvious in retrospect (ibid. 1982, 32).

Last, it is often claimed that *threats to personal reputation and status* account for the failure to probe the plan more closely. Many of Kennedy's advisers were generalists who did not feel it was their place to challenge the experts in the CIA and the military. Objecting to the plan might expose them to ridicule or embarrass-ment if they were shot down in meetings by those in the know. Arthur Schlesinger admits to feeling like this, noting that others would regard it as presumptious if he—a mere college professor—were to challenge someone like Dulles or Bissell (ibid. 1982, 32) This too, is not a fully satisfying explanation, though. Janis notes that while some junior members of the administration might well have felt intimi-dated, the old hands probably would not have. It is inconceivable that forceful figures like Robert Kennedy or Robert McNamara would have been struck dumb by the fear of losing their status. They could also have expressed their doubts one-on-one with the president, if they had felt sufficiently concerned.

If these official accounts do not fully account for what happened, what does? Janis traces the fiasco to a deeply flawed and dysfunctional decision-making process. Applying the theory of groupthink to the case (see chap. 3), he argues that the following symptoms manifested themselves:

- *An Illusion of Invulnerability*: As Janis sees it, the New Frontier people (a term often used to describe Kennedy's officials) believed that they were winners and that they almost couldn't fail. Kennedy had beaten the odds and been elected to the White House in November 1960. The President himself was unaccustomed to losing at anything in his life, as was the case with most if not all of his key advisers; they had all been chosen because they were young, can-do figures who had been highly successful across a range of endeavors. Robert McNamara, at the age of forty-four, had been the youngest ever President of the Ford Motor Company, and McGeorge Bundy was the youngest dean of the faculty at Harvard University at twenty-seven. This was the dawn of the optimistic 1960s; a sense of euphoria and a can-do attitude that anything was possible was pervasive within the administration, and a number of Kennedy's advisers seem to have felt that they possessed what Kennedy's close political adviser Theodore Sorensen later called "the magic touch." But this "nothing can stop us!" philosophy is frequently dangerous, Janis notes. It bred in this case a concurrence-seeking tendency and a belief that even a long-shot plan like the Bay of Pigs strategy could succeed. They overestimated the group's own capabilities and stereotyped the enemy as weak and unpopular, even though a more objective look at the facts would suggest that neither of these assumptions was accurate. They viewed themselves as the good guys, moral men facing an immoral enemy, and they seem to have assumed that simply being on the right side of history would make the plan successful.
- *An Illusion of Unanimity*: Apart from Senator William Fulbright, whose objections were not taken seriously by the group, no one raised significant doubts about the invasion plan in the many formal meetings that were held to discuss it. Drawing on the accounts of Sorensen and Schlesinger, Janis argues that an atmosphere of consensus and concurrence pervaded these gatherings, fostering the assumption that "silence gives consent" (ibid. 1982, 38). In reality, however, men like Rusk and McNamara must have harbored private doubts about the plan, since even a cursory acquaintance with Cuban politics revealed that Castro was in fact quite popular with his own people and that any invasion was unlikely to spark a popular uprising against him.
- *The Suppression of Personal Doubts*: Some of Kennedy's advisers—most notably Arthur Schlesinger—revealed in the years after the failed invasion that they had harbored significant doubts about the plan, which they failed to voice at the time in key meetings. Although, as already noted, Schlesinger

did send JFK several memoranda in which he questioned a number of assumptions that underlay the plan, he reveals in his memoirs that when the opportunity to speak up in official meetings was presented to him, he simply remained silent; in Janis's memorable phrase, Schlesinger engaged in "self-censorship." Influenced by social pressure and driven by the perception that he could not speak out against the plan, he never did (ibid. 1982, 39–40).

- *The Emergence of Self-Appointed Mindguards*: Janis argues that in cases of groupthink, self-censorship is reinforced by the emergence of what he memorably termed "mindguards." Mindguards are individuals who take it upon themselves to police the presumed consensus within the group by knocking down the objections of dissenters (that is, those who *do* dare to speak out). Just as bodyguards protect us physically from threats, mind-guards act as forceful guardians of the group's seemingly watertight consensus. In this case, Robert Kennedy and Dean Rusk in particular seem to have acted as mindguards. Robert Kennedy is said to have told Schlesinger not to voice his doubts in meetings, since the president had already decided to go ahead with the plan. "The president has made his mind up. Don't push it any further," RFK reportedly told the dissenting Schlesinger. Similarly, Chester Bowles was also a strong opponent of the invasion plan. He sent Rusk a strongly worded memorandum questioning the various assumptions behind the plan. Rusk, however, simply decided not to pass on Bowles's reservations to the president (ibid. 1982, 40–42).

- *Docility Fostered by Suave Leadership*: Sometimes, the behaviors of leaders can foster the concurrence-seeking tendency behind groupthink as well, Janis argues. In particular, he contends that John Kennedy himself may have encouraged a sense of complacency and docility by allowing the CIA to dominate the discussion. He also failed to encourage his advisers to ask the tough questions which might have exposed the plan's flaws. For instance, at the April 4 meeting at which Bowles was sitting in for Rusk, JFK failed to ask the undersecretary of state for his own views (ibid. 1982, 43).

- *A Taboo against Antagonizing New Members*: Allen Dulles and Richard Bissell were both strongly in favor of the plan and were held in high esteem by the group. Janis argues that in such a situation, it becomes socially difficult to challenge the wisdom of those who appear to know what they are doing. The two men were treated as valuable new members of the in-group, not as representatives of an agency seeking to push its own pet projects (ibid. 1982, 44–46).

Janis argues that "my tentative conclusion is that President Kennedy and the policy advisers who decided to accept the CIA's plan were victims of groupthink. . . . If the facts I have culled from the accounts given by Schlesinger, Sorensen and the others are essentially accurate, the groupthink hypothesis makes more understandable the deficiencies in the government's decision-making that led to the enormous gap between conception and actuality" (ibid. 1982, 47).

Although Janis does not mention it in his own account, there is some independent evidence that some of Kennedy's advisers felt browbeaten into accepting the CIA's optimistic assessments of its own plan. There is at least one important and early dissenter against that plan whom we have not so far discussed, Thomas Mann, the assistant secretary of state for Inter-American affairs . Mann left Washington just before the invasion to become U.S. Ambassador to Mexico. But in February 1961, he sent Rusk a list of sharp objections to the plan, which were strikingly similar in character to those of Bowles and Fulbright. Mann cast strong doubt upon the likelihood of a popular uprising against Castro, warned that the President would face a choice of escalating to full-scale war or abandoning the brigade in the event of the plan's failure, and questioned the legality of the operation as well as its political wisdom in general. He also thought that even a successful operation would be met with riots in Latin America and would damage the administration's image abroad. The National Security Adviser McGeorge Bundy forwarded Mann's memorandum to the President, but it was apparently ignored altogether. Kennedy never called Mann to discuss these points, and he was never asked to discuss them in the official meetings. Mann was clearly disheartened by this, and at the meeting on April 4, 1961, at which the President asked everyone to vote yes or no on the plan, Mann surprisingly voted in favor. Although he still had strong doubts about the whole thing, he did not mention these at the meeting (Gleijeses 1995, 24–32). This looks very much like an instance of what Janis called self-censorship. It is also clear, as Janis suggests, that Richard Bissell was held in very high esteem by the group. "All of us—Kennedy and Bundy and the rest—were hypnotized by Dick Bissell to some degree, and assumed that he knew what he was doing. In this, Kennedy made a great mistake. One thing Kennedy learned was never again to take the CIA, or the Joint Chiefs of Staff, very seriously," Schlesinger recalls (quoted in Blight and Kornbluh 1998, 64).

As we noted in chapter 3, some analysts of foreign policy decision-making have also looked beyond groupthink, reexamining the wider literature on group behaviors within social psychology for clues as to how other theoretical frameworks might be developed ('t Hart, Stern, and Sundelius 1997). One such approach has become known as the *newgroup syndrome* (Stern 1997). Newly formed policy groups, Stern argues, can become prey to a particular pathology. Stern and Sundelius hypothesize that groups go through a number of developmental stages during the lifetime of their existence from their initial formation to the point where they formally adjourn, and that a differing kind of dynamic operates at each. Stern and Sundelius are especially interested in the beginning of a group's life, where a new administration comes to power or a significant turnover in membership (through resignations, hirings, and firings) in effect creates a new group dynamic. While dysfunctional decision-making is not inevitable at this early stage—it all depends on the kind of norms that the group leader encourages at the outset— there is a tendency toward caution and *conformity* (and a corresponding lack of open, critical thinking) at this early stage.

Stern applies this approach to the Bay of Pigs case study, and we may usefully contrast his own approach with that of Janis. Like Janis, he argues that conformity was a particular problem in the decision-making, but he traces this to the fact that Kennedy—having swept away Eisenhower's decision-making structures and a foreign policy apparatus, which is now highly regarded by many scholars (see for instance Burke and Greenstein 1989)—operated in a way that was too informal and ad hoc. The major players did not know one another well and were only beginning to find their feet in their jobs. Moreover, the president himself had little management or executive-level experience, having been a member of Congress and then a senator. "Given Kennedy's relatively laissez-faire management style, he did not attempt to guide consciously and clarify the group decision culture in order to reduce uncertainty and promote critical interaction," Stern concludes. "He appears to have been unaware of the effect of his person and the weight of his office upon his colleagues. Similarly, the evidence suggests that he was insufficiently conscious of the emergent group norms (unwittingly reinforced by his own conduct) of deference to the president and to 'experts'" (Stern 1997, 182).

Homo Psychologicus

An analyst working in the *Homo Psychologicus* tradition examines the beliefs, both collective and idiosyncratic, held by the decision-makers being studied. He or she tries to trace causal linkages between those beliefs and foreign policy behavior, or between the personalities of the policymakers and how they act. This kind of analyst also looks for evidence of cognitive shortcuts and other cognitive processes used by those same decision-makers, again attempting to trace a link between those processes and the behavior of the decision-makers. In short, we look for evidence that *dispositional* as opposed to *situational* factors drive foreign policy behavior (Houghton 2009). *Homo Psychologicus* assumes that beliefs, personalities, styles, and other aspects of our personal dispositions, as opposed to the demands of the situation or political context, best account for how foreign policy decision-makers behave. Unlike both *Homo Bureaucraticus* and *Homo Sociologicus*—both of which emphasize the organizational or group dynamics, and hence place much of the weight for explaining decisions on the situational environment in which policymakers operate—this third perspective assumes that individual decision-makers play the critical role in shaping foreign policy and works at the individual level of analysis (or the smallest *matryoshka* doll in the series, to return to the analogy we utilized in chap. 1).

What beliefs did Kennedy and his advisers *share*? Blight and Lang have ably traced the collective beliefs that Kennedy and his contemporaries held in common, emphasizing five ideas in particular: (1) they strongly believed that there should be no more "Munichs." Neville Chamberlain's appeasement of Adolf Hitler at the Munich conference of 1938 had exerted a huge pull on the minds of Kennedy and his generation, convincing them that attempting to appease evil was wholly counterproductive; (2) they believed that only the demonstration of overwhelming military force could contain a determined adversary; (3) they believed in the domino theory first articulated explicitly by Dwight Eisenhower. Allowing one country to fall to Communism would lead to surrounding nations falling as well, much like a row of dominoes. This powerful mental image/metaphor fed in part on the image of European states falling to Fascism during the 1930s; (4) Kennedy's generation believed that Vietnam was the critical domino, at least in Southeast Asia and perhaps in a global sense as well; and (5) they believed that America must lead the free world and fight Communism globally regardless of the cost (Blight and Lang 2005, 142–43).

These core beliefs certainly encouraged the idea that allowing Fidel Castro to control Cuba's destiny was simply unacceptable. Presidents from Eisenhower to George H. W. Bush shared the view that Castro's regime was both morally reprehensible and a threat to economic and political freedom in the region. They also shared the belief that appeasing Castro might lead other domino nations to fall in Central America and perhaps throughout the hemisphere. It was therefore vital that U.S. power and influence be used to contain the export of Castro's revolution, a view that would later be articulated with special vigor by the Reagan administration. As we saw in chapter 3, Reagan and his advisers thought it was critically important to head off the expansion of Marxism to Nicaragua, El Salvador, and beyond because they saw all this as part of a process in which the Central American dominoes were finally and ominously toppling, one by one.

Nevertheless, while it is clear that these collective beliefs lay somewhere behind the Bay of Pigs decision-making, it is difficult to explain particular foreign policy decisions at this rather abstract level. Why did this particular administration go ahead with a plan to invade Cuba? Why were the decision-makers so blind to the plan's defects? Why were Dulles and Bissell in particular so convinced that it would succeed, in spite of all the evidence to the contrary? And why did they discount Kennedy's own warning that he would never allow American troops to become directly involved in an invasion of the island? For this reason, accounts of the Kennedy administration's decision-making during the Bay of Pigs from a *Homo Psychologicus* perspective focus on the more detailed cognitive processes in which the decision-makers appear to have engaged.

Working in part within this tradition, Lucien Vandenbrouke has argued that three such processes were especially evident in this case. First, it is hard to explain the tenacity with which the decision-makers deluded themselves into believing that the plan would succeed without recognizing the extent to which human beings strive for *cognitive consistency*. As we saw in chapter 4, one body of theorizing within psychology deals with the manner in which our minds frequently dismiss information we do not want to hear. Cognitive consistency theory suggests that beliefs often prove resistant to uncomfortable facts; while individuals use different strategies to cope with inconsistencies that emerge between beliefs, one common approach is to ignore or manipulate information that might lead to cognitive inconsistency or dissonance. This approach, as Deborah Welch Larson notes, "provides one possible explanation of the imperviousness of preconceived opinions to rational disconfirmation" (Larson 1985, 29). It is clear that many of the decision-makers ignored dissonant information, such as the fact that key details of the plan had been published in the *New York Times*, which should have led them to conclude that the whole operation was no longer plausibly deniable. The CIA planners also ignored evidence from their own organization's intelligence branch that Castro was highly popular on the island and that a popular uprising against him was therefore unlikely (Vandenbrouke 1984, 488; Wyden 1979, 99).

Second, there is some evidence that the decision-makers also employed a cognitive mechanism known as *defensive avoidance*. This is one technique for dealing with a highly stressful decision-making context; it involves maintaining the present course of action or existing policy because there seems to be no hope of finding a better solution to a problem, and avoiding further consideration of an issue because of this (Janis and Mann 1977, 57–58, 107–33). Kennedy appears to have practiced this kind of avoidance. Because there appeared to be no better option available for getting rid of Castro and addressing the Cuba problem, the President seems to have stuck to his existing course for want of anything better (Vandenbrouke 1984, 488–89). He also seems to have put the shortcomings of the CIA's plan out of his mind. At one point during the final stages of the Bay of Pigs decision-making, Arthur Schlesinger asked Kennedy what he thought about the invasion plan. "I try to think about it as little as possible," Kennedy is said to have replied (Schlesinger 1965, 94).

Third, wishful thinking seems to have played a decisive role here as well. This is an emotional state of mind in which the decision-maker confuses what he or she hopes will occur with what is realistically possible. Kennedy's winning streak may have encouraged such overoptimism, Vandenbrouke argues, as might the spectacular past successes of others who shared an apparent overconfidence in their own abilities, such as Richard Bissell and Tracy Barnes within the CIA. As Schlesinger suggested, there was a feeling within the administration early on that the young President possessed "the Midas touch" (Vandenbrouke 1984, 489; Schlesinger 1965, 259). This is very similar to the point Janis made about the existence of an illusion of invulnerability, but from the perspective of *Homo Psychologicus* it might perhaps best be seen as a tempting delusion held by particular individuals, rather than the product of group dynamics per se.

In addition to the three cognitive mechanisms identified by Vandenbrouke, a fourth one—the pull of analogical reasoning—also seems to have played a significant role in the genesis of Operation Zapata. In 1954 the CIA had successfully overthrown the Guatemalan leader Jacobo Arbenz in Operation PB Success, replacing him with the more politically appetizing junta (from an American perspective) of Colenel Castillo Armas. Like Castro, Arbenz was seen as a threat to U.S. interests in the region, even though the latter's credentials were less convincing than his willingness to stand up to the American-owned United Fruit Company. As it developed, the Bay of Pigs operation was almost a carbon copy of the 1954 operation, especially in terms of its leadership and operational plan. Many of those involved in 1954 were deliberately brought back into the 1961 operation, with Allen Dulles, Richard Bissell, and Jacob Esterline again taking major planning roles, and the likes of Howard Hunt (later made famous by Watergate) and "Rip" Robertson once more involved operationally. Adolf Berle, a State Department official during the Bay of Pigs and that department's liaison to the CIA, had also held a similar position during the Truman administration. There he had tried unsuccessfully to get Eisenhower's predecessor to mount the operation that would become PB Success, and he now became an advocate of the Bay of Pigs plan. Operationally, the planners simply transferred the blueprint used in the Guatemalan case to suit Cuba. Most notably, in both cases an exile force was organized to invade with U.S. backing, and in both cases the invasion was intended to succeed by means of psychological warfare rather than military prowess. As in 1961, the small, ragtag forces of Armas were expected to overthrow a government simply by generating fear rather than utilizing actual might.

Trumbull Higgins describes Operation PB Success as a "successful practice run for the Bay of Pigs" noting that it "greatly influenced" the CIA's planners in a number of cases, Operation Zapata included (Higgins 1987, 13–35). Rather than a group-derived invulnerability generated by Kennedy and those around him, the real source of the wishful thinking, overconfidence, and can-do attitude that the CIA planners felt in 1961 may well have been the success of Operation PB Success, combined with the influence of victory in World War II. As Jacob Esterline later put it, "Allen Dulles, Bissell and so on were marked by the experience of World War II: the U.S. always wins! Then the Guatemalan thing stumbled to success. It reinforced the feeling that anything the U.S. did would succeed" (quoted in Gleijeses 1995, 41). The analogy proved so powerful in 1961 that the same organizational structures within the Agency were employed as in 1954, and the Cuban exiles were even trained in Guatemala.

The Agency may well have seen overthrowing Castro in 1961 as a "cakewalk"—to employ a term one Bush official later used prior to the Iraq invasion—because they were so taken with the Guatemalan precedent; after all, if it had worked once, why shouldn't it work again? But the comparison, of course, proved deeply misleading, since Guatemala had been "a dangerously facile victory" (Higgins 1987, 34). A less superficial reading of Operation PB Success would have revealed the flaws inherent in the Guatemalan scheme that were simply being transferred to the Cuba case; as Higgins notes, "Castillo Armas's widely scattered forces, too weak for any deep or effective penetration of their homeland, waited in vain under CIA orders for a revolt, or even local desertions, by the Guatemalan army" (Higgins 1987, 31). Nevertheless, the operation had finally worked, in large part because Arbenz fled in 1954 when presented with the threat of U.S. force being used against him. This would not be the case with Castro in 1961.

Indeed, Castro had clearly learned a great deal himself from the 1954 case, in part because Che Guevara, the perennial traveling revolutionary and a close advisor to Castro by 1961, had been present in Guatemala in 1954 and had observed events at firsthand. The lessons he drew from his perspective had to do with how one utilizes guerilla warfare to repel an invading foreign power. At one meeting following the failure of the mission, McGeorge Bundy (who had happily gone along with the plan once various changes were made) mused, "well, I guess Che learned more from Guatemala than we did" (Hersh 1998, 219). The decision-makers also ignored a far more telling analogy, that of Indonesia in May 1958, where the same techniques employed in 1954 subsequently failed spectacularly to unseat the government of President Sukarno (Vandenbrouke 1984, 474). As at the Bay of Pigs, the CIA set up a small group of rebels and armed them with a fleet of B-26 bombers. As in 1961, the Agency failed in its effort to force an "undesirable" foreign leader out of office, and Sukarno remained in power for another decade. These mixed results for what was fast becoming the Agency's modus operandi in covert actions during the 1950s ought to have given the planners pause, but it was the success of 1954 that they remembered and not the failure of 1958.

The grip of the Guatemala analogy on the minds of the decision-makers also helps to explain why the CIA planners remained so convinced that Kennedy would send in the U.S. military if the exiles ran into difficulty. This is something of a puzzle, since Kennedy repeatedly made it clear in planning meetings that under no circumstances would he do so. Why didn't Dulles and Bissell take this more seriously? In part, the answer probably lies in the fact that they could not imagine *any* U.S. president leaving the invaders to their fate and pulling out of the situation. Experience generally had taught Dulles that operations on paper often get expanded and amended in the field. But the Guatemala analogy probably played a role here too. Eisenhower had told the CIA on that occasion that the full force of the U.S. government would be placed behind Operation PB Success in the event of difficulties with the CIA's plan, and both Dulles and Bissell may have been so taken with the comparison that they assumed that Kennedy would in reality be willing to act in 1961 as Eisenhower had been prepared to do in 1954.

Equally important at this psychological level, perhaps, was the general role of misperception. Analysts working in this tradition have long studied what can happen when we misperceive the actions and intentions of our adversaries (Jervis 1976). The work of Piero Gleijeses, however, suggests that the most important misperception during the Bay of Pigs affair occurred not between Cuba and the United States but between the White House and the CIA. Gleijeses walks a line between two rival views we have mentioned already, the notion that the CIA deliberately entrapped the President and the charge that Kennedy deliberately betrayed the exiles for political reasons. He makes clear, moreover, that a third position is possible: the view that Kennedy and the CIA were simply talking past one another and had fundamentally different ideas of what the invasion plan actually entailed. "My research has led me to conclude that the Bay of Pigs was launched not simply because Kennedy was poorly served by his young staff and was the captive of his campaign rhetoric, nor simply because of the hubris of the CIA," Gleijeses argues. "Rather, the Bay of Pigs was approved because the CIA and the White House assumed they were speaking the same language when, in fact, they were speaking in utterly different tongues" (Gleijeses 1995, 2). For Kennedy, the plan represented a small, politically deniable infiltration, and he assumed that if the invaders were unsuccessful, they could flee to the Escambray Mountains and join the guerilla movement there.

For the CIA, though, failure would mean an out-and-out military intervention by the U.S. Marines. The White House and the CIA were like "ships passing in the night," neither truly understanding the other (Gleijeses 1995, 39).

ASSESSING THE THREE APPROACHES: SOME POINTS TO CONSIDER

It will be left to the reader to reach a judgment as to which of the three perspectives seems to best account for the decision-making in this case study. But the reader is also entitled to hear some of the criticisms that have been (or might plausibly be) directed at each account. Starting with *Homo Bureaucraticus*, there are at least three potential problems with the account presented from that perspective which the reader might like to consider. First of all, Dean Rusk is by most accounts said to have harbored only minor doubts about the plan, and most of these related to its so-called noise level. When asked by Kennedy to vote a straight yes or no on the plan, Rusk voted in favor and went along with the plan. We also know that his deputy Chester Bowles opposed it, as did Thomas Mann (while voting in favor) and Arthur Schlesinger (both of whom also worked for the State Department). Why the differences in view if indeed "where you stand determines where you sit"? If organizational culture exerts such a forceful causal effect on where one stands, why the variation in support expressed by Rusk as opposed to the others? In *Essence of Decision*, Allison and Zelikow stress that bureaucratic position is only one force— albeit the most important—exerting an influence on bureaucratic position, and that an individual's prior personality and beliefs count as well. But if this is so, we have effectively smuggled *Homo Psychologicus* into the story via the back door. In other words, to explain the variation in policy views among the four State Department officials, we quite possibly need to move beyond the *Homo Bureaucraticus* perspective and analyze the personal beliefs and personalities of each player.

A second criticism which might be raised of this approach is that the Bay of Pigs plan may not actually have represented a genuine bureaucratic compromise between the CIA and the State Department. The *Homo Bureaucraticus* view, it has often been argued, seems to relegate the president to the position of just one actor among many, acting as an arbiter or referee between different organizations (Krasner 1972). The reader may want to ask whether Kennedy was really acting as such a referee in this instance. Kennedy's own strong feeling, as we have seen, was that the noise level of the CIA's original plan was too high. While this was also Dean Rusk's position, it is plausible to argue that the decisions were ultimately the product of Kennedy's own mind-set and calculations rather than the product of pulling and hauling.

Third, it is difficult to explain the manner in which the key decision-makers deluded themselves about the Bay of Pigs plan without looking at the individual psychologies of the individuals concerned. As Vandenbrouke notes:

> Neither the goals and values of individual actors nor the pulling and hauling of the players seem adequate to explain the decision-makers' persistent refusal

to face up to unpleasant facts. For instance, once Richard Bissell and his aides opted for invasion, they never seem to have reconsidered their assumption that a judicious application of pressure would topple Castro's regime, despite numerous indications to the contrary. Instead, the operatives ignored the agency's own analysts, who stressed the regime's control over the island, as well as the outside experts who confirmed that Castro retained considerable support (Vandenbrouke 1984, 487).

Similarly, the *Homo Sociologicus* interpretation of the Bay of Pigs decision-making has also been subjected to some trenchant criticisms in the years since it was first proposed. The journalist Peter Wyden, author of what is probably the best general account of the Bay of Pigs affair, has argued that many of the key decisions were not actually made in a group environment at all:

> Too much can be made of group dynamics. The five key decisions of the Bay of Pigs were not made in a group, nor even, for the most part, in a group setting: (1) the decision to escalate the adventure from a plausibly deniable infiltration effort into an invasion was made in Bissell's head; (2) the decision to weaken the first air strike and make it "minimal" was made unilaterally by Kennedy; (3) the decision to cancel the second strike was made by Kennedy late on a Sunday night by phone in consultation with Rusk and Bundy; (4) the decision to give the "go" order was made by Kennedy after extensive lonely soul-searching; (5) the decision not to escalate the invasion in the face of great temptation posed by incipient disaster—to become a "bum," not an aggressor—was made by the President, sparring fiercely with Admiral Burke; other advisers were practically silent (Wyden 1979, 316).

It is possible to criticize the *Homo Sociologicus* account in other ways as well. One criticism relates to Janis's claim that Kennedy and his advisers were gripped by an illusion of invulnerability. Robert McNamara has suggested that the dominant emotion within the Kennedy administration on taking office was not one of omnipotence or invulnerability, as Janis's account suggests, but rather a strongly *defensive* feeling. Kennedy had indeed won the 1960 presidential election, but he had done so by the narrowest margin in electoral history, and he faced a southern bloc within the Democratic Party in Congress which stood ready to thwart many of his domestic initiatives. In foreign policy terms, moreover, the dominant feeling was one of being on the defense against an ever-expanding Communist threat (McNamara, Blight, and Brigham 1999, 25–31). Similarly, Roderick Kramer argues that Janis's interpretation of the Bay of Pigs case sits poorly with what we now know:

> When making a case for the argument that Kennedy and his advisors displayed symptoms of overconfidence and an "illusion of invulnerability" when deciding to proceed with implementation of the CIA operation, Janis did not have access, of course, to the classified records of top secret briefings and meetings. This evidence, now available to scholars, indicates that Kennedy's assessments were undoubtedly influenced not only by deliberately misleading intelligence assessments provided by the CIA, but also by disingenuous, and politically motivated

comments made by President Eisenhower to the new president during private, top-secret briefings (Kramer 1998, 245).

Instead of being unduly influenced by group processes, Kramer suggests, Kennedy may simply have had a great deal of difficulty in believing that Dwight Eisenhower, "the organizational genius behind the largest, most complex, and most successful amphibious military invasion in U.S. history" would have supported a much smaller and less ambitious amphibiously based invasion that had little chance of success (ibid. 1998, 245). Kennedy also engaged in a number of behaviors which seem inconsistent with the groupthink approach, including privately consulting with at least two trusted journalists and bringing in Senator William Fulbright as an outsider who he knew in advance opposed the majority view.

Finally, the *Homo Psychologicus* approach also faces some potential problems. First, the same point that Kramer makes about the absence of a general illusion of invulnerability within the Kennedy administration may also be used to critique the claim that Kennedy and others engaged in wishful thinking. Perhaps the real root of the problem lay in the CIA's presentation to the President of what were supposedly facts, rather than any fanciful thinking on his part; after all, JFK was generally known as a level-headed and cautious pragmatist, and from this perspective it is unlikely that he would have allowed himself to be carried away by his narrow electoral victory in 1960. Second, the confidence that Kennedy and his advisers had in the CIA may well have stemmed from the agency's success in the overthrow of Giacomo Arbenz in Guatemala in 1954. JFK and his advisers expected that Castro would flee the country when presented with a U.S. plan for his overthrow, just as Arbenz had done some seven years earlier. However, for all the similarities between the two cases, there were differences as well, which means that logically the Cuban plan can only have been partly driven by the Guatemalan analogy. For one thing, Guatemala did not involve an amphibious landing. This part of the plan obviously had to be developed sui generis rather than analogically. Finally, it remains unclear whether the differences between the CIA and White House were really ones of misinterpretation and misunderstanding. It is worth noting that although *Homo Psychologicus* (and especially cognitive consistency theory) tends to assume the best about the motivations of the various actors, the more sinister CIA entrapment thesis associated with administration insiders like Arthur Schlesinger as well as the presidential betrayal argument of commentators like Grayston Lynch both assume the worst.

CONCLUSIONS

History does not speak for itself, and a strong argument can be made for each of our three models of decision-making. It is of course too early in the book for the average reader to have formed a permanent idea as to which of the models best captures empirical reality, and you are encouraged to keep an open mind as to which works best as a general explanation. On the other hand, you should by now have some idea as to which account of the Bay of Pigs case you think seems most useful. We turn next to the Cuban missile crisis, one of the most analyzed and, as some have suggested, overanalyzed cases in the study of foreign policy and international relations. In the next chapter, we shall see that theoretical accounts that seem to work well for one case study do not necessarily work well in another, but equally powerful arguments can and have been made in this instance for each of our general perspectives.

CHAPTER 6

To the Brink:
The Cuban Missile Crisis

MRBM LAUNCH SITE 3
SAN CRISTOBAL, CUBA
29 OCTOBER 1962

A photograph taken by U-2 overflights of the missile sites in San Cristobal, Cuba, October 29, 1962. SOURCE: © CORBIS

Was the world on the brink of a holocaust? Was it our error?
A mistake? Was there something more that should have been
done? Or not done? His hand went up to his face and covered his
mouth. He opened and closed his fist. His face seemed drawn, his
eyes pained, almost gray. We stared at each other across the table.
For a few fleeting seconds, it was almost as though no one else
was there and he was no longer the President.

—ROBERT KENNEDY 1968, 54.

It is one of the most written about and studied events in the history of international relations, thirteen days in October 1962 when the two nuclear superpowers stood on the brink of nuclear disaster. In fact, it has received so much attention from scholars that there have even been calls to stop studying it (Cohen 1985/86). Others maintain that there are still fundamental lessons to be drawn from the Cuban missile crisis that remain largely unlearned by today's policymakers. One recent White House Press Secretary—born about ten years after the crisis—has admitted to being enormously embarrassed at a press briefing in 2007 when asked about the Cuban missile crisis: she did not even know what it was![1] Although most Americans possess only a dim memory of the actual event or have never acquainted themselves with its details, it remains the most famous and minutely studied event of Cold War history. The crisis effectively began on the morning of October 16, when National Security Adviser McGeorge Bundy showed President John F. Kennedy photographs taken the day before by an American U-2 aircraft flying over Cuba (see photo 2) . To the untrained eye the photos look innocent enough, but the CIA's expert photo interpreters knew that they were looking at Soviet medium-range ballistic missile (MRBM) sites under various stages of construction. The pictures provided irrefutable evidence that the Soviet Union was placing nuclear missiles on the island, which could potentially hit a large number of targets within the United States.

The United States government already knew that the Soviet Union was shipping a considerable number of arms to Cuba, and Kennedy had publicly warned the Russians that "the gravest issues would arise" if offensive weapons were found to have been placed there. While there had been many rumors that the Russians were placing missiles in Cuba (Senators Kenneth Keating and Everett Dirksen had been among those warning that this was taking place) the administration had been assured by the Soviet Ambassador Anatoly Dobrynin that any Soviet armaments on the island were purely defensive in nature. The U-2 photos, however, provided the first solid evidence that nuclear weapons capable of hitting the U.S. mainland were being installed, and President Kennedy is said to have been "shocked" by the news. "It sure surprised all of us," Kennedy's close presidential confidant Theodore Sorensen later stated. "The Sovietologists were convinced that the Soviets would never put missiles outside the Soviet Union" (Neustadt and May 1986, 4; Blight and Welch 1989, 35).

Just how much President Kennedy knew about the missiles before October 16, 1962—and hence how surprised he really was—has long been a matter of dispute among the administration's defenders and detractors. Kenneth Keating, who ironically lost his Senate seat to Robert Kennedy two years after the crisis, claimed in 1964 that his information had come from someone inside the administration. This is certainly a possibility. In September, the Defense Intelligence Agency (DIA) learned of an eyewitness sighting of objects "which resembled large missiles" being transported by truck across the island, and there had been earlier reports of similar sightings in August. It was precisely such rumors that led the President to authorize U-2 overflights of the area (see Thompson 1992, 15; Dallek

2003, 542–43). By early October, the administration also possessed intelligence gleaned from U.S. spy ships, which suggested that missiles were being installed (Bamford,1983, 276).

CIA Director John McCone had warned the White House during August and September that the Soviets might be planning to place MRBMs in Cuba. Although he had no hard proof at this stage, he had raised this scenario as a possibility in a meeting on August 10 (Fursenko and Naftali 1997, 200). Curiously, however, his own analysts issued a Special National Intelligence Estimate on September 19 contradicting McCone's personal view and arguing that this scenario was unlikely (Fischer 1998, 158–59). Keating and Dirksen may have been 'cherry picking' leaked intelligence reports—getting it right by mistake, as it were—and McCone's view was also based on a theoretical hunch rather than on hard intelligence.[2] There had in fact been hundred of reports of missile 'sightings' in Cuba, even before the Soviets had actually placed them there. It is understandable, then, why subsequent reports of *real* sightings might have been discounted at the time and the U.S. intelligence community slow to respond (Garthoff 1998, 22–23).

For other reasons, though, Kennedy and his advisers should probably not have been surprised. While we will probably never know for sure why Soviet Premier Nikita Khrushchev placed the missiles in Cuba, there are several plausible hypotheses as to why he engaged in what to the Americans seemed like a dangerous and reckless action. For instance, the Soviet Union at the time had only about six missiles capable of striking the U.S. mainland. The Americans, on the other hand, had hundreds, including missiles stationed in Great Britain, Italy, and in Turkey close to the Soviet border. Placing missiles in Cuba may have been seen as a quick and easy way of evening up the nuclear balance, or at least bolstering Soviet deterrence. In his memoirs Khrushchev even writes of giving the United States "a little of their own medicine." To many within the Soviet leader's circle, it would be an outrageous double standard if the United States were to complain of Russian missiles on their doorstep, given that the Soviets had lived with this situation themselves for some years, and this may be one reason why Khrushchev believed that the Americans would simply accept the new status quo. As Michael Dobbs notes, it was as if the Soviet leader was "acting out of a deep-seated psychological pique" since the Turkish missiles had only become fully operational that year, but among Kennedy's advisers only Ambassador Averell Harriman seems to have discerned a direct linkage between Cuba and Turkey (Dobbs 2009, 18; Lebow and Stein 1994, 48). As we saw in chapter 5, the United States had also attempted to invade Cuba the year before. Soviet leaders believed that another invasion was imminent, and the missile placement may well have been intended to forestall this. Furthermore, Khrushchev may have been playing a dangerous political game with Cuba, designed to extract some sort of political or strategic victory from it. He may have been using it as a bargaining chip in order to get rid of the missiles in Turkey, for example, or in order to extract concessions from the Americans on Berlin (Allison and Zelikow 1999, 104). Or, as Lebow and Stein have argued, Khrushchev seems to have believed that placing the missiles in Cuba would force the United

States to take the Soviet Union seriously, thereby (he hoped) compelling its leaders to pursue a policy of detente. All of these considerations, as well as others, seem to have played on the Soviet leader's mind, and they may well have been mutually reinforcing rather than there being any single reason why he acted as he did.

Unbeknown to JFK and his colleagues at the time, a substantial number of the nuclear weapons were already operational by the time of the U-2 overflight, which makes the whole incident even more dangerous in retrospect than the participants suspected at the time. As former Defense Secretary Robert McNamara later recalled in conjunction with his colleague James Blight, he experienced a great surprise during a January 1992 conference held with Fidel Castro in Havana on the missile crisis:

> While in Havana, we were told by the former Warsaw Pact chief of staff, General Anatoly Gribkov, that in 1962 the Soviet forces in Cuba possessed not only nuclear warheads for their intermediate-range missiles targeted on U.S. cities but also nuclear bombs and tactical warheads. The tactical warheads were to be used against U.S. invasion forces. At the time the Central Intelligence Agency was reporting no warheads on the island. They believed the first batch was to be delivered by a Russian ship named the Poltava (McNamara and Blight 2003, 189).

The Russian press subsequently reported later that year—almost exactly thirty years after the crisis had ended—that there had in fact been a total of 162 nuclear warheads on the island, including at least ninety tactical warheads. Had the United States invaded—and there were already extensive preparations to do just that, should negotiations fail—U.S. troops armed only with conventional arms would have been confronted by tactical nuclear weapons.

None of this was known at the time on the American side, at least as far as we can tell. Kennedy's first reaction on the morning of October 16 was to call a meeting of his most trusted advisers, a group that became known as ExCom (Executive Committee of the National Security Council). Although JFK purposely did not sit in on many of the ExCom's meetings, he taped its deliberations in secret without the knowledge of the participants, and this group would form the president's key source of advice throughout the crisis. The various advisers disagreed as to whether the Soviet placement altered the balance of power between the United States and the Soviet Union, but a consensus quickly emerged that the presence of the missiles so close to American shores was unacceptable. The central task of the decision-makers was thus to get the missiles out of Cuba but to do so in a way that would avoid escalating the crisis into war.

On October 17 the ExCom discussed a range of possible U.S. responses, from doing nothing to launching a full-scale military invasion. The discussion quickly boiled down to just two options: launching a "'surgical'" air strike to take out the missile sites from the air, and mounting a naval blockade (or "'quarantine'") of the island to prevent further Soviet supplies and equipment from getting to Cuba. Robert Kennedy, Robert McNamara, and George Ball became the champions of the blockade option, while Dean Acheson, Paul Nitze (assistant secretary of defense), and John McCone argued strongly for the air strike. The latter alternative, together with a full-scale invasion, was also preferred by the Joint Chiefs' of Staff.

Throughout the crisis, Kennedy seems to have seen the presence of missiles in Cuba as primarily a political problem rather than something that could be addressed militarily. This was also the view put forward by McNamara. In opposition to the Joint Staffs, both the President and his Defense Secretary agreed that the placement did not alter the nuclear balance, since the Soviets already had enough Intercontinental Ballistic Missiles (ICBMs) to destroy one or more U.S. cities, and the Americans enjoyed a vast strategic advantage. McNamara told the ExCom early on in their deliberations that "a missile is a missile." But this did not mean that he found Khrushchev's action acceptable. From his perspective, this was an unacceptable challenge to U.S. superiority in the region and to its status as a bulwark against Communism. Kennedy had forcefully pledged to prevent the global spread of Communism in the election campaign of 1960 and in his inaugural address, where he posed as a tough Cold Warrior. He had been humiliated at the Bay of Pigs, and had been challenged by Khrushchev at a meeting in Vienna and when the Soviets erected the Berlin Wall. To do nothing was simply unacceptable politically to the President, in both a domestic and an international sense.

Kennedy's first instinct, like that of many of his advisers, had been to go with the air strike. By October 18, however, he was obviously leaning heavily toward the blockade, and late that evening he had instructed the military to prepare to implement this option. Moreover, other advisers who had begun the crisis as 'hawks'—such as Treasury Secretary Douglas Dillon—became more doveish as the arguments against the air strike were heard. Three days later, under continued pressure from his brother Robert not to launch an air strike and after hearing the Joint Chiefs admit that bombing the missiles from the air could not be assured of 100 percent success, JFK formally made the decision to mount a blockade. On October 22 the President went on national television to announce the presence of the Soviet missiles to the American public (who had not been informed of the crisis up until this point) and told them of the decision to institute a blockade:

> This Government, as promised, has maintained the closest surveillance of the Soviet military buildup on the island of Cuba. Within the past week, unmistakable evidence has established the fact that a series of offensive missile sites is now in preparation on that imprisoned island. The purpose of these bases can be none other than to provide a nuclear strike capability against the Western Hemisphere. ... The characteristics of these new missile sites indicate two distinct types of installations. Several of them include medium range ballistic missiles, capable of carrying a nuclear warhead for a distance of more than 1,000 nautical miles. Each of these missiles, in short, is capable of striking Washington, D. C., the Panama Canal, Cape Canaveral, Mexico City, or any other city in the southeastern part of the United States, in Central America, or in the Caribbean area. Additional sites not yet completed appear to be designed for intermediate range ballistic missiles—capable of traveling more than twice as far—and thus capable of striking most of the major cities in the Western Hemisphere, ranging

as far north as Hudson Bay, Canada, and as far south as Lima, Peru (Chang and Kornbluh 1998, 160).

The blockade was set up by the morning of October 24, as Soviet ships steamed toward Cuba. Although some of the ships were allowed through after it was determined that they were carrying no military equipment, it was reported that twelve had actually turned back. As Dean Rusk commented, "We're eyeball to eyeball and I think the other fellow just blinked."

On October 26 the Soviets, working through informal intermediaries, made an offer to the United States: if Kennedy would agree to make a public pledge not to invade Cuba, Khrushchev would agree to remove the missiles from the island. A second offer arrived the next day, proposing an exchange: the Soviets would remove the missiles in Cuba in return for the United States removing the Jupiter missiles it had placed in Turkey as part of a NATO commitment. This led to the secret deal that was eventually arrived at, a compromise which effectively ended the crisis: RFK met with Soviet Ambassador Dobrynin on October 27 following the ExCom meeting of that day and offered to remove the Jupiter missiles in Turkey—together with the President's assurance not to invade Cuba—in exchange for the removal of the Soviet missiles. This the Soviets agreed to, and the crisis was essentially over by the following morning when the deal was publicly broadcast over Radio Moscow. By mutual agreement, the part about removing the American missiles in Turkey was kept secret by both sides, however, since each knew that making a public statement about removing the Turkish missiles would prove politically embarrassing to the Kennedy administration. Neither Turkish nor NATO officials were informed of the deal at the time, but the Jupiter missiles were quietly decommissioned the following year and replaced by sea-born Polaris missiles.

RATIONAL DECISION-MAKING?

At first sight, the missile crisis might seem to illustrate the epitome of reasoned, rational decision-making. Having gotten themselves into a situation in which the imperatives of 'the game' threatened to take over—circumstances in which the whole event threatened to spiral out of control, driven by their own horrifying momentum—each side pulled back from the brink. The missiles, we now know, were already on site and the warheads were operational, but although not effective in a military or strategic sense, the blockade option bought Kennedy time and gave Khrushchev an 'out', an opportunity to pull back and claim victory without resorting to dangerous and potentially disastrous escalation. But as Lebow and Stein note, Khrushchev's original decision to place the missiles in Cuba was anything but rational. In particular, his perception that Kennedy would simply accept the placement represented a staggering miscalculation:

> Foreign-policy analysts expect statesmen to have consistent preferences and to choose policies most likely to advance their preferences. Khrushchev violated both these expectations. He did not choose the appropriate means, given his

ends, nor did he recognize the contradictions among his objectives. The missile deployment threatened some of his most important foreign-policy goals. It was a singularly inappropriate means of advancing his proclaimed objectives. The secret deployment of missiles raised rather than lowered the risks of an American invasion of Cuba. It was also illusory for Khrushchev to believe that a missile deployment would compel the United States to move toward détente (Lebow and Stein 1994, 62).

It is also unlikely that rigorous group processes lay behind the Soviet move. As Aleksandr Fursenko and Timothy Naftali note, the decision was essentially Khrushchev's to make and although the plan was certainly discussed internally within various groups, it encountered relatively little dissent and there seems to have been little discussion of potential alternatives to it (Fursenko and Naftali 1997, 179–83). There are some indications that groupthink may have lurked behind the Soviet decision. There are also aspects of both the Soviet deployment and the American response that seem explicable only through the lenses of bureaucratic politics and psychological shortcuts. Moreover, a convincing case can be made that Kennedy and the ExCom failed to rigorously assess all the available alternatives to a blockade, and that dissenters were excluded from the process.

Our knowledge of the thirteen days has increased enormously over the last twenty years or so, aided by three developments in particular: (1) the declassification of all the ExCom's deliberations on the missile crisis was complete by the mid-1990s; (2) several historically important conferences were held during the late 1980s and early 1990s during which surviving Soviet, Cuban, and American leaders confronted one another and recalled their decision-making processes (see Blight and Welch 1989; Blight and Welch 2002); and (3) the end of the Cold War has made former Soviet officials more available to Western researchers, and many materials within the Soviet archives have been opened as well (Lebow and Stein 1994; Fursenko and Naftali 1997). As a result we now possess an unusually rich treasure trove of empirical materials upon which our three approaches have drawn. They provide a fascinating insight into the deliberations of the U.S. government in particular, and they allow us to provide answers to a puzzle which has vexed students of the missile crisis for many years: How did the two sides come so close to war over the tiny island of Cuba?

Homo Bureaucraticus

Graham Allison and Philip Zelikow's *Essence of Decision* is by far the most famous statement of the *Homo Bureaucraticus* approach, and it was initially developed on the basis of this case study. Unsurprisingly, then, it is a relatively straightforward matter to apply this perspective to the Cuban missile crisis. However, the reader should note one especially important theoretical point before we proceed. Throughout this book, we have been treating the bureaucratic politics approach as a single, unified model of decision-making, but in *Essence of Decision* it is actually divided into two largely compatible but separable approaches. Allison and Zelikow term these Models II (Organizational Process) and Model III (Governmental

Politics). Although *Homo Bureaucraticus* merges Models II and III as many scholars of bureaucratic politics have done since the book was first published, it is worth briefly emphasizing the subtle differences between them.

Briefly stated, Model II sees foreign policy as the product of organizational *outputs* (emphasizing the importance to decision-making of what organizations 'can do'), while Model III sees foreign policy as *resultants* (policy as that thing which results from bargaining, compromising, and wheeling and dealing by the most powerful actors). In Model II, government policies are best seen as a series of *outputs* produced by organizations. Government policy is less the product of deliberate, well-thought-out *choices* by politicians and more what organizations are accustomed to doing. Organizations are wedded to standard operating procedures (SOPs), and they operate according to their own logic and culture once created, only partially controllable by elected politicians. They also pursue incrementalism rather than radical change, and as we have seen they tend to resist political control. This can lead to behavior that is less than fully 'rational' and/or to unintended consequences, which can have very harmful effects (especially when misconstrued by the other side).

In Model III, on the other hand, decisions are essentially *collages*. Decisions emerge as *resultants* in a process of bargaining and compromise (pulling and hauling). Again, we have seen this dynamic operating in previous chapters. If power is widely dispersed within the government, what state X does may simply be what everyone *can agree upon* (the lowest common denominator). The positions players occupy shape their views/outlooks, moreover—"where you stand depends on where you sit"—and parochial players tend to see their own organization's interests as synonymous with the national interest. As with Model II, Model III can lead to decisions which are only boundedly rational and may be misunderstood by an adversary or even an ally.

Allison and Zelikow actually begin their analysis of the decision-making on the American side by looking at why Kennedy chose a naval blockade from the Rational Actor Model (RAM), which they term Model I in *Essence of Decision* (what we have been calling *Homo Economicus* in this book). Again, we have discussed this approach in chapter 1, but just to remind you, recall that in Model I decision-makers are rational in the sense that they are assumed to have clear objectives and that they weigh up the costs and benefits of each alternative. Having performed this mental weighing process, they then select the "utility-maximizing" choice. We further assume that the state is a unified, purpose-driven actor; in other words, we treat states as if they were individuals capable of purposive action.

A Model I analyst reasons in simple fashion, and as Allison and Zelikow show, there are essentially three processes involved (Allison and Zelikow 1999, 49). First of all, we look at the *action* we are interested in (e.g., the Soviets place missiles in Cuba, George W. Bush invades Iraq). We then reason backwards to examine the *objectives* the state must plausibly have had in mind. Last, we *link* the two: "given this objective, it is little wonder that state X acted as it did," we might tell ourselves. We have now 'explained' the decision. Consider, for instance, George W. Bush's decision to invade Iraq in 2003. Why *did* we invade? We will examine this question in detail in chapter 10, but for now consider briefly how we might answer that question. We have an action, the U.S. invasion. The typical analyst will then reason backwards and examine the objectives that the Bush administration must have had in mind. "Bush invaded in order to spread democracy" might be one answer. "Bush invaded to destroy Iraq's Weapons of Mass destruction (WMDs)" might be another. Still another analyst might posit other objectives, such as "Bush invaded to show he was tougher than his father," "Bush invaded to ensure U.S. access to oil," or "Bush invaded to remove a thorn in America's flesh." But whatever the objective posited, we then create a mental linkage between the action and the objective(s): "no wonder Bush invaded given that he [fill in the blank]."

There is a very satisfying symmetry to all of this, and it is easy to see why this is essentially the default and almost knee-jerk way of explaining decision processes we cannot directly observe. Indeed, this was what the ExCom itself did when scrambling to explain the Soviet decision to place the missiles. Re-creating the kind of reasoning that the decision-makers used, Allison and Zelikow offer four competing explanations (Allison and Zelikow 1999, 78–109):

1. Cuban Defense
2. Cold War Politics
3. Missile Power
4. Berlin—Win, Trade, Trap.

Of these, Allison and Zelikow prefer the fourth explanation, based on their own view of evidence which has come to light since the first edition of *Essence of Decision*.[3] The first explanation accounts for Khrushchev's placement of the missiles by pointing to his desire to forestall what he seems to have thought was an imminent U.S. invasion. Allison and Zelikow contend that while the *Cuban defense* explanation seems plausible at first blush, however, putting strategic weapons in was 'overkill' in the sense that it was not necessary to place MRBMs on the island to prevent a Cuban invasion. Similarly, they contend that the idea that Khrushchev was playing *Cold War politics* with the island is unlikely, for why choose Cuba to play political games with as opposed to some other issue? While they find the *missile power* argument—the notion that placing the missiles provided a quick and easy means of evening up the nuclear balance—more plausible, they suggest that the fourth (*Berlin—Win, Trade, Trap*) explanation is probably the most apt. No matter how JFK responded, Khrushchev would get something out of the deployment. As Allison and Zelikow put it, "if the Americans did nothing, Khrushchev would force the West out of Berlin, confident that the missiles in Cuba would deter the Americans from starting a war. If the Americans tried to bargain, the terms would be a trade of Cuba and Berlin. Since Berlin was immeasurably more important than Cuba, the trade would also be a win for Khrushchev." Alternatively, if Kennedy decided to blockade Cuba or invade the island, he would fall into a trap, since the Soviet Premier would then have a perfect excuse to blockade or invade Berlin (ibid. 104).

Turning to the U.S. decision-making from a *Homo Economicus* perspective, they note that the ExCom weighed the costs and benefits of six different options (ibid. 109–20):

1. Do Nothing
2. Diplomatic pressure
3. Secret approach to Castro
4. Invasion
5. Air strike
6. Blockade

First of all, doing nothing (1) was simply not considered a viable alternative: this would appear to indicate a lack of resolve and might encourage Soviet boldness over Berlin. Moreover, domestic political considerations foreclosed this option as well; how would it play with Congress—already armed with reports that the Soviets were placing MRBMs in Cuba—if Kennedy simply accepted the new situation as a fait accompli? Similarly, they ruled out a diplomatic option (2) early on; bargaining over the missiles would have meant offering something in return (for instance, the U.S. missiles then stationed in Turkey). They reasoned that this would have weakened the NATO alliance and hence undermined U.S. credibility with its allies. Their initial reaction was also that a diplomatic solution would have smacked of weakness. A secret approach to Castro (3), which is a variation on the diplomatic theme, was ruled out because the Cuban leader did not have control of the missiles, and the ExCom members reasoned—correctly, as it later turned out—that Castro was unlikely to accept some sort of deal over the missiles in any case.

This, then, left only the 'harder' military-based options. One obvious solution in this regard was an all-out invasion (4). Why not do the job right this time, using U.S. forces instead of exiles? While this option had some advocates (the Joint Chiefs' were especially sympathetic to this idea), most of the decision-makers ruled this out as too risky. America's conventional military superiority would surely prevail in the end, but the invading force might well become involved in a long, slow war of attrition. Most importantly, this seemed a sure way to escalate the conflict. The Soviets would be certain to intervene, expanding a conflict over a tiny Caribbean island into a full-scale war between the superpowers. This was something Kennedy wanted to avoid at all costs.

What, then, of a more limited military action, such as an air strike (5) launched against the missile sites? As noted earlier, this was initially the President's favored option. Indeed, his initial reaction upon being shown the U-2 photographs by McGeorge Bundy was that "we are probably going to have to bomb." Further debate produced second thoughts. Striking the missiles from the air would mean taking out Soviet MiGs capable of attacking Florida; Soviet troops might well be killed in such an attack and so the risks of escalation were high for this option too.

The air strike would not be too 'surgical' in this sense, and the Joint Chiefs could not guarantee that they would be able to destroy all of the missiles. Even if only a single warhead were left, it might be used to obliterate a U.S. city. Alternatively, the Soviets might just replace the bombed missiles. Finally, Robert Kennedy and others argued that it would be morally unacceptable not to give a warning to the Cubans that an attack was imminent, while giving that warning might well destroy its whole effectiveness.

In the end, then, the ExCom settled on a blockade (6) or naval 'quarantine' of the island. The U.S. ships would create a ring around Cuba, policing a '"no-go zone"' in order to prevent the Soviets from shipping any more weapons to the island. This carried a number of advantages, as the decision-makers saw it. First of all, it conveyed firm resolve but with a lesser risk of escalation. Second, it put the burden on Khrushchev to make next move, buying time in a way that was designed to allow 'cooler heads' to prevail. Finally, it left the other options open; an invasion could still be tried if the blockade did not work, as could 'softer' measures like negotiation. In this sense, the blockade provided an interim measure.

Model I provides a rather satisfying explanation for the U.S. decision-making, which many readers will find convincing. What is so wrong with this approach, then, from Alison and Zelikow's perspective? Examining the case study from Model IIs vantage point, they return to the point made earlier in this book: some government actions are the product of relatively 'mindless' bureaucratic routines. In particular, there are some puzzles about the Soviet deployment, which Model I finds it hard to explain. Why, for instance, was no effort made to camouflage the missile sites during the construction process? The Soviets knew that the U-2 flights could detect these, so why didn't they construct the sites during the hours of darkness? Why not construct the MRBM sites first, and why in general weren't the missile sites more protected?

Reasoning now from a Model II perspective, Allison and Zelikow argue that all of these oddities are at least partially attributable to Soviet SOPs. The Soviets had no SOP for camouflaging missile sites. Lacking such a procedure, the military simply proceeded to do things the way it did them in the Soviet Union. Organizations, as we have seen, tend to operate according to their own logic and culture once created, developing routines that can be hard for anyone to change. This is essentially Allison and Zelikow's explanation for the otherwise almost inexplicable failure on the part of the Soviets to hide the presence of the MRBMs:

> At the sites, each team did what it knew how to do –emplace missiles – literally according to the book. ... No attempt was made to harden the missile sites, not because of any intention to launch a first strike, but rather because no Soviet missiles sites had ever been hardened. ... The failure of camouflage made it certain that if a U-2 flew over the site the U.S. would discover the missiles. ... A serious effort to camouflage the operation was possible. But the units constructing the missiles had no routine for camouflage, having never camouflaged construction activity in the Soviet Union (Allison and Zelikow 1999, 212–13).

On the American side, too, there is plenty of evidence that bureaucratic routines influenced the decision-making, or at least how the decisions were implemented. Indeed, McNamara has argued that such routines came very close to precipitating nuclear war, and that Admiral George Anderson, the head of the U.S. Navy, had to be dissuaded from following potentially disastrous bureaucratic procedures before McNamara intervened. As he relates, the ExCom members knew that Soviet submarines were lurking close to the quarantine line, and there was a risk that Navy SOPs would unleash a chain of events that leaders would be powerless to reverse. "The point was that our quarantine was intended to be a political signal, not a textbook military operation, and trying to get that across to the military caused us all a lot of headaches," he later recalled. McNamara literally lived in the Pentagon for most of the missile crisis, fearful that this message might be forgotten and making sure that control of the military remained in the hands of the President. One evening, McNamara met Anderson to discuss the implementation of the blockade, provoking a now-famous exchange about what they would do when the first ship approached the quarantine line:

> I asked Admiral Anderson, "When the ship reaches the line, how are you going to stop it?"
> "We'll hail it," he said.
> "In what language—English or Russian?" I asked.
> "How the hell do I know?" he said, clearly a little agitated by my line of questioning.
> "I followed up by asking, "What will you do if they don't understand?"
> "I suppose we'll use flags," he replied.
> "Well, what if they don't stop?" I asked.
> "We'll send a shot across the bow," he said.
> "Then what, if that doesn't work?"
> "Then we'll fire into the rudder," he replied, by now clearly very annoyed.
> "What kind of ship is it?" I asked.
> "A tanker, Mr. Secretary," he said.
> "You're not going to fire a single shot at anything without my express permission,"
> I said (Blight and Welch 1989, 63–64).

This was not the end of the discussion, however. According to McNamara, Anderson replied that the Navy had been conducting blockades "since the days of John Paul Jones, and if I would leave them alone they would run this one successfully as well." McNamara was now clearly angry as well, repeating his point about civilian control and forcing Anderson to state that no shot would be fired without his direct orders or those of the President (Blight and Welch 1989, 64).[4]

This kind of bureaucratic resistance, where organizations try to do things the way they have always done them, is of course highly characteristic of Model II. How do Allison and Zelikow explain the U.S. decision-making using Model III, then, in which decisions are seen as the outcome of bargains or *compromises* between the representatives of agencies rather than simply organizational outputs? They do not claim that the decision to mount a naval quarantine was a direct compromise, but they do suggest that bureaucratic politics indirectly conditioned the choice, making it in effect the only alternative still viable by the time it was chosen. Pulling and hauling between White House, State Department, and CIA, they argue, determined the *timing of the discovery* of the missiles. Timing was critical since an air strike could have been taken more seriously if the military had had more time to plan it. McCone (who, as we have seen, already had a strong hunch that the Soviet were placing nuclear missiles on the island) wanted to authorize U-2 overflights to examine what was really happening in Cuba. Dean Rusk, though, was deeply concerned that a U-2 might be shot down and that this might jeopardize forthcoming talks with the Soviets (Allison and Zelikow 1999, 329).

In the short term Rusk won the debate, and the U-2 overflight that discovered the existence of the MRBMs was delayed until October 14. This indirectly conditioned the subsequent debate about whether an air strike or blockade was more feasible, according to Allison and Zelikow. Moreover, the participants in the ExCom debates stood where they sat and advocated the solutions that their respective organizations 'could do'. On the overflight issue, McCone was preoccupied with gathering intelligence, and Rusk with diplomacy. Later on, when decisive intelligence had been gathered, the debate about how to respond was shaped by bureaucratic politics as well. From his vantage point in the White House, JFK was preoccupied with the political effects of the missile installation. The domestic political consequences of not being seen as 'resolute' could be catastrophic at the forthcoming midterm congressional elections, and hence the option of simply doing nothing and accepting the new status quo was unacceptable to him. The State Department and the U.S. ambassador to the UN Adlai Stevenson, meanwhile, saw the issues primarily in diplomatic terms. From his vantage point at UN headquarters in New York, it is no coincidence that Stevenson was the most enthusiastic advocate of a diplomatic solution. Equally, it is not surprising that representatives of the CIA and the U.S. military argued for an air strike and/or an all-out invasion (Allison and Zelikow 1999, 329–30).

Some of the most compelling evidence in favor of a *Homo Bureaucraticus* interpretation—especially the extent to which the Joint Chiefs were in near rebellion over the decision to blockade rather than launch an air strike—does not appear in *Essence of Decision*.[5] While it has long been known that the Joint Chiefs favored the air strike and invasion options over a blockade, the sheer depth of their feelings became clear only in the late 1990s, when the transcript of an October 19 meeting between Kennedy and the Joint Chiefs (secretly tape recorded without the knowledge of anyone except the president) was finally declassified. In this meeting Kennedy was openly challenged by Air Force Chief Curtis LeMay, who even compared the President in a roundabout but not-so-subtle way to former British Prime Minister Neville Chamberlain (who had famously attempted to 'appease' Hitler at the Munich conference of 1938). "This blockade and political action, I see leading into war," LeMay told JFK. "This is almost as bad as the appeasement at Munich. ... I just don't see any other solution except direct military action right now." Among those attending were LeMay, Joint Chiefs' Chairman Maxwell Taylor, George Anderson, Army Chief of Staff Earle Wheeler, and Marine Corps Commandant David Shoup, and the judgment of all the service chiefs was broadly similar:

> **WHEELER:** Mr. President, in my judgment, from a military point of view, the lowest-risk course of action ... is to go ahead with a surprise air strike, the blockade, and an invasion, because these series of actions progressively will give us increasing assurance that we really have gone after the offensive capability of the Cuban/Soviets corner. Now, admittedly, we can never be absolutely sure until and unless we actually occupy the island.
>
> **SHOUP:** If there is a requirement to eliminate this threat of damage, then it's going to take some forces, sizable forces, to do it. And as we wait and wait and wait, then it will take greater forces to do it.
>
> **LeMAY:** We (you) made pretty strong statements ... that we would take action against offensive weapons. I think that a blockade, and political talk, would be considered by a lot of our friends and neutrals as being a pretty weak response to this. And I'm sure a lot of our own citizens would feel that way, too. You're in a pretty bad fix, Mr. President.
>
> **PRESIDENT KENNEDY:** What did you say?
>
> **LeMAY:** You're in a pretty bad fix.
>
> **PRESIDENT KENNEDY:** You're in there with me. Personally (Naftali and Zelikow 2001, 588; May and Zelikow 1997, 180–82).

The tension is almost palpable, especially when one listens to this exchange on tape. When Kennedy and Taylor leave, the extent of the bad feeling that the Joint Chiefs harbor toward the President becomes even clearer. Unaware that their remarks are being tape recorded for history, LeMay, Anderson, Wheeler, and Shoup vent their frustration with the White House. Shoup in particular expresses the view that Kennedy is simply getting in the way of sound military policy, and his barely suppressed rage and contempt is all too clear on the tape as he tells LeMay he agrees with him "a hundred percent":

> **SHOUP:** Somebody's got to keep them from doing the goddamn thing piecemeal ... you're screwed, screwed, screwed. ... Either do this son of a bitch and do it right, and quit friggin' around. That was my conclusion. Don't frig around and go take a missile out ... you can't fiddle around with hitting the missile sites and then hitting the SAM sites. You got to go in and take out the goddamn thing that's going to stop you from doing your job (Naftali and Zelikow 2001, 597–98; May and Zelikow 1997, 188).

Homo Sociologicus

The reader might be expecting Irving Janis to diagnose 'groupthink' in this case. It is important to note at the very outset of our discussion, however, that he considered the missile crisis decision-making an ideal *counterpoint* to groupthink—its very opposite. Analyzing the U.S. response during the missile crisis from a rather approving perspective, Janis coins the term "vigilant appraisal" to describe what he sees as the more rigorous group decision-making procedures used by the ExCom. The notion of vigilant appraisal is very similar to the RAM approach and is characterized by four major features: (1) acknowledgement of grave dangers even after arriving at a decision; (2) explicit discussion of moral issues; (3) reversals of judgment, and (4) non-stereotyped images of enemy. Kennedy and the other members of the ExCom were clearly cognizant of the danger that even the naval blockade could easily produce nuclear escalation, and they explicitly discussed the morality of their actions. For instance, Robert Kennedy compelled the ExCom to consider the morality of an air strike against tiny Cuba, explicitly comparing it to what the Japanese had done at Pearl Harbor. Some members reversed their initial judgments, most notably Douglas Dillon, and the decision-makers never fell into the trap of believing that Khrushchev was either 'stupid' or 'irrational' (Janis 1982, 148–53).

According to Janis, Kennedy's handling of the missile crisis differed fundamentally from the way he approached the Bay of Pigs. First of all, by creating the ExCom the President quite deliberately brought in a much broader range of advice this time, including outsiders to the normal decision-making process such as Dean Acheson, former Defense Secretary Robert Lovett, and Ambassador Stevenson. A full range of options was considered from doing absolutely nothing to launching an all-out invasion. The costs and benefits of all these alternatives (at least as Janis sees it) were carefully weighed. Most members of the ExCom also kept an open mind and proved willing to change their initial estimates of the situation. The President avoided groupthink by consciously encouraging the ExCom's members to remain independent thinkers. This was partly a result of the legacy of Bay of Pigs: Kennedy believed that he had relied too heavily in "Cuba I" on the Joint Chiefs and the CIA, and he resolved not to repeat this mistake in "Cuba II." This led to a number of interesting innovations. Each member was asked to be a generalist rather a representative of his or her organization, and each was deliberately encouraged to step on the bureaucratic turf of other members. No formal agenda was imposed in meetings with the intention that discussions be more freewheeling and the ExCom was broken into groups, each of which would examine a particular option in depth. Leaderless sessions were held, from which the President deliberately absented himself to avoid unduly influencing the thinking of ExCom members or inhibiting them from speaking out. Moreover, Robert Kennedy and others seem to have acted as devil's advocates, deliberately taking unpopular positions in order to make sure that all conceivable options were given proper consideration (Janis 1982, 137–48).

We are in no way bound to accept Janis's own account of what an account of the missile crisis in the spirit of *Homo Sociologicus* should include. Primarily, the groupthink approach may well have been relevant on the Soviet side. Janis certainly cannot be faulted for failing to mention evidence which was unavailable to him even at the time that the revised edition of *Groupthink* appeared in 1982. Nevertheless, the more recent account provided by Aleksandr Fursenko and Timothy Naftali, for instance, provides some suggestions that groupthink may have underlain the Soviet decision-making process within the Kremlin (see Furskenko and Naftali 1997, 179–83). While it might be argued that the decision Khrushchev made was essentially his own, his initiative was of course discussed in various forums and was not simply taken unilaterally or without discussion. In this vein, there is evidence that some of the Soviet decision-makers appear to have held private reservations about the missile deployment which they failed to voice in key meetings, suggesting the presence of the kind of self-censorship Janis identified as critical to groupthink; there is also evidence of dissenters, since both Soviet Ambassador Aleksandr Alekseev and foreign policy adviser Anastas Mikoyan expressed doubts and reservations about Khrushchev's plan; and last, Defense Chief Rodion Malinovsky seems to have acted as a mindguard, taking it upon himself to defend the consensus that a deployment to Cuba was advisable. When Alekseev spoke out against the deployment at one early meeting, for instance, Malinovsky is said to have aggressively knocked him down (ibid. 179–80).

Turning back to the American side of the equation, was Janis really correct in presenting this as a 'non-example' of the groupthink phenomenon? Ned Lebow in particular has suggested in *Between Peace and War* that Janis presented far too idealized an account of Kennedy's deliberations within the ExCom. Lebow notes that Kennedy's group "has received the most extensive praise from both practitioners and theorists" (Lebow 1981, 298). While he concedes that the President instituted a number of innovations in this case, "it would nevertheless be an exaggeration to describe the ExCom as an open decision-making environment" (ibid. 299). It is not clear that the option of doing nothing and simply accepting the new status quo was ever seriously contemplated by the ExCom members; for example, As Lebow argues:

> The Ex Com's mandate was a narrow one: to consider the pros and cons of the variety of coercive measures that could be employed to get the Soviet missiles out of Cuba before they became operational. From the very outset the President made clear to the group that he would neither acquiesce to the presence of the missiles nor seek to remove them by purely diplomatic means. He was intent on using force to overcome the threat posed by the missiles and charged the ExCom with recommending what military option was best suited to the task. In effect, he made the most important policy decision before the Ex Com even convened. The group never debated the wisdom of using force, despite the realization by all of the participants that such a course of action risked triggering a nuclear war (ibid. 299).

The majority of the ExCom's time, Lebow notes, was spent on considering which military option to pursue. But there was a significant dissenter from a rather unexpected source: Robert McNamara. With his "a missile is a missile" argument, McNamara stated—setting himself against the opinion of the military chiefs within the Pentagon—that the Soviet deployment did not meaningfully alter the strategic nuclear balance between the superpowers. It did not matter, he said, whether an American city was obliterated by a nuclear missile fired from Cuba or from a Soviet nuclear submarine; the effect would be precisely the same, and the Soviets already had the capacity to do the latter. The implication, as Lebow sees it, was that the United States should do nothing, yet Kennedy brushed this view aside. Even more tellingly, the President himself may have acted as a classic mindguard in dismissing the views of Adlai Stevenson, the member of the ExCom most disposed toward negotiation and diplomacy. Kennedy made it clear at the outset that he felt negotiation alone would send the wrong message and would not work in any case. Stevenson's argument was also rejected as too soft by John McCone and Robert Lovett. Lebow argues that "there seems little doubt that Stevenson was ostracized by the core of the ExCom" and that "the president's cavalier treatment of him probably encouraged other members of the group to give vent to their emotions" (ibid. 301). In short, Lebow argues, the myth has been created that Kennedy used the ExCom as a genuine decision-making device, but in reality it was little more than "a relatively pliant tool," which "was brought into being less to make policy than to legitimate it" (ibid. 302). Kennedy decided to go with the blockade option, and when no consensus appeared within the ExCom in favor of this move, he simply had Robert Kennedy and Theodore Sorensen railroad it through.

It is also possible that Janis—because he was not privy to information about American internal debates which only came to light years after his death—may have missed other evidence that symptoms of groupthink (rather than vigilant appraisal) were prevalent on the American side of the decision-making. H. R. McMaster, for instance, has suggested that key dissenters were deliberately excluded from the missile crisis, though he focuses on the way that JFK excluded hawks rather than doves. As already noted, Kennedy distrusted the Joint Chiefs after the Bay of Pigs, and he tended to rely on his personal adviser Maxwell Taylor for military advice. Rather than appointing George Anderson to become Chairman of the Joint Chiefs, Kennedy bypassed the usual rotation processes among the services on October 1, 1962, and simply appointed Taylor, who had retired from active military service four years earlier, to the top position. As McMaster notes, Taylor was the only professional military officer permitted to attend the ExCom's deliberations. The pro-air strike and pro-invasion preferences of the service chiefs were already well known to Kennedy, but he may have used Taylor to filter these out of the process. "The JCS resented being excluded from the ExCom meetings," McMaster writes. "Every evening during the crisis, Taylor found the Chiefs anxiously awaiting his return from the White House." They suspected that Taylor was not faithfully conveying their arguments to the President, and while JFK gave the appearance of consulting with them in a White House meeting on October 19, this was held simply to keep them on board (McMaster, 1998, 26–27). We know that groupthink *can* on occasion lead to a favorable decision-making outcome within Janis's framework—after all, what Dean Acheson memorably called "plain dumb luck" can intervene (Acheson 1969)—and so the possibility exists that this may have occurred in the missile crisis case, or that at least one or two symptoms of groupthink were present.

Homo Psychologicus

Considering the roles that individuals play—most obviously those of President Kennedy and Chairman Khrushchev—poses some interesting issues, many of them having to do with the issue of counterfactual reasoning that we briefly examined in chapter 4. Imagine, for instance, that the president in 1962 had been Richard Nixon rather than John Kennedy. This is a plausible counterfactual, involving only a 'minimal' rewrite of history; after all, the 1960 presidential election was one of the closest in American electoral history, and had only a few hundred thousand voters switched from Kennedy to Nixon, this would have placed the latter in the White House after January 1961. It has often been argued that Nixon would have adopted a far more forceful stance toward the Soviets than Kennedy did, perhaps giving a good deal more weight to the preferences of the Joint Chiefs'. You may find this possibility rather plausible, but the issue is more complex than this: when we mentally 'change' one aspect of history, we always have to attend to the other ways in which the alteration we have made might affect the outcome we are interested in (Lebow and Stein 1996, 119).

Consider how many other things might have changed before we even got to October 1962, had Nixon been president. One obvious change we have to make is to consider the Bay of Pigs operation. Had Nixon been at the helm in early 1961, it is quite possible (though not certain) that he would have provided the air cover that Richard Bissell and Admiral Burke requested. This would have made the invasion an openly U.S. operation, making it more likely that other American forces would be committed (exactly what Kennedy feared, and his justification for rejecting the advice he was given). Had this occurred, it is again conceivable that one of three scenarios would be in place in October 1962: either a U.S.-backed government formed by the Cuban exiles as the CIA had hoped, or an ongoing civil war between Castro and the exiles, or some combination of the two. In any of these scenarios, it is hard to imagine Khrushchev sending missiles to Cuba. Even in a civil war scenario with Castro still at the helm, it is hard to imagine the Soviets being able to construct the missile sites in such secrecy; and even if successful, such a move would have risked bringing the Soviet military into direct conflict with American forces (something Khrushchev would surely have avoided). And even leaving the Bay of Pigs issue aside, we also have to consider how Nixon would have reacted at the Vienna conference and to the building of the Berlin Wall.

Looking at the substance of psychological processes employed by the decision-makers, four approaches seem especially useful in understanding the thirteen days of the Cuban missile crisis: (1) cognitive consistency theory, motivated wishful thinking, and other cognitive biases may help us understand why many in the CIA and the White House took so long to accept the evidence that the Soviets were placing MRBMs in Cuba, and why Khrushchev discounted the very real possibility that Kennedy would not simply accept the missile deployment; (2) the analogical reasoning explanation in particular seems to provide a useful approach to understanding the debates that went on inside the ExCom, since it is precisely under crisis conditions, and other circumstances which engender high uncertainty, that the resort to analogizing is most likely; (3) prospect theory may also be particularly useful in accounting for Khrushchev's decision to send the missiles and Kennedy's blockade response; and (4) newer research on the utility of emotional processes and their centrality to decision-making may throw considerable light on the reasons why both sides pulled back from the nuclear brink.

First of all, both motivated biases and cognitive psychological theory can indeed shed light on the question of why it took so long for the CIA to detect the missiles. As Beth Fischer notes, "the United States had been monitoring the buildup of Soviet weapons in Cuba closely. It is therefore unclear how could it have missed the transshipment of missiles and supporting equipment, and the construction of weapons sites which so scarred the Cuban landscape" (Fischer 1998, 159). While Allison and Zelikow are puzzled by the Soviet failure to camouflage the missile sites, the failure of the U.S. intelligence community to detect such blatantly undisguised weapons for so long presents us with an equally vexing puzzle. There was no lack of evidence that the missiles were being transported and constructed, and yet there was an obvious reluctance within the American intelligence community to take this evidence seriously. The CIA held an image of the Soviets as expansionist but risk-averse. As Fischer puts it, they held that "while the Soviets constantly sought to expand their influence, American officials believed, they avoided taking great risks in pursuit of that goal. Since U.S. analysts assumed that a Soviet deployment would not occur, they may well have been relatively insensitive to the vast amount of human intelligence—such as refugee reports and sightings by operatives in Cuba—that suggested such a deployment was underway. The CIA may have failed to detect the missiles earlier in part because they did not expect the missiles to be there at all" (Fischer 1998: 160–61). Instead of taking the intelligence reports seriously, officials may have dismissed these from their mind because they did not comport with long-established beliefs within the Agency.

Similarly, Kennedy and his advisers believed false assurances from Khrushchev (made privately through Ambassador Dobrynin, Soviet intelligence official Georgi Bolshakov, and others) that no offensive weapons were being placed in Cuba, and that the Soviets would do nothing to sour the air between the superpowers prior to the November midterm elections. The administration's critics have therefore suggested that Kennedy was rather naively duped (see for instance Hersh 1998, 349–50). There is a sense in which this is undeniably true; Robert Kennedy later admitted that "we fooled ourselves," and even Dobrynin was misled by his own government on this issue (Kennedy 1968, 23). But rather than consciously disregarding evidence to the contrary, the president and his advisers may have engaged in wishful thinking. They had strong *motives* to believe that what the Soviets said was true, especially since Kennedy was hoping to negotiate a major peace agreement with Khrushchev at the time, and he also worried that he would be greatly hurt in November if the allegations of Keating and other Republicans should prove correct. As Fischer notes, information processing models stressing the cognitive economy of human reasoning contend that "we see what we *expect* to see," while cognitive consistency theory and other motivational approaches suggest that "we see what we *want* to see" (Fischer 1998, 153, my italics; see also chap. 4 of this book). Put simply, the CIA may have seen what it expected to see, while the White House saw what it wanted to see. Equally, Khrushchev evidently wanted to believe that he could get away with placing missiles in Cuba, and disregarded evidence to the contrary.

Second, research on one particular type of information processing, analogical reasoning, suggests that high uncertainty places a premium on cognitive heuristics which are designed to overcome the unpredictability associated with the situation being confronted. One of the first and most prominent historical analogies to surface in the ExCom's discussions was the comparison with Pearl Harbor (Neustadt and May 1986, 1–16). As discussion of the air strike option proceeded on the first morning, it became very clear that Robert Kennedy in particular was highly skeptical of the claim that the missiles could be taken out 'surgically'. He doubted the ability of the Joint Chiefs to do what they said they could do, but his main argument—remembered and emphasized by many of the key participants after the event—was that such a surprise attack would be not only difficult to pull off but *morally* wrong. Early on in the crisis when an initial consensus had developed around the air strike as the only realistic hope of getting the missiles out, Robert Kennedy notes that he made his viewpoint privately very clear to his brother. "Most felt, at that stage, that an air strike against the missiles sites could be the only course. Listening to the proposals, I passed a note to the President: 'I now know how Tojo felt when he was planning Pearl Harbor'" (Kennedy 1968, 9).

From Wednesday October 17 on, RFK was to draw the analogy between the proposed air strike and the actions of the Japanese before World War II much more openly, forcefully, and explicitly. To warn the Soviets and/or the Cubans in advance of the air strike might constitute military suicide and would certainly deprive U.S. forces of the element of surprise, so the raid would have to be conducted without prior notification. But as Theodore Sorensen notes, this "would be, as the Attorney General pointed out, a Pearl Harbor in reverse and regarded by the world and by history as an attack by a leading power against a tiny nation without any warning or any effort to solve the matter without force" (Sorensen 1964, 50).[6] Moreover, "notes on the Wednesday meetings prepared for the President by Sorensen referred several times to 'Pearl Harbor' (Neustadt and May 1986, 6). Robert Kennedy was to return repeatedly to the analogy until the crisis was resolved. At a meeting in the Oval Office on Sunday October 21 between the President, Robert Kennedy, General Maxwell Taylor, General Sweeney, Robert McNamara, and John McCone, the Attorney General stated again that there should be no air strike against the missiles because "it would be a Pearl Harbor type of attack" (see Chang and Kornbluh 1998, 145; McNamara 1964, 27). Similarly, Maxwell Taylor in almost identical words recalls RFK arguing on this occasion that "we could not allow the United States to become involved in a Pearl Harbor type attack" (Taylor 1964, 54; see also Blight and Welch 1989, 78).

Pearl Harbor was an event of considerable significance in Robert Kennedy's life. Arthur Schlesinger, who had access to the Kennedy's private papers in Hyannis Port, writes that the young Kennedy corresponded regularly to his parents on this subject while at school:

> Pearl Harbor found Robert Kennedy, just turned sixteen, in his third year at Portsmouth Priory. The school, only a few miles from the naval base at Newport, responded quickly to the tremors of war. The headmaster decreed a blackout. "We all had to go sit in the basement for 20 minutes." When the aircraft carrier *Ranger* steamed into Narragansett Bay, the boys watched planes practicing dive-bombing in the hazy distance (Schlesinger 1979, 40).

Much as many middle-aged people nowadays can remember being placed under emergency conditions during the Cuban missile crisis RFK could clearly recall the same thing happening in relation to Pearl Harbor during his own youth. His impassioned comparison between the two episodes clearly had a profound impact on at least some of the members of the ExCom. George Ball states that "I thought at the time that it altered the thinking of several of my colleagues" (Ball 1982, 291). Robert McNamara, for instance, concluded that the blockade option "avoided the Pearl Harbor approach of a sneak attack and a war without warning on a small nation. It was really the only course of action compatible with our principles and our standing as a free world leader" (McNamara 1964, 25). Here Kennedy was almost certainly preaching to the choir, for Roswell Gilpatric, the deputy secretary of defense, states that he and McNamara had already reached the conclusion that the blockade was the best option via a process of hypothetical reasoning, in the form of war gaming. However, the effect upon the hawkish Douglas Dillon is, by his own admission, beyond much doubt. Dillon reports that at the ExCom meeting that took place on the morning of Friday October 19, "Bobby Kennedy brought out the parallel with Pearl Harbor. That impressed me a very great deal." At that meeting, Bobby Kennedy argued that "for 175 years we had not been that kind of country. A sneak attack was not in our traditions. Thousands of Cubans would be killed without warning, and a lot of Russians too" (Schlesinger 1979, 549; Chang and Kornbluh 1998, 125).

In later years, Dillon has frequently cited this comparison as the decisive factor that led him to change his mind. At the beginning of the Wednesday meeting, Dillon stated the view that "he agreed that there should be a quick air strike" (Chang and Kornbluh 1998, 125). Yet after the Pearl Harbor analogy had been drawn, "I felt that we just couldn't live with that, so I moved into the camp advocating the blockade" (quoted in Blight and Welch 1989, 50). "I finally agreed that a surprise attack on Cuba at that time was unacceptable because it was too much like the Japanese attack on Pearl Harbor. If we attacked like that, we would be forsaking the ideals for which I believed we had fought in World War II" (ibid. 152).

Dillon suggests that the use of that analogy was so convincing to him because he came from the generation of Americans that had experienced the events preceding America's entry into World War II:

> At first, I didn't think of the Pearl Harbor analogy. It never occurred to me. I guess I focused on the provocation of the Soviets putting the missiles in and what I saw as the strong need to get rid of them as soon as possible. ... After the first day or two, Bobby Kennedy began talking about the analogy very passionately. I could see that this analogy could be exploited by the Soviets as a propaganda weapon that could be used against us. Because of this consideration, I concluded that it was probably worthwhile to give up the military benefits of the immediate air strike (ibid. 167).

The analogy may well also have been instrumental in converting CIA Director John McCone to the blockade. According to McNamara's notes on his meeting with the President of October 21, for example, after RFK stated his argument against the air strike "McCone agreed with the Attorney General, but emphasized he believed we should be prepared for an air strike and thereafter an invasion" (Chang and Kornbluh 1998, 145). George Ball has also stated that RFK's use of that analogy "had a tremendous effect on him" (Blight and Welch 1989, 141). Indeed, Ball may have been the first to draw this parallel during the crisis. In the second ExCom meeting held on the evening of October 16, Ball stated that "this, uh, come in there on Pearl Harbor just frightens the hell out of me as to ... what happens beyond that. You go in there with a surprise attack. You put out all the missiles. This isn't the end. This is the beginning, I think" (Chang and Kornbluh 1998, 112). In a memorandum outlining his support for the blockade dated on or around October 18, Ball argued that an air strike "would, in fact, alienate a great part of the civilized world by behaving in a manner wholly contrary to our traditions. ... We tried Japanese as war criminals because of the sneak attack on Pearl Harbor" (ibid. 121). Theodore Sorensen also clearly agreed with the comparison. In a memorandum to the president written on October 20, Sorensen argued that "an air strike means a U.S.-initiated 'Pearl Harbor' on a small nation which history could neither understand nor forget." The naval blockade would be "a more prudent and flexible step which enables us to move to an air strike, invasion or any other step at any time it proves necessary, without the 'Pearl Harbor' posture" (ibid. 133).

There were, of course, those who remained utterly unconvinced by the comparison. "Frankly, I thought it was all nonsense," recalls Paul Nitze, and he later disparaged "these everlasting debates on the morality of a big country attacking a small country" (Blight and Welch 1989, 141–42). Dean Acheson—like Nitze, one of the leading hawks—found the Pearl Harbor analogy similarly unconvincing. At a Wednesday October 17 meeting of the ExCom, RFK "had it out loudly with Dean Acheson," and Acheson reportedly denounced Robert Kennedy's Pearl Harbor as "so much poppycock" (O'Donnell and Powers 1970, 317). As Acheson himself later recalled:

> This seemed to me to obfuscate rather than clarify thought by a thoroughly false and pejorative analogy. I said so, pointing out that at Pearl Harbor the Japanese

without provocation or warning attacked our fleet thousands of miles from their shores. In the present situation the Soviet Union had installed ninety miles from our coast - while denying that they were doing so -offensive weapons that were capable of lethal injury to the United States (Acheson 1969, 76).

In other words, there were important differences between the two situations that justified differing responses in each. Acheson, who was Truman's secretary of state, reports that he conveyed similar remarks to JFK in a private meeting the next day, on Thursday, October 18. He took the view that there were profound differences between the two cases, and that he regarded the Monroe Doctrine and previous statements by President Kennedy on the issue as ample warning of what could be expected if missiles were placed so close to U.S. shores, so that "whatever we did could not be regarded as a surprise attack" (ibid. 44–45, 76–77). George Ball reports that Acheson considered Robert Kennedy "an upstart" who "was talking sentimental nonsense" (Ball 1982, 291). Apart from this personal disregard, though, Acheson seems to have found the Munich analogy a good deal more applicable to the missile case. As Richard Reeves notes, "Acheson and some of the others preferred the 'Munich' metaphor, the British appeasement of Hitler in 1938" (Reeves 1993, 378). Curtis LeMay in particular was also a strong advocate of this position, going so far as to directly confront the President with the comparison.

Another analogy which seems to have shaped President Kennedy's thinking, is the comparison with World War I; indeed, this analogy may have affected his whole understanding of what was occurring during the Cuban missile crisis. He had recently read Barbara Tuchman's bestselling book *The Guns of August*, which describes how the various combatants in World War I had stumbled almost inadvertently into a war no one really wanted. JFK saw the potential for something very similar to happen during the Cuban missile crisis. Kennedy was so impressed by the parallels between the two situations that he had his advisers read it as well. On Tuesday October 23, after a 6 p.m. ExCom meeting was over, JFK, RFK, Theodore Sorensen, and Kenneth O'Donnell (one of JFK's top aide) sat in the president's office and discussed both the World War I analogy and Tuchman's book. On Saturday October 26, the President talked again to his brother about the parallels. He was determined not to repeat those errors in this instance, where the stakes were now nuclear. Accordingly, he would constantly place himself in Khrushchev's position during the crisis, and resolved to never put his adversary in a situation where he faced the stark choice of escalation versus humiliation. Briefly stated, his whole emphasis on the necessity of a peaceful, negotiated settlement can be seen as a logical consequence of his understanding of what had happened in 1914.

Prospect theory offers us a third way of understanding the deliberations of both Premier Khrushchev and those of President Kennedy. Working separately, Beth Fischer and Mark Haas have each argued that the Soviet leader in particular acted in ways consistent with prospect theory. The reader will recall that within this perspective, a decision-maker who perceives himself or herself to be in a domain of loss is likely to be risk-acceptant, while someone who sees themselves in a domain of gains is likely to be risk-averse. In other words, when we believe that we are facing great losses, we are more likely to try to recoup these in one quick but risky swoop. With this in mind, the Soviet leader had suffered a number of recent losses in October 1962: Perhaps rather unwisely, a speech by Roswell Gilpatric had publicly exposed the notion that the missile gap favored the Soviets as a myth; the Soviets believed that the United States was about to invade its only ally in the Western Hemisphere; relations with China were strained; and Khrushchev faced challenges to his leadership and domestic agenda from within the Soviet government. Operating within such a domain of losses, his willingness to take the enormous risk of placing missiles in Cuba becomes a good deal more explicable (Fischer 1998, 161; Haas 2001, 253–57).

The same theory has also been used to account for U.S. decision-making during the missile crisis. Haas notes that "the discovery of ground-to-ground missiles on Cuba plunged President Kennedy deeply into a loss frame. ... Kennedy and his subordinates in the fall of 1962 had explicitly and repeatedly stated that the placement of offensive missiles in Cuba by the Soviet Union was unacceptable to American interests and security" (Haas 2001, 257). Kennedy also believed (wrongly, as we now know) that Khrushchev doubted his resolve, and he was under fire domestically on the Cuban issue as we have seen. The President was so concerned about the missiles in Cuba that he became convinced that if he did not act in a strong and decisive manner on this issue, the Soviets might well make a move on Berlin. Haas accepts that Kennedy did not respond to this domain of loss by choosing the *most* risky option, a position that at first sight seems contrary to prospect theory. Haas argues that when decision-makers assess the probability of war associated with a given option as *certain*—as most did with regard to the alternatives of both an invasion and an air strike—they will not select those options. Instead, Kennedy selected an option that, while still very risky, did not seem certain to produce war (Haas 2001, 259–60). Put differently, while decision-makers are not as rational as *Homo Economicus* would have us believe, they will not choose disaster if that seems certain to be the outcome of their actions. Both an invasion and an air strike seemed certain to lead to war, as Kennedy and most of his advisers saw it.

It may be, of course, that a purely cognitive approach to the Cuban missile crisis—treating the decision-makers as if they were simply cool processors of information, which both analogical reasoning and prospect theory tend to—does not really capture the real flavor of the event itself, or explain how and why it was resolved. Equally important, if not more so, may have been the *emotions* that the decision-makers experienced, and we can think of this as a fourth kind of individual-level explanation. James Blight, for example, has stressed what he sees as the productive and adaptive role of fear in his book *The Shattered Crystal Ball*. Fear seems to have played a far more positive role within decision-making during the Cuban missile crisis of October 1962 than it would during Johnson's fateful 1965 decisions about Vietnam (see chap. 7). Sheer, unadulterated fear was arguably the predominant factor that helped the decision-makers pull back from the brink, not cold or cerebral calculation of the alternatives. In fact, the naval blockade that the ExCom eventually selected as its first option did not do very much of a practical nature; as we now know, the Soviet nuclear missiles on the island were already operational, and the blockade or naval quarantine seemed not to affect the course of events directly, even at the time. The Joint Chiefs can today be heard on one of the secretly recorded missile crisis tapes berating Kennedy for supposedly lacking backbone, and one military man (David Shoup) can be heard saying "we're screwed, screwed, screwed." But the blockade was a way of signaling resolve while in effect doing little, a way of buying time in the hope that "calmer heads would prevail," as Theodore Sorensen later put it.

As Blight suggests, the emotion of fear seems to have sharpened the reasoning processes of President Kennedy and those around him rather than blunting them, as research on stress and decision-making has shown is indeed possible at the low to moderate end of the scale. "Fear was pervasive, from the American President and the Soviet Chairman to the ordinary citizens, and fear was efficacious. Without the rise of what I have called the intensifying crystal ball effect, it is hard to imagine that the missile crisis could have been resolved peacefully" (Blight 1990, 150). He notes that most of the accounts of the missile crisis, including those given by the participants themselves, vividly recall the fear that the decision-makers experienced but make no linkage between that emotion and the successful resolution of the crisis. In reality, though, one cannot hope to understand the missile crisis decision-making on either side without also understanding what Blight calls "the adaptive role of fear" (ibid. 149–67).

Ralph White's classic work on empathy is also worthy of note under this heading. White often explained that empathy is very different from sympathy, or at least each represents an opposite point along a continuum. The latter implies active approval, while the former simply entails putting oneself in the shoes of another in order to better understand his or her motives. Empathy, White notes, is "defined as a realistic understanding of the thoughts and feelings of others," while sympathy is "defined in accordance with its Greek derivation, as *feeling with* others—being happy because they are or unhappy because they are—which often implies doing what one can to help them." White argued in his own work that empathy is primarily cognitive while sympathy is affective (White 1986, 82), but this distinction breaks down a good deal given what we now know about the intertwined nature of emotion and cognition. Kennedy and his colleagues had to *feel* what Khrushchev and his associates were feeling in order to truly empathize with them, and as Thagard and Shelley argue, empathy is a form of analogical reasoning in which emotions are transferred instead of information: "In empathy, I try to understand your emotional reaction to a situation by transferring to you my emotional reaction to a similar situation" (Thagard and Shelley 2001, 335–62). Nevertheless, White's insights remain exceptionally useful, once we accept that empathy is emotionally based.

Empathy is important because it is, in White's phrase, "the *great* corrective for all forms of war-promoting misperception" (White 1984, 160). It is also a potential corrective to fundamental attribution error, since it forces the decision-maker to appreciate the situation that the adversary is confronting. White's work helped pioneer a rich tradition of work in the study of international relations on empathy, perception, and misperception, which continues today. Empathy with one's adversary is possible to achieve when decision-makers consciously and deliberately make an effort to place themselves in the shoes of that adversary, and the policymakers know the opponent well enough for realistic empathy to be possible. The success of the Oscar-winning documentary film *The Fog of War* has brought the importance of empathy with one's adversary as a means of conflict resolution renewed attention in international relations and foreign policy, a theme echoed in McNamara's book *Wilson's Ghost*, co-authored with James Blight, and in the book by James Blight and Janet Lang that accompanies the film (McNamara and Blight 201; Blight and Lang 2005). The film features a notably successful case of empathizing: John Kennedy's handling of the Cuban missile crisis. What got us out of the Cuban missile crisis and pulled us back from the brink, apart from "sheer dumb luck," to use Dean Acheson's memorable phrase, was JFK's ability to empathize with Khrushchev, McNamara argues. Spurred on by U.S. Ambassador to the Soviet Union Llewellyn "Tommy" Thompson, Kennedy was able to successfully place himself in the shoes of the adversary and thus avert nuclear disaster. Thompson realized that Khrushchev almost certainly knew several days into the crisis that he had made a serious miscalculation in placing missiles in Cuba, and that he would be looking for some sort of face-saving way out of the crisis; successful resolution of the situation would therefore require a negotiated solution from which both sides could claim some sort of victory.

ASSESSING THE THREE PERSPECTIVES

As with the other case studies we examine in this book, our three perspectives have not gone without criticism in the literature. In a classic and much-discussed critique of *Essence of Decision's* take on the Cuban missile crisis, Stephen Krasner argues that both Models II and III greatly underestimate the part played by the President (Krasner 1972; see also Art 1972). Model III in particular appears to suggest that the chief executive is simply one of a number of equals, but Krasner notes that the president is at a minimum "the first among equals"; in other words, not all the actors in the bargaining game of bureaucratic politics enjoy equal resources, and those of the president presumably far exceed the bargaining powers of his cabinet members or other advisers. Moreover, presidents to some extent create—or at least have the opportunity to mold and shape—the bureaucratic structures and routines around them. Presidents who have chosen to bypass the State Department and rely more on the national security adviser and/or make foreign policy out of the White House may often do so, as we saw in chapter 2.

Krasner also points to other problems with Model III. Most tellingly, he notes that the U.S. decision to go with a blockade was not actually a compromise or deal between the decision-makers; rather, it reflected the president's feeling that the naval quarantine represented the *best way* of showing that the United States meant business but with less risk of military escalation than the other hawkish alternatives. Indeed, Krasner feels that the decision can easily be explained using the RAM approach. Unlike Lebow but in common with Janis, Krasner views the ExCom as having undertaken a thorough consideration of options. Finally, he suggests, the major participants do not stand where they sit in this case study. For example, Robert McNamara should have been likely to propose a military solution to the crisis, but he instead goes against his bureaucratic position. And many of the ExCom's members lacked a bureaucratic position—they do not sit anywhere, as Krasner voices—while others change their minds about the best course of action. In the first category, Dean Acheson, Robert Lovett, and Robert Kennedy occupied no formal foreign policy positions and hence possessed no bureaucratic axes to grind, while within the second category Douglas Dillon began by favoring the air strike but then switched to the blockade.

Originally, the first edition of *Essence of Decision* contained much bolder claims on behalf of Models II and III than can be found in the revised (1999) edition. For instance, Allison suggested in 1971 that Kennedy had ordered the State Department to remove the Jupiter missiles in Turkey the year before, and that he had been angry when his order was ignored. This account, in fact, turned out to be inaccurate and was removed from the 1999 version, as was Allison's original claim that the Navy had refused to move the quarantine line during the blockade of Cuba. Both of these arguments were originally used to bolster the case for Model II, and what remains is in effect a watered-down version of Allison's original argument. Equally, some critics have alleged that Model III does no better on the Soviet side. The original version of *Essence of Decision* devoted about fourteen pages to this question, but in the latest edition (co-authored with Philip Zelikow) the Model III account is missing altogether. Was this excised because it does not comport with what we now know: that hardly anyone was opposed to the idea within the Soviet government and that the decision was essentially Khrushchev's, or was there some other reason (Houghton, 2000)?

Turning to the *Homo Sociologicus* account, one evident weakness of the group-think/vigilant appraisal dichotomy is that it is difficult to decide on which side of the division a given case falls. Critics have noted that Janis's case studies are open to different interpretations. In this case, Janis saw ample evidence of rigorous and systematic decision-making procedures, but Lebow notes the ways in which what he sees as "the myth of the ExCom"—fueled perhaps by wishful thinking about the slain president's management capabilities—has distorted our thinking not only about the missile crisis and how it was handled but whether it is possible to construct decision-making processes which bypass or nullify the cognitive limitations of decision-makers themselves. According to Lebow, it is ironic that some of the foremost critics of the RAM (*Homo Economicus* in this book) fall back upon this assumption when trying to design procedures which purportedly produce substantively better decisions (Lebow 1981, 298).

Finally, we can find potential weaknesses in the *Homo Psychologicus* account as well. The evidence is overwhelming that the Pearl Harbor analogy was used repeatedly by RFK, for instance, and the World War I analogy by the President. What does this mean, though? *Why* did Kennedy use the Pearl Harbor analogy? Had he decided that he didn't want an air strike *before* using the analogy to his brother and later in front of his colleagues? Perhaps RFK had decided—on the grounds of being a classic dove—that he was opposed on ideological grounds to taking the missiles out this way, and he searched around for some alternative argument that would convince hawks not to go with the air strike option, thereby achieving his desired goal but avoiding alienating the hard-liners with "soft talk." Or perhaps he had decided against the air strike *solely* on the grounds that it might not work and that it risked escalation of the conflict. He may then, in similar fashion, have grabbed a justification from the history books, which he thought would convert those who had more faith in the ability of the military to accomplish what it promised. In both of these instances, talk of Pearl Harbor would constitute an *ex post* justification, designed to persuade the other ExCom members after the fact, rather than an *ex ante* source of understanding and categorization.

Equally, an account based on prospect theory seems somewhat weak on the American side, perhaps even suggesting that the theory itself may be open to question as applied to political decision-making. While it might seem to be merely stating a truism—surely it is no more than common sense that leaders are more likely to act recklessly when they are losing, or think they are losing—it may be that the perception of loss does *not* automatically lead to risk taking in real world decision-making. First of all, it may be that Khrushchev's risk-taking behavior was more a matter of his personality than his perceptions of losses or gains; the Soviet leader in fact had a long history of risk-taking behavior, which U.S. decision-makers appear to have missed in their assessments of his likely behavior (Fischer 1998, 161). More problematically perhaps, while one can infer as Haas does that John Kennedy was almost certainly operating in the domain of loss by October 1962, he proved relatively risk-averse. There was a congressional election coming up, the Republicans were hammering him on the missile issue, Kennedy had seemed relatively weak in some in his confrontations with Khrushchev, and the discovery of the missiles had been a slap in the face on the international stage. However, one can argue that he chose the *least* risky of the feasible options: the naval blockade. While Haas has an explanation for this (see our earlier discussion), it does seem to weaken the predictive force of the theory. This suggests at least the possibility that in political decision-making the notion that risk aversion equates with loss and risk acceptance with gain may be too simplistic. On the other hand, the choice of a blockade was still relatively risky, and certainly presented a dangerous roll of the dice when compared with the kind of diplomatic options proposed by Stevenson and Thompson.

CHAPTER 7

An Agonizing Decision: Escalating the Vietnam War

President Lyndon B. Johnson is visibly crushed by his torment over Vietnam.
SOURCE: LBJ Library photo by Jack Kightlinger

Technically, America's military involvement in the Vietnam War lasted from 1965 to 1975, covering the presidencies of Lyndon Johnson, Richard Nixon, and Gerald Ford. This country's first involvement in Vietnam, though, can actually be traced as far back as the administration of Harry Truman. Truman provided economic and military aid to the French in 1950, when Vietnam was still a French colony (the French were then fighting a war against Communist insurgents led by Ho Chi Minh). France withdrew from Vietnam in 1954 after defeat at the battle of Dien Bien Phu, and a peace conference in Geneva then theoretically granted the country its independence but split it into two: North Vietnam, led by the Marxist-Leninist regime of Ho, and South Vietnam, under the weak but pro-Western government of Ngo Dinh Diem. From the late 1950s on, Ho began aiding the Vietcong, pro-Communist revolutionaries based in the South, who were seeking to a united Vietnam under Ho's rule. Eventually, the United States tried to prop up Diem's regime, but by the early 1960s South Vietnam appeared on the verge of collapse.

Fearing that the South would fall to the Communists and that the rest of the region would soon succumb to a similar fate thereafter (the infamous domino theory), both Eisenhower and Kennedy sent a steadily increasing number of military advisers to Vietnam. By the time of JFK's death, there were 16,000 such advisers in the South. The role of these personnel was to provide military assistance and training to the South Vietnamese, without actually engaging directly in the fighting themselves. The Americanization of the war had thus begun long before Lyndon Johnson took office after the assassination of Kennedy in 1963. Yet it was under Johnson that the U.S. role in the conflict became a direct one and thus committed to a full-scale war against Communist North Vietnam. Faced with the imminent collapse of the South Vietnamese regime and the victory of Ho's forces, Johnson was soon faced with a stark choice: escalate the U.S. role in the conflict or withdraw. In March 1964 the United States began secretly bombing selected military targets in the North in what later became known as Operation Rolling Thunder.

Then in August of that year came the event that triggered the major escalation of America's role: the Gulf of Tonkin incident, in which the North Vietnamese allegedly attacked two U.S. ships. What actually occurred during the attack. and, indeed, whether there was an attack at all, remains unclear to this day and provides a topic of heated debate for historians. There is a general consensus that the first attack certainly did occur, however, while the second almost certainly did not. Regardless of what really did happen, however, the episode provided LBJ with the opportunity to escalate the U.S. role more openly. The president had Congress approve the Gulf of Tonkin resolution of 1964. To its detractors in later years, the resolution came to be seen as a blank check, since in practice it granted Johnson virtually unlimited authority to respond to the North Vietnam's actions in whatever manner he saw fit.

During the latter part of 1964 the administration considered various possible options in relation to Vietnam, ranging from a limited bombing campaign to full-scale bombing to the commitment of thousands of ground troops. But it was in 1965 that the Johnson administration took two momentous decisions which effectively committed America to winning the war, and which were to soon to make any withdrawal short of this goal immensely difficult: (1) in February 1965 LBJ ordered a major bombing campaign in the North in retaliation for a Vietcong attack on U.S. military advisers in the South; and (2) this was followed in April by the decision to send in 82,000 ground troops, initially with the limited mission of protecting U.S. bases from attack and engaging in minor combat. More troops were added incrementally, and by the end of 1965 there were more than 180,000 American soldiers in Vietnam. The American troops would remain in Vietnam for the next eight years. Although there were a few dissenting voices within the administration at this critical stage of the decision-making—most notably that of George Ball, who argued that the United States could not win in Vietnam—the vast majority of Johnson's advisers supported the decisions taken in 1965.

The President had won a landslide victory in the election of 1964, but public opinion was turning against 'Johnson's War' by the middle of 1966, and this trend intensified over the course of 1967 and 1968. Although he had repeatedly predicted in public that the United States was about to prevail over the enemy, there was in fact very little evidence to support the claim that the North or the Vietcong were close to defeat. Massive and repeated bombing raids of North Vietnam produced few discernable results, and if anything the resolve of the Communist forces seemed to harden. Opinion polls showed mounting disapproval of Johnson's handling of the war, and the public began to believe that the United States should end their involvement in Vietnam, either through an all-out push for military victory (which would devastate the country) or a straight withdrawal of our forces. And within the administration itself, many previously steadfast supporters of the Vietnam policy voiced their opposition to the war in private, or else quietly resigned from office and returned to private life: between 1966 and 1968 George Ball, presidential adviser and speechwriter Richard Goodwin, McGeorge Bundy, Press Secretary Bill Moyers, Deputy Defense Secretary Cyrus Vance, and finally Vance's boss Robert McNamara, all left office disillusioned to varying degrees by Johnson's Vietnam policies.

The final nail in the coffin for the administration's Vietnam policy came in January 1968 with a massive and sudden attack on the South by the North which became known as the Tet Offensive. This attack, mounted in conjunction with a similar effort by the Vietcong, represented an attempt by North Vietnamese forces to win the war and sap the will of the adversary. Although this attempt failed militarily, the Tet Offensive brought home to the American people just how unsuccessful the efforts of the previous years had been: the North and the Vietcong were seemingly as strong as ever. In itself, even this event did not entirely convince Johnson that America's present course could not be continued. The reactions of his most trusted advisers to Tet did eventually change his mind, however. After Tet, LBJ held a meeting orchestrated by his new Defense Secretary Clark Clifford, a strong supporter of U.S. withdrawal from the war, with a group of experienced and highly distinguished former American statesmen and military personnel known as the "Wise Men." This group contained many of the architects of the idea of containment, men who had been very supportive of Johnson's policies before the Tet offensive. It was instrumental in convincing LBJ that he needed to find a way to get the United States out of the war, since most now favored military disengagement. On March 31, 1968, Johnson made a televised speech in which he announced a partial suspension of the bombing, but he knew that his presidency was effectively over: to the surprise of most of his closest advisers, he closed his speech with the announcement that he would not be seek re-election in the forthcoming presidential election of 1968. It had become all too obvious that he could not win the election, given what had happened in the rice paddies of Southeast Asia.

The war had cost Johnson the White House, and Vice President Hubert Humphrey was then defeated at the 1968 election by Republican Richard Nixon. Nixon came to office promising to end the war but did not specify how he would do this. Committed to a policy of détente and a thawing of relations with China and the Soviet Union, Nixon announced that there would be a "Vietnamization" of the war and engaged in peace talks with the North Vietnamese in Paris. These talks eventually produced a cease-fire, but not before the United States had mounted a highly expanded and intensified bombing campaign of the North (including the Christmas bombing of Hanoi in December 1972). In 1973 a peace agreement was reached. Under the terms of the deal, U.S. troops were withdrawn from Vietnam in return for the return of American POWs. The last U.S. personnel left Saigon in 1975, when it finally fell to the North. The striking scenes of American helicopters taking off from the roof of the U.S. embassy in Saigon, evacuating the country with only a few belongings as North Vietnamese tanks prepared to roll in to the city, present a vivid contrast with the hopes and rhetoric of six American presidents: Truman, Eisenhower, Kennedy, Johnson, Nixon, and Ford, all of whom had all committed themselves to not losing Vietnam.

The war had come with a terrible cost, both human and financial. It destroyed Johnson's economic and social policies at home, draining American coffers of the funds necessary to wage what he called his War on Poverty. More importantly, the conflict destroyed millions of lives and continues to take a terrible physical and psychological toll among the survivors today. The names of 58,000 U.S. casualties, most of them lost during the presidencies of Johnson and Nixon, are today writ-ten on the Vietnam Wall in Washington. Hundreds of thousands if not millions of Vietnamese died, and more bombs were dropped on North Vietnam than were dropped in all of World War II. There is a broad consensus today among political scientists and historians that the war was a terrible mistake, a disproportionate response to an issue whose ramifications were largely regional if not altogether local. It was also waged in the vain attempt to stave off an outcome which could, it was later suggested, have been prevented back in 1945 if the United States had supported Ho Chi Minh's declaration of independence from the French. Both on that occasion and at various points along the way, there had been various lost opportunities which could have been taken to avoid war (see McNamara, Blight, and Brigham 1999).

One such opportunity came in the immediate aftermath of World War II. During the war, Ho's Communist forces had allied themselves with the United States against Japan, and his organization (known as the Viet Minh) had actually assisted in the recovery of downed American pilots over Vietnam, Cambodia, and Laos. In 1945 the British returned control of Vietnam to its French colonizers, but

Ho unilaterally chose to declare Vietnam's independence. As he did so, members of the American OSS—the predecessor of today's CIA—looked on in approval, and Ho even began his declaration using the first few sentences of the American Declaration of Independence. Tragically, however, the decision was made in Washington to side with the French; many in the State Department reasoned that the United States should support France in its efforts to regain control of its former colonies, since failing to do so might jeopardize French support for NATO in Europe. At that time, moreover, Europe was considered a far more significant theater of interest than Southeast Asia.

WHY DID JOHNSON ESCALATE?

Identifying the factors that led the Johnson administration to escalate U.S. involvement in the war is our primary objective in this chapter. Why, first of all, did the U.S. government choose to initiate a bombing campaign of North Vietnam, and why were ground troops then committed to the conflict? Second, why did the Johnson administration persist with its policies toward Vietnam in the face of evidence that strongly (if not unambiguously) suggested that these policies were failing? Like the Cuban missile crisis case, the decisions behind the war have been extensively analyzed, and there is a very large primary and second literature on this case study, only some of which we can do justice to here. Briefly stated, *Homo Bureaucraticus* finds evidence of bureaucratic resistance to change and organizational parochialism. The State Department, CIA, and Pentagon all developed parochial interests in the Vietnam intervention, and bureaucratic tussles hampered the ability of the service chiefs within the Pentagon to offer coherent military advice. Unfortunately for those who argued against the 1965 escalation, the dissenters tended to occupy relatively lowly bureaucratic positions or else no position at all, thus hampering their ability to play the bureaucratic game. From the viewpoint of *Homo Sociologicus*, there were powerful pressures toward conformity and consensus within the key decision-making group, and those who did dissent were gradually domesticated (to use Janis's memorable phrase) or excluded altogether. Vietnam may represent a textbook case of groupthink. Finally, *Homo Psychologicus* places particular emphasis upon the individual characteristics of Lyndon Johnson and those around him, as well as the historical lessons that key decision-makers had drawn from previous episodes. The role of misperception and wishful thinking also comes out strongly in this type of account.

Homo Bureaucraticus

Although Graham Allison's *Essence of Decision* was about the Cuban missile crisis rather than the Vietnam escalation, the bureaucratic politics approach is sufficiently well specified that applying it to the latter is a fairly straightforward matter. The "where you stand depends on where you sit" axiom predicts that State Department officials should be doves and Defense Department representatives hawks. The views of Dean Rusk sat poorly with this kind of prediction; his belief that U.S.

diplomacy hinged on the sincerity of its international commitments, including the one that successive U.S. presidents had made to Vietnam, somewhat paradoxically led him to the conclusion that the Vietnam situation could be resolved only by the use of military force. Nevertheless, the State Department in general was less enthusiastic than the Pentagon about this prospect. Although not solely an argument about bureaucratic politics, James Thomson's classic critique of the Johnson administration's Vietnam policies is full of interesting observations from the perspective of *Homo Bureaucraticus*. Thomson had an ideal view of the policy process from his perch as an East Asia hand in the State Department and then the White House, working for the National Security Council. From Thomson's perspective, the State Department and other organizations within the government lacked expertise in Southeast Asia, primarily because during the 1950s the McCarthyites had systematically removed anyone who knew anything about China and the Far East from State's ranks. The State Department was also hampered in its ability to offer informed advice about Vietnam by its own ingrained cultural habits:

> Below the level of the fatigued executives in the making of Vietnam policy was a widespread phenomenon: *the curator mentality* in the Department of State. By this I mean the collective inertia produced by the bureaucrat's view of his job. At State, the average desk officer inherits from his predecessor our policy toward country X; he regards it as his function to keep that policy intact—under glass, untampered with, and dusted—so that he may pass it on in two to four years to his successor. And such curatorial service generally merits promotion within the system (in other words, maintain the status quo and you will stay out of trouble.) In some circumstances, the inertia bred by such an outlook can act as a brake against rash innovation. But on many issues, this inertia sustains the momentum of bad policy and unwise commitments, momentum that might otherwise have been resisted within the ranks. Clearly, Vietnam is such an issue (Thomson 1968).

In addition to this kind of organizational parochialism, Thomson argues that bureaucratic language bred a kind of detachment from the conflict itself, together with a failure to squarely confront the reality of what was happening in Vietnam and the true nature of war itself:

> As a further influence on policy-makers I would cite the factor of *bureaucratic detachment*. By this I mean what at best might be termed the professional callousness of the surgeon (and indeed, medical lingo— the "surgical strike" for instance— seemed to crop up in the euphemisms of the times). In Washington the semantics of the military muted the reality of war for the civilian policy-makers. In quiet, air-conditioned, thick-carpeted rooms, such terms as "systematic pressure," "armed reconnaissance," "targets of opportunity," and even "body count" seemed to breed a sort of games-theory detachment. Most memorable to me was a moment in the late 1964 target planning when the question under discussion was how heavy our bombing should be, and how extensive our strafing, at some midpoint in the projected pattern of systematic pressure. An Assistant Secretary of State resolved the point in the following words: "It seems to me that our orchestration should be mainly violins, but with periodic touches of brass" (Thomson 1968).

In one view, bureaucratic parochialism about Vietnam was evident across a whole range of organizations within the U.S. government. While organizations initially proved resistant to the change that a major commitment to Vietnam involved, once they became engaged in that issue they developed various vested interests in Johnson's policies. "The bureaucracy became like a cement block in the trunk of a car," argue Leslie Gelb and Richard Betts in *The Irony of Vietnam*. "It added tremendous momentum. Cautious, sometimes resistant, in the earlier years, each bureaucratic organization then had its own stakes. The military had to prove that American arms and advice could succeed. The Foreign Service had to prove that it could bring about political stability in Saigon and build a nation. The CIA had to prove, especially after the Bay of Pigs fiasco, that it could handle covert action and covert paramilitary operations lest it chance having its operational missions in general questioned" (Gelb and Betts 1979, 239).

From this perspective, bureaucratic divisions within the Pentagon were just as significant, if not more so, than interdepartmental disputes at the cabinet level. As H. R. McMaster has argued, the Joint Chiefs agreed that President Johnson's strategy of graduated bombing—designed to bring the North Vietnamese to the bargaining table—was fatally flawed. Army Chief General Harold Johnson, for instance, predicted that it would take 500,000 men and five years to produce a victory in Vietnam (McMaster 1998, 261). He thought LBJ's bombing strategy would fail, as did the other members of the Joint Chiefs of Staff such as Navy Chief Admiral David McDonald. But they largely did not communicate their doubts to the civilian leadership of the Pentagon, and bureaucratic rivalries between the various services got in the way of their attempts to offer coherent military advice. As we have seen in previous chapters, JFK in particular distrusted the Joint Chiefs after the Bay of Pigs, and both he and LBJ were only too happy to cut the Joint Chiefs out of the decision-making process. Secretary McNamara seems to have even adopted a policy of "divide and conquer" with them at one point. As McMaster states, service parochialism was so great that each organization wanted to fight the war in Vietnam using its own resources, using what it could do:

> The administration could not seriously evaluate proposals from a service chief that relied almost exclusively on the resources of his particular service … General [Wallace] Greene thought that the Marine Corps was ideally suited for occupying Vietnam's seaboard and proposed that it establish secure enclaves along the coast. [Air Force Chief Curtis] LeMay remained a zealot for air power. McDonald emphasized mining ports, riverine patrols in the Mekong Delta, and using navy aircraft to conduct reconnaissance and air strikes (McMaster 1998, 81–82).

During the decision-making process on Vietnam, Lyndon Johnson occasionally brought in Clark Clifford, a presidential adviser from outside his government and a seasoned Washington veteran. Clifford argued in his memoirs that the critical decision to escalate U.S. involvement in Vietnam was made on the weekend of July 25–26 at Camp David. Johnson had invited all of his key foreign policy advisers to spend Saturday and Sunday with him at the presidential retreat outside DC, and while the purpose was ostensibly relaxation, the real objective was to debate the business of Vietnam one last time (Clifford 1991, 418–22). Although Clifford was not formally part of LBJ's foreign policy team, the President knew that his old-friend and adviser was opposed to escalation and set up a debate that weekend between Clifford and the main civilian advocate of the troop increase, Robert McNamara.[1] Clifford essentially made the following points, gathering his notes together and using his legal training to present the case as if LBJ were a judge:

- You'll be admired for withdrawal, since it will be seen as a noble attempt to follow a lost cause.
- Bombing hasn't worked, and you will have to resort to horrific measures if you expand the war.
- You will be seen as criminal by those you most admire, and a hero to those you hate, if you escalate our involvement.
- The Vietminh (the North Vietnamese Communists) will not tire and will wait until our own appetite for the war declines.
- Political disaster lies ahead, and Vietnam will destroy your presidency.
- This is a problem that should be dealt economically, not militarily.
- This is a year of minimum political risk for withdrawal (LBJ had won a landslide victory at the 1964 presidential election).

Secretary McNamara did not agree and presented the following counterpoints:

- The *domino theory* applies here: if we back down in Vietnam, we will encourage the regional and global spread of Communism.
- We have made pledges and commitments to Vietnam, which will be very costly to break.
- Our international prestige will be greatly harmed by withdrawal, the United States will be viewed as weak, and our Allies will lose faith.
- We can win the war if we greatly expand the bombing targets.

While the personal beliefs of the participants clearly mattered in explaining Johnson's decision to escalate, we also need to take account of bureaucratic role if we are to explain why one argument proved more appealing than another. Bureaucratic status and position in the foreign policy hierarchy make a difference, and it matters *who* is arguing a particular case. In July 1965, as Johnson approached the irrevocable and fateful decision to commit 100,000 U.S. troops to a land war, Dean Rusk, McGeorge Bundy, and McNamara were all lined up in favor of the escalation. Within the formal foreign policy circle, George Ball was the champion of the argument against escalation. Indeed, among Johnson's official advisers he was practically the only decision-maker who made this case. Here a little counterfactual reasoning may prove useful in bolstering an argument in favor of *Homo Bureaucraticus*. What if Ball's boss Dean Rusk had argued against escalation as well? Had that scenario occurred, President Johnson might well have found it much more difficult to reach the decision to escalate. Ball's relatively lowly bureaucratic position, together with the numbers ranged against him on the other side of the argument, can have exerted no little impact on the outcome. Equally, what if Clark Clifford had been the Secretary of Defense in 1965 (a position he later accepted in 1968), or if Robert McNamara had held the views in 1965 that he did in 1967 (by which time he had changed his mind about Vietnam)? Clifford was hampered by at least one significant factor in his arguments to the president: he had turned down Johnson's early offers to join the administration. Despite his long experience as an adviser to several presidents, he was an outsider in this instance. He was dependent on the memoranda that Ball leaked to him and lacked the bureaucratic clout that his opponents possessed, but what if he had been (say) CIA director in 1965? LBJ had offered him this position in 1964, but he had turned it down. The possibilities and 'what ifs?' are endless, of course, but they all point toward the same conclusion: bureaucratic role may influence the reception with which different arguments are greeted.[2]

Another problem for those who opposed the escalation within the White House is that they tended to be relatively junior figures, constrained by their bureaucratic roles. Although the constraints are predominantly informal and unwritten rather than formal-legal, in most administrations the president's immediate staff also tend to be constrained by the expectations that foreign policy is not their job. Former Johnson administration press secretaries George Reedy and Bill Moyers both had very strong feelings about Vietnam, and but only Reedy tried to convey these directly to the President (and when he did so, LBJ would essentially ignore him). Moyers's approach was more subtle; as David Halberstam reports, the latter's technique was to encourage those who occupied more accepted foreign policy roles and who doubted the wisdom of Johnson's Vietnam policies to speak for him, rather than attempting to persuade the President directly. Moyers "showed his own doubts on Vietnam largely by encouraging other doubters to speak and by trying to put doubters in touch with one another" (Halberstam 1969, 497). According to Clark Clifford, Moyers did so because he "felt he could not play an open role in policymaking because his job as press secretary constrained him from active policy formulation" (Clifford 1991, 416).

In a sense, the decision to escalate may well have involved a bureaucratic compromise. As Clifford relates, while Robert McNamara "won" the July 1965 debate in a substantive sense, Johnson effectively split the difference between his advisers in at least one way. He approved the troops as McNamara had wanted, but he also followed the advice of Ball and Clifford to do so very quietly:

> We both had argued that we should "underplay" any public announcements so as to maintain maximum flexibility for future withdrawal, while arguing, of course, against any escalation at all. In the actual event, the president turned down our strategic objective, but handled the public announcement in a manner consistent with our suggestion. Instead of a nationally televised speech in primetime, the President simply disclosed the buildup during a midday press conference on July 28 (Clifford 1991:422).

In a statement that would return to haunt Johnson in later years since it was plainly untrue, when the President was asked whether the troop commitment meant that the administration was changing its policies toward Vietnam, he simply replied rather flatly that it did "not imply any change in policy whatsoever." After this, he ground to a sudden, rather awkward verbal halt, presumably since he knew the statement was false.

Homo Sociologicus

Irving Janis argues that the decision to Americanize the war in Vietnam in 1965, made by Lyndon Johnson and his advisers, represents one of the clearest examples of the groupthink phenomenon that we have (Janis 1982, 97–130). Together with the Bay of Pigs case, the Vietnam escalation forms one of the two centerpieces of his book. Janis does not look at the war in an especially broad context, but he does examine in a fair amount of depth Johnson's discrete decision to commit land troops to the war, as well as resistance to change within the administration once the war was underway. What was so interesting to Janis as a social psychologist was that Johnson and his advisers exhibited the same kinds of conformist behaviors in groups to those shown in numerous laboratory experiments. These were the individuals whom David Halberstam called "the best and the brightest," experienced and highly regarded men Johnson had inherited from his predecessor John Kennedy (Halberstam 1969). And yet the vast majority of these individuals wholeheartedly supported the escalation of a war which ultimately proved disastrous for the country.

Janis's groupthink account draws partly on James Thomson's rich account of the decision-making process, since that article actually contains points useful to all three of our approaches. He notes that Thomson called the Vietnam process "a slow-motion Bay of Pigs," immediately suggesting that this case study might be a good candidate for the application of the theory of groupthink (Thomson 1968). While America's commitment to Vietnam drew from a complex series of causes, the decision-making group at the very top was insulated from the experts. Vietnam policy was made by generalists, "can do" men who knew little about Southeast Asia and who were under excessive time pressure and stress. Dissenters were treated as "troublemakers," Thomson argues, and the decision-makers held stereotypical images of Communists and Orientals, including the racist notion that Asians supposedly do not place a high value on human life. This was a rather contradictory position to take given the bombing campaign then underway, since the success of that campaign rested on the notion that heavy casualties among the Vietminh and Vietcong forces would ultimately force the North Vietnamese to the bargaining table.

The primary forum for Johnson's Vietnam decision-making, Janis notes, was the Tuesday Lunch Group. This was a small, highly cohesive but informal collection of individuals whose judgment Johnson trusted the most, men like Dean Rusk and Robert McNamara. Within this rather clubby group, Janis observes the presence of a number of tell-tale symptoms that can lead to the emergence of groupthink:

- *Effects of stress on group cohesiveness.* The Vietnam decisions were made by a small, cohesive group of like-minded decision-makers who valued unity and consensus. They cultivated a warm atmosphere, almost like a gentleman's club. This was enhanced by the stress of the Vietnam decision-making process and the time pressure they faced, since social psychological experiments have shown that groups become more internally cohesive when they collectively perceive some kind of external threat.

- *Effects of commitment to prior group decisions.* As the group became more cohesive, a homogenization of views took place within the inner circle of advisers. There was also a general unwillingness to revisit old decisions or reassess their wisdom. Instead, group members became increasingly committed to the course of action they were pursuing.
- *Conformity pressures.* This involved the "domestication" or outright exclusion of dissenters like George Ball and the emergence of mindguards (Walt Rostow). The suppression and self-censorship of personal doubts by group members took place and potentially useful outside advice was avoided or ignored.
- *Unanimity within the group.* There was, for the most part, general agreement on the war policy within Johnson's inner circle, and even dissenters often felt a strong sense of kinship and consensus with the group.
- *Overlooking the risks.* An illusion of vulnerability and complacency prompted by Johnson's 1964 landslide victory emerged, similar to the "magic touch" feeling that the Kennedy decision-makers experienced in 1961 prior to the Bay of Pigs. The group persuaded itself that the bombing campaign was working and would work, displaying a great deal of overoptimism about the chances that Ho Chi Minh could be bombed to the negotiation table.

Janis devotes the most attention to conformity pressures, and this factor is worth discussing in particular detail. Even within Johnson's inner circle, there were a handful of important dissenters. When one of the original architects of the war, Robert McNamara, began to have doubts about the wisdom of the war and started to express these outside the group, Johnson compared him to a son who had let slip to prospective buyers of a house that there are cracks in the basement (Janis 1982, 118). "He is just short of cracking up," Johnson is reputed to have told advisers in 1967 when McNamara was not present (D. K. Goodwin 1976). More generally, Janis uses Thomson's argument about the "effectiveness trap" to describe how the advice of dissenters was dismissed out of hand. "I'm afraid he is losing his effectiveness," implying that the decision-maker is somehow burned out, became a standard phrase used to denigrate dissent by devaluing the dissenter. As long as transgressors keep their dissent within the group and within tolerable bounds, they are accepted. But as soon as they take dissent outside the group, they may be excluded altogether. Janis sees the firing of McNamara as a classic example of this (Janis 1982, 117–20).

Most famously, George Ball, as undersecretary of state, harbored significant doubts about Americanizing the war and repeatedly expressed these doubts in meetings. But Janis argues that the group employed rather ingenious means in order to defuse Ball's dissent: they began referring to him as a "devil's advocate." This term originates from the Roman Catholic Church, referring to a cardinal within the Vatican who is chosen to argue against the beatification of a saint, in effect making the "Devil's case." Much like a lawyer who must defend a notorious criminal in a court trial, the other cardinals know that the devil's advocate is not committed to his position, but he is nevertheless *required* to take this position as part of the process. Similarly, many of those who favored escalating the war maintained that Ball was not serious in his dissent but was merely arguing against the majority position in order to ensure that all positions were heard in the debate.

For the rest of their lives, many of Johnson's decision-makers who had favored our involvement in Vietnam—William Bundy, assistant secretary of state for East Asian affairs, is an especially good example—would continue to maintain that Ball had been a devil's advocate. This was probably wishful thinking, though. Ball harbored very real and heartfelt disagreements with the others. But dismissing or domesticating the dissenter in this way is exactly what one would expect if groupthink were present, Janis's analysis suggests. Similarly, Lyndon Johnson himself would defuse the criticism of Press Secretary Bill Moyers by announcing "here comes Mr. Stop the Bombing!" whenever Moyers walked into the room, thus blunting anything Moyers might say against the war before he even uttered a word (Janis 1982, 115). And when James Thomson expressed his doubts about the Vietnam policy in front of his superiors, one of them would refer to him as our "favorite dove" (Thomson 1968).

Homo Psychologicus

Would any American president have escalated U.S. involvement in Vietnam? Over the years, this question has been endlessly analyzed and re-analyzed, but one especially prominent argument recently has come from Robert McNamara himself. Reasoning counterfactually, McNamara argued in his memoirs *In Retrospect* that individual leadership was critical, and that had he lived, John F. Kennedy would not have taken the United States into war as Johnson did. "Having reviewed the record in detail, and with the advantage of hindsight," McNamara argued, "I think it highly probable that, had President Kennedy lived, he would have pulled us out of Vietnam. He would have concluded that the South Vietnamese were incapable of defending themselves, and that Saigon's grave political weaknesses made it unwise to try to offset the limitations of South Vietnamese forces by sending U.S. combat troops on a large scale" (McNamara 1995, 96). We will never know for sure whether this is true. However, by looking at a range of cases where Kennedy had the opportunity to militarize disputes but chose diplomacy and negotiation instead, Blight, Lang, and Welch conclude that it is likely that Johnson's leadership attributes and characteristics did make a difference (Blight, Lang, and Welch 1999). If this is true, then the question becomes: *Which* attributes made a difference?

Various authors have argued that Johnson's personality in particular was critical to the Vietnam decision-making. Johnson had an especially fascinating Jekyll and Hyde personality, often charming one moment, but crude or bullying the next. He has often been described as exceptionally insecure—he seems to have felt ashamed of his own modest education in Texas when compared with colleagues whom he called his "Harvards"—and has also been described as a narcissist, a paranoid, and even a manic-depressive. In *The Presidential Character*, James David Barber describes LBJ as an "active-negative personality." Barber's book was one of the first to analyze American presidents in a comparative way, and the first to come up with a generalizable framework that could be applied to all presidents, no matter what their background or beliefs. He was interested above all in explaining why some presidents succeed while others fail, and in predicting who is likely to succeed or fail before it actually happens. In so doing, Barber generated a famous fourfold distinction between personality types, and he places LBJ in the "least desired" category of presidential personality, that of active-negative. These presidents, Barber argues, are driven individuals who have vast amounts of energy, and while they throw themselves enthusiastically into the job, they derive little or no emotional satisfaction from it. They often retreat into themselves, hunkering down in the face of opposition. Johnson, Barber argued, did precisely this with regard to Vietnam; he stubbornly pursued a course of action in Southeast Asia which led directly to his own downfall, refusing to change course until it was too late and losing many of his closest advisers in the process.

One of the best psychological analyses of Johnson was written by the presidential historian and former Johnson White House intern, Doris Kearns Goodwin. In her *Lyndon Johnson and the American Dream*, first published just three years after LBJ's death, Goodwin applies a somewhat psychoanalytical approach to Johnson. She suggests that his early upbringing, especially his relationship with his mother, shaped his future interactions with his staff and others in the political world. Johnson's rather intellectual and ambitious mother felt robbed of a promising career by Sam Johnson (Lyndon's father), by all accounts a boorish man who was often drunk. She compensated for this by using her son as a substitute for her own ambitions, Goodwin argues, withdrawing her love when Lyndon didn't live up to her high expectations. She argues that a striking link is apparent between the way his mother alternately extended and withdrew love, and the manner in which Johnson himself treated his own staff and indeed "nearly all his adult relationships." LBJ was capable of incredible warmth and generosity toward his friends, colleagues, and subordinates, but they uniformly recall how swiftly this warmth could turn to anger and hostility when they failed to live up to the high standards he set for them. Johnson "demanded a measure of gratitude and loyalty so high that disappointment was inevitable. And when the disappointment came, Johnson tended to withdraw his affection and concern—the 'Johnson freezeout'—hurting others in much the same as his mother had hurt him years before" (Goodwin 1976, p. 7). The duality in Johnson's personality, often acting in boorish ways as his father had, then behaving in a more kind and even genteel fashion, may have come from his father *and* his mother respectively.

Another distinguished presidential historian, Robert Dallek, views Johnson as a textbook case of political paranoia. While in no sense a full-fledged psychobiography, Dallek's *Flawed Giant* argues that "at times, Johnson came frighteningly close to clinical paranoia" (Dallek 1998). As … "an irrational conviction that his domestic opponents were subversives intent of undermining national institutions. Johnson's paranoia raises questions about his judgment and capacity to make rational life and death decisions. I do not raise this matter casually. It is a frighteningly difficult issue, which the country has never seriously addressed" (Dallek 1998, 627). Dallek confirms Bill Moyers's view, previously attributed to him by Richard Goodwin, that Johnson suffered from spells of intense paranoia and quotes Moyers's belief that Lady Bird Johnson was more concerned about her husband's paranoia than anyone else (Dallek 1998, 283). He also offers evidence that Dean Rusk too was worried. Like his successor Nixon, Johnson saw conspiracies everywhere, both from the Left and the Right. But the beliefs Johnson expressed about his enemies, though sincerely held, were unfounded, no more than "cranky nonsense" in Dallek's words (Dallek 1998, 283). This certainly affected his handling of the situation that followed JFK's assassination, but it may also have influenced his Vietnam policies through his tendency to see global Communism as a vast, coordinated conspiracy.

Similarly, Richard Goodwin has argued that Johnson exhibited increasingly strange behavior at the time of the key decisions about Vietnam:

> During 1965, and especially in the period which enveloped the crucial midsummer decision that transformed Vietnam into an American war, I became convinced that the president's always large eccentricities had taken a huge leap into unreason. Not on every subject, and certainly not all the time. ... There is no question in my mind that both the atmosphere of the White House and the decisions taken until 1965 (the only period I personally observed) were affected by the periodic disruptions of Lyndon Johnson's mind and spirit (ibid. 393) (R. Goodwin 1989).

Based on several years of observing Johnson first hand, Goodwin concludes that LBJ "experienced certain episodes of what I believe to have been paranoid behavior" and that this observation "was shared by others who also had close and frequent contact with the president" (ibid. 394). In 1965 both Dick Goodwin and Bill Moyers began—independently and without each others' knowledge—consulting psychiatrists about the president and reading psychology textbooks in an effort to make sense of the mental deterioration they observed.

It is clear that in a general sense various emotions, especially fear, played a profound role in Johnson's Vietnam decision-making. One of his most compelling fears was the feeling that if he *didn't* go into Vietnam, he would provoke a debate in America similar to the "Who Lost China?" debacle which would destroy his domestic agenda (in other words, the thing that he really cared about) and might well even destroy his presidency; sadly, as we know that with hindsight, this proved to be a self-fulfilling prophecy, but to Johnson the fear, obviously based on a potent analogy with a major event in his own past, seemed all too real. And he seems to have been trapped between two fears. On the one hand, Johnson knew that major wars often destroy the best-laid plans for domestic change. "Oh, I could see it coming all right," LBJ told Doris Kearns Goodwin after he left office.

"History provided too many cases where the sound of the bugle put an immediate end to the hopes and dreams of the best reformers: the Spanish-American War drowned the populist spirit; World War I ended Woodrow Wilson's New Freedom; World War II brought the New Deal to a close. Once the war began, then all those conservatives in the Congress would use it as a weapon against the Great Society" (D. K. Goodwin 1976, 252).

But a second fear proved more compelling to Johnson. As he told Goodwin, "everything I knew about history told me that if I got out of Vietnam and let Ho Chi Minh run through the streets of Saigon, then I'd be doing exactly what they did in World War II. I'd be giving a big fat reward to aggression. And I knew that if we let Communist aggression succeed in taking over South Vietnam, there would follow in this country an endless national debate—a mean and destructive debate—that would shatter my Presidency, destroy my administration and damage our democracy." The rise of McCarthyism and the debate which had followed the loss of China, Johnson predicted in a particularly vivid analogy, "were chickenshit compared with what might happen if we lost Vietnam" (ibid. 252–53; see also Berman 1982, 147). Ultimately, Johnson's greatest fear may have been the risk of becoming the first American president to lose a war.

Once he was deeply embroiled in Vietnam, another fear LBJ mentioned often to his subordinates was the prospect that he might inadvertently set off World War III by bringing China into the war. "In the dark at night, I would lay awake picturing my boys flying around North Vietnam, asking myself an endless series of questions," Johnson told Goodwin. "What if one of those targets you picked today triggers off Russia or China? What happens then?" (D. K. Goodwin 1976, 270). This comparison set off strong emotions in Johnson, which must inevitably have affected his policymaking. Blema Steinberg's analysis of U.S. decision-making on Vietnam also suggests that the emotions of shame and humiliation were very much behind the reasoning of both LBJ and his successor Nixon. "Lyndon Johnson and Richard Nixon were two highly narcissistic individuals who suffered from painful feelings of shame and humiliation," she argues. "It was these feelings, in the overall context of their narcissistic character structures, that played an important role in shaping their presidential decisions on Vietnam" (Steinberg 1996, 7). While not everyone would agree with her psychoanalytic characterization of the two men, it seems beyond doubt that these emotions (and others) had a strong impact on the policymaking process in general.

Johnson's decision-making on Vietnam was also notable for the absence of one emotion that had been evident during the missile crisis: empathy. While obviously a laudable goal for policymakers to pursue, empathy is especially difficult to achieve under some circumstances. It is patently easier to achieve in retrospect than it is at the time, and as Errol Morris's outstanding film of Robert McNamara's life, *The Fog of War,* makes clear, one has to *know* the adversary sufficiently well to put oneself in their shoes. By McNamara's own admission, this was not the case with Vietnam. Lyndon Johnson and the principals in the Tuesday Lunch Group had little familiarity with the history of Vietnamese-Chinese relations; if they had,

McNamara notes, they would have been far less likely to see the North Vietnamese as a mere satellite of the Chinese. Greater familiarity with the nationalist aspects of Ho Chi Minh's thinking, as opposed to his Communist beliefs, might equally well have discouraged a tendency to see North Vietnam as a mere puppet of the Soviets. What American leaders saw as a war to prevent falling dominoes in Southeast Asia, North Vietnamese leaders saw as just one episode in a struggle against colonial invasion, which stretched back thousands of years (Blight and Lang 1995, 52–57). Sadly, those who did have the capacity to empathize with Ho were largely marginalized and came to be regarded, in James Thomson's memorable phrase, as "troublemakers." In essence, LBJ and his colleagues seem to have fallen victim to a variety of misperceptions about what the North Vietnamese wanted and what the likely repercussions of a North Vietnamese victory would be both regionally and globally (White 1968).

Yuen Foong Khong's book *Analogies at War* is probably the leading analysis of the Vietnam decision-making from the perspective of *Homo Psychologicus*. Like another work about analogical reasoning in policymaking, Neustadt and May's *Thinking in Time,* the book's title has an interesting double meaning: it is both about the use of analogies in wartime decision-making, and the ways in which those analogies compete with one another for the attention of the president (Neustadt and May 1986; Khong 1992). Like Janis, Khong examines the decisions by the Johnson administration to escalate U.S. involvement in the Vietnam War in 1965. Rather than examine conformity within Johnson's group, however, Khong's focus is on the ways in which different decision-makers perceived the situation they faced in contrasting ways, assessing the stakes and national interests involved differently and proposing different policy prescriptions. His major finding is that historical analogies played a decisive role in the reasoning processes of those who opposed the escalation and those who advocated it. Three analogies in particular, Khong finds, exerted a critical effect upon the decision-making process: Korea, Munich, and Dien Bien Phu.

For the first group, Korea was the analogy of choice. This faction included President Johnson and many of his advisers, such as Dean Rusk. As Khong puts it, "Johnson was informed by many lessons of many pasts, but Korea preoccupied him. ... Whatever it was that attracted Johnson to the Korean precedent, a major lesson he drew from it was that the United States made a mistake in leaving Korea in June 1949; the withdrawal emboldened the communists, forcing the United States to return to Korea one year later to save the South. Johnson was not predisposed toward repeating the same mistake in Vietnam" (Khong 1992, 110–11). The United States had successfully repelled the Communists "the last time," when North Korea had invaded its Southern neighbor. For Johnson and Rusk, this analogy suggested that they could fight a limited war in Southeast Asia, as long as the military did not push too hard; China had at some point become involved, an eventuality with which LBJ would be constantly concerned during the Vietnam War. The president clearly did not want to repeat errors of June 1949, when U.S. troops had left Korean only to return after the Northern invasion. As Khong finds, this analogy was the one most often cited in public and private by Johnson administration officials in the run-up to war.

A second group, partially overlapping with the first, was more taken by the parallel with Munich, a comparison (see chap. 6) which was especially popular during the missile crisis with figures like Curtis LeMay and Dean Acheson, and would much later influence the thinking of Madeleine Albright regarding Kosovo (see chap. 10). In the Vietnam decision-making, both McGeorge Bundy and the U.S. Ambassador to Vietnam Henry Cabot Lodge drew on the perceived lessons of the Munich–World War II experience in predicting the scenarios they believed would occur if the United States did *not* intervene (Khong1992, 134). For those who advocated this comparison, the image of Neville Chamberlain at the Munich Conference in 1938 (where the British Prime Minister had made concessions to Adolf Hitler in an effort to avert war) played on their minds. This analogy was something to which LBJ gave a great deal of thought. In his conversations with Doris Kearns Goodwin he expressed the view that if he appeased the North Vietnamese, he would be giving "a big fat reward to aggression" (D. K. Goodwin 1976, 252).

The third analogy was advocated mainly by one man, George Ball. He argued that increased American involvement in Vietnam would soon lead to "another Dien Bien Phu," a repeat of the disastrous French experience in Indochina in which the French increasingly proved unable to defeat Communist and nationalist insurgents in a guerilla war and were eventually forced to relinquish their former colony. At the battle of Dien Bien Phu in 1954, the French had been roundly defeated, outwitted by General Vo Nguyen Giap after attempting to maneuver the North Vietnamese into fighting a conventional war. If U.S. forces were committed to Vietnam, they would be no more successful than the French had been at defeating an enemy which was often invisible, Ball argued rather presciently. While Ball was mostly alone in arguing for the relevance of the Dien Bien Phu analogy, President Johnson occasionally brought in Clark Clifford as an outside adviser. Clifford also seems to have found this comparison compelling, and his argument that the North Vietnamese Communists would not tire seems to have been based on the French experience.

Moreover, for both Ball and Clifford Vietnam was no Korea, since they saw many meaningful differences between the two situations. First of all, Korea had been a clear "war of aggression by North against South." Vietnam, however, was far more complicated. The country had been artificially divided at Geneva in 1954, and the dividing line was not so clear since there was an indigenous, pro-Communist guerilla group in the South (the Vietcong). There was a good case to be made, then, that this was essentially a civil war. Second, Korea and Vietnam did not involve a similar kind of fight. Korea had been fought out in the open using conventional military means, but fighting in Vietnam would involve a counterinsurgency against an enemy whose means were anything but conventional. Indeed, it was unlikely that the enemy would oblige the United States by choosing to fight a conventional war, since they knew they would lose such a fight. Instead, they would use guerilla tactics, melting into the jungles of Southeast Asia. Third, Korea had been fought as a UN operation using a multinational force. In Vietnam, by contrast, the United States could expect little help from its European allies, most of whom were opposed to the war. Unlike in Korea, we could expect little help in Vietnam, and would therefore have to fight the conflict more or less unilaterally. And finally, Ball cast doubt on the stability of South Vietnam's government. While the South Korean administration was relatively strong and entrenched, Vietnam's government was notoriously unstable. One general after another had stepped into the leadership role, with very little success.

What specific roles do analogies perform, and why are they so useful in decision-making? Khong argues that we can think of analogies as "diagnostic devices," which assist policymakers in performing six crucial functions: they "(1) help define the nature of the situation confronting the policymaker, (2) help assess the stakes, and (3) provide prescriptions. They help evaluate alternative options by (4) predicting the chances of success, (5) evaluating their moral rightness, and (6) warning about dangers associated with the options" (Khong 1992, 10). He develops what he calls the "AE Framework," essentially a shorthand term for the belief that analogies are genuine cognitive devices, which perform the tasks specified above. The primary research purpose of Khong's book is to argue against the view that analogies are used solely to "prop up one's prejudices" or to justify decisions which have already been decided upon using some other rationale, and he finds that the Johnson people tended to use historical analogies which drew upon recent events such as the missile crisis, the Berlin crises, Korea, Pearl Harbor, and Munich. Khong also shows rather convincingly that in choosing a historical analogy which seemed to make sense of Vietnam, Johnson's advisers picked a historical example on the basis of its superficial or surface similarities to the case in hand (Khong 1992, 217–18).

This in turn raises the issue of why leaders choose particular analogies, and Khong draws upon cognitive psychological theory to do this. As we saw in chapter 4, attribution theory is useful for addressing this issue. First of all, we commonly employ the *representativeness heuristic* when searching for analogies, looking for a fit (or superficial similarity) between situations. Korea and Vietnam were superficially similar: both were in East Asia, for instance, thus making the analogy appealing at some level. We also make use of the *availability heuristic*, which suggests that an analogy is most likely to be used if it can be easily recalled (either because it happened recently, or because it is an especially vivid experience in one's life). For instance, Dien Bien Phu was probably especially available to Ball because of his experience as lawyer for the French during the 1950s, while Rusk had been in the State Department at the time that the Korean war was won. For him, the lesson was that stubborn perseverance wins out in the end (Khong 1992, 215–19).

In the end, Korea was the comparison that won the analogical war, Khong argues, and he notes that it is the only one of the analogies that can account for the specific choices LBJ made. In the February 1965 decision to launch an air war (Operation Rolling Thunder), the option of a "slow squeeze"—that is, graduated bombing of selected targets—was chosen because it involved decisive action, but with the least danger of bringing China into the war (and it was therefore most consistent with lessons of the Korean analogy). In the July 1965 ground war decision, on the other hand, Johnson also selected the only option on the table that was fully consistent with Korea. Correspondingly, few within LBJ's circle were impressed by the Dien Bien Phu analogy, which was never used in public. The parallel was consistently shot down when Ball mentioned it in private meetings, and U.S. decision-makers may have had difficulty seeing a moral equivalence or military similarity between themselves and France.

ASSESSING THE THREE PERSPECTIVES

While each of our approaches seems to add something useful to our understanding of America's Vietnam decision-making, it is instructive to examine their weaknesses as well. In the case of *Homo Bureaucraticus*, for instance, there are some obvious problems in applying Allison's "where you stand" proposition to this case. While it seems to work exceptionally well for the service chiefs within the Joint Staff, how do we explain the division within the State Department between Dean Rusk and his deputy George Ball? If the axiom is correct, one would expect both men to advocate diplomacy over military force, not just Ball. Moreover, how do we explain the division between Robert McNamara and the Deputy Secretary of Defense John McNaughton (who was skeptical about the war until his tragic death in a helicopter crash)? And how do we explain variation in preferences within a single individual while he or she occupies the same role? Why in particular does Robert McNamara later become so dovish? In short, several participants stood where they sat (the Joint Chiefs) while others plainly did not (Dean Rusk) and others had no bureaucratic position or organizational interests to defend (Clark Clifford). Moreover, as Khong notes, the decision to escalate was primarily Lyndon Johnson's to make rather than reflecting some sort of bureaucratic compromise (Khong 1992, 197–200).

Of the three perspectives we have discussed in this chapter, *Homo Sociologicus* is the one that has been subjected to the most criticism. Attempts to test the groupthink model more rigorously than Janis himself did, it must be said, have met with mixed results (Tetlock et al. 1992). More generally, some have critiqued the theoretical coherence of the model Janis developed, while others have used more recently declassified materials to undermine the empirical arguments he made. As Philip Tetlock and his colleagues note, four broad criticisms have been raised against Janis's work on the theoretical side: first of all, Janis relied on qualitative case studies, a method that frequently tempts the researcher to emphasize evidence which fits a theory and to discard information which does not. Second, there is a "suspiciously perfect correlation" between the presence of groupthink and flawed decision-making in Janis's book, even though he himself concedes that process is not everything and that it is possible (by sheer luck) for a good decision to emerge from flawed procedures. Third, there is an equally suspicious

all-or-nothing quality to the way that Janis's cases fit so neatly into the categories of groupthink or vigilant decision-making; and last of all, there are various
conceptual problems with the model itself, especially those having do with dis-
tinguishing the causes from the consequences of groupthink. In their classic critique, Longley and Pruitt question (among other things) the inclusion of "a belief
in the inherent morality of the group" and "stereotyped views of out-groups" in
the list of symptoms of groupthink, since unlike the other factors these appear
to have little to do with consensus formation or concurrence-seeking (Longley
and Pruitt 1980, 91). In short, one does not need to hold a simplistic view of one's
enemy or an exalted view of one's own moral position to engage in hasty or premature decision-making which excludes minority views.

David Barrett has notably challenged the notion that Lyndon Johnson neither
sought nor received competing advice on Vietnam. *Most* of his advisers, Barrett
concedes, certainly did argue for escalation, but a significant minority did not.
He highlights six advisers in particular who argued against escalation. There was
George Ball as we know already, but Senator William Fulbright, Vice President
Hubert Humphrey, Senator Mike Mansfield, Senator Richard Russell, and Clark
Clifford all expressed strong misgivings about the war directly to Johnson as well.
The picture of a president stubbornly ignoring outside advice and relying exclusively upon a tiny group of like-minded individuals, then, does not really fit what
actually occurred, Barrett suggests (Barrett 1988, 1993). Of course, we have long
known that it was not just Ball who expressed reservations about escalation; many
in the CIA, Defense Departments, and State Departments also harbored strong
doubts, although dissenters tended to occupy positions lower down the bureaucratic hierarchy or (like Clifford) lacked any bureaucratic power base within the
government at all.

Even more significant, perhaps, is the evidence we now have that Johnson
himself agonized over the decision to escalate the war. Johnson secretly taped a
large number of his phone calls, and the declassification of many of these calls
since the late 1990s has revealed a president who was almost always pessimistic about the chances of military success, rather than exhibiting any illusion of
invulnerability. We now know that Johnson and his colleagues were, as Barrett
puts it, "reluctant warriors" (Barrett 1993; Beschloss 1997, 2001). In similar vein,
Roderick Kramer has noted that the major dissenter, George Ball, never felt inhibited from speaking his mind and did not self-censor his thoughts (Kramer 1998,
256). Indeed, even Dean Rusk took great pains to make sure that the views of his
deputy, which were very much contrary to his own, were given a fair hearing, as
did Lyndon Johnson himself. This behavior does not seem consistent with Janis's
groupthink hypothesis.

Finally, *Homo Psychologicus* can be criticized on the grounds that it is impossible to determine whether individuals mattered in this case study. It is also notoriously difficult to trace the linkages from personality types to particular decisions.
We will never know for sure whether Lyndon Johnson's personality really made a
difference, or whether John Kennedy would have waged war in Vietnam just as

LBJ did. It is possible, of course, that Kennedy apologists are themselves engaging in wishful thinking about the slain president. Noam Chomsky, for one, argues that Kennedy was in fact a virulent Cold Warrior hell-bent on taking America into Vietnam. According to this view, JFK believed in an undifferentiated Communist menace, and the notion that he was some sort of dove is pure myth spread by pro-Kennedy propagandists. JFK, Chomsky concludes, had no intention whatsoever of pulling out of Vietnam (Chomsky 1993; see also Hunt 1996). If the doctrine of containment preordained American involvement in Vietnam, the issue of personalities becomes moot. Even if we concede that Johnson's leadership did matter, moreover, there is some disagreement as to whether cognitive or motivational factors played the key role, and whether Johnson really wanted to fight a war in Vietnam at all.

CHAPTER 8

Disaster in the Desert:
The Iran Hostage Crisis

The abandoned wreckage of the failed Iran hostage rescue mission. SOURCE: AP Photo

It is comparatively rare for foreign policy issues to bring down a presidency. We encountered the most obvious example in chapter 7 when discussing Lyndon Johnson's difficulties over Vietnam, but a good case can be made that the Iran hostage crisis powerfully contributed to the downfall of America's thirty-ninth president, James Earl "Jimmy" Carter. On November 4, 1979, Iranian radicals seized the American embassy in Tehran, initially taking sixty-six Americans hostage. This was the beginning of the longest and most protracted crisis in the relations between Iran and the United States. For 444 days, the hostages were held in close confinement by students acting in the name of the man who would become Iran's new Supreme Leader, the Ayatollah Ruhollah Khomeini. Politically, Jimmy Carter's inability to obtain the release of the hostages and his near obsession with the issue made him look weak and contributed to the perception that America had lost its way during his presidency. Nothing Carter did, neither trying to open direct diplomatic channels, nor reaching out to Iranian moderates through the UN and other third parties, nor imposing economic sanctions, nor (at one point) launching an ill-fated rescue mission, worked. In a deliberate snub to the departing president, the hostages were finally released only hours after Jimmy Carter left the White House, as Ronald Reagan—promising to renew American power and its sense of patriotism and vitality—took the reins of power.

Behind the Iran hostage crisis lay one of the most embarrassing and ultimately eventful intelligence failures in the history of the United States. The CIA failed to predict the downfall of Mohammed Reza Pahlavi, the Shah of Iran, a leader allied with the United States who for a number of years had found it increasingly difficult to maintain his grip on the country. The Shah had been placed in office following a CIA-inspired coup in 1953, which deposed the democratically elected Mohammed Mossadegh. Although by the 1970s the Shah's hold on the country was getting more and more tenuous—he had resorted by this time to the use of brutal secret police tactics to maintain that slippery hold—many in the U.S. intelligence community apparently believed up until the very last moment that the Shah would survive the profound undercurrent of discontent with his leadership. Embarrassingly, Carter even made an address on December 31, 1977 in which he described Iran as "an island of stability in one of the more troubled regions of the world." In August 1978, a draft version of the annual National Intelligence Estimate (NIE) predicted that the Shah would survive for another ten years. And on December 12 of that year, Carter stated that "I fully expect the Shah to maintain power in Iran … the predictions of doom and disaster that come from some sources have certainly not been realized at all" (quoted in Bill 1988, 259). On January 16, 1979, barely one month after Carter's "'doom and disaster'" quote, just five months after the NIE, and less than thirteen months after the President's "'island of stability'" speech, the Shah would flee the country and go into exile. On February 1, Ayatollah Khomeini arrived at Tehran airport to the jubilation of a fanatical welcoming crowd, estimated by some to number six million people. Khomeini's arrival signaled the emergence of a new chapter in Iran's history and the beginning of what is now commonly known as the Islamic Revolution in the region.

Decision-making about the Shah was characterized by flawed and dysfunctional interagency processes, and Carter generally received poor and only intermittent advice about Iran (Moens 1991). And if the president did not exhibit much understanding of what was transpiring within the country, neither, it must be conceded, did the U.S. intelligence community. Stansfield Turner, then CIA director, later admitted:

> We let him down badly with respect to our coverage of the Iranian scene. We had not appreciated how shaky the Shah's political foundation was; did not know that the Shah was terminally ill; did not understand who Khomeini was and the support his movement had; did not have a clue as to who the hostage-takers were or what their objective was; and could not pinpoint within the embassy where

the hostages were being held and under what conditions. As far as our failure to judge the Shah's position more accurately, we were just plain asleep (Turner 2005, 180).

James Bill traces the complacent attitude among Iranian experts within the CIA to what he calls "the supershah myth." Many American intelligence officials who had spent time in Iran came to see Pahlavi as a permanent and unmovable fixture within the Iranian political system. To those who had done several tours of Iran and had seen the Shah shake hands with presidents from Eisenhower to Carter, "the Shah seemed to have been around forever," Bill notes. "They had witnessed his many close brushes with disaster and had come to view him as indestructible. They could not envisage an Iran without the Shah" (Bill 1988, 403). Similarly, ignorance of Khomeini and his objectives even seems to have been widespread among U.S.-based academics working on the Middle East. While some of them—most notably Richard Cottam, a longtime expert on Iran and professor at the University of Pittsburgh—knew all about Khomeini,[1] others had no idea who he was. Bernard Lewis, a professor of Middle Eastern Affairs at Princeton University later to achieve renown as an informal adviser to Vice President Dick Cheney, has admitted that he knew very little about Khomeini before the latter's return to Tehran. Lewis recalls that in early 1979 he went straight to his university library to look Khomeini up, finding a book by Khomeini he had never read before called *Islamic Government*.

Having gotten Iran wrong the first time, President Carter was somewhat quicker this time to appreciate the formidable risk that admitting the Shah to the United States might cause a backlash among Iranian radicals, especially the possibility of violent moves against American citizens living in Iran. After fleeing Iran in January, the Shah moved through a succession of countries in search of a safe haven. Heading first for Egypt and then Morocco, the Carter administration reluctantly agreed to allow him to enter the United States after it was learned that the longtime American ally was suffering from cancer. Carter had consistently opposed allowing the Shah to enter in the face of determined pressure from powerful friends like Henry Kissinger, and the President was effectively the "last holdout" within the administration on this issue. Rather presciently, Carter foresaw trouble ahead, although this was one instance where the President was well advised; numerous experts on Iran, as well as key U.S. diplomatic staff stationed in Tehran, had warned that the embassy might well be attacked if the Shah was admitted (Pollack 2004, 160). As Carter recalls in his memoirs, he agreed very reluctantly to allow the Shah to come to New York for medical treatment. But he rather pointedly, and with obvious annoyance, asked his advisers in a meeting held on October 19, 1979 "what course they would recommend to me if the Americans in Iran were seized or killed" (Carter 1982, 455).

THE HOSTAGES ARE TAKEN

Instinctively, Carter turned to negotiation and diplomacy as his first or "default" policy in attempting to get the hostages back. While a variety of diplomatic and economic measures were employed to try to get Khomeini to sanction the release of the hostages, the primary technique was to reach out to the regime by setting up some sort of direct or indirect negotiation channel. Initially, the direct route was tried. Carter sent the congressional staffer William Miller and former U.S. cabinet member Ramsay Clark to Iran in the hope that they would be able to talk to the Ayatollah directly. Clark was an outspoken former attorney general from the Johnson years whose vocal criticisms of past American foreign policies were mistakenly thought to lend him some sort of credibility with Islamic revolutionaries, but Khomeini simply refused to meet with either Miller or Clark. Later on, Carter sought the intercession of the UN Secretary General Kurt Waldheim; while Waldheim did visit Tehran, he was similarly unsuccessful in setting up a negotiation channel, and he reportedly felt lucky afterwards to have made it out of Tehran alive. The White House Chief of Staff Hamilton Jordan then tried to create an alternative channel using two lawyers who were said to have some access to Khomeini. At the same time, the administration tried to open talks by using U.S. academics with in-depth experience of Iranian affairs, most notably Richard Cottam. All of these attempts came to naught, however. The strongest ties America possessed were to Iranian moderates, but the latter were increasingly not in control of events within Iran.

By March 1980—clearly exasperated and falling behind in the polls during an election year—President Carter was finally losing patience with these attempts to open negotiations. The underlying problem was that for much of this period there was no recognized Iranian government with which to negotiate, and consequentially no political authority with both the will and the capacity to hand the hostages back. Khomeini in particular had no political incentive to talk to the United States about the hostage issue; in fact, the hostages were a valuable political tool in his attempt to wrest control of the government from more moderate elements within Iranian society. Although the Ayatollah was enormously popular at the time, and while broad anti-Shah and anti-U.S. sentiment certainly existed within Iran, it was by no means preordained that Khomeini would be able to create an Islamic state under his control. First he had to defeat or sideline other anti-Shah forces such as secular nationalists and pro-democratic moderates, and the presence of U.S. hostages in the embassy as a symbol of "'the Great Satan'" and reminder of past American involvement in internal Iranian affairs was a useful tool in this struggle.[2] While there is little evidence that Ayatollah Khomeini sanctioned the seizure of the embassy beforehand, he was certainly aware of the political utility of the whole event once it had gone ahead. He is said to have told Iran's president at the time, for instance, that the seizing of the hostages "has many benefits. ... This has united our people. Our opponents do not dare act against us. We can put the constitution to the people's vote without difficulty, and carry out presidential and parliamentary elections" (Moin 1999, 228).

Secretary of State Cyrus Vance reasoned that it was highly unlikely that Khomeini would do anything to harm the hostages, given the enormous political value they held for him; he also believed that the hostages would be released as soon as their political value dissipated (that is, as soon as Khomeini's political grip on Iran was consolidated). Faced with this seemingly endless and intractable situation, however, President Carter began to seriously consider giving the go-ahead for a bold but risky rescue mission. The mission had been planned from the first days of the hostage crisis as a contingency measure, to be used in the event that the hostages were harmed by their captors. Early on, it had been ruled out as virtually impossible to do by the Pentagon. Almost all rescue operations to that point had been conducted at airports, for instance, making it relatively easy to fly a rescue team in and then extract the hostages. The U.S. embassy, on the other hand, was in the center of a densely populated city, teeming with people and in the grip of a revolution. Could such a mission be done quickly and quietly enough to avoid starting a war?

Moreover, Tehran was then thousands of miles away from any American military base, meaning that a rescue force would have to fly enormous distances to even get close to the hostage site. The location of the hostages meant that helicopters would have to be used, but the helicopters that the Pentagon possessed were not designed to fly such great distances; some unorthodox means would have to be found to refuel them, presumably within Iran itself. There was also very little human intelligence available on the precise whereabouts of the hostages; many of the CIA's representatives on the ground were themselves hostages inside the embassy, and the agency could not guarantee that the embassy officials were all still inside the walls of the building. While they could provide the president with abundant satellite images showing that the building was still standing, that was about the limit of the intelligence they could provide. One participant later recalled that "we had a zillion shots of the roof of the embassy ... anything you wanted to know about the external aspects of that embassy we could tell you in infinite detail. We couldn't tell you shit about what was going on inside that building" (Emerson 1988, 20; Vandenbrouke, 127).

A small, secretive group of planners had gone to work on these various problems, and by early 1980 the four-man planning group—usually composed only of the National Security Adviser Zbigniew Brzezinski, CIA Director Stansfield Turner, Defense Secretary Harold Brown, and Chairman of the Joint Chiefs David Jones—believed that they had come up with an operation which could overcome all or most of these difficulties. As Brzezinski later put it, "our target was far from the United States, remote from any American-controlled facilities, and helicopters were not usually used for long-distance assault missions," but "the military went to work overcoming these difficulties" (Brzezinski 1982, 28). At first they gave active consideration to the idea of smuggling a military rescue team into Iran man by man. This was an idea modeled on a successful but much smaller operation masterminded by the Texan billionaire H. Ross Perot. In February 1979, shortly after the Iranian revolution began, Perot had ordered the rescue of two of his employees being held in an Iranian prison. The rescue team had entered the Tehran airport one by one using fake passports. The two employees were spirited away while a diversion was created, and the rescue team and hostages then left Iran by sneaking over the border.

On November 12, 1979, the planning group actively considered putting Delta Force into Iran the way Perot had suggested—indeed, members of the group even discussed such an idea with Perot himself—but it soon became clear that the operation they had in mind was of such a substantially larger scale that the rescue team would be easily detected by passport authorities in Iran. There were far more hostages, and the rescue team would have to be much bigger than Perot's had been. This meant that a more conventional military approach, involving planes and helicopters, would have to be used. But that created further difficulties. Where would the rescue team land within Iran? And if helicopters were to be used in the raid, how would they be refueled? It was soon realized that the secrecy of the operation might be compromised by problems encountered at this stage. Eventually, therefore, the planners settled on a site in Iran's Dasht-E-Kavir desert. One stretch of this desert was flat and firm enough to land aircraft on; moreover, it had the advantage of not needing to be seized by force (Gabriel 1985, 88). "Desert One," as the location would become known, was by no means a perfect choice, since the stretch of sand the planners identified adjoined a main road regularly used by Iranian vehicles, but it appeared to the group to carry relatively *less* risk of jeopardizing mission security. It was selected as the initial landing site for the rescue force and the place where the helicopters would refuel prior to proceeding with the main part of the mission.

Many of the CIA's top agents in Iran were *themselves* hostages, and so intelligence contacts had to be built up from scratch in Iran; so too did the gathering of precise intelligence on the hostages' whereabouts, but by January 1980 the CIA was at last "reasonably sure" that all the hostages were being held within the embassy compound (Turner 1991, 87). The plan as it evolved would have to be highly complex, and large transport aircraft as well as helicopters would have to be involved in the long-distance operation. The mission would be exceptionally risky *and* especially demanding for the pilots. Under cover of darkness and avoiding Iranian radar, eight RH-53D helicopters would fly from the aircraft carrier USS *Nimitz* to Desert One. There the eight helicopters would meet up with eight waiting *Hercules* C-130 transport planes, which had flown in secretly from Masirah Island in Oman. The C-130s would carry fuel for the helicopters as well as the substantial rescue team needed to extract the hostages from the embassy. Having refueled the helicopters, the plan was to have the rescue team spend the next day at a secret hideout codenamed "Desert Two." After nightfall, they would transfer to vans and trucks, which had been procured in Iran by local U.S. agents and then storm the embassy in downtown Tehran. If all went well, they would take the hostages to a nearby football stadium, where they would be met by the refueled helicopters. The hostages would then be flown out of Iran and into safety. Impressed by the extensive planning that had gone on during the previous few months, President Carter gave the final go-ahead for the mission at three critical meetings held on March 22, April 11, and April 15, 1980.

As the reader will have already surmised, the operation required a large measure of luck since it contained a considerable number of moving parts, each of which had to come together perfectly for the mission to be a success. The central problems the planners had faced—the absence of an airport or landing place near the embassy, the absence of a convenient refueling point, the distances involved, and the problem of getting the rescue force into Tehran undetected and then out again—had been overcome on paper but only at the cost of generating an incredibly complex operation, which depended on every single stage going exactly to plan. This made the whole enterprise even more risky, since only one element of the plan had to go wrong for the whole mission to be jeopardized.

Operation Eagle Claw finally went ahead on April 24, 1980. In a series of fiascoes which almost immediately drew comparisons with the Bay of Pigs operation, almost everything that *could* go wrong with the mission *did* in fact go wrong (Taylor 1980; see also chap. 5). Two of the original eight helicopters developed mechanical problems before they even reached Desert One; one of these had to be abandoned in the Iranian desert when it malfunctioned, while another encountered such a severe dust storm that it almost crashed, and its pilot decided to return to the Aircraft Carrier *Nimitz* shortly thereafter. To make matters worse, there was an almost inexplicable miscalculation involving the journey of the C-130s from Oman to Desert One, and the planes entered Iranian airspace while it was still daylight rather than under the cover of darkness. The remaining six helicopters— the minimum required to transport the hostages and rescue team back to safety— all arrived at Desert One an hour late. Other near-disasters then followed. Since the landing site was very close to an unexpectedly busy main road, members of the rescue team were forced to shoot out the tires of an Iranian bus which passed alongside the landing site and take its passengers hostage.[3]

All of this was bad enough, but there was far worse to come. Once at Desert One, the C-130s and RH-53Ds together created a massive dust storm and an almost deafening amount of noise; indeed, conditions were so bad that members of the rescue force could barely see or hear one another. On arriving at the landing site, moreover, one of the remaining six helicopters developed mechanical difficulties and could no longer be flown. With only five helicopters now available, the mission's de facto on-scene commander Colonel Charles Beckwith was compelled to cancel the mission altogether. As the rescue team prepared to begin the long, demoralizing flight back to base, one of the RH-53D helicopters collided with one of the C-130 transport planes (a direct result of the lack of visibility created by the sandstorm). Eight U.S. servicemen died in the resulting explosion and fire, and a number of others were seriously injured. The following morning, an obviously distraught and sleep-deprived President Carter was compelled to go on live television in the United States announcing the failure of the mission. In gruesome fashion, supporters of the Ayatollah triumphantly displayed the remains of the deceased Americans in the Iranian media.

As one might expect, the postmortems began almost immediately in the American media, but there were of course also more formal internal investigations conducted to determine what had gone wrong. One leading problem was that the planners had been so concerned about operational security (OPSEC) that there had never been a full-scale dress rehearsal prior to the mission. In previous rescue operations (the Son Tay raid of 1970, conducted behind enemy lines in North Vietnam, provides one example), the rescue team had been permitted to train as a single unit and in a single location. In this instance. though, the planning group was so concerned about the prospect that the operation might leak that such a rehearsal was never permitted, but it obviously had deadly consequences. Had the whole team come together at a practice site in the United States—say, for instance, at a remote spot in the deserts of Arizona or Nevada—the sandstorm created by the rescue force itself might well have been foreseen long before it ever reached Desert One.

The official postmortem report chaired by Admiral James Holloway found that "critical concern for OPSEC at all levels tended to dominate every aspect of mission planning, training and execution. From the outset, task force members were imbued with the absolute need for total secrecy. Planning was strictly compartmentalized; plans review was performed largely by those involved in the planning process; individuals were generally restricted to that information they actually required to play their particular roles." Another result of the overriding concern with OPSEC was that it led to an almost obsessive desire to keep the number of planes and helicopters small. As the Holloway report states, "there were pressures clearly felt by all involved to keep the force small in order to decrease the risk of detection" (Special Operations Review Group, 13). The obsession with secrecy also led to an unwillingness to subject the final plan to the scrutiny of outside experts, and it was the overriding emphasis on this factor that led to a desire on Zbigniew Brzezinski's part to plan the mission within a very small and insulated group, which bypassed a vast reservoir of organizational expertise within the administration. Serious discussion of military options was avoided in the full NSC meetings, the progress of the rescue planning process was a closely guarded secret known only to a handful of people, and the whole decision-making process was compartmentalized into two rival tracks, one based on negotiation and the other on the rescue mission. This meant that those who were primarily concerned with one track had little knowledge of what those working on the other track were doing.

Many media commentators and former policymakers expressed surprise that the mission had gone ahead at all. According to Philip Keisling, "its failure had almost been assured by the military's process of planning the raid, analyzing it for defects, and choosing the man to lead it. The military systematically ignored or downplayed intelligence that suggested the difficulty—if not the impossibility—of the task. The plan for the raid ... violated a fundamental tenet of military strategy, which holds that the possibility of failure increases exponentially with a plan's complexity and size" (Keisling 1983, 52). In similar vein Colin Powell, during the hostage crisis a military assistant at the Pentagon but not privy to the planning itself, later voiced a number of criticisms from a military viewpoint:

> Helicopters are notoriously temperamental. For a mission this demanding of men and machines, far more than eight helos should have been launched to make sure

that six would still be airworthy to carry out the demanding second leg of the mission. Desert One also erred in counting on a "pickup" team drawn from all four services and brought together just for this mission in which men from one service flew helicopters of another. Weaknesses in the chain of command, communications, weather forecasting, and security further contributed to the failure" (Powell 1995, 249).

Still others attribute the failure of the operation to a misguided faith in the power of technology to overcome military and political problems. As a former engineer who was widely seen as believing that science could solve any problem, President Carter was especially open to this kind of criticism. Daniel Greenberg, for instance, opined not long after the failure of the mission that "the risks and consequences of something going wrong get much bigger when desperate politicians turn hopefully to 'technological fixes' for difficult political problems." In the United States, he argued, there is a particular cultural belief in these kinds of solutions, a popular notion that "clever and vigorous application of far-out techniques and equipment can bring a desired solution out of an otherwise intractable problem" (Greenberg 1980).

What would have happened had the rescue mission *not* run aground at Desert One is probably anyone's guess. Some of the hostages, on hearing much later the details of how a plan to rescue them had gone badly awry, expressed relief that it had gone no farther. But the planners were exceptionally confident that the later stages would be the easiest once the rescue team had been infiltrated. Brzezinski and Jones, for instance, both expressed the view at a critical NSC meeting held on March 22 that "the extraction of the hostages was probably the easiest part of the operation" (Sick 1985, 223). Why the planners were so confident remains something of a mystery, but part of the explanation probably relates to the preparations that the CIA had already made for the rescue force. We know, for instance, that the retired U.S. military operative Richard Meadows had been sent into Tehran in advance to supervise the Iranian agents, and that he had already obtained a hideout and purchased the trucks that would transport the rescuers into the city. The CIA might have obtained the agreement of moderates to "look the other way" while the raid was launched. According to Amir Taheri, there was a team of locals in place, which "consisted of four air officers who had trained in San Antonio, Texas, and twenty-five cashiered members of the Imperial Guard who believed they were recruited for an anti-Khomeini operation, which was to serve as a prelude to a coup d'etat." Apparently, the four officers would have been airlifted out of Iran with the embassy hostages (Taheri 1988, 133). While the details remain sketchy at the time of writing, it is clear that some arrangement along these lines must have been made in advance.

EXPLAINING CARTER'S DECISIONS

Can the decisions that Carter and his advisers arrived at during the Iran hostage crisis be defended as comprehensively rational? It might seem to the reader that the answer must inevitably be no. Surely it was less than rational for Carter to spend so much time attempting to negotiate with a government which did not yet exist; surely it was irrational to launch a rescue operation whose chance of success seemed so low even at the time; and surely it was also irrational for the President to devote so much of his time to this issue, elevating in the eyes of the public an issue which he probably should have handled more quietly behind the scenes. When we make assessments like these, we are referring to the concept of *substantive rationality*. Viewed from our perspective today and with the benefit of hindsight, the decisions Carter reached may seem to us irrational in some ways. But that does not mean that his decision-making processes were flawed. Perhaps, based on the information he and his colleagues possessed at the time, the decisions he reached were in fact quite rational.

While certainly entertaining from the perspective of the armchair historian, debating this issue is inevitably going to be a fruitless exercise in the sense that supporters of the RAM approach can always retrospectively defend *any* decision as substantively rational, even when the decision (as we saw in chap. 7) involved a choice that led to the deaths of 58,000 Americans and millions of Vietnamese. It is ultimately more useful, then, to examine whether the decision-making might be portrayed as *procedurally rational*; we might examine, in other words, whether a thorough review of goals and objectives was conducted. Having established an objective, were all the conceivable options for addressing the issue fully canvassed and the costs and benefits of each thoroughly weighed?

From one perspective, the answer appears to be yes. One might contend that the decisions to negotiate and then to mount a rescue mission were rational in the sense that *all* feasible options were considered and the merits of each weighed. On November 6, 1979, for instance, a number of critical meetings were held, which would set the agenda for much of the later discussion and debate. The first full meeting of the NSC on the hostage issue took place that afternoon, and the battle lines began to be drawn in a crisis which would drag on for 444 days. Cyrus Vance made it clear from the outset that he favored a negotiated settlement to resolve the crisis, while Zbigniew Brzezinski argued for a more forceful stance. At this meeting and the one that preceded it, Vance suggested two options which might be used to pressure the Iranians into releasing the hostages: (1) encouraging the Shah to leave the United States, and (2) negotiating with Khomeini.

Brzezinski focused instead on possible military options, suggesting a number of alternatives, which included a military rescue mission. Added to Vance's proposals, this gave the decision-makers a list of seven options to consider:

1. Encourage the Shah to leave United States.
2. Negotiate with Khomeini.
3. Institute a naval blockade of Iran.
4. Launch an air strike on the oil refinery at Abadan.
5. Mine the Iranian harbors.
6. Seize the oil depots on Iran's Kharg Island.
7. Launch a rescue mission.

Weighing the seven options, only items two and seven seemed likely to result in the direct release of the hostages. Negotiation, a RAM approach might point out, was chosen initially because it was the only alternative that could conceivably release the hostages, or because it achieved the benefit sought at the least cost. Arguably, the rescue mission option—the only other alternative judged likely to result in the release of the hostages—was later resorted to when, and only when, it actually became feasible, and when a reasonable cost-benefit analysis suggested that it had more chance of gaining the hostages' release than did continued negotiation.

Broadly speaking, then, *Homo Economicus* appears to offer us a satisfactory account of the decision-making. This approach is lacking in at least two ways, though. First of all, this is largely a descriptive account of the decision-making, rather than an explanation for it. It is empty in the sense that it largely fails to tell us *why* the decision-makers came to view negotiation and the rescue mission as the only feasible or workable options, and *why* the costs associated with these were considered relatively lower than those of the rival alternatives. By offering no clues as to what determined the content of the decisions reached, the RAM in effect provides us with only a superficial account of what occurred as opposed to the more thoroughgoing explanation we are looking for. While *Homo Economicus* simply takes actors' preferences as given ("they are what they are"). our three alternative models or perspectives seek to uncover the source of these preferences and the ways in which decision-making processes biased the reception of various options one way or another.

Second, it is also not entirely clear that the costs and benefits of all available options in the early meetings *were* comprehensively weighed in the manner that *Homo Economicus* expects. Some of the options in the list seem to have been examined in only a very cursory way, not least because the President thought of most of these as punitive measures which could be taken if negotiation did not succeed or in the event that some of the hostages were killed by their captors. These options were also not fully discussed because of the initial expectation that the crisis would soon be over. As Stansfield Turner notes, "there was almost no interest" in these options at the November 6 meetings (Turner 1991, 32). Presenting the military alternatives to the SCC and NSC, Secretary Harold Brown merely "ticked off several possibilities," recorded the NSC notetaker Gary Sick. In fact, according to Turner, military options other than a rescue were discussed "only once" at the NSC, SCC, and rescue planning group sessions at which he was present *during the entire hostage crisis* (Sick 1985, 245; Turner 1991, 72). A naval blockade might have bought the President time on this issue—just as it had for Kennedy during the Cuban missile crisis—but this comparison does not seem to have been raised. Equally, mining Iranian harbors—an option that Turner, as a former U.S. Navy Admiral, secretly favored—might have cut off importation and exportation early on, but there were was very little discussion of this option either. Nor is it clear that the costs and benefits of the rescue mission were fully weighed later on in 1980. The advice of Cyrus Vance against a rescue mission, together with his prescient warnings of imminent military and political disaster, was later ignored by the other decision-makers, and President Carter (as we shall see in the following sections) took the decision to proceed with the operation while Vance was away from Washington. Different members of the bureaucracy were attuned to see different sides of the Iran issue, leading them to offer very contrasting advice to the president. Their differing personal experiences and beliefs also predisposed them to give this contrasting advice.

It is always tempting to dismiss those who criticize operations like the Bay of Pigs and the Iran hostage rescue mission as victims of what Baruch Fischoff termed "hindsight bias," known more colloquially as the tendency to be "wise after the event." As Susan Fiske and Shelley Taylor note, hindsight bias research has shown that "it is very difficult to ignore knowledge of an actual outcome and to generate unbiased inferences about what could or should have happened." We often misremember what we originally thought, believed, or predicted in order to fit the new wisdom that the actual course of events brings (Fiske and Taylor 1984, 376). Nevertheless, as in the Bay of Pigs case, it can be argued that the failure of the operation should have been largely predictable on the basis of facts that were already available to the decision-makers. Cyrus Vance, for instance, argued that even in the event of a successful operation, the Iranians could react by simply taking more Americans hostage. Somewhat bizarrely, there were dozens (and perhaps even hundreds) of U.S. media personnel encamped outside the American embassy in Tehran, there with the tacit approval of whatever Iranian government existed. So even a perfectly executed rescue mission could very easily have led to the seizure of more American hostages, taking Carter and his colleagues right back to square one. Critics of the mission also predicted *prior* to the operation that there were too many moving parts to the plan and that it had a very high probability of failure because of this.

As the reader will certainly by now appreciate, it is often possible to account for the same decision at a number of different levels of analysis, using different kinds of foreign policy decision-making theory. This case study has generated an especially rich array of explanations, many of which can be classified under the headings of our three models. As usual, we begin by examining the kind of organizational-level theories highlighted by *Homo Bureaucraticus,* then turn to the group-based approaches of *Homo Sociologicus* and conclude with an examination of how various perspectives within the *Homo Psychologicus* camp have explained the Iran hostage crisis decision-making.

Homo Bureaucraticus

Although Graham Allison originally developed the theory of bureaucratic politics as an explanation for aspects of the Cuban missile crisis, which seemed puzzling from a RAM or *Homo Economicus* perspective, later scholars working in this area have picked up his mantle and applied the approach to other case studies. It has been used to explain the case of the Iran hostage rescue mission by Steve Smith, for instance (Smith 1984). While he does not attempt to explain the initial decisions Carter reached at the outset of the crisis, Smith offers an account of the decision to mount the rescue mission that follows the Allisonian model quite closely. In particular, he suggests that it is possible to attribute the policy preferences expressed by the leading players primarily to their bureaucratic positions, the famous "where you stand depends on where you sit" axiom. Although Smith admits to harboring some doubts about the perspective's applicability to the case, he nevertheless shows that it is able to account rather well for the viewpoints taken by the various participants in the policy debate about whether to launch the rescue mission. Harold Brown, Zbigniew Brzezinski, David Jones, and Stansfield Turner, for instance, all favored the rescue mission, and their positive stance toward the idea seems to have derived in part from their bureaucratic roles.[4] Smith argues that "the positions adopted by those classified here as 'hawks' could have been predicted in advance. What is striking about the evidence is the consistency with which these four men—Brown, Brzezinski, Jones, and Turner—proposed policies that reflected their position in the bureaucratic network" (ibid. 16).

Then there are the policy positions adopted by the presidential supporters, individuals like the vice president, the White House press secretary, and the White House chief of staff, whose first loyalty is to the president and who are especially attuned to the politics of foreign policy. Steve Smith argues that these three individuals—Walter Mondale, Jody Powell, and Hamilton Jordan—"show that their concern was first and foremost with the effect of the crisis on the Carter presidency," and they tended to advocate whatever they saw as being in the president's domestic political interests (ibid. 17). The evidence does suggest quite strongly that Hamilton Jordan and Jody Powell in particular behaved throughout the crisis in the manner predicted by the bureaucratic politics approach. Jordan always seems to have viewed his role in this way during his time in the Carter administration. He notes, for instance, that at foreign policy meetings "I would try to raise political objections, problems, and concerns with Vance, Brzezinski, and the president as they talked about how they were going to change the world," something he did when Vance suggested that the administration should essentially "wait Khomeini out" on the hostage issue (Jordan 1981, 53). This kind of bureaucratic position may play a particularly powerful role in shaping foreign policy preferences, since it involves a job description or role which is more sharply circumscribed than other positions. It is of course left to the individual to decide what constitutes a defense of the President's interests, so that bureaucratic position may not exert as much predictive power in determining preferences as initial appearances might suggest. Yet being a presidential supporter does appear to exert great influence upon receptivity to the arguments of others (Houghton 2001, 184–85). It is natural for a White House press secretary, for instance, to see foreign policies through the lens of domestic politics, for he or she must constantly defend those policies at the White House podium and must constantly present the president in the best possible light both domestically and to the outside world.

Finally, Smith contends that "the evidence that bureaucratic role determines policy stance is strongest of all in the case of the 'doves': Cyrus Vance, the Secretary of State, and Warren Christopher, the Deputy Secretary of State" (Smith 1985, 8). With the exception of one of two individuals attached to the CIA or Pentagon, the hostages were predominantly State Department employees, and Vance almost certainly felt a special responsibility for his own people. Both Vance and Christopher displayed the commitment to negotiation and diplomacy that one would expect from an Allisonian perspective. At the critical NSC meeting held on April 11, for instance, Christopher sat in for Vance, who was away in Florida. Vance did not know what his boss's feelings were about going ahead with the mission, although he was of course aware of his previous opposition to it. Christopher assumed (erroneously, as it turns out) that Vance must have known that the mission was about to be approved and so was uncertain as to whether the Secretary of State had changed his mind. Christopher nevertheless listed a number of diplomatic alternatives to the mission at the April 11 meeting. These were summarily dismissed by the hawks and the presidential supporters, all of whom felt that the time had come for stronger action.

Conceivably, one could argue that Vance and Brzezinski in particular were predisposed by their bureaucratic positions to see their side of the issue and hence were unreceptive to other views. Nevertheless, they still needed to construct arguments which would sell their favored alternatives to the other decision-makers. If bureaucratic position determines where one stands on a given issue, then the arguments and beliefs of policy actors are more properly seen as *effects* rather than causes; Vance's pro-negotiation stance during the hostage crisis might have been determined by the fact that he headed the State Department and was consciously or unconsciously defending his own bureaucratic corner, in which case one would then expect him to search around for some argument that would support the State Department's stance on this issue (and which might help impress upon other decision-makers the desirability of a nonbelligerent approach to the problem). Decision-makers know that to be seen to defend the narrow, parochial interests of one's own organization over and above the national interest—especially during a major crisis, where such concerns are meant to be held in abeyance—will delegitimize them in the eyes of their colleagues, so alternative justifications must be found that support the same conclusion but then reach it via some more socially respectable route.

To what extent can the hostage rescue mission option be seen as the product of bargaining and compromise? While it is difficult to make the argument that this general option was itself the resultant of bargaining between, say, the CIA and the Pentagon, from a bureaucratic politics angle the decision could easily be seen as stemming from the formation of a coalition between the hawks and the presidential supporters. The hawks had been frustrated by their inability to act early on in the crisis, particularly when it became clear that the U.S. military did not in early November 1979 have the capability to mount a rescue mission in Tehran, and they may have been determined to demonstrate their bureaucratic clout. The presidential supporters, on the other hand, may well have felt the need to do something dramatic in a domestic political sense to stem Carter's rising unpopularity at home. By 1980 the proportion of Americans saying that they approved of president's performance generally had fallen to only 40 percent, and only 30 percent approved when asked about his foreign policy performance in particular. The CBS news anchor Walter Cronkite was signing off his nightly newscast with an announcement of the number of days that the hostages had been held, and over on ABC, a nightly update show presented by Ted Koppel discussed the crisis in depth.[5] Carter was also facing a challenge within his own party for the presidential nomination from Senator Edward Kennedy. By the end of March, Kennedy had won the New York primary by 59 percent to Carter's 41 percent, and on April 22—just two days before the rescue operation went ahead—Kennedy managed a narrower win in Pennsylvania (Gartner 1993). Overall, the presidential supporters in particular must have felt that their backs were very much against the wall by the time that the decision was taken to launch the mission.

In a broader sense, the long-distance nature of the operation was also necessitated by what might be seen as bureaucratic obstinacy. One obvious option would have been to fly in the helicopters from Turkey, a U.S. ally which has a border with Iran; another would have been to fly the aircraft from a carrier stationed in the Persian Gulf. In the end, either of these options would have cut down the distances involved considerably or would have allowed the rescue team to use helicopters they were more accustomed to flying, but both ideas met with bureaucratic resistance. Stansfield Turner later recalled that the Pentagon "refused" to put a carrier in the Persian Gulf, and the State Department "refused" to ask Turkey if a mission could be launched from their soil. The Navy in particular argued that placing a carrier closer to Iran might be too risky and might alert the hostage-takers to the imminent possibility of a rescue mission. Turner argued that the helicopters could take off from NATO bases in Turkey instead, since U.S. aircraft were already stationed there. The State Department objected to the Turkish option, though; they argued that we would have to warn Turkey in advance, and that permission would not be given because both Turkey and Iran are Muslim nations. The CIA wanted to proceed anyway, but State successfully argued that diplomatic relations would be hampered by failing to inform the host nation in advance (Turner 1991, 42–43, 69). In the end, the helicopters were launched from the *Nimitz* in the Gulf of Oman, close to the border between Iran and Pakistan. There was a distance of approximately 1,200 miles from the takeoff point to Desert One, and about 1,600 miles to Tehran from the *Nimitz*.

The notion that intra-Defense bureaucratic politics were at play in generating the precise form the mission took is also plausible, not least because the final operation resembled something of a patchwork quilt. Marine pilots, for instance, were selected to fly the Navy RH-53D minesweeping helicopters used in the rescue operation. This was a problem, however, because the Marines were trained to fly CH-53s (a different model of the same helicopter) and were wholly unfamiliar with the RH-53Ds they were asked to fly. Edward Luttwak notes that personnel from all four services were involved in the mission as a whole, and he suggests that this was primarily due to each agency wanting its piece of the action. "Not one of the services (except the Coast Guard) could be deprived of its share," Luttwak suggests. "The Army, Air Force, Navy, and Marine Corps were all present in the rescue force." If the mission had been planned and executed by a single service, he argues, it would have stood a much greater chance of success. The British, French and Israelis "had learned long ago to avoid any mixture of men," he notes (Luttwak 1984, 44).

Since he felt that the Navy pilots who came with the RH-53Ds were not up to the job, Delta Force commander Colonel Charles Beckwith himself felt that there had to be a mixture of men to some extent, but he also felt that bureaucratic politics lay behind the choice of Marine pilots instead of the Air Force special operations people who had been his first preference. As Mark Bowden puts it:

> The Air Force already had its piece of the mission, flying the fixed wing aircraft. Beckwith suspected, rightly, that the marines were given the choppers to fly to satisfy their need for a role. ... As far as he was concerned, he was getting second-string pilots because the brass was less interested in success than in keeping things collegial in the Pentagon dining halls. This suspicion, that Pentagon politics was being given a higher priority than excellence, would continue to influence morale. Delta believed the men recruited to deliver them and fly them out were not in their league (Bowden 2006, 228).

The insistence of various agencies in being involved—if indeed this is truly what occurred—may have contributed to the failure of the entire operation. This is potentially the dark side of *Homo Bureaucraticus*, suggesting that interorganizational politics can on occasion cost human lives.

Although Beckwith ended up making the decision to abort the mission—or at least recommending to President Carter via General Jones and Harold Brown that the mission be abandoned—there were in fact four military commanders overall in what must have amounted to a confusing leadership structure, especially in the noise and dust of Desert One. This command structure was singled out for particular criticism by the Holloway report. Major General James Vaught of the U.S. Army was officially the mission's commander, working directly under the chairman of the Joint Chiefs. This reflected the Pentagon's SOPs, since it is normal to appoint an overall commander when several agencies within the military are involved (Turner 1991, 68). In a practical sense, however, there was no single military authority in charge. Vaught was in Egypt during the mission and was therefore dependent on the judgment of three other on-site commanders who variously headed the pilots and rescue team: Air Force Colonel James Kyle, Lt. Colonel Edward Seiffert of the Marines, and Army Colonel Beckwith. Kyle, Seiffert, and Beckwith all reported to Vaught by radio, but Vaught does not seem to have made it clear which of the men would make the key decisions on the ground. Nominally, he designated Kyle to play this role rather than Beckwith; Vaught is said to have disapproved of Beckwith's "flamboyant style," since the latter, who was nicknamed "Chargin' Charlie" and had a sign on his desk bearing the legend "Kill 'em All and Let God Sort 'em Out," had a reputation for recklessness. But Kyle does not seem to have believed that he had the authority to give Beckwith or Seiffert orders. There is also some evidence of tension between Beckwith and Kyle, or at least between the rescue team and the pilots. Reportedly, Kyle "told his C-130 pilots not to go near Delta's tent area because he thought the people there were about to explode" (Turner 1991, 138). In the end, it was Beckwith, not Kyle, who made the decision to cancel the mission when things went terribly wrong, but this probably derived more from Beckwith's charisma and appeal to his men than from any organizational chart about who was supposedly in charge.

Homo Sociologicus

Is there any evidence that the Carter decision-makers may have been victims of groupthink as they went about the process of deciding to launch the hostage rescue mission? Irving Janis in the revised (1982) version of his book was the first to suggest that this might indeed be the case. Although Janis does not examine this example as a full-fledged case study in *Groupthink*, he does argue that there are some rather suggestive initial indications of the groupthink syndrome present in the Iran hostage crisis decision-making and that this is therefore a good candidate for further analysis. Noting that Cyrus Vance was excluded from the April 11 meeting, Janis asks the following questions:

> Was Secretary Vance excluded from the crucial meeting in which the final decision was made because, as a lone dissenter who would not give in, he was being "treated as a deviant who was violating the group's norms"? Had those who admitted—after it was too late—that he was raising important objections been suppressing their own doubts, as loyal members of an in-group often do when they are prematurely striving for concurrence rather than for a critical evaluation of the available options? Were other symptoms of groupthink also manifested? These are not intended as rhetorical but as genuine questions that might profitably be pursued along with other key questions essential for a complete examination of the groupthink hypothesis in a detailed case study (Janis 1982, 182).

Janis described the symptoms of groupthink in a newspaper op-ed published shortly after the failure of the rescue mission. "If the dissenter does not give in, he is treated as a deviant who is violating group norms, his advice is ignored, and he may be excluded from the crucial meeting at which the final decision is made (one cannot help but wonder whether the way Cyrus R. Vance was treated was an instance of just such a symptom)," he wrote (Janis 1980, E21). While the author of *Groupthink* never undertook any published attempt to answer questions like these beyond that brief op-ed and a couple of pages in his book, Steve Smith and Betty Glad in particular have both built considerably upon Janis's suggestions (Smith 1984; Glad 1989, 49–53). As the reader will recall, this approach suggests that we can divide most group-level processes into one of two categories: *vigilant* decision-making (which corresponds rather closely to the RAM), and *groupthink*. We have seen that the groupthink effect—a kind of "premature concurrence-seeking"—typically occurs where opinionated leaders, the pressure to maintain unanimity, and the exclusion of outside advice combine to ensure that the full range of policy alternatives is not fully or rationally appraised. An analyst approaching this case would look for a number of symptoms which aid identification of the syndrome, including the exclusion of dissent, the emergence of one or more mindguards who police the decision-making process, a belief in the inherent morality of the group, and a belief in the group's invulnerability.

According to Smith, there is a strong case to be made that the decision to launch the rescue mission derived, at least in part, from groupthink. First of all, he notes, "it is evident that those who made the decisions did not critically evaluate the probability of success. The mission was an extremely risky one, and because those who made the decisions wanted a rescue attempt to go ahead, they did not look at the very obvious weak points in the plan" (Smith 1984, 118). There is evidence that the group shared an illusion of invulnerability, which led it to take reckless risks, that it viewed itself as inherently moral, and that dissent was internally suppressed. There is also evidence of the kind of assertive leadership that breeds conformist group behavior. Glad notes that while Carter usually employed rather exhaustive decision-making procedures, often letting debate go on too long for the taste of some group participants, he deviated from this pattern in the rescue mission case. For example, on April 11, 1980—the key decision point in the rescue mission deliberations—the President began the meeting by announcing that he was "seriously considering an attempt to rescue the hostages," adding that the experts working on the plan were now confident that it could succeed (Glad 1989, 49). Although the decision-makers went through the motions of a group discussion, it was apparent to many of the members that the President had already made up his mind.

Smith and Glad also find compelling evidence that dissenters from the majority view were excluded from the group and that their advice was discounted when they were included. With respect to the exclusion of dissenting advice, Smith notes that the decision of April 11 was taken while Vance—known to disagree with the notion of launching the operation—was on vacation in Florida. Smith infers from this that Carter used Vance's absence as a kind of bureaucratic opportunity, a chance to push ahead knowing that no one else would speak out against the decision. While it is difficult to tell at this point whether this claim is true, it is certainly an extraordinary coincidence that Carter picked this precise moment to give the go-ahead; after all, Vance was in Florida for only a very brief vacation of no more than a couple of days. As already noted, he was replaced at the April 11 meeting by Warren Christopher, Deputy Secretary of State, who was uncertain as to how he should proceed. As Smith notes, Christopher "was shocked to find that the rescue mission was to go ahead, and assumed that his boss had accepted it" (Smith 1984, 120). While he fully realized that his boss was opposed to the mission, he nevertheless went along with the plan. Christopher reminded the group that various diplomatic avenues remained and stressed that these had not yet been exhausted, but the available record suggests that he was simply shot down on this.

When Vance found out about the meeting, he was angered and amazed that a decision of this importance had been taken in his absence. Given the opportunity on April 15 to express his doubts about the decision, Vance made a number of arguments that seem rather prescient in retrospect:

First, "I was very worried about the helicopters," he remembers. "It was entirely possible that we weren't going to be able to get in there without losing some helicopters, and what then?"; second, "I was also very concerned that if we did get in, that we would have to bomb, and if we bombed, then the consequences of that in terms of the response that would take place"; third, Vance worried that "we would have to do this without notifying our allies—particularly the British—about this, and I knew that this would have a very negative effect"; fourth, "I was also worried about what the effects might be in so far as what the Russians would do in response to this"; fifth, "the climate which we were involved in at that particular period of time, the whole situation in that part of the Middle East, was extremely fragile, and that we might indeed cause a real breakout of major warfare. That worried me a lot." For Vance, these five concerns added up to an inescapable conclusion: "when you look at all of these things, you couldn't help but come to the conclusion that this is something that cannot and should not be done, because it's against the national interest. That was my view, and I said what my strong views were" (Houghton 2001, 129).

No one spoke up to support Vance, though. The participants in the meetings have described what followed as a painful silence, and it was if the members were simply going through the motions: listening to the Secretary of State because he was someone who deserved a hearing rather than attending to the substance of his arguments. Moreover, once Vance had tendered his resignation in protest at the decision, it became easy for the other group members to dismiss him as someone who wanted to resign anyway. Vance had previously talked of serving only one term as secretary of state, and it must have been relatively easy to downplay the nature of his dissent for this reason. As Glad has noted, the one factor most consistent with the groupthink hypothesis in the Iran case is the fact that "Vance's views were dealt with by deprecating Vance–a man most other observers would describe as unusually mature in his ability to hold firmly to positions he felt right. At this time, however, Jordan saw him as a pathetic figure—alone, isolated—his eyes begging for support. The president saw him as 'emotionally overwrought'". Similarly, National Security Adviser Brzezinski viewed Vance as 'traumatized' (Glad 1989, 51). Thus, two processes seem to have occurred in parallel with one another, each of which had the effect of undermining Vance's dissent: one a presumably conscious attempt to take advantage of his physical absence, the other a probably more unconscious attempt to downplay the substance of his advice by deprecating Vance himself.

Last, Smith suggests that at least one "self-appointed mindguard" emerged to bolster the decision to go ahead with the military rescue: Stansfield Turner, who was one of the advocates of the mission. Turner apparently suppressed a long-infamous March 1980 CIA report which suggested that 60 percent of the hostages would lose their lives if the mission went ahead (see Salinger 1981, 237–38). Smith rightly notes that "there is no record of Turner raising this report at any of the meetings," and Turner has subsequently confirmed that he never showed it to President Carter (Smith 1984, 122; Houghton 2001, 188–89). As Smith suggests, there is a real possibility that in failing to pass on the CIA report, which suggested that the mission was just as likely to fail completely as it was to succeed completely, Turner might have been playing just this kind of subtle mindguard role, protecting the group from any unfavorable information that might challenge the prevailing consensus. The reader will recall from chapter 5 that Dean Rusk, as secretary of state, is said to have done something similar when confronted by a memorandum from his deputy Chester Bowles; Bowles criticized the Bay of Pigs plan on a number of counts, but there is no evidence that Rusk ever showed this memorandum to the President. From the perspective of *Homo Sociologicus*, the fact that the CIA report remained in Turner's desk and was never shown to anyone outside the agency evokes an eerie parallel with Kennedy's Cuban fiasco of 1961. Equally, the way in which Vance was written off personally and his advice downplayed as the product of a man under great psychological strain is highly reminiscent of the way Lyndon Johnson is said to have treated Vance's former boss Robert McNamara on the issue of Vietnam. As we saw in chapter 7, LBJ described McNamara in 1968 as "just short of cracking up" and compared him to a son telling prospective purchasers of the family house that there are leaks in the basement.

Homo Psychologicus

Did personal beliefs, personalities, experiences, and other psychological factors stemming directly from the individual play a more powerful role in Iran decision-making than bureaucratic politics or group-based perspectives would suggest? As the reader will have guessed by now, from the perspective of *Homo Psychologicus* the answer would obviously be yes. Unlike the RAM, proponents of this approach would concede that the bureaucratic politics approach does at least offer us a theory as to *why* given actors propose the policy positions they do and of *who* is likely to propose what position. However, they suggest that both Rational Actor Model and bureaucratic politics perspectives share a common failing, in the sense that, as Robert Axelrod has written, neither provides any clear account of just how decision-makers estimate the probability that a given policy option will succeed or fail (Axelrod 1977, 728). *Homo Sociologicus*, on the other hand, is silent altogether on the question of where leaders' preferences come from; it merely suggests that once a given option has been selected, perhaps by an overassertive leader, it can be very difficult in certain groups to reverse course or reconsider options that were initially rejected.

The *Homo Psychologicus* camp is far less dominated by a single theoretical approach than the other two, and it is more internally diverse as a result. In fact, at least three different approaches within this general perspective have been offered to try to account for Jimmy Carter's decision-making during the hostage crisis: one examines the personality and beliefs of Jimmy Carter himself, another uses prospect theory to explain why Carter decided to go ahead with the rescue mission, and a third (like the approach offered by Khong in chap. 7) focuses on analogical reasoning and other cognitive processes of the key decision-makers. We will take each approach in turn.

One traditional if rather controversial form of individual-level explanation centers on the *personality traits* of leaders (see, e.g., George and George 1964). In the Iran case, Betty Glad has proposed that Jimmy Carter's personality—and in particular what she terms his "ego-defensive" traits—caused him to act rashly in proposing the hostage rescue mission. Although she does see positive aspects to his personality, Glad argues that Carter dramatically "overplayed" the situation. His "narcissistic, expansionist personality structure" led him to become obsessed by the hostage issue, elevating it to a point where it became self-defeating. He launched the rescue mission, she suggests, in large part because he was a "risk taker" who flirted with danger, arguing that "expansionist types, with their seem-ingly boundless self-confidence, are apt to take risks, where others fear to tread." Carter also exhibited a "self-defeating self-centeredness" (Glad 1989, 54–55). Where Smith traces the failure to fully consider the defects inherent in the rescue mission solely to groupthink, for Glad this failing derived at least equally from flaws within Carter himself. "The processes he set up for planning the rescue operation ... almost guaranteed that vulnerabilities in the operation would not be seriously explored. Certain problems that might have been discovered were not corrected, and the decision was made without a clear understanding of the risks it entailed. ... Carter's personal interests and distinctive style and personality led to these results," she concludes (ibid. 58)

Glad's analysis is not exclusively individual level as we have seen, but much of her work suggests the power of personality in decision-making. In this instance, she contends that the decision to mount the rescue mission was primarily related to Carter's personality, and that a different personality might have led to different policy choices and a different reaction to the external and domestic constraints that Carter faced. In a similar kind of analysis that reaches a rather different conclusion, James David Barber argues that Carter's handling of the hostage crisis issue was essentially a success, and attributes this to what he sees as the strength of the president's per-sonality. "The Carter character was, I think, severely tested by the Iranian hostage crisis and not found wanting. ... Unlike Wilson, Hoover, Johnson, and Nixon, this president did not freeze onto some disastrous line of policy and ride it to the end. Rather he kept his head, kept his mind open, flexibly and energetically pursuing some way out of an apparently success-proof situation." While Barber admits that Carter made mistakes, he argues that "he could have done a great deal worse." All in all, he claims, Carter had the best kind of personality for the job of president: he was what Barber calls an "active-positive," someone who both works hard in the Oval Office and derives positive enjoyment from the role (Barber 1985, 456–57).

It is also probably impossible to understand Jimmy Carter's overall approach to the Iran hostage crisis without recognizing the powerful moral beliefs that ani-mated him as president. As Erwin Hargrove states, for Carter "religious faith was central to his life. Faith shaped his understanding of himself and others, his belief about the political purposes of government, and his style of authority ... he saw politics as a moral activity" (Hargrove 1988, 8). He instinctively opposed the use of military force, at least as a first resort. He was also driven by idealism or liberalism in foreign policy, which led him to prefer negotiation and the pursuit of human rights as a policy goal. Carter famously remarked at a White House meeting in 1978 that "human rights are the soul of our foreign policy, because human rights are the very soul of our sense of nationhood." Carter's actions early in the crisis, especially to negotiate rather than bombing Tehran, are obviously compatible with these beliefs. A strong argument can be made that the ideological worldviews or belief systems of Vance and Brzezinski in particular also predisposed them toward the positions they took during the crisis. Brzezinski was known for his hawkish worldview, which probably would have prevailed irrespective of the bureaucratic position he happened to occupy within the administration. And we know that Vance's doveish worldview predisposed him against any use of military force to resolve the crisis, and he too would probably have clung to his existing views regardless of the bureaucratic position he held.

Both poliheuristic theory and prospect theory have been employed in recent years in the effort to understand why Jimmy Carter rather uncharacteristically decided to launch a military rescue mission to save the hostages. Recalling the discussion from chapter 4, remember that in poliheuristic theory, decision-making is a two stage process in which options are first ruled out using simple heuristics or shortcuts and then the remaining options are assessed more systematically for the costs and benefits they seem to imply. Using this kind of approach, it has been argued that Carter first of all ruled out all options that would have been unacceptable in terms of domestic politics, and then went ahead with a rescue mission when he calculated that this was the best option available in terms of both costs and benefits (Brulé 2005).

The reader will recall from chapter 4 that in order to use prospect theory, we need to know whether the decision-maker (to use McDermott's vivid analogy) is feeling 'hot' or 'cold'. In other words, is the policymaker operating in a domain of gains, like a gambler on a lucky streak, or a domain of loss where everything is going wrong? In the case of Carter in March and April 1980, it seems rather easy to gauge the president's subjective assessment in this regard, and McDermott has used this to apply prospect theory to the decision to mount the hostage rescue mission. Summarized briefly, she argues that Carter was clearly operating in a domain of losses by March 1980, and this made him acceptant of risks that he would not have undertaken—and obviously did not undertake—when the hostages were first seized in November 1979. Carter's personal popularity was in sharp decline five months into the crisis, he had just lost two presidential primaries to Senator Edward Kennedy, and negotiations seemed to have run aground. "By the time of the rescue mission," McDermott suggests, "Carter was a leader ready to take a gamble to return things to the status quo, with the hostages safely at home, national pride and international honor restored, and his political fortunes turned upward ... in terms of prospect theory, he was a man operating in the domain of losses" (McDermott 1992, 241–42).

Finally, as a third position within *Homo Psychologicus,* we can consider the application of an analogical reasoning approach to this case study. In many ways, the debate about what to do about the American hostages in Iran resembled the kind of analogical warfare that we observed in chapter 7 on Vietnam. Brzezinski is said to have favored the rescue mission in part because he had the recent historical precedent of the Entebbe rescue mission in mind. This was a highly successful Israeli commando mission launched in 1976. Very famous indeed during the late 1970s, the Israeli raid succeeded in rescuing almost all of the hostages being held by Palestinian hijackers at Entebbe airport in Uganda. While pretending to negotiate with the hostage-takers, the Israeli Prime Minister Yitzak Rabin and his Foreign Minister Shimon Peres were secretly planning a daring raid on the airport terminal where the hostages—most of them Israeli citizens—were being held. The raid succeeded and was considered a great success despite the loss of a few of the hostages and that of Jonathan Netanyahu, the operational chief of the mission and brother of a future Israeli prime minister.

Entebbe was a demonstration that "daring works," and Brzezinski freely admitted in later years that the analogy influenced his decision-making (Houghton 1996, 2001). Brzezinski subsequently defended the small number of helicopters used in the Tehran raid by reference to the Entebbe analogy as well. "Some have argued subsequently that the mission should have been composed of, say, twice as many helicopters," he noted. "But if the Iranians had discovered the mission as a result of the size of the air armada penetrating their airspace, we all would doubtless have been charged with typically excessive American redundancy, with unwillingness to go in hard and lean—the way, for example, the Israelis did at Entebbe" (Brzezinski 1983, 495). Sometimes doing nothing is more costly than the alternatives, Brzezinski argued, and he held this to be another major lesson of Entebbe.

Using Kahneman and Tversky's heuristics, it is easy to see why this particular analogy popped into many people's heads at the time (Tversky and Kahneman 1974). First of all, the Entebbe analogy was *available;* it was recent at the time and had made international headlines. It had even been rather hurriedly made into no less than three television movies, with international stars like Peter Finch and Anthony Hopkins playing Rabin. By coincidence, Brzezinski had been dining at the home of Shimon Peres during the Entebbe crisis, and even suggested to his (rather suspicious) dining companions that they were being somewhat soft in negotiating with the terrorists instead of storming the airport terminal. Although there were in reality many differences between Tehran and Entebbe—for one thing, the Israeli raid had been conducted at an airport, while the embassy was in the center of a major city teeming with protestors—it also seemed at least superficially *representative* of the situation in Iran.

For Vance, on the other hand, the relevant historical analogies were the *Pueblo* hostage crisis from 1968 and the Angus Ward case from 1949. In both cases, the hostages were extricated using diplomacy and without bloodshed or the necessity for a risky rescue operation. In 1968 the North Koreans had seized a lightly armed U.S. intelligence ship, the USS *Pueblo,* which was monitoring radar installations off the coast of the country. They took the crew hostage, and the whole incident lasted almost a year. President Johnson had ruled out a rescue mission as too risky and likely to result in the deaths of the hostages. As in 1979, LBJ was also hampered by a lack of intelligence on the precise whereabouts of the hostages, and the decision-makers knew or strongly suspected that the Americans would be released once they lost their political utility to the hostage-takers. As Carter would later find in the Iranian hostage crisis, negotiation eventually succeeded in obtaining the hostages' release. Similarly, the Angus Ward case involved the seizure of U.S. diplomatic personnel during a revolution—this time in China—and the distances involved as well as other military and strategic considerations made a rescue mission nearly impossible to implement successfully. As in 1979, the Chairman of the Joint Chiefs ruled out a military solution early on, and negotiation was again used successfully (Vance 1983, 498–500). While neither the Ward nor the *Pueblo* case was especially available to most of the decision-makers in a cognitive sense, something which may partially explain their lack of appeal to many, there was again a personal linkage here. Vance had been a negotiator during the *Pueblo* hostage crisis, and so was familiar with the case in a way that most of Carter's advisers (especially those who had worked for him in Georgia when he was the governor there) were not. He also argued that both analogies were strongly representative of the Iran situation.

Vance was clearly thinking of *Pueblo* when the hostages in Iran were seized, but for some members of the military the *Mayaguez* raid provided an even more apt parallel. David Jones had been especially reluctant to mount a quick rescue operation in the Iran case, in part because he had felt unduly rushed by President Ford and his Secretary of State Henry Kissinger during the *Mayaguez* crisis. As we saw in chapter 4, Jones had been the acting Chairman of the Joint Chiefs during that episode. Ford and Kissinger had overridden Jones's judgment that extra time was needed to plan a successful rescue operation and Jones must have felt somewhat vindicated when poor intelligence and rushed planning led to the loss of more U.S. service personnel than there were hostages. When Jones next planned a rescue operation, he would at least try to ensure that more rigorous processes were followed. "General Jones looked back on the *Mayaguez* as a model of how not to plan a rescue mission," Neustadt and May relate. "When he next faced such a task, in 1980 … he would insist on controlling the timetable and on centralizing both planning and command in his own Joint Staff. In doing so … he would sometimes refer explicitly to the *Mayaguez* analogy" (Neustadt and May 1980, 65).

Finally, the analogical reasoning perspective has the advantage of being able to explain why President Carter—widely known for a predilection for micromanagement of problems—failed to intervene during the implementation of the rescue mission. It is conceivable that Carter could have decided to override the judgment of Colonel Beckwith and proceeded with the mission, since the mission *could* have proceeded with only five helicopters if some equipment and personnel were left behind at Desert One or Two and picked up later. Nevertheless, Carter did not attempt to second guess his military commanders. Interestingly, this was a lesson, which both Brzezinski and Carter had drawn from the Bay of Pigs episode (see chap. 5). Following conversations Carter had earlier conducted with Brzezinski, who urged him not to follow Kennedy's example in modifying a military plan already in progress, the Bay of Pigs analogy reportedly weighed so heavily on the President's mind during the Iranian rescue mission that his first response after its failure was to ask what Kennedy did next. He asked his Press Secretary Jody Powell for a copy of JFK's post–Bay of Pigs speech about "victory having a hundred fathers," and the phrases that Carter uttered in 1980 were eerily similar to those spoken by Kennedy in 1961 (Jordan 1983, 256).

ASSESSING THE THREE PERSPECTIVES

How are we to assess the worth of each of our three approaches? In his analysis of the hostage crisis decision-making from the *Homo Bureaucraticus* perspective, Smith is careful to avoid a hard version of the bureaucratic politics model; in other words, he recognizes that policy preferences of decision-makers cannot solely be the product of where you sit, and that the kind of prior beliefs that a student of *Homo Psychologicus* would emphasize matter as well. On the one hand, there is a clear correlation or relationship between bureaucratic position and policy preferences among the decision-makers when one examines decision-making in the immediate run-up to the rescue attempt: those in hawkish positions take a hawkish view, those in dovish positions take a dovish view, and the presidential supporters all uniformly back whatever they think is in the interest of the presidency. But there is an old saying in statistics and social science that "correlation is not causation." To understand this principle, consider a simple example, which you may find entertaining. Most people who have taught at the college level for a number of years have observed that there is a noticeable tendency for some students to apparently fall ill at examination time or when a term paper is due! In other words, there is a statistical relationship between exam/paper deadlines and apparent illness. But does this mean that professors are making their students ill by assigning examinations? In most cases, one should hope not. A more likely causal explanation for this relationship, which may be real enough if we were to chart it on paper, is that some students routinely pretend to be ill in order to avoid taking an exam they think—or know—they might fail! In other words, there is a correlation between exam times and illness, but it is probably not a *causal* relationship on the whole, because there is a third (intervening) factor doing the causation. Equally, while bureaucratic position certainly correlates with position in this case, it is hard to say whether this is a genuinely causal relationship. Perhaps Vance and Christopher were appointed to the State Department in the first place precisely because they were both practiced lawyers and diplomats who were already known to be dovish.

One way to think about the where-you-stand debate is to again employ counterfactual reasoning. As we saw in chapter 4, counterfactual propositions often begin with the phrase "what if?" and can be thought of as "imagining something that you know *did not* happen in order to better understand what *did*". While counterfactuals are of course difficult to prove one way or the other, we can engage in the same kind of imaginative counterfactual reasoning with the positions of Vance and Brzezinski. Imagine, to begin with, that Vance had been appointed to the post of secretary of defense when Jimmy Carter took office in 1977 instead of that of secretary of state. This is not altogether hard to imagine, and it counts as a plausible counterfactual since Vance had served as deputy secretary of defense under Lyndon Johnson. It is also said that if Hubert Humphrey had won the 1968 presidential election, Vance would probably have been offered the top post at the Pentagon. If where you stand does indeed depend on where you sit, Vance as defense secretary would have been a strong advocate of the rescue mission in 1980. Is this plausible? Certainly, Vance himself cited the personal *experiences* to which he had been exposed as the decisive factor influencing his position on the hostages. Similarly, imagine a Brzezinski as secretary of state arguing for negotiation and restraint in the face of provocation. Is it plausible that either man would have changed his policy preferences on the hostage issue if these were the bureaucratic positions each held? In fact, Smith is quite aware of this difficulty, and his own view is that Brzezinski, for instance, would probably have been a hawk regardless of the position he held (Smith 1985, 23).

A second difficulty is that even the connection between position and preference seems to disappear for Harold Brown and David Jones when one examines their positions during the *initial* phase of the crisis. As defense secretary and chairman of the Joint Chiefs respectively, these were the very two men whom the bureaucratic politics model predicts would advocate military measures, and yet they were especially vocal in ruling out such options at the outset. For *Homo Bureaucraticus* to account for his policy preferences, Brown perhaps ought not to have been so skeptical about the prospect that military options might succeed in this case. A similar point applies in the case of General Jones, whose hesitancy to mount a rescue operation is difficult to explain without knowing that he had planned a similar mission only four years earlier, which had been judged a monumental failure by many observers.

Finally, while the mixture of personnel involved in the hostage rescue mission may well have been the result of bureaucratic infighting, this factor has also been convincingly explained as a matter of technical necessity. Since the U.S. military in 1980 lacked the capability to conduct the kind of operation that political officials were demanding of them, some sort of unit had to be put together from scratch. By necessity, this involved putting together what Colin Powell termed a "pickup team," which blended elements of different services and capabilities. As Stansfield Turner has noted, the fact that Marine pilots were required to fly Navy minesweeping helicopters (to address one prominent example) is largely explicable in terms of the experience of the pilots and the technical demands of the situation. Even though they had not trained in the RH-53D helicopters, the Marine pilots were more accustomed to combat conditions and to flying over land under cover of darkness, while the Navy pilots were used to mostly straightforward minesweeping exercises over water. The CH-53s in which the Marine pilots *had* trained, moreover, could not be flown for the distances required. In fact, the planners initially did try to use the Navy pilots in the RH-53Ds, but they found that the Marines were far better suited to the requirements of the mission (Turner 1991, 87–88; Bowden 2006, 227–28). In short, then, this aspect of the decision-making may in fact be explicable from the perspective of *Homo Economicus*.

Turning to the *Homo Sociologicus* perspective, the evidence that other decision-makers deprecated Vance is clear and hard to question. The evidence that Vance was deliberately excluded, however, is more open to interpretation, and others have viewed Carter's behavior in a much less sinister way. James David Barber, for instance, suggests that the fact that Vance was away on April 11—the day Carter decided to launch the mission—was coincidental, since only the day before "Carter noted in his diary that Iranian terrorists were threatening the kill the hostages if Iraq—in their eyes an American puppet—attacked Iran" (Barber 1985, 455). Barber implies that it was the existence of this threat (whether real or imagined) that led Carter to decide in Vance's absence rather than an attempt to keep the major dissenter out of the loop. One can counter, probably with some justification, that this was an instance of rationalizing after the fact on Carter's part; it is certainly astonishing that a President would make a decision of such import in the absence of his Secretary of State, and it left Vance with little option but to resign.

A second potential problem with the groupthink interpretation in this case lies with the notion that Stansfield Turner might have acted to insulate others from information to which they should properly have had access; in other words, the claim that the CIA Director acted as a mindguard. In its classic form, this involves "putting social pressure on any member who begins to express a view that deviates from the dominant beliefs of the group, to make sure that he will not disrupt the consensus of the group as a whole," in the words of Janis (1982, 40). Yet Turner never seems to have exerted such pressure. Moreover, he has subsequently defended his role in discounting the report, and has accounted for his decision not to draw it to the attention of the other decision-makers in a way that at least casts doubt on the idea that he was consciously or unconsciously preventing the opinions of a doubting subordinate within the CIA from being heard. Turner said in an interview in 1994 that the (still classified) report examined "a social scientific theory," which suggested that the rescue attempt had a high probability of failure. Turner recalls that the report concluded that "this is not something on which you should make a decision." He considered the whole matter of little significance, and he adds that "the whole thing could be cleared up by having the report declassified." Similarly, then Deputy CIA Director Frank Carlucci has "a vague recollection of some report on potential casualties based on assumptions that most people questioned" (Houghton 2001, 188–89). Neither Turner nor Carlucci seems to have felt that this was something worthy of the President's attention or that of other NSC members. After all, any theoretical estimate of casualties in a highly complex operation of this sort would have to be mostly speculation and conjecture.

Finally, it is also difficult to tell whether the mistakes that Smith refers to were the result of *group level* processes, or whether these were simply the outcome of psychological misperceptions at the individual level. Using the findings of the Holloway report, Smith shows quite convincingly that Carter and his associates engaged in a great deal of wishful thinking as to whether a rescue mission could succeed. But we know that wishful thinking can also be induced by analogy—in this case, perhaps, by the tempting mental image of another Entebbe or by the simple need to do something in the face of Carter's mounting unpopularity. It is also unclear how many conditions or symptoms of the phenomenon need to be present before groupthink can be reliably diagnosed. This is a particular problem because the evidence suggests that some signs of groupthink (like the exclusion of dissent) are present, while other symptoms (for example, the presence of mindguards or an illusion of invulnerability) are not (see also Tetlock et al. 1992; McDermott 1992, 252).

Turning to *Homo Psychologicus*, one advantage of the analogical reasoning perspective is that it can explain why Carter decided not to micromanage, why Brzezinski was so taken with the idea of a rescue mission, why Jones wanted to take his time in planning such a mission, and why Vance was always so dead-set against it. On the other hand, perhaps simple belief-system approaches can explain the decisions taken during the hostage crisis. Some of the participants in the hostage crisis decision-making doubt whether the analogies used by Vance, for instance, had a fundamental impact on his thinking; perhaps the *Pueblo* and Ward analogies were just ex-post justifications, designed to dress up arguments Vance had reached on ideological grounds, and perhaps Brzezinski's Entebbe comparison played the same role. Indeed, Vance and Brzezinski might well have adopted the positions they took had Entebbe, *Pueblo,* or the Ward case never happened. If this is so, then we need not examine the historical analogies the decision-makers employed in order to arrive at a reasonable theoretical account of events. On the other hand, as we argued in chapter 7, it is probable that analogies, which derive from the personal experiences of the decision-makers, really did exert an impact on their thinking, and analogies certainly lend a degree of precision to decision-making that general beliefs do not. Knowing that Brzezinski is a hawk, for instance, tells us that he is likely to advocate a military solution of some kind, but it does not tell us which of a wide array of possible military options he is likely to favor; the Entebbe analogy, on the other hand, can potentially do this.

Some other elements within this approach can also be used to critique one another. Was the kind of risk-taking behavior observed in President Carter when he approved the mission a fundamental aspect of his personality (as Glad argues), or did it have more to do with his changed perception of the situation he faced (essentially McDermott's view)? The latter approach has the advantage of being able to explain why Carter's risk-taking behavior *changed* from November 1979 to April 1980; since Carter's personality presumably did not change fundamentally during this period, an obvious problem, which occurs with Glad's account, is why he did not take bigger risks earlier if risk taking was simply an aspect of his personality. Apart from the correlation-is-not-causation axiom, there is another old adage that states "you can't explain variation with a constant." In other words, if the phenomenon you are interested in explaining changes but what you think is causing it stays the same, your theory is probably mistaken. This is also potentially a problem for the analogical reasoning approach, for if Entebbe proved alluring as an analogy in 1980, why didn't it earlier on? Equally, Jimmy Carter's moral belief system seems useful in explaining his overall approach, but it would have proved a poor predictor of his decision to launch the rescue mission. Arguably, McDermott's account is quite useful to us here, since it uses an explanation which does vary with the decision taken.

Equally, prospect theory is admittedly difficult to test in many situations since we cannot always tell whether a decision-maker believes himself or herself to be operating in a domain of losses or gains, as McDermott admits. While it is relatively easy to infer that a person feels cold in a freezing room or that he or she feels hot on a sweltering beach, in political decision-making the indicators are usually more ambiguous, and so we cannot know for sure in any given instance whether gain or loss is what is being perceived. We may also find it difficult to tell how risky a decision-maker thought various policy alternatives were. While it seems fairly obvious that Carter saw himself operating in a domain of loss by March 1980, it is less clear whether the President saw the rescue mission as the riskiest of the options available. Jack Levy suggests that it is unclear whether "Carter, given his high estimates of success of a rescue mission, perceived that a rescue mission involved more risks than did allowing the hostage crisis to continue, with all of its unpredictable consequences for his own upcoming reelection campaign as well as for the image and influence of the United States in the world" (Levy 1992, 302). Another problem, as we saw in chapter 6, may be that the perception of loss does not automatically lead to risk taking in all cases; during the Cuban missile crisis Kennedy chose what appears to have been the least (rather than the most) risky of his available options.

CHAPTER 9

NATO Intervenes:
Seventy-Eight Days Over Kosovo

Protestors call for an end to the NATO bombing of Kosovo.
SOURCE: Time & Life Pictures/Getty Images

This chapter covers a rather less well-known but more contemporary case study, the Kosovo crisis with which the Clinton administration grappled in 1999. This brief conflict—NATO's first ever military engagement—was fought between that organization and Serbia from March to June 1999. Following the failure of peace talks at Rambouillet over the status of the Yugoslav province of Kosovo and the decision of Serbian president Slobodan Milosevic to step up the 'ethnic cleansing' of Albanians living there, the United States and NATO began a seventy-eight-day bombing campaign against Serbia, conducted almost exclusively from the air. The bombing lasted from March 22 until June 11, 1999, and involved some 1,000 aircraft, flying more than 38,000 combat missions and operating mainly from bases in Italy, from submarines, and from aircraft carriers in the Adriatic. Although it looked for a long time as if Milosevic would weather the storm, he eventually gave in to NATO's demand that he pull his forces from Kosovo and agree to the stationing of a NATO peacekeeping force there. With the exception of Greece, all nineteen NATO members played some role in the campaign, including Germany's Luftwaffe, participating in its first armed conflict since World War II.

On March 24, 1999, President Clinton went on live television to announce the beginning of the NATO bombing campaign and explain the decision to the American people:

> My fellow Americans, today our Armed Forces joined our NATO allies in air strikes against Serbian forces responsible for the brutality in Kosovo. We have acted with resolve for several reasons. We act to protect thousands of innocent people in Kosovo from a mounting military offensive. We act to prevent a wider war; to diffuse a powder keg at the heart of Europe that has exploded twice before in this century with catastrophic results. And we act to stand united with our allies for peace. By acting now we are upholding our values, protecting our interests and advancing the cause of peace.

Clinton explained that Milosevic and the Serbs had defied the international community and committed atrocities on a scale that simply could not be ignored. "Now, they've started moving from village to village, shelling civilians and torching their houses," the President said. "We've seen innocent people taken from their homes, forced to kneel in the dirt and sprayed with bullets; Kosovar men dragged from their families, fathers and sons together, lined up and shot in cold blood. This is not war in the traditional sense. It is an attack by tanks and artillery on a largely defenseless people, whose leaders already have agreed to peace." Clinton made the case that intervention was in America's national interest, while also making the moral case for war. "Ending this tragedy is a moral imperative," he said. But Clinton also attempted to calm those who feared that this would become a land war and/or an open-ended American commitment. "I do not intend to put our troops in Kosovo to fight a war," he added in his speech, in a phrase that would later return to haunt him.[1]

The declared goal of the NATO operation was summed up by its spokesman as "Serbs out, peacekeepers in, refugees back." The Serbs would have to remove their troops from Kosovo, and they would be replaced by international peacekeepers who would guarantee that Albanian refugees—who had fled to the forests and mountains to avoid Milosevic's attempts at ethnic cleansing—could return to their homes. Initially Serb air defenses and high-value military targets were hit. Many within NATO and within the U.S. administration believed that Milosevic would give in within a few days, but this proved to be little more than wishful thinking. The air campaign was also hampered by some calamitous military errors. On one occasion NATO planes struck an unarmed convoy of Kosovars attempting to flee ethnic cleansing, with horrifying results. On another occasion, NATO bombs hit the Chinese embassy in downtown Belgrade, leading to accusations by Chinese officials that it had been deliberately targeted (it was later admitted that the CIA had used an old map of the city in drawing up the target list). Rather than surrendering quickly, Milosevic responded by stepping up the ethnic cleansing, which led to accusations that NATO was causing far more deaths than it was preventing, and a flood of refugees moved out of Kosovo into neighboring Albania. So-called dual use targets (used by both civilians and the military) such as electrical power stations, TV stations, and bridges were also targeted, and the resulting death of Serb civilians led to accusations that NATO was itself violating international law.

As the conflict dragged on into April with no end in sight, U.S. decision-makers in particular began to seriously contemplate invading Kosovo using ground troops. Contingency plans were made early on for an invasion, though these were never actually implemented (Priest 1999a). The Pentagon in particular was especially reluctant to back such an operation, and President Clinton had always been equally reluctant to commit American forces to a ground offensive (Myers 1999). However, NATO credibility was on the line, and there was particular concern that the conflict needed to be resolved before the winter; many Kosovars were hiding in the forests and hills but would starve or freeze to death as the colder months set in (Perlez 1999). Fortunately, Finnish and Russian negotiators were finally able to persuade Milosevic to back down before plans for a ground offensive were implemented. The Russians made it clear that they would not intervene to defend the Serb leader against a NATO ground invasion, and Milosevic accepted a peace deal in which his own troops would be withdrawn and replaced by NATO troops (essentially the same arrangement that the U.S. special envoy to the Balkans Richard Holbrooke had offered the Serb leader the year before the war began).

THE HISTORICAL BACKGROUND TO THE CONFLICT

Although the historical background to the Kosovo War was long and complex, the basic political problem in Kosovo was very simple: although roughly 90 percent of its population of two million people are ethnic Albanians, two peoples claimed the same piece of territory. For both Serbs and ethnic Albanians, Kosovo is sacred ground and has been so for centuries. In 1389 the Serbs lost the Battle of Kosovo, and their leader Prince Lazar was killed. The only historical accounts of this we have are unreliable since they are highly biased in favor of one side or the other, but we do know that this event marked the beginning of the decline of Slav power in the region, and a vivid mythology grew up around it (Malcolm 1998, 58–80; Schwartz 2000, 35; Hosmer 2001, 8–11). Today, nationalist Serbs are motivated to avenge the death of Lazar, and Milosevic presented himself as Lazar's modern heir. For centuries, Serbia was ruled by the Ottoman Empire, and after a relatively brief period of independence it became part of Yugoslavia after World War I. In 1974 Yugoslavia's then leader Marshal Tito granted Kosovars a measure of political independence, and Kosovo existed as a kind of semi-autonomous region within Yugoslavia with its own shadow government and political institutions. In 1989, though, Slobodan Milosevic took this status away when he became

Yugoslavia's leader, embracing the Serbian nationalist cause in Kosovo. As a former Communist official who came to power riding the nationalist wave in the region, Kosovo was the crown jewel of his Serbian nationalist strategy. In adopting this approach, Milosevic was almost certainly a political opportunist rather than a genuine nationalist; like many demagogues, he had found an issue and was cynically exploiting the nationalist tide that engulfed Yugoslavia in the late 1980s and early 1990s (Glenny 1996, 60). But in a practical sense, the effect was the same: politically, Milosevic could not afford to give Kosovo up, and he needed to retain the power base that he had so carefully and skillfully nurtured.

Kosovars chafed under Milosevic's rule as he systematically removed their economic and political rights, and sided with Kosovo's Serbian minority. This led to the rise of both violent and nonviolent protest movements in the region: of the latter, the most significant was the Kosovo Liberation Army (KLA), but Kosovo's elected leader, Ibrahim Rugova, espoused a peaceful approach inspired by figures like Mahatma Gandhi. During the summer of 1998 the Serbs, apparently believing that the KLA was about to step up its attacks on its military forces, increased its campaign of ethnic cleansing in a move often known as the "Summer Offensive" (Posen 2000, 43). This caused a refugee crisis as Albanians left their homes and fled to the hills and forests to avoid Serb death squads. With a major humanitarian crisis in the making, the Clinton administration sent Ambassador Richard Holbrooke to Belgrade in the hope that he could broker a peace deal. This led to the so-called October Agreement, but its failure was very soon apparent since neither side kept to its provisions. There was until January 1999 very little appetite within NATO or the U.S. administration to go to war over this issue, but then came the Racak massacre. Forty-five innocent Albanians were found murdered, their bodies maimed in hideous ways. President Clinton and NATO leaders gave diplomacy one last shot, and they tried again to negotiate a settlement at Rambouillet, France. This too failed as Milosevic refused to budge, and the reluctant warriors of NATO began their bombing campaign in March 1999.

The West had long been concerned with Kosovo but until the ethnic cleansing of the late 1990s, this small area—about the same size as Connecticut—had always been treated in a strictly hands-off manner by the United States and the European powers. Part of the reason lay with a kind of pessimistic resignation about the Balkans. Robert Kaplan in his highly influential book *Balkan Ghosts* argued that ancient ethnic hatreds were endemic to the region, and that little could be done by Western governments to assuage these (Kaplan 1994). This was a view widely shared by many European leaders. It contributed to the West's slow response when Yugoslavia dissolved and ethnic violence erupted there in the early 1990s, although the disintegration of the state probably had as much to do with the economic dislocation caused by Yugoslavia's overnight abandonment of socialism and sudden leap into the icy waters of market capitalism than it did with ingrained ethnic hatreds (Woodward 1995). Kosovo was left out of the Dayton Accords of 2005, which brought peace to Bosnia and reined Milosevic's Serbs in (albeit temporarily). Aside from the popularity of the ancient hatreds view, the primary reason for the hands-off approach had to do with *realpolitik*; as in the Kurdish region of Iraq, the interest of most Western powers lay in maintaining the status quo and dissuading the Kosovars from pushing for independence. As former National Security Adviser Brent Scowcroft noted, "a number of powers had very strong interests in Kosovo and in that general region. The Albanians did, the Greeks did, the Turks did, the Bulgarians did, as well as the Serbs. And therefore, something happening there could have brought about a wider war, even with the possibility of some of our NATO allies on opposite sides."[2] Russia was a particular concern since it possessed a historical affinity with Serbians as fellow Slavs, but in a more practical sense Russia's leaders feared that independence for the Kosovars would hamper them in their own fight with Chechen separatists.

Unlike the examples we have covered up to this point, there is still only a very small theoretically developed literature on this case study, so our observations must be more speculative in nature. No gatherings of the decision-makers similar to those undertaken in the missile crisis case have so far been undertaken, and no transcripts of official meetings on either the U.S. or the Yugoslav side have yet been made public. Nor is it likely that we will ever have anything similar to Kennedy's ExCom transcripts in the Kosovo case, since U.S. decision-makers have generally not taped their deliberations since Nixon's Watergate tapes helped bring down his presidency in 1974. We accordingly have to rely primarily on the memoirs of various American policymakers, including those of Bill Clinton, Secretary of State Madeleine Albright, NATO Supreme Allied Commander Europe (SACEUR) Wesley Clark, and Chairman of the Joint Chiefs Hugh Shelton, and on second-hand accounts of the decision-making gleaned from documentaries, newspaper accounts, and the relatively small number of books written on this topic.

Nevertheless, there are some interesting indications already that our three approaches can inform an empirical understanding of this case. Bureaucratic struggles between the State Department and the Pentagon, tussles between Shelton and Clark, and indications that individuals within the White House had little appetite for a war based on their own vantage point at the time all provide some support for a *Homo Bureaucraticus* approach. From a *Homo Sociologicus* perspective, meanwhile, there is some evidence that the decision-makers may have been victims of groupthink, collectively convincing themselves that Milosevic would back down if confronted by the mere threat of force. Finally, from the *Homo Psychologicus* perspective President Clinton was reluctant to commit ground troops to Kosovo, in part because of the Vietnam syndrome that had heavily influenced his thinking throughout his presidency and the shattering experience of the Somali "Black Hawk Down" incident in 1993. Madeleine Albright, on the other hand, was heavily influenced by U.S. inaction during the first Balkans crisis over Bosnia and frequently used the Munich analogy, both of which suggested that if Milosevic was not stopped early on, the United States would simply have to confront him later. The underlying World War I analogy also suggested that regional conflict in the Balkans could spill over into a major conflagration, just what the West most wanted to avoid. The Albanians, the Greeks, the Bulgarians, and the Turks—and most troubling of all, the Russians—might be dragged into a far broader regional and perhaps even global war if the conflict should spread.

Homo Bureaucraticus

This is in many ways precisely the kind of case where an advocate of *Homo Bureaucraticus* would expect bureaucratic infighting and SOPs to shape decision-making. Jerel Rosati has argued that one of the factors that increases the importance of this phenomenon is presidential inattention. While he concedes that the structure of a decision-making unit is far from being the only factor that determines the outcome or result of the debate, he maintains that it nevertheless matters a great deal. On some issues, presidential involvement and attention is high and organizational involvement low. Richard Nixon's overture to China, as we saw in chapter 2, might be a good example of this, since he largely cut the State Department out of the process and made decisions on this issue from the White House. On issues like this, presidential dominance often trumps bureaucratic maneuvering. Equally, presidential dominance is also likely to be high when White House attention *and* organizational attention is heavily focused on the issue; Kennedy's decision-making on the Cuban missile crisis (see chap. 6) might be regarded as a good example of this scenario. But where presidential attention is lacking but organizational involvement is high, we can expect bureaucratic politics—or what Rosati calls "bureaucratic dominance"—to prevail (Rosati 1981, 248–51). In this instance, we know that presidential attention was generally low, but the State Department, the CIA, and the Pentagon played active roles. As Myers and Schmitt put wrote at the time, "although President Clinton also reviews the most sensitive [bombing] targets and weighs in on significant decisions, his direct participation in the military planning is said to be episodic" (Myers and Schmitt 1999; Sciolino and Bronner 1999). Indeed, the very fact that this conflict was often referred to as "Madeleine's War" rather than "Clinton's War" is in itself rather revealing (Isaacson 1999).

A good case can be made that President Clinton was only intermittently attentive to foreign policy issues in general, especially (though not exclusively) at the outset of his presidency. He began his term in office in early 1993 hoping that he could act as the primary manager of domestic policy, and that foreign policy issues could be relegated to the backburner and delegated to an experienced foreign policy team, headed by then Secretary of State Warren Christopher and Clinton's first National Security Adviser, Anthony Lake. This made a kind of intuitive sense at the time: first of all, despite the impressive foreign policy credentials of Clinton's predecessor George H. W. Bush, the latter was widely perceived as having neglected the kind of bread-and-butter economic issues with which Bill Clinton was especially comfortable. Clinton had been elected in 1992 on the memorable slogan, "It's the Economy, Stupid!" Second, the widespread expectation across the political spectrum after the end of the Cold War was that a new peace dividend would prevail. With few direct threats to U.S. security on the horizon, this common assumption held at the time, America could retreat inward and focus on pressing domestic issues like unemployment and health care. Again, these were areas on which George H. W. Bush was perceived as weak, but where the young governor of Arkansas Bill Clinton was strong. As David Halberstam notes, "clearly the country wanted some kind of reward for having soldiered through the hard years of the Cold War, an economic and psychological, if you will, peace dividend. To emphasize that point, there was Clinton, out of the hustings, attacking Bush again and again for paying too much attention to the rest of the world and not enough to his own country" (Halberstam 2002, 158).

Over time, Clinton realized that he could not simply delegate these issues to his national security team. By the early 1990s, the President was forced to confront a whole host of disparate and often unconnected foreign policy problems: in Iraq, Saddam Hussein began a continual game of cat and mouse with UN weapons inspectors; North Korea became a nuclear threat; in Somalia, the warlord Mohammed Farah Aideed defied the United States by intercepting UN food consignments to his own people, producing a disastrous attempt to kidnap him in 1993 (generally known as the "Black Hawk Down" incident); and in Bosnia, the emergence of ethnic cleansing, primarily by Serbs against Bosnian Muslims and presided over by Milosevic, pressed for the attention of both American and European leaders. In the case of the later Kosovo War, however, Clinton's attention to foreign policy was inevitably only intermittent because of his impeachment trial in the House and Senate. The President himself was preoccupied with domestic scandals, and for a long time did not wish to do anything that smacked of a *Wag the Dog* effect (named after a Hollywood movie in which a fictional White House manufactures a war in order to distract attention from a sexual scandal). As Ivo Daalder notes, "the early part of 1998, the White House is preoccupied with very different things. The Monica Lewinsky story has just broken. The notion that at this point you engage in another foreign adventure, that you start using force in a kind of *Wag the Dog* scenario, was one that was not generally supported in the White House."[3]

Although Clinton's memoirs are not especially forthcoming on this issue or on the internal debates that raged over whether and in what fashion to intervene in Kosovo, it is well established that the White House had little political appetite for a second war in the Balkans. Both Clinton and Gore were especially opposed to putting American ground troops in Kosovo, knowing that there was strong opposition in Congress (which still complained of a seemingly endless commitment to the peacekeeping effort in Bosnia) and little support among the American people for such an engagement. Clinton later expressed this view strongly in his memoirs, arguing that putting ground troops into Kosovo would have produced far more casualties than the subsequent air war did (Clinton 2004, 859). He also believed that the commitment of American troops would be hard to defend domestically, and he seems to have felt that this was a bad time politically for his administration to become involved in a major war. As Ivo Daalder and Michael O'Hanlon note, apart from concerns that an air war might fail or lead to the second open-ended commitment of U.S. troops to the Balkans for years, "most officials were also concerned about the political impact of a decision to use force in an atmosphere poisoned by the impeachment procedures that were then ongoing. With the House having voted to impeach the president and the Senate in the midst of deciding on his possible removal from office, this was hardly a propitious time to lead NATO into war" (Daalder and O'Hanlon 2000, 65). In short, the White House tended to view the issue of Kosovo in terms of what would play politically.

Rather ironically perhaps, given the early influence of Vietnam upon his own thinking, Bill Clinton insisted on approving the selection of bombing targets during the air war in a manner similar to Lyndon Johnson (who obsessed over each target, fearful that a stray bomb would trigger a conflict with the Soviets or Chinese). This practice is said to have greatly irritated Gen. Wesley Clark; instead of being able to order the quick air strikes that he felt he needed to as the overall commander of an air war, he had to wait at least forty-eight hours to clear each target with the White House and the Pentagon (Myers and Schmitt 1999; Smith 2004). Even if he was not actually frustrated, moreover, he was certainly very surprised to learn that the president would be signing off personally on each target (Clark 2001, 202). From Clark's perspective, military officials and politicians in Washington were second-guessing what their commander on the ground was trying to do, further complicating what was already a complex NATO decision-making process.

Again, however, the reason Clinton micromanaged the process may have been related to political concerns. Although the President rarely seems to have paid very close attention to the implementation of his foreign policy decisions, he may well have done so in this case because of the political embarrassment that (probably faulty) U.S. intelligence had caused him the year before. On August 20, 1998, the U.S. military had bombed the Al-Shifa pharmaceutical plant in Sudan, in conjunction with an attack on Al-Qaeda camps in Afghanistan. One person was killed and eleven injured in the Sudanese attack, which seems to have been manufacturing not a VX nerve gas agent—as Clinton was told by the CIA—but aspirin and other medications. It was later claimed that thousands of Sudanese citizens also suffered as a result of their lack of access to the products that the company had manufactured, although this claim is hard to assess. Clinton maintains in his memoirs that the intelligence was in fact accurate and that he had done "the right thing," but he also complains that many in the media speculated that he ordered the strikes in order distract attention from the Monica Lewinsky scandal (Clinton 2004, 805). This was first time that Clinton was accused of following the *Wag the Dog* scenario, since the bombing came just two days after he had admitted in a live television address to an "inappropriate" relationship with the former White House intern.[4] Stung by the criticism, it is easy to see why he would try to make sure that no similar mistakes occurred in Kosovo (although, sadly, similar mistakes occurred anyway, including the accidental bombing of what turned out to be the Chinese embassy).

Several years after the war ended, indications emerged that Vice President Al Gore in particular may also have viewed the war partly through the lens of domestic politics, as the "where you stand depends on where you sit" axiom would suggest for members of the White House. Former SACEUR Gen. Wesley Clark made his official papers available in 2004 and suggested in these that there were individuals in the White House who were pressuring him to end the air war in Kosovo before Gore began his formal campaign for the presidency in 1999. Clark took a notably hawkish position throughout the Kosovo crisis. By the time a peace agreement was reached, he still favored escalating the war rather than ending it quickly, since he felt that Clinton was giving up too much in the agreement. He also favored the use of ground troops, though he realized that neither the White House nor the Allies shared this position.

General Clark had specified June 10, 1999 as the date on which he would be formally recommending an escalation of the bombing campaign, but this brought him into conflict with (unnamed) Clinton administration officials. "There were those in the White House who said, 'Hey, look, you gotta finish the bombing before the Fourth of July weekend. That's the start of the next presidential campaign season, so stop it. It doesn't matter what you do, just turn it off. You don't have to win this thing, let it lie,'" Clark stated in a January 2000 interview with a NATO historian. At the time that the papers were released, Clark was himself running for the Democratic party's nomination. According to Jeffrey Smith, "some top Clinton administration officials wanted to end the Kosovo war abruptly in the summer of 1999, at almost any cost, because Gore's presidential campaign was about to begin."[5] Gore, who is alleged to have expressed a concern at one point that the war might "interfere" with his political plans, formally announced his campaign for the presidency on June 16, 1999, less than one week after the end of the air war (Smith 2004).

Bureaucratically speaking, Clark was in an exceptionally delicate position, in large part because—like all SACEURs since the position was created—he was not only part of NATO's chain of command but also working under the orders of President Clinton and the Pentagon. In his public speeches, for instance, he had to simultaneously balance the preferences of both masters, and the two were usually far from identical. President Clinton chose to personally sign off on every bombing target, but so too did representatives of all the other members of NATO. In this "war by committee," Clark was therefore continually concerned that—with all nineteen members of NATO taking part in some form and thus potentially hundreds of people having to be informed—news that a particular target was about to be hit would leak; indeed, this had happened on at least one occasion. But by his own account, he was often just as frustrated by interservice rivalries within his own Defense Department back in Washington as he was by resistance coming from America's allies. According to Clark, his requests often fell victim to such disputes. "Washington couldn't help much, either," he later recalled. "Although the Joint Staff was working with us in the development and advance approval of bombing targets, the subject of Kosovo had become a political football among the Joint Chiefs themselves, as they argued about whether our national interests in southeast Europe justified military action" (Clark 2007, 209).

The organizational culture of the Pentagon, and to some extent that of the State Department also, had changed since Vietnam. Largely as a result of that scarring experience, the gung-ho generals who told John Kennedy that they could launch a highly surgical air strike and assured Lyndon Johnson that victory was just around the corner in the rice paddies of Southeast Asia had been replaced by more cautious, innately conservative military leaders who were highly reluctant to use military force. To some extent, a can-do culture was replaced by a no-can-do one at the Pentagon, while the State Department became more activist and interventionist (Halberstam 2002, 37–38). Although it occurred before she became secretary of state, the famous Albright and Colin Powell confrontation early on in the Clinton administration was perhaps emblematic of the cultural changes that had occurred. As Walter Isaacson relates, "it was early in Clinton's first term, back when she was UN ambassador during the first showdown with Serbia over Bosnia, that Albright showed her stripes on foreign policy. At a 1993 meeting with Joint Chiefs Chairman Colin Powell—who gave his name to the doctrine that the military should be used only after a clear political goal has been set, and then only with decisive force—she challenged the general: 'What's the point of having this superb military that you're always talking about if we can't use it?' As Powell later recalled, 'I thought I would have an aneurysm'" (Isaacson 1999).

Nowhere within the Defense Department was this new culture more strongly imbued than in the Army, whose personnel would bear the brunt of humanitarian, peacekeeping missions since it would be their boots on the ground. By the time of the intervention in Bosnia, the Army had to be forced into taking on additional and unfamiliar responsibilities, while simultaneously fending off cuts to its budget. Reportedly, it took all the bureaucratic skills of then Chairman of the Joint Chiefs John Shalikashvili to persuade the Army Chief of Staff, Gen. Dennis Reimer, to provide 20,000 troops to go to Bosnia to police the Dayton Accords. Reimer was not enthusiastic about the task (Halberstam 2002, 391). As a hawkish activist in foreign policy, Clark was often regarded as a discordant figure within the Army, and he was passed over for promotion at least twice by General Reimer. As Halberstam notes, "he was in some way alien to the military culture" (ibid. 394). This was to have important consequences for the management of the air war: with peacekeeping troops already in Bosnia, Reimer wanted at all costs to avoid becoming embroiled in a second Balkan war. Clark, on the other hand, was one of the most interventionist, activist military leaders of his generation. He clearly favored escalation to a ground war if that proved necessary, which he increasingly began to feel that it would be. As Dana Priest notes, Clark "repeatedly warned the White House that jets could not reliably destroy troops and tanks on the ground" (Priest 1999c).

Bureaucratic infighting between Clark and the Army came to a particularly contentious head over what became known simply as "the Apache issue." Later on in the air campaign, Clark requested the use of AH-64 American Apache helicopters to be used to attack Serbian ground forces, but the whole issue became in his words "a real saga" (Clark 2007, 215). In fact, while the Pentagon did eventually ship twenty-four Apaches to Albania, they were never actually used in the war. From a *Homo Economicus* perspective this is rather puzzling, not least because the helicopters were especially well-suited to the task of destroying Milosevic's ground forces and might have shortened the war considerably. Bombers three miles over the ground or cruise missiles fired from ships could do the job if the target were a fixed entity such as a building, but they were not nearly so accurate or useful in destroying mobile targets like tanks and troops sections. As Dana Priest noted after the war ended:

> The Army has spent $15 billion over the past two decades to make the Apache the most lethal and least vulnerable attack helicopter in the world. It had proved its tank-killing capabilities in the Persian Gulf War. One Apache, carrying 46 rockets and missiles, can fly at night, just above the tree tops, at 100 miles per hour, without a single visible light. Armored flaps on the side windows shield the control panel's illumination, curved rotor blade tips dampen its noise and the exhaust system cools the engine quickly to fool heat sensors. The Apache can also fly in the kind of rainy, cloudy weather that was grounding so many jets in the first month of the Kosovo war (Priest 1999c).

After the Joint Chiefs initially agreed to provide the helicopters, the Army then resisted the idea, and their resistance was especially critical since they controlled the Apaches. General Reimer feared that Clark was using the Apache request as a prelude to the introduction of ground troops, much as escalation in Vietnam had proceeded by increments (a phenomenon known in the U.S. military as "mission creep"). The Army's standard operating procedure for using the Apaches also involved ground troops; Apaches are designed to be used in conjunction with troops on the ground, who act as target spotters for the Apaches and provide them with intelligence. In the absence of land forces, Clark argued, the target spotting could be done by unmanned drones and satellite technology, but Reimer in particular was uncomfortable with this innovation. It would be like "looking through a soda straw," he is reported to have stated in arguing against sending the Apaches. "The army didn't want to be involved because they were afraid of being embarrassed or afraid of taking risks or whatever," Clark later stated rather bitterly in his papers. "The navy didn't have a dog in the fight but [wasn't] too interested. And the air force, well, they would support me, but then they sent their henchmen down to make sure the [Apaches] would never fly" (Smith 2004). Of all the services, the air force sometimes seemed to be on Clark's side, though he would often clash with their officials on the ground as well, not least because the political demands of maintaining cohesion meant bombing in a piecemeal, incremental fashion in a way that violated the Air Force's SOPs (Priest 1999b).

The Joint Chiefs were divided, and in the end the result was a classic bureaucratic compromise. As Priest notes, Hugh Shelton and Joseph Ralston, then air force chief, "came up with a compromise. They recommended to Defense Secretary William S. Cohen that the Apaches be sent to Albania but not used in combat until the Pentagon generals were convinced that the mission made sense. Shelton would then make a recommendation to President Clinton, who had the final say. Cohen bought the idea and on April 3 Clinton signed the order sending the Apaches to Albania" (Priest 1999c). Almost immediately Shelton and Ralston began arguing against actually using the Apaches once they got there, however, claiming that they would cause unacceptable casualty rates (Gordon and Schmitt 1999). Predictably, Clark was infuriated by this, but the Apaches seem to have been sent to keep all parties minimally happy. Sending the helicopters but not using them seems to have been the least common denominator in this case, and a rather expensive one at that. It reportedly cost half a billion dollars to put the Apaches in Albania, but the Joint Chiefs seem to have convinced Bill Clinton that their use was not feasible and would cause an unacceptable casualty rate. Later on, Clark even clashed with the President himself on this issue. During a visit by Clinton to Brussels in 1999, Clinton apparently told Clark—in a phrase highly reminiscent of General Reimer's arguments and the Army's organizational culture—"well, I guess the Apaches are too high-risk to use." The NATO commander then responded that this simply wasn't the case. "Boy, he didn't want to hear that! He turned his head away," Clark recalls, "and that was the end of the discussion" (Smith 2004).

Wesley Clark often differed with the National Security Adviser Samuel "Sandy" Berger and with other officials at the Pentagon as well—including William Cohen and Hugh Shelton—expressing the view that "I know this region a whole lot better than a lot of these guys back in Washington do" (Smith 2004,1). By design, William Cohen rarely spoke to the SACEUR directly, and Clark's aides are said to have referred to him sarcastically as "Senator Cohen," since he seemed to spend most of his energy to selling the administration's policies on Capitol Hill rather than making policy in the executive branch (Myers and Schmitt 1999).[6] Clark had equally tense relations with Shelton. In his memoirs, for instance, Clark notes that Shelton "had little experience in Europe" (Clark 2007, 202). From Shelton's perspective, on the other hand, Clark simply did not know how to run an air war and "had developed a very weak battle plan, one without a strategic plan and corresponding targets" (Shelton 2010, 370). According to the hawkish Clark, Sandy Berger did not see what was happening in the Balkans as a real threat to European security, and was always in favor of a solely diplomatic solution. The National Security Adviser, Clark suggested later, believed at the time that the risks posed by Milosevic were "not real" and failed to constitute a "serious problem." While Berger was prepared to "jerk this guy's [Milosevic's] chain," he was no longer interested in pursuing the issue of Kosovo as soon as it became "too embarrassing politically," Clark contended (Smith 2004).

For his part, Shelton viewed Clark as intelligent but less than competent for the job he had been selected for. He also saw the NATO Supreme Commander as a "loose cannon" who often acted recklessly and without the permission of his civilian bosses, a view that he says Secretary Cohen shared (Shelton 2010, 373). The reader will recall that a major concern of Kennedy and his advisers during the Cuban missile crisis was that a U.S. military commander would act on his own and that war might occur in some inadvertent fashion because of this. Indeed, fear of this bureaucratic tendency is central to the *Homo Bureaucraticus* approach in general and to advocates of what Allison and Zelikow call Model II in particular. While the stakes were probably not as high in this case as they were in 1962, the concern that bureaucratic operatives might act without civilian control seems to have been at least partially realized in a well-known incident at the end of the air war, after Milosevic had finally succumbed and agreed to a cease-fire. Russian forces briefly took over Pristina airport in Kosovo. Although their motives for doing so are still unclear, President Clinton later argued that military hard-liners may have taken this action in a half-hearted and ill-advised effort to influence the course of events. In a confrontation, which was widely publicized at the time, Clark told British Gen. Sir Michael Jackson to place helicopters and armored personnel carriers in the way of the Russians so that they could not land, and he seems to have been more than willing to fire upon the Russian forces holding the airport if that should prove necessary. The NATO commander was apparently unconcerned by the prospect of a direct clash between the rival forces, simply assuming that the Russians would back down in *Homo Economicus* fashion when confronted by a show of force. "Yes, they could shoot. When they shoot, we're gonna shoot. And guess what, there's a lot more of us than there are of them," Clark later related. "So my guess is, they're not gonna shoot!" (Smith 2004).

General Jackson, however, was very much concerned by this prospect and famously refused to obey his commanding officer, stating that "I'm not going to start World War III for you." Although it is still not clear precisely what occurred during this incident, Clark seems to have had no authorization from Washington, London, or NATO HQ in Brussels for his actions. In his memoirs, Clinton merely notes that General Clark was "livid" over the Russian action and states that Jackson was quickly able to bring the situation under control, but he fails to mention what orders (if any) Clark was acting under (Clinton 2004, 859). Clark was later dismissed from his position by William Cohen, probably in no small part because of this incident. His opposition to the 1999 peace agreement and seeming desire to continue the war cannot have helped either. "People knew I was fighting this thing [an early draft of the cease-fire agreement] as it was being dragged to the conclusion, because I felt we were giving too much away", Clark later recalled. "And what was coming from Washington was, get an agreement at any price" (Smith 2004).

Homo Sociologicus

Is there any evidence of collective, group-level delusions among the Clinton administration's national security team either prior to or during the air war? Is there any evidence of the emergence of mindguards to bolster these delusions, or of the self-suppression of dissent from important players in the decision-making process? Again, our conclusions must be tentative on this point, especially since no published account has yet examined this case study from a groupthink or other group-based perspective. Nevertheless, there is some suggestive evidence of group-level delusions in this case study. First of all, the decision-makers—especially but not solely Ambassador Richard Holbrooke—may have been victims of groupthink, collectively convincing themselves that Milosevic would back down if confronted by the mere threat of force. This of course proved to be incorrect. There are some suggestions also that the one or two policymakers who disagreed with this assessment were effectively sidelined, at least until diplomacy failed. Second, once the air war commenced, the general assumption within the administration and within NATO was that it would only be a few days before Milosevic backed down. This proved equally incorrect.

Within the Clinton administration, the clearest advocate of a sustained bombing campaign—with perhaps the exception of Wesley Clark, whose thinking was very similar to hers—was Madeleine Albright. As Daalder and O'Hanlon note, "from the very beginning of the conflict in Kosovo, Madeleine Albright believed that a strategy relying solely or even mainly on negotiations with Milosevic was likely to fail." However, she knew that she was very much in a minority in 1998. President Clinton decided to bring Richard Holbrooke, a successful troubleshooter who had dealt with Milosevic before and who had negotiated the Dayton Accords in 2005, back from private life. According to one source, Albright was unhappy with the idea of bringing Holbrooke in, probably in large part because she felt that simply talking to Milosevic would not work unless the credible threat of NATO force lay fully on the table (something that was not there at that stage). Throughout that year "her perspective failed to prevail in Washington's corridors of power," as Daalder and O'Hanlon put it, and she effectively deferred to Holbrooke on the issue of Kosovo, knowing that she could not win the debate at this stage. Convinced that negotiations without a credible threat of force would fail but realizing that her views were not supported in the White House or the Pentagon, Albright may have censored her own views in policy debates to some extent and bowed to group pressure (Judah 2000:,144; Daalder and O'Hanlon 2000, 69).

If there is some suggestive evidence of such self-censorship, one of Irving Janis's symptoms of groupthink, there is also some evidence of what looks like mindguarding and of group pressure toward conformity, at least before the Racak massacre transformed the debate and persuaded the key players that a change of course was overdue. Early on in the crisis, on April 23, 1998, the then chief negotiator in Kosovo Bob Gelbard sat down in the White House with Sandy Berger, Albright, and her deputy Strobe Talbott. As Albright relates, Gelbard warned the others at the meeting that negotiations would go nowhere unless they could get NATO to use military force against the Serbs. Without this, Milosevic would simply not back down. Berger cut Gelbard off in the middle of his statement. "You can't just talk about bombing in the middle of Europe," he stated with great consternation and some rudeness. "What targets would you want to hit? What would you do the day after? It's irresponsible to keep making threatening statements outside of some coherent plan. The way you people at the State Department talk about bombing, you sound like lunatics." Albright fought back somewhat weakly—stating that "I'm going to insist we at least have this discussion"—but she knew that no one apart from her was interested in what Gelbard had to say on this, at least at this stage (Albright 2003, 383–84). According to Daalder and O'Hanlon's account—based on an anonymous interview they conducted with one of the attendees at the meeting—"after Berger's outburst, no one else—not Albright nor her deputy, Strobe Talbott—came to Gelbard's support" (Daalder and O'Hanlon 2000, fn. 283).

Almost nine months later, the basic dynamic in the meetings had not changed. On January 15, 1999, the day before news of the Racak massacre broke in the United States, the Principals Committee met to consider a revised strategy. Clinton was absent from this meeting, preoccupied with his State of the Nation Address and with the Senate vote on his impeachment. In her memoirs, Albright relates just how isolated she still was in meetings of the national security team, even at that late stage. She argued forcefully for NATO air strikes, reiterating her view that Milosevic would not budge without at least the credible threat of force. But she was a lonely voice, since her natural ally, General Clark, was thousands of miles away at NATO headquarters and was only occasionally brought in the meetings of the national security team. Albright's status as the lone dissenter was by now well established, and the others were clearly weary of hearing her position articulated once more. "As I looked around the table, I saw 'there goes Madeleine again' glances being exchanged." Her remarks, as she puts it, "weren't received with much enthusiasm," and she failed to make any real headway in changing policy on Kosovo (Albright 2003, 392). The next day news of Racak reached the U.S. decision-makers, transforming the debate almost overnight. The slaughter of forty-five Albanians by a Serb killing squad proved to be a real turning point in the debate, convincing everyone that the basic strategy had to change (Halberstam 2002, 409–10).

Second, once the debate swung toward military intervention and Albright's view, another collective delusion—that the United States and NATO would not have to bomb the Serbs for very long before Milosevic capitulated—seems to have gripped the minds of many of the principals. Daalder and O'Hanlon call this the "quick-war assumption," noting that it was highly prevalent within the administration at the outset of the war (Daalder and O'Hanlon 2000, 90–96). Within NATO, there were those who apparently believed that the air campaign would last as little as three days. Wesley Clark would later say that he thought there was about a 40 percent chance that things would work out that quickly, although he may have rated the possibility rather more highly at the time (Priest 2003, 266). The intelligence reports provided to Clinton by the CIA also suggested that Milosevic would quickly back down in the face of NATO air strikes. A January 1999 interagency report concluded that "Milosevic doesn't want a war he can't win. After enough of a defense to sustain his honor and assuage his backers he will quickly sue for peace" (quoted in Sciolino and Bronner 1999). Naturally enough, this kind of assessment—which was exactly what many of the key decision-makers wanted to hear—was appealing throughout most of the government (with the clear exception of the Pentagon itself). Albright, stated on the day that the bombing campaign started, "I don't see this as a long-term operation. I think that is something … that is achievable within a relatively short period of time" (quoted in Daalder and O'Hanlon 2000, 91). Naturally enough, after the fact many of those same decision-makers denied that they had ever "got it wrong" on this issue, perhaps genuinely but unconsciously revising their recollections of their own feelings at the time to comport with what actually happened.

According to one unnamed State Department official who spoke while the war was still in full swing, "as we contemplated the use of force over the past fourteen months, we constructed four different models. One was that the whiff of gunpowder, just the threat of force, would make [Milosevic] back down. Another was that he needed to take some hit to justify acquiescence. Another was that he was a playground bully who would fight but back off after a punch in the nose. And the fourth was that he would react like Saddam Hussein." In Iraq, Hussein had hunkered down and tried to ride out allied bombing, which is essentially how Milosevic behaved for those seventy-eight days. Albright expected that the third outcome was by far the most likely, with Milosevic behaving like the bully until "a few punches were thrown" and then capitulating (Lipmann 1999). This general feeling was shared in many European capitals. As Daalder and O'Hanlon note, "NATO did not expect a long war. Worse, it did not even prepare for the possibility" (Daalder and O'Hanlon 2000, 103).

Homo Psychologicus

According to Michael Hirsch, "historians may one day rank Kosovo alongside the Bay of Pigs as a diplomatic and military miscalculation" (Hirsch 1999, 65; see also Mandelbaum 1999). While this may be overstating the case somewhat, there were certainly plenty of miscalculations and misperceptions to go around, on all sides. Indeed, the Kosovo case provides us with an excellent example of what might be termed "mutual misperception." From the perspective of *Homo Psychologicus*, misperception first of all played a clear role on the Yugoslav side. Milosevic misjudged NATO intentions and appears to have done so repeatedly. Most obviously, he did not take the threats that American envoys like Richard Holbrooke issued seriously, since he judged that the United States lacked any vital interest in what he saw as a primarily internal Yugoslav matter. President Clinton himself made what military planners regarded as a key strategic error in this regard; when he delivered his speech on March 24 announcing the beginning of the war, he stated rather pointedly that "I do not intend to put our troops in Kosovo to fight a war." Although the language was deliberately ambiguous, this was obviously done to reassure members of Congress and skeptical NATO allies that he did not wish to put U.S. ground troops in Kosovo. Nonetheless, Milosevic may well have interpreted this to mean that Clinton lacked resolve. Surely the President did not intend to fight a war without using troops? As we have noted, Western leaders had long treated Kosovo as a domestic matter for their own (largely self-interested) reasons, and Holbrooke had reaffirmed that the United States saw Kosovo as an internal matter in his meetings with the Serb leader (although he simultaneously made it abundantly clear that ethnic cleansing there was unacceptable). Milosevic at one point suggested that the United States would be "crazy" to go to war over Kosovo. While Holbrooke told him in response that "we are just crazy enough to do it," the Serb leader clearly did not find this threat credible. Milosevic may also have believed, with some justification, that Clinton would not intervene because he already had too many problems at home. This was the view expressed by the former Senator

Bob Dole, for instance, after he was sent to Yugoslavia as a special envoy of the president in 1998. Upon his return, he visited Clinton in the White House:

> I told the president that there have been so many empty gestures that I don't believe Milosevic really believes anything will ever happen. That was sort of my message. But let's face it, the president was preoccupied with Monica Lewinsky. And I think it's fair to say, without disclosing what was said, that we talked about that. So I think it was a distraction, I think the whole Lewinsky thing. I've said I think Kosovo was maybe the first casualty of the Lewinsky affair.[7]

Correspondingly, because Milosevic made this key miscalculation early on, many U.S. and NATO decision-makers then seriously underestimated his will to resist the bombing. The Serb leaders obviously assumed—or simply hoped—that the all-too-evident splits in NATO's unprecedented war by committee would become gaping chasms. Since both President Clinton and NATO leaders also signaled that they were highly reluctant to use land troops in this case, the Serbian leader may well have calculated that he could ride out bombing from the air, and that the NATO political consensus would not last long enough to do serious military damage. By skillfully manipulating divisions within Western alliances as he had done many times before, he could drive a wedge between the United States and its allies, thereby ensuring that nothing of any consequence would occur to stop his plans. These were probably reasonable inferences for him to have made based on the information available to him, and the signals many Western leaders were sending him can only have reinforced these.

Faced with cognitive complexity—and the Yugoslav case certainly invoked that, involving as it did a long story of conflict and coexistence, which few in the West understood—human beings often fall back on historical analogies. We cut through all the detail and reach for a device that simplifies everything. The U.S. decision-making process about Kosovo in both the executive and the legislative branches was replete with analogies (Hehir 2006; Paris 2002), and the analogical reasoning approach may be especially helpful in explaining why American and European policymakers were so convinced that Milosevic would back down quickly not long after NATO began the bombing. Part of the answer, as we have seen, probably lies in the faulty intelligence assessments provided to the President. This, however, merely restates the problem: *why* were representatives of the CIA—and for that matter, individuals from the State Department—so convinced of this? As Daalder and O'Hanlon note, it probably had a great deal to do with the fact that many administration officials were relying so heavily on the (faulty) analogy with what had happened in Bosnia in the early 1990s (Daalder and O'Hanlon 2000, 92–93). Yugoslavia had come apart at the seams, taking many Western observers by surprise. The Clinton administration had advocated a strategy of "lift and strike," lifting the arms embargo that the United Nations had placed on all parties to the conflict and striking Serbia from the air. Most of the European powers (many of whom had peacekeepers on the ground) opposed both of these measures, however, and what resulted was effectively a policy of "rift and drift" (Drew 1994, 159).

The British Foreign Secretary Douglas Hurd famously stated that lifting the embargo would be like "heaping fuel on the flames," a phrase that outraged many in Washington. The result had been a long stalemate—broken only in 1995 when NATO, under U.S. prompting, finally bombed the Serbs, and Richard Holbrooke brokered the Dayton Accords—and for the first half of the 1990s, the West had looked helplessly on as Slobodan Milosevic and his Bosnian Serb allies accelerated their campaign of ethnic cleansing against Bosnian Muslims and Croats.

Albright in particular was affected by the "Bosnia syndrome," which suggested that obfuscation by the international community in the face of a genocide and a humanitarian disaster merely defers decisive action to a later date, after the damage has already been done. In her view, the United States needed to act immediately and decisively this time. "I believe in learning lessons," she later recalled, "and I believed that it was very important to make clear that the kinds of things that Milosevic does—which is decide that because you are not his ethnic group that you don't deserve to exist—is unacceptable. And it is not just a lesson for Kosovo, but it is—and it is not American to stand by and watch this kind of a thing." In March 1998 there was a massacre at Prekaz, in which Serb units slaughtered more than fifty members of the KLA's chief Adem Jashari's family, including women and small children. "I came down pretty hard, in terms of saying that we had learned a lot of lessons out of Bosnia, where we had waited too long to do something, and that we would be judged very harshly if we allowed something like this to happen again," Albright recalled. Equally, when Serb forces rampaged through Racak in early 1999, she had another strong sense of déjà vu. For Albright, "when the pictures showed up of these massacres and there was this sense—the sense that I'd had from the very beginning of the year, that we had—were reliving the stories of Srebrenica[8] and the terrible things that had happened in Bosnia, and that we knew better now, that we shouldn't be allowing these kinds of things to happen."[9]

Unfortunately, while the comparison may have been apt in some ways, it was misleading in others. Ambassador Holbrooke in particular seems to have believed that if he could negotiate a peace deal with Milosevic at Dayton, he could do so again in Belgrade (Hehir 2006, 74–75). Milosevic had caved in after two weeks of bombing in 1995, and there was a general feeling that he would do so again in 1999. But as Daalder and O'Hanlon note, the analogy was flawed for a number of basic reasons. First of all, while Kosovo had long been recognized internationally as an integral part of Serbia, Bosnia was a separate entity within Yugoslavia. The United States recognized that Bosnia was an independent entity in April 1992 when it declared its independence. Second, Kosovo was "special" to the Serbs in a way that Bosnia was not. It is often compared to a kind of southeast European Jerusalem. As Daalder and O'Hanlon note, "Kosovo is the cradle of Serb nationalism: it is the site of Serbia's historical defeat by the Ottoman empire, it is home to numerous important Serb monasteries, and it contains the seat of the patriarchate of the Serb Orthodox-Christian Church." And third, U.S. decision-makers misread the lessons of Dayton. Contrary to popular belief, the NATO bombing campaign began *after* Milosevic had already decided to capitulate; what really convinced the

Serb leader that he had to sue for peace in 1995 was the massive Croatian offensive that occurred in August of that year (Daalder and O'Hanlon 2000, 92–93).

In a less proximate but still very significant sense, Albright's life history exerted an important impact on her Kosovo strategy as well. She repeatedly referred during to Kosovo crisis to the lessons of Munich, which had helped shape her whole worldview. "My mind-set is Munich," as she has succinctly put it (Dobbs 1999, 34; see also Hehir 2006, 96). Her family had fled both fascism and communism, and she twice became a refugee in her early life. Albright consequently developed a somewhat hawkish view toward foreign policy, especially when it came to the use of military force against brutal dictatorships. Although she obviously came from a different time and place, the lessons of appeasement—"fight aggression early," "never reward a bully"—were no less significant in Albright's experience than they had been for Kennedy and Johnson. The danger of appeasing Milosevic played in a key role in her thinking about Bosnia and then Kosovo. On one especially memorable occasion, which she relates in her memoirs, she upbraided her assistant Jamie Rubin at a meeting in Europe for daring to suggest that she compromise on one issue. "Jamie do you think we're at Munich?" she asked him (Albright 2003, 386). Similarly, Wesley Clark—in many ways even more hawkish than Albright—used the World War II analogy in opposing a quick peace deal during the NATO bombing campaign, and he thought that the eventual deal reached with Milosevic gave too much away at a point when Clark believed he had the Serbian dictator on the ropes. "All along, I always had a terrible feeling about Milosevic, that we were really sort of making a compromise with Hitler in 1943," Clark recalled (Smith 1994).

Although he talked about it less, for President Clinton and his generation—which included Secretary Cohen—Vietnam rather than Munich was clearly uppermost in his mind. The Vietnam syndrome suggested somewhat contrasting lessons, but the main lesson Clinton had taken was the same one that influenced the Joint Chiefs: avoid the use of military force overseas, unless it absolutely cannot be avoided (Lebow 1995, 239–40). In this sense, the tension between the young President—who had been accused of dodging the draft during the Vietnam War, and who had pushed the Chiefs to allow gays in the military—was ironic, since they both shared the same hesitancy to employ U.S. power abroad and wield the big stick. Former Clinton State Department official Bruce Jentelson joked that while Theodore Roosevelt's maxim in foreign policy had been "talk softly and carry a big stick," Clinton's was "talk loudly and carry a small stick" (quoted in Berman and Goldman 1996, 300). While Albright's Munich experience caused her to develop into a strident moral idealist, Clinton was less ideologically driven and more pragmatic, taking each case on its practical and political merits. In 1994 he had refused against Secretary Albright's advice to intervene to halt the genocide then taking place in Rwanda, only the year after an attempt to capture the Somali warlord Mohammed Farah Aideed went badly wrong in the "Black Hawk Down" incident (Bowden 1999). While the events in Rwanda must have weakened his resistance to using military force somewhat—again, the United States had mostly stood by while a horrifying genocide took place—Somalia was clearly seared into Clinton's memory, and it must have reinforced the lessons he had taken from Vietnam (Halberstam 2002, 261–65).

Hanging over everything—perhaps in the background, but important never-theless—was the specter of a repetition of World War I, which had after all begun in precisely the same region. Richard Holbrooke may have been seduced by the Bosnia-Dayton analogy, where NATO bombing and his own negotiating skills had opened, or appeared to open, the door to the greatest diplomatic success of his career. But he also had a heavy sense of the history of the place, and worried that neighboring states and their separatist movements could be sucked into the conflict, just as the parties had appeared to literally fall into war in 1914. "We pre-sented the ultimatum to Milosevic that if he didn't sign the agreement, the bomb-ing would start," Holbrooke recalled. "And he said, 'No.' We stayed in Belgrade overnight. In the morning, I went back completely alone to see him, because I was very conscious of the fact that, in August of 1914 in that part of the world, a huge war had started through an avoidable misunderstanding. World War I was not inevitable, as many historians say. It could have been avoided, and it was a diplo-matically botched negotiation. I didn't want to have a repetition of that, even at a lower level."[10]

What other psychological approaches might be useful in understanding the Kosovo decision-making? Although its application to this case may be controver-sial, prospect theory might be relevant here. Bill Clinton was certainly operating in a domain of losses by the summer of 1998 and well into early 1999. While we cannot know for sure that this was what he was perceiving at the time, one may reasonably infer that the deluge of political trouble that had descended on his presidency had caused him to frame the situation he faced in this way. The Monica Lewinsky scandal had broken in early 2008, adding to the President's troubles over the Whitewater investigations. Republicans were also attacking what they saw as Clinton's feeble response to Saddam Hussein's continual defi-ance of UN weapons inspections, and NATO's credibility was under grave threat. Although the impeachment process was over by March 1999 when the air war in Kosovo was initiated, Clinton was still at a politically low ebb. As we have seen, some critics alleged that a *Wag the Dog* effect was occurring whenever the admin-istration launched a bombing raid. In international relations theory, this is more formally known as the "diversionary theory of war" (see Levy 1989 for a review and critique). Faced with difficulties at home, the theory suggests, leaders may be apt to manufacture conflicts or escalate preexisting ones in order to distract attention from these difficulties. In the United States, the incentive to do so may be exacerbated by the tendency of Americans to rally around the flag when the president undertakes a major military initiative abroad. Since presidents know that this effect will occur in any foreign policy crisis—regardless of whether the outcome is good or bad—they may have particular incentives to engage in diver-sionary behavior in a domain of loss. In somewhat similar though not identical vein, Steven Redd has argued that poliheuristic theory may be useful in explaining

Clinton's decision-making in this case, arguing that domestic political considerations prompted the President to respond in some way. Fear of casualties—again, largely a domestic consideration—then dictated his decision to fight from the air rather than putting boots on the ground (Redd 2005).

ASSESSING THE THREE PERSPECTIVES

From the perspective of *Homo Bureaucraticus*, there is plenty of evidence of infighting between the representatives of various organizations, especially over the Apache helicopter issue. Moreover, this is in many ways an easiest case to prove for this perspective, since the literature suggests that bureaucratic politics are likely to be most significant when presidential attention is lacking and where lower-level officials play a greater role. The facts concerning some aspects of bureaucratic behavior during the decision-making are still unclear, however: Did Wesley Clark really face political pressure from the White House to end the bombing as soon as possible, for instance, or was this a misinterpretation of his comments? Moreover, a simple version of the where-you-stand axiom seems especially weak here. President Clinton and Vice President Gore appear to behave in ways consistent with that rule, and the White House was clearly reluctant to go to war. And yet rather than advocating diplomacy, Secretary of State Albright was always the *strongest* advocate of the bombing campaign. Equally, Secretary of Defense Cohen was the *weakest* advocate of military intervention, and Chairman of the Joint Chiefs Shelton was lukewarm at best.

There are two different ways of looking at this result: on the one hand, this case study (like other examples we have seen) suggests that the classic where-you-stand view is simply incorrect or works only on occasion. On the other hand, a more sophisticated version of the proposition would accept that organizations can and do change their preferences over time, and that the Pentagon seems to have gotten more risk-averse over time just as the State Department has moved in the opposite direction. Equally, it often seems as if the preferences of the players stemmed more from their personal life experiences than from their bureaucratic positions in this case study, an argument that strengthens *Homo Psychologicus*. Sandy Berger has noted that William Cohen was the only member of the national security team who saw no particular need to intervene militarily into Kosovo, and he attributes this to the fact that Cohen was the only one who had not been in the administration during the gut-wrenching experience of Bosnia, where the conflict dragged on for several years and hundreds of thousands of casualties mounted before the United States and NATO finally bombed Milosevic to the negotiation table (Halberstam 2002, 443). Moreover, the analogical reasoning approach helps explain why the U.S. decision-makers believed that the Serb leader would capitulate quite quickly in the face of NATO's bombing campaign.

At the same time, some aspects of *Homo Psychologicus* seem weak here as well. Against prospect theory, it has to be noted that Bill Clinton for a long time responded to the domain of loss he faced not by engaging in a reckless foreign policy behavior but by exhibiting restraint. Moreover, a president who *knows* (as Clinton certainly did) that his opponents are expecting him to act in a diversionary fashion in foreign policy has considerable disincentives to fulfill the prophecies of his political adversaries. Obviously, confirming these predictions risks courting further disaster and increasing losses. In fact, the Lewinsky affair and ongoing impeachment trial both appear to have inhibited the president's behavior for a long time. Only when the impeachment process was over did he finally approve a bombing campaign, which also suggests a distracting and politically inhibiting effect to the process initiated by Special Prosecutor Kenneth Starr. The effect, in other words, may have been precisely the opposite from that predicted by prospect theory, where decision-makers are only too prepared to take considerable risks or gambles in order to restore the previous status quo. Arguably, the theory suggests that Clinton should have been willing to risk a broader war, possibly including the use of ground troops, but this did not happen. Again, the conclusion of this case study seems to be that real-world political decision-making is more complex than prospect theory would suggest.

With reference to *Homo Sociologicus*, we should also be careful about automatically diagnosing groupthink in this case. For one thing, *Sociologicus* is at its best when dealing with conditions of group conformity, where decision-makers essentially agree with one another and feel some pressure to do so. Although there were some indications of this early on, during the air war dissensus rather than consensus—especially a difference of opinion between State and Defense as to how effective air power would be—seems a more apt description of the decision-making processes in this case (an area where *Bureaucraticus* clearly has the edge). The mere presence of collective delusions at the group level is probably not sufficient to diagnose groupthink reliably, since as we saw in chapter 3 several rather specific conditions need to be present. There is some evidence of self-censorship on Albright's part, of the exertion of group pressure on her as a dissenter, and some indications of mindguarding on Berger's part. In remaining largely silent on the use of military force early on, Albright may simply have been biding her time rather than bowing to group pressure, and her own views ultimately prevailed in any case. Berger, on the other hand, may simply have been reflecting the President's own views at that time, which were essentially that a war in Kosovo was the last thing he needed during this scandal-ridden phase of his presidency.

Equally, is there any evidence that the decision-makers were laboring under an illusion of invulnerability, for instance? While this is hard to assess, it seems unlikely. Yugoslavia was widely seen as an intractable no-win issue, which would be exceptionally difficult for Western leaders to resolve, and most of the decision-makers seem to have felt vulnerability, not its opposite, for the political reasons already given. Although Bill Clinton had been acquitted by the Senate, many members of his national security team felt let down by the President's behavior, and more generally key individuals like Cohen and Berger appear to have felt highly constrained by the political situation they faced vis-à-vis Congress, especially on the issue of the former Yugoslavia. If anything, they may have felt more constrained than they actually were, since Clinton plausibly *could* have made his case to NATO and the American people more forcefully, confident in the short-term at least that Americans would rally around the flag and that European members would have followed decisive U.S. leadership on the issue. As Daalder and O'Hanlon note, the administration probably need not have gotten a congressional authorization for the war either, and probably would not have attempted to do so had the President ultimately decided to put U.S. troops into Kosovo (Daalder and O'Hanlon 2000, 97–100). Nor does it seem likely that Congress would have utilized the appropriations process to cut off funding for a land operation if the President had committed U.S. soldiers abroad.

CHAPTER 10

Into Iraq: A War of Choice

U.S. Army soldiers in the streets of Najaf, Iraq. SOURCE: AP Photo/Jim MacMillan

WHY DID THE UNITED STATES DECIDE
TO INVADE IRAQ?

On the last day of 2006, Saddam Hussein, the former leader of Iraq, was executed at an Iraqi army base after being found guilty of crimes against humanity. He was found hiding in a manhole near a farmhouse, unkempt and disheveled, a mere shadow of the man who had ruled Iraq with savage ferocity since 1979. His demise marked the end of a long and tortuous saga, with more twists and turns than the plot of a Tom Clancy novel, and George W. Bush's confrontation was a war that was "twelve years in the making" (Purdum 2003, 9–31). During the 1980s, Iraq had actually been an ally of the United States, and Donald Rumsfeld—ironically, later to become secretary of defense in George W. Bush's (Bush 43) administration, when the United States invaded the country—had actually shaken hands with the Iraqi dictator. This was during the administration of

Ronald Reagan, at a time when the United States aligned itself with Iraq because its neighbor Iran (with whom Hussein had gone to war in 1980) was judged the greater enemy. Since that time, Saddam had become a thorn in the flesh of successive American presidents, especially since George H. W. Bush (Bush 41) became president. Most notably, the Iraqi leader had invaded his neighbor Kuwait in 1990, taking control of the country and its oil fields. Bush 41 had responded by going to war with Iraq, creating a substantial international coalition to fight Saddam in what is now known as the first Persian Gulf War (1990–91). The United States and its allies quickly forced Hussein's troops to leave Kuwait, although the war stopped at the border of Iraq. Bush 41 had no particular interest in deposing Saddam or changing the landscape of the Middle East; as a cautious realist in foreign policy— very much like Nixon and Kissinger in an earlier era—he sought merely to reestablish the status quo or balance of power that had existed prior to the invasion of Kuwait. Bush was also concerned that invading Iraq itself would shatter the coalition he had created against Saddam, an alliance which included not only Israel but Arab states like Saudi Arabia.

Since that time, Iraq had been subject to stringent economic sanctions and UN weapons inspections. To many critics during the 1990s, however, it did not seem as if these attempts to rein in Saddam's regional ambitions were working. Iraq was continually defying the weapons inspectors, on one occasion throwing them out of the country altogether. The Clinton administration tried to contain Saddam, but neoconservatives within the Republican Party were especially dissatisfied with U.S. foreign policy during this period. They also believed that Bush 41 had failed to stand up for the Iraqi people, ignoring an issue they saw in fundamentally moral terms. Some of them, like Paul Wolfowitz, had been members of Bush 41's administration and were appalled when the he failed to move on to Baghdad and remove Hussein from power. They were equally appalled when Bush 41 encouraged Iraqis to rise up against the dictator, but then stood by as Hussein ruthlessly and bloodily put down all dissent.

While some saw Saddam as little more than an annoyance, others viewed him as a mortal threat. He had used Weapons of Mass Destruction (WMDs) against his own people—most notably when he used poison gas against the Kurds in the northern region of Iraq in the 1980s, and had gunned down the Kurds and Shiites in 1991 when they tried to rise up against his rule—and many critics began to worry that the United States was simply not doing enough to prevent the Iraqi leader from re-creating what was assumed to be his new stock of chemical and biological weapons. During the 1990s Clinton's critics began to talk of regime change, and they persuaded a reluctant President to pass the Iraq Liberation Act in October 1998, committing the United States to regime change and support for democratic movements in the country. Although the congressional declaration was partly symbolic, Clinton followed this up less than two months later with a four-day bombing campaign of Iraq known as Operation Desert Fox.

When George W. Bush (43) arrived in the White House in 2001, the hawks saw their opportunity. The politically cautious Bill Clinton was never going to invade Iraq or seriously attempt to depose Saddam Hussein, any more than Bush 41 had been willing to go to Baghdad. But Bush 43 looked far more promising in this respect. Where his father had been a realist, Bush 43 displayed all the characteristics of a moral idealist. A novice in foreign affairs, he tended to be moved by moral instinct and passionate conviction rather than the cool calculation of national interest. While he surrounded himself with some of the realists who had worked for his father—including Colin Powell, who would become secretary of State during W.'s first term—key positions within the Pentagon and White House were occupied by neoconservatives, with whom the president more readily identified (Mann 2004). Following some attempts at addressing the problem of Saddam diplomatically, in March 2003—backed by a much smaller, narrower alliance that Bush 43 referred to as "the coalition of the willing"—the president went to war in Iraq. The war was deeply unpopular in Europe and in the Middle East, and there were even large-scale protests against the war in the United Kingdom (probably Bush's staunchest ally during the conflict).

We may *never* be able to answer the question of why the Bush 43 administration chose to invade Iraq, at least not in any definitive way.[1] Richard Haass—at that time Director of Policy Planning for the State Department—has said that he "will go to his grave not knowing the answer." Haass insists that "it was an accretion, a tipping point. A decision was not made—a decision just happened, and you can't say when and how" (Packer 2005, 45–46). The decision to invade Iraq, Haass suggests, was never properly staffed out to the various agencies—the State Department in particular seems to have played a lesser role in the decision-making than the Pentagon's Office of Special Plans or the Vice President's office, and hence the administration never drew upon the variety of expertise and advice available to it. The debates in the National Security Council were all about how and when to invade Iraq, never about *whether* it should be done (Suskind 2004, 76).

It is now clear that the decision, such as it was, was made at a very early stage in the life of the administration. A variety of knowledgeable sources make this apparent. Former Counterterrorism Chief Richard Clarke, for instance, notes that both Donald Rumsfeld and Paul Wolfowitz had been arguing for an invasion of Iraq for some years and that both seized on 9/11 as an opportunity to make their case for this. "Since the beginning of the administration, indeed well before, they had been pressing for a war with Iraq" (Clarke 2004, 30). Similarly, former Treasury Secretary Paul O'Neill recalls an invasion of Iraq being the leading topic of discussion in the NSC only ten days after Bush 43's inauguration. On January 30, 2001, Iraq was a prominent topic on the agenda, and the NSC meeting that day featured a presentation of grainy intelligence photographs supposedly showing Saddam's chemical and biological weapons facilities (Suskind 2004, 73). In O'Neill's own words, "from the very beginning, there was a conviction that Saddam Hussein was a bad person and that he needed to go. It was all about finding a way to do it. That was the tone of it. The president saying 'Go find me a way to do this.' For me, the notion of pre-emption, that the U.S. has the unilateral right to do whatever we decide to do, is a really huge leap."[2]

"Ten days in, and it was all about Iraq," O'Neill says (ibid. 75). The administration seems to have managed to conceal this from its allies until the summer of 2002, when the British were surprised to learn that the decision to invade Iraq had effectively been made already. The famous "Downing Street Memo" of July 23, 2002, tells much the same story as Clarke and O'Neill (albeit just over a year after the two Americans discovered what was in the works). In the memo Sir Richard Dearlove, head of Britain's MI6, reported the following in regard to the talks he had been holding with Bush officials in Washington:

> There was a perceptible shift in attitude. Military action was now seen as inevitable. Bush wanted to remove Saddam, through military action, justified by the conjunction of terrorism and WMD [weapons of mass destruction]. But the intelligence and facts were being fixed around the policy. The NSC had no patience with the UN route, and no enthusiasm for publishing material on the Iraqi regime's record. There was little discussion in Washington of the aftermath after military action. (see Danner 2006, 88–89)

It is difficult to present this case study as an example of procedural rationality, for the simple reason that there was never any comprehensive examination of different options for dealing with Saddam, and no proper discussion of alternatives to an outright invasion. In this sense, it perhaps most closely resembles the Bay of Pigs case study, discussed in chapter 5. The reader will recall that in that case also, there was no comprehensive analysis of different ways of getting rid of Castro; rather, the decision was essentially "do we go ahead or not?" From very early on, there was a widespread perception within the administration—from which only Colin Powell and his staff deviated—that all other options had been exhausted, and therefore that no reexamination of alternatives was necessary.

As in the Kosovo case, only a relatively small theoretically driven literature exists on the decision to invade Iraq at this time. Nevertheless, we have a huge wealth of empirical materials to draw upon in making arguments from our three perspectives. An extraordinary number of books and articles have now been published about the invasion and occupation of Iraq, in addition to the works by Clarke, Danner, Suskind, and Packer already cited (see, e.g., Bamford 2004; Bremer 2006; Chandrasekaran 2006; Diamond 2005; Galbraith 2006; Gordon and Trainor 2006; Isikoff 2006; Mann 2004; Olson 2006; Ricks 2006; Risen 2006; Suskind 2006; Wilson 2004; and Woodward 2002, 2004, 2006, 2009). We now also have a memoir by Bush 43, which seeks to explain why he acted as he did (Bush 2010). Reading many of the works cited above, as well as talking to some of the individuals involved in the earliest days of the Iraqi reconstruction process, provides a fascinating window into the decision-making processes we are interested in.

How would each of our approaches account for the Bush administration's decision-making regarding Iraq? As usual, each argues that decision-making processes we can observe failed to live up to the exalted standards that *Homo Economicus* (or the RAM approach) expects, but each traces this shortfall to different processes. There is obviously much we still do not know about the manner in which the decision to invade Iraq in 2003 was made. There are some interesting indications from the vantage point of *Homo Sociologicus*, however, that groupthink may have played a prominent role in that decision. Colin Powell seems to have played the role of a somewhat subdued dissenter in this instance. Those who argued against an invasion were soon excluded from Bush's inner circle, which became an "echo chamber" in Ron Suskind's memorable phrase. From the perspective of *Homo Bureaucraticus*, meanwhile, it is interesting that those who sat in the State Department—most notably Powell, his deputy Richard Armitage and his Chief of Staff Lawrence Wilkerson—were *least* enthusiastic about a military invasion, arguing that sanctions, weapons inspections, and diplomatic pressures needed to be given more time, while those in the Pentagon exhibited an almost reckless can-do attitude. Bureaucratic infighting between State and Defense (and between State and Cheney's office) during the postinvasion reconstruction phase has been widely reported. Finally, various cognitive and motivational errors also seem evident in the decision to go into Iraq, including misperceptions about the adversary, the so-called drunkard's search (looking for data in psychologically convenient places), the use of Munich/Hitler as an analogy, the resistance of entrenched beliefs in the face of disconfirming evidence, and the impact of wishful thinking in general. We can thus make a good case that *Homo Psychologicus* adds a great deal to our understanding of the decision-making as well.

Homo Bureaucraticus

As various accounts attest, there was extensive bureaucratic infighting between State, Defense, and the VP's office over Iraq. Many observers assumed at the time that nobody in the U.S. government had prepared for what would happen after the war, for instance. But Bush 43 makes it clear in his memoirs that there were extensive preparations made for the postwar reconstruction of Iraq. As he recalls, "two of our biggest concerns were starvation and refugees. Sixty percent of Iraqis were dependent on the government as a source of food. An estimated two million Iraqis could be displaced from their homes during war" (Bush 2010, 237). He also notes that beginning in the fall of 2002, the administration began to draw up extensive short-term and long-term plans for what would happen to Iraq after an invasion, including plans to ensure that education, health, water, and electricity would be available to ordinary Iraqis, and ideas for redesigning Iraq's political system. A new office of Reconstruction and Humanitarian Assistance (ORHA) was to be created, headed by Lt. General Jay Garner. Garner had some experience of dealing with Iraqis from the first Persian Gulf War, and he initially found favor with Rumsfeld.

Not long after the invasion, news reports began to emanate from Iraq that the country was in chaos. In fact, even Bush admits that Baghdad descended into "a state of lawlessness" (ibid. 247). With no government in place, looting of shops and businesses was widespread, and Bush has conceded that he made a basic error in not responding to this more quickly (ibid. 256). Basic necessities went unattended as well. Power stations were not running, electricity had been turned off through much of Baghdad, and food and water were often in short supply. Moreover, the war created a health care crisis, and the country's infrastructure buckled under the strain of the war. What had happened to all these much-vaunted preparations?

No doubt some of the disarray was the inevitable by-product of war, and a certain amount of dislocation was always likely. In many ways, however, much of the chaos was directly attributable to bureaucratic politics. In somewhat similar fashion to Bill Clinton in his autobiography, Bush essentially airbrushes over some of the key debates going on behind the scenes, especially the fact that these plans fell victim to bureaucratic "knife-fighting" between Powell and Rumsfeld. The State Department's Future of Iraq project was a particular bone of contention, and its rejection arguably had very damaging consequences (Phillips 2005, Diamond 2005, Olson 2006). The extensive planning to which George W. Bush refers in his memoirs is probably a reference to this, since State was the only organization prior to the war that had drawn up any preparations. Indeed, members of the Future of Iraq project had been thinking about Iraqi reconstruction as early as October 2001 (Diamond 2005, 27). But there was a problem from the Pentagon's perspective: Rumsfeld thought that State would engage in too much nation building, the very thing for which Bush 43 had criticized his predecessor during the 2000 campaign. He apparently believed that the State Department would not be sufficiently pro-democracy in Iraq. As we saw in chapter 9, the Pentagon also did not wish to become embroiled in the kind of lengthy, open-ended peacekeeping operations which it had performed only with extreme reluctance during the Clinton era. Rumsfeld envisioned a quick in-and-out operation, with no real occupation and certainly no long-term commitment to the people of Iraq.

Rumsfeld successfully lobbied the President to take postwar reconstruction out of the hands of the State Department and the Future of Iraq project, and make this the responsibility of the Pentagon. But there was an obvious problem: Defense had no postwar plans of its own, in part because it does not "do" postwar reconstruction, and in part because it had always been assumed that this would be the State Department's role in Iraq. At the same time, the Pentagon was extremely reluctant to provide the kind of troop numbers that the situation required. One member of the NSC staff estimated that based on the Kosovo model, it would take about half a million troops to police Iraq after the government dissolved. Since many of America's allies had not been on board with the idea of invading Iraq in the first place, it was unlikely that these numbers could be made up with a predominantly multinational force. Inevitably, the implication was that half a million U.S. troops would be needed. This was unacceptable to the Pentagon, and so the whole idea of postwar planning became a casualty of the bureaucratic war (Packer 2005, 110–11).

Eventually, however, something had to fill the void. Rather than draw upon the planning already done, Rumsfeld insisted that a new office, ORHA, be created at the eleventh hour under Pentagon control. It would be headed by Jay Garner, who Rumsfeld knew slightly and apparently trusted. The unfortunate by-product of this bureaucratic tussle, though, was that all the work that had been done already was essentially tossed out of the window, and Garner was left in the unenviable position of making up policies and plans on the hoof. Indeed, Garner has spoken of making up the plans "on the back of an envelope" on the way to Iraq (Garner 2007).

Sadly, the bureaucratic knife fight even continued after the United States had nominally "won" the war and the reconstruction phase had begun. Garner quickly realized to his surprise that others in the government had already been thinking about the scenarios that postwar Iraq would face, and he naturally sought to bring them on board. Like any good leader, he realized that he did not know everything, and that the best way to overcome one's own limitations is surround oneself with people who know the things we do not. ORHA was created only in late January 2003 and did not even have office space until the following month. One of the first things that Garner did, however, was to call various experts on Iraq and postwar construction together at the National Defense University, located in DC and run by the Department of Defense in late February. Together with the historian Paul Rudd, Garner happened to stumble upon a man called Tom Warrick, who seemed to know far more about the issues than they did. It turned out that Warrick had been the head of the Future of Iraq project for the State Department, and Garner immediately hired him for ORHA. He also hired Meaghan O'Sullivan, who worked for State's policy planning team (Packer 2005, 123–24).

At this point, however, Rumsfeld created another bureaucratic block. He got Warrick and O'Sullivan thrown off the team, claiming that the order had come from Cheney. When Colin Powell heard about this, he was furious and told Rumsfeld that he wanted his employees back on ORHA's team. "I can take prisoners too," he reportedly told him. Rumsfeld refused, although he later quietly agreed to let O'Sullivan back on the team. An ORHA request for thirty-four State Department experts on Iraq was turned down by Rumsfeld (Phillips 2005, 127). Other State department employees that Garner had asked for would be held up for months by the Pentagon and the VP's office, and Tom Warrick—the man who knew more about Iraq postwar planning than anyone else in the government—was only allowed to go to Iraq one full year after the war began (Packer 2005, 123–26).

Moreover, from the *Homo Bureaucraticus* perspective, the traditional where-you-stand approach seems to at least partially account for the preferences of the players in the debate. Although "correlation is not causation," the positions of the key decision-makers were all fairly predictable prior to the discussion about whether to invade. The Pentagon representatives were all in favor. Paul Wolfowitz was one of the most visible proponents of the war against Saddam, while another official serving on the Defense Review Board, Kenneth Adelman, had famously suggested that the invasion would be a "cakewalk." On the other hand, Powell, Lawrence Wilkerson, and Richard Armitage were all in favor of continuing with diplomatic efforts. If Saddam Hussein was little more than a "toothache" for Powell, as he memorably put it on at least one occasion, from the White House perspective, Saddam was a significant thorn in the flesh, a cancer that had to be excised. While the story was probably more complex than this account might suggest, each of the players tended to see the Iraq issue from his or her vantage point within the government. Each organization argued for what it could do. Powell, Rumsfeld, and Cheney, moreover, were all accomplished bureaucratic knife fighters, highly accustomed to the ways of Washington (Purdum 2003, 34–37).

It may be that there was no single reason behind the decision to invade Iraq, and this is the explanation to which George Packer gives most weight. Paul Wolfowitz, for instance, has suggested in an extraordinary admission that the famous WMD justification was simply a least common denominator, that thing onto which everyone could sign but by implication not the real motivation. "The truth is that for reasons that have a lot to do with the U.S. government bureaucracy," Wolfowitz rather revealingly admits, "we settled on the one issue that everyone could agree upon, and that was weapons of mass destruction" (Packer 2005, 60). Outside the administration and among those intellectuals on the Right and Left who supported the war—and certainly for the administration's own intellectuals like Wolfowitz—the Iraq intervention was principally an opportunity to remake the Middle East and advance the cause of liberalism in a region that has so far seen little of it:

> The whole appeal of the idea lay in its audacity. It would, with one violent push, shove history out of a deep hole. By a chain reaction, a reverse domino effect, war in Iraq would weaken the Middle East's dictatorships and undermine its murderous ideologies and begin to spread the balm of liberal democracy. The road to Jerusalem, Riyadh, Damascus, and Tehran went through Baghdad. To persist with caution toward the sick, dangerous status quo of the Middle East would be contemptible, almost unbearable. Who wouldn't choose amputation over gangrene? With will and imagination, America could strike one great blow at terrorism, tyranny, underdevelopment, and the region's hardest, saddest problem (Packer 2005, 58).

But not everyone thought in these terms, Packer notes. There were relatively few geostrategic, neoconservative intellectuals in the president's immediate ambit even in the run-up to the war. Wolfowitz was a "big ideas" man, but most within the Bush administration were not. For them, Saddam was an existential threat, a menace to other states in the region such as Israel. This was probably true for Rumsfeld and certainly for Cheney also, who was convinced that an intimate link existed between Iraq and al-Qaeda. This made not one *casus belli* but three: (1) to set off a pro-democratic version of the domino theory, (2) to protect U.S. regional partners and ultimately America itself from WMDs, and (3) to strike back at Saddam for what some saw as his role in 9/11. From the White House's perspective, the war had to be sold to the American people in clear and simple terms, and so—at least according to Wolfowitz—they just split the difference and chose the WMD rationale. Since many Americans and Europeans shared the belief that Saddam had such weapons, it also made sense to compromise on this message. There was also an internal consensus on this rationale. While the CIA was unwilling to tell those officials who saw a link between Al-Qaeda and Saddam what they wanted to hear—the general finding was that no such link existed, and that if it ever did, it never amounted to much—the CIA, the Pentagon, and even the State Department all agreed that Iraq had WMDs. On December 21, 2002, CIA Director George Tenet told President Bush that the case against Saddam and WMDs was solid. Tenet famously called this a "slam dunk" (Tenet 2007, 359–67).

Homo Sociologicus

As Peter Galbraith has suggested, it is difficult to see Iraq as anything other than the product of miscalculation. The Bush 43 administration tried with some success to silence critics by demanding that they answer the simple question—"are we better off without Saddam Hussein or not?"—pointedly suggesting that this end was justified by whatever means were at hand, and that it took priority over all other desirable ends (Bush 2010, 257). Nevertheless, critics have argued that the invasion had a host of highly unfavorable consequences for the United States, many of which were foreseen by the war's critics early on. As Galbraith writes:

> A war intended to eliminate the threat from Saddam Hussein's nonexistent weapons of mass destruction ended up with Iran and North Korea much closer to having deployable nuclear weapons. A war intended to fight terror has helped the terrorists. A war intended to bring freedom and democracy to Iraq now has U.S. troops fighting for pro-Iranian Shiite theocrats and alongside unreformed Baathists. A war intended to undermine Iran's ayatollahs has resulted in a historical victory for Iran. Iranian-backed political parties control Iraq's government and armed forces, giving Iran a role in Iraq that it has not had in four centuries. A war intended to promote democracy in the Middle East has set it back. (Galbraith 2008, 1)

Galbraith goes on to list six more unintended consequences, including the adverse effects that the war in Iraq has had on American power and leadership around the globe. While we may quibble with some of these—some may be more temporary than others, for instance—it is beyond dispute that the war has had many adverse effects within the Middle East and beyond, a possibility to which George W. Bush and many of his colleagues seem to have been oblivious at the time the decision to invade was taken.

From the perspective of *Homo Sociologicus*, this leads us to pose the same question that Irving Janis asked about the Kennedy administration and the Bay of Pigs. Why did a collection of such intellectually gifted (and in this case, highly experienced) decision-makers get Iraq so badly wrong? It is ironic that the Iraq decisions of 2003 were made by a collection of individuals with such a rich store of decision-making experiences. On the one hand, it seems unlikely that George W. Bush himself thought about the issue of Iraq in sophisticated strategic terms. As Packer relates, Bush was so ill-informed about the country that Iraqi exiles like Kanan Makiya and Ahmed Chalabi apparently wasted one meeting in the Oval Office explaining to the president that the Iraqi population was divided between Kurds, Sunnis, and Shia (Packer 2005, 96). But W. surrounded himself with key advisers who had collectively amassed some two hundred years of decision-making experience, both inside and outside government.

Dick Cheney, for instance, had served Ford and Bush 41, while Colin Powell had experience from the Carter, Reagan, Bush 41, and Clinton years. Perhaps most notably, Donald Rumsfeld—already the youngest secretary of defense on record from his years in the Ford administration, and then the oldest under George W. Bush—was known for hard thinking about decision-making processes in general. "Reports that say that something hasn't happened are always interesting to me, because as we know, there are known knowns; there are things we know we know," Rumsfeld once ruminated from a podium at the Pentagon. "We also know there are known unknowns; that is to say we know there are some things we do not know. But there are also unknown unknowns— the ones we don't know we don't know. And if one looks throughout the history of our country and other free countries, it is the latter category that tend to be the difficult ones."[3] While the complexity of this statement was predictably lampooned by the late-night comedians, it does reveal a capacity for abstract thinking which is uncharacteristic of most previous secretaries of defense. The consequences of invading Iraq, ironically, presented the decision-makers with a whole network of what were in effect "unknown unknowns"; nobody really knew what the consequences of the invasion would be, although the critics proved prescient in highlighting how things would probably turn out well in advance of the invasion and occupation. "Unknowns" were also treated as "knowns" as certainty substituted for healthy skepticism.

Though he had never studied decision-making in an academic sense, Rumsfeld had clearly derived a whole series of decision-making rules from his time in business and government. As Rowan Scarborough notes, "Rumsfeld has an ever-evolving list, called 'Rumsfeld's Rules,' of bon mots and proverbs—some his, some overheard or read" (Scarborough 2004, 64). By the time he retuned to government in 2001, these had evolved into a full-length handbook. Rumsfeld himself published some of these "rules" prior to joining the Bush 43 administration, and while not all of them have to do with decision-making procedures, many of them do (see Rumsfeld 2001). He clearly viewed himself as a rigorous thinker who constantly challenges unstated assumptions and outdated bureaucratic SOPs, and sought to bring the management of the Pentagon and the policy process more generally closer to the RAM, or what Graham Allison and Philip Zelikow would call Model I–type decision making (Allison and Zelikow 1999). Rumsfeld became famous for his "snowflakes" or "Rummygrams," the unsigned commands and requests for information with which he peppered his subordinates, continually questioning the Pentagon's modus operandi. What is curious, though, is the extent to which he failed to examine his *own* assumptions about Iraq in the wake of 9/11. While the decision to go to war in Iraq was of course the president's, there is little if any evidence that Rumsfeld—or anyone else high up in the Bush 43 administration, for that matter—ever questioned the assumption that Saddam Hussein *had* weapons of mass destruction. He seems to have simply assumed that this was a "known," while any reasonably rigorous analysis of Iraq's capabilities in 2003 would have indicated that it was a "known unknown."

Were Irving Janis still alive, he would doubtless find many reasons to conclude that groupthink was operative among what has been termed the "Praetorian Guard" around President Bush (Levine 2004; McQueen 2005). While groupthink has been much criticized as a theory in recent years, it remains an instructive place to begin thinking about the Iraq decision-making process at the group level (Janis 1982). As we have seen repeatedly in this book, Janis defined the groupthink phenomenon as a process through which a group reaches a hasty or premature consensus and then becomes closed to outside ideas. In Janis's own words, groupthink is "a mode of thinking that people engage in when they are deeply involved in a cohesive group, when the members' strivings for unanimity override their motivation to realistically appraise alternative courses of action" (Janis 1982, 9). High group cohesion can develop, for instance, where the members have known each other for many years and/or think very much alike. While such a group *can* make effective decisions—group cohesion is a necessary but not sufficient condition for groupthink to occur—it can become prey to this pathology where members of the group come to prize "concurrence-seeking" over the full and rational consideration of all available courses of action.

A brief reminder of Janis's theory is probably in order here. He argued that groupthink has a number of causes in addition to high group cohesiveness, including insulation of the group from outside advice, aggressive and opinionated leadership, a lack of norms requiring methodical procedures, and homogeneity of members' backgrounds/ideology. Such groups develop a risk-taking illusion of invulnerability, collectively rationalize away warnings, fail to reconsider their core assumptions, believe themselves to be inherently moral, and develop excessively simplified, stereotyped views of out-groups. Moreover, the false consensus that develops in cases of groupthink is policed by direct pressure exerted on dissenters, self-censorship, and the emergence of self-appointed mindguards—members of the group who take it upon themselves to protect the leader and other members from dissenting views and information that might challenge the group's cherished consensus.

The fact that Bush does not appear to have used the formal apparatus of decision-making to go into Iraq does not mean that group processes are irrelevant, since the president seems to have interacted more informally in a group format with various individuals. What signs are there of dysfunctional group processes in this example, then? As Schafer and Crichlow have concluded, there was little if any decision-making structure in place on Iraq, but what structure existed was insulated, dominated by biased leadership, and subject to few if any methodical decision-making processes. There was also an illusion of invulnerability and evidence of the existence of "gatekeepers," or what Janis preferred to call mindguards (Schafer and Crichlow 2010, 227–30). During the days before the *Challenger* shuttle disaster in 1986—a case now used to train managers and other decision-makers in the perils of groupthink—one top-level manager at Morton-Thiokol, a private company working close with NASA, exhorted another to "take off your engineering hat and put on your management hat." On engineering grounds, there were very real concerns about taking off in unseasonably cold temperatures in January 1986—no shuttle had ever launched at such low temperatures—but pressure was exerted on doubters like Roger Boisjoly and others to set their concerns aside and "join the team." In classic cases of groupthink like this one, such mindguards emerge to preserve the illusion of consensus and to prevent the group from reconsidering rejected alternatives or outside advice. In the Iraq case these processes seem to have been mirrored in micro-format within particular organizations, such as the Coalition Provisional Authority (CPA), the CIA, and most of all the Pentagon's Office of Special Plans.

The CIA struggled to come up with impressive intelligence indicating that Iraq actually possessed WMDs, and on at least one occasion President Bush pushed for better evidence. In a meeting in December 2002 he noted, "surely we can do a better job of explaining the evidence against Saddam" (Bush 2010, 231). George Tenet seems to have agreed, but neither he nor the President ever seems to have questioned whether that evidence existed. Instead, he notes that there was an almost unquestioned consensus, especially within the administration itself but outside it as well, that it did. "The conclusion that Saddam Hussein had WMD was nearly a universal consensus," Bush recalled. "My predecessor believed it. Republicans and Democrats on Capitol Hill believed it. Intelligence agencies in Germany, France, Great Britain, Russia, China, and Egypt believed it. … If anything, we worried that the CIA was underestimating Saddam, as it had before the Gulf War" (ibid. 231). Later on in his memoirs, W. concedes that "we were all wrong" (ibid. 251).

If both Bush and Tenet failed to question the basic assumption that Saddam had WMDs, so too did the President's inner circle as a whole. In this case the leading dissenter—in fact, the only senior policymaker who raised real concerns about the accuracy of the intelligence they were receiving on WMD—was Colin Powell. Powell famously regarded Saddam as a "toothache," a minor problem which would come and go—and which was painful to endure on occasions—but not a major national security threat. As Bush recalls, Powell "had the deepest reservations [about the use of military force]. In a one-on-one meeting in early 2003, he had told me he believed we could manage the threat of Iraq diplomatically" (ibid. 241). Powell was also less than happy about the plans that General Tommy Franks had drawn up for the invasion. The whole operation flew in the face of the "Powell Doctrine," which advocated the use of overwhelming and unambiguous force against a security threat and drew from the lessons Powell had deduced from Vietnam. Large as it was, however, this would be a far more pared-down operation, based on Rumsfeld's ideas about a leaner military.

To some extent, George W. Bush himself appears to have acted as a mindguard (or at least one of them) in confronting Powell's dissenting advice. Woodward claims that dissenters of any kind on the Iraq issue were judged to be "not on the team" and tended to lose access to the president, an unstated but very real pressure that caused those in disagreement with the invasion (as well as those who merely disagreed with the way it was being implemented) to remain silent. Powell's deputy, Richard Armitage, reportedly felt this pressure especially strongly (Woodward 2006, 328). Both he and the Powell considered themselves completely bypassed by the White House and Pentagon and "about as influential as a couple of potted plants" on the Iraq issue. On one occasion, then Deputy National Security Adviser Stephen Hadley—in an example of mindguarding par excellence, which might even have astonished Janis himself—objected to Armitage's "body language" in meetings, which he rightly surmised conveyed deep unease with the whole decision-making process (Woodward 2006, 230).

Strikingly, even the phrase that Bush used in one meeting with Powell was reminiscent of the *Challenger* decision-making. On January 13, 2003, Bush and Powell met for a brief meeting in the Oval Office, during which Bush announced that he had decided to invade Iraq. According to Woodward, Powell—by now known by all to be at best lukewarm on the idea of invading Iraq—raised a few objections, but Bush responded with a point about the importance of consensus and team play:

> "Are you with me on this?" the president asked his secretary of state. I think I have to do this. I want you with me."
>
> "I'm with you, Mr. President," Powell replied.
>
> In case there was any doubt—and there really couldn't be for Powell, the good, obedient soldier—the president explicitly told the former chairman of the Joint Chiefs: "Time to put your war uniform on" (Woodward 2006, 106; see also Bush 2010, 241).

Indeed, George W. Bush has offered some evidence that he may have been mindguarded himself by Vice President Cheney! At one point shortly before the decision to invade was made, Cheney and the President were having one of their regularly scheduled weekly lunches. By this point, Cheney was clearly exasperated with the diplomatic process and with ongoing efforts to obtain another UN resolution prior to using military force against Hussein. At one point, Cheney asked the President rather pointedly "are you going to take care of this guy or not?" Bush notes that this was "blunt advice" and states that Cheney quickly noted that as VP this was not his decision to make, but the message was clear enough (Bush 2010, 239).

A particular problem within the Bush administration seems to have been the tendency to generate self-reinforcing analyses among the group of like-minded individuals established by Douglas Feith inside the Pentagon to find evidence of Iraqi WMD. According to David Levine:

> One force that can fight against groupthink is independent analysis. For example, the CIA's core competence is finding the well-supported arguments within vast amounts of noise and rumor. Before the decision to invade Iraq, however, these safeguards were short-circuited. The Pentagon established its own intelligence agency largely to bypass the more independent CIA. Under pressure from the White House, the CIA then abandoned some of its independence and delivered

a partial view of the information it held. The resulting reports gave credence to sources the CIA had historically (and apparently correctly) discounted, and down-played cautions the CIA had (correctly) emphasized in the past (Levine 2004, 2).

In the view of Brad Swanson, there were many signs of groupthink within Paul Bremer's Coalition Provisional Authority; Swanson felt that no one wanted to ask difficult questions or puncture the false consensus that all was going well (Packer 2005, 319). The Senate Intelligence Committee also identified groupthink operating within a single organization, pinning most of the blame for the errone-ous intelligence about WMDs on the CIA. More generally, however, the atmos-phere at the top levels in the administration seems to have encouraged a broader, *inter-* (not just *intra-*) organizational form of groupthink. As the groupthink hypothesis would predict, dissenters were rapidly snatched out of the public's view and then reprimanded or dismissed. The most prominent public dissenter within the Army, General Eric Shinseki, was rebuked by Paul Wolfowitz in congressional testimony before the war for suggesting that the postwar occupation force would likely have to be on the order of 200,000–300,000 troops; his advice was ignored by the civilian officials at the Pentagon, and he soon retired (Ricks 2006, 96–100). When Lawrence Lindsay, Bush's economic adviser, predicted before the war that it could cost $200 billion (a woeful underestimate, as it turned out) he was mar-ginalized and then fired. According to Packer, "the administration systematically kept forecasts of the war's true cost from the public and, by the insidious effects of airtight groupthink, from itself. This would be historic transformation on the cheap" (Packer 2005, 116).

Former Treasury Secretary Paul O'Neill has proved to be an invaluable source on questions such as these, providing an early glimpse into the operations of those at the top. His conclusion about the typical inner workings of the administration, as related to Ron Suskind, is worth quoting at length:

> The president was caught in an echo chamber of his own making, cut off from everyone other than a circle around him that's tiny and getting smaller and in concert on everything—a circle that conceals him from public view and keeps him away from the one thing he needs most: honest, disinterested perspectives about what's real. ... It was clear to O'Neill that Cheney and a handful of others had become "a praetorian guard" that encircled the president. In terms of bring-ing new, transforming ideas to the Oval Office, "that store is closed" (Suskind 2004, 293).

O'Neill argues that Dick Cheney played a particular role in "closing the store," and his well-documented and unprecedented number of visits to the CIA dur-ing the run-up to the war—during which some intelligence officials say they felt pressured to come up with intelligence that retrospectively supported the admin-istration's drive toward Iraq (Pincus and Priest 2003)—can be interpreted a par-ticularly effective exercise in policing dissent. Some intelligence officials "felt a continual drumbeat, not only from Cheney and ['Scooter'] Libby, but also from Deputy Defense Secretary Paul D. Wolfowitz, Feith, and less so from CIA Director

George J. Tenet, to find information or write reports in a way that would help the administration make the case that going into Iraq was urgent" (Pincus and Priest 2003). It is interesting that the term "praetorian guard"—the bodyguards who protected the emperors of ancient Rome—came to mind for O'Neill, just as the term "mindguard" seemed most apt to Janis.

In short, there is enough prima facie evidence of groupthink in this case to make further study eminently worthwhile, and the evidence of self-censorship and mindguarding in this case study—the two main factors Janis highlights as primary mechanisms by which a fake consensus is preserved—is especially suggestive. With regard to the latter, we know that on at least two occasions, Cheney even confronted Colin Powell after a meeting and physically poked him in the chest, although most of the pressure seems to have been more subtle than this. Others appeared to have censored their doubts in a manner similar to Arthur Schlesinger in the Bay of Pigs case. Lawrence Wilkerson, Powell's former Chief of Staff, recalls that in the meetings where he was present, no one really voiced the doubts that almost everyone in the State Department was feeling at the time. Asked in an interview with the author why he never spoke up in the meetings, Wilkerson expressed puzzlement at his own inaction. "I don't know ... I don't know why," was his simple reply (Wilkerson 2007). In recent years, Wilkerson has been anything but reticent about speaking out and is widely seen as the public voice of Powell himself (who has largely refrained from public comment on the Bush administration's internal decision-making style). The fact that Wilkerson was unwilling to do so at the time, however, suggests that like Armitage he felt pressured by group dynamics to remain quiet, not least because this is one variable which is obviously missing now that he has left government.

Homo Psychologicus

Throughout this book, we have seen that Homo Psychologicus stresses the manner in which even decision-makers who are aware of the standard potholes into which policymakers often fall frequently fail to apply the lessons learned in real-life contexts, blind to empirical examples of the theoretical rules they espouse. No amount of experience can compensate for the ways in which the human mind shorts out the decision-making process through a variety of common cognitive and emotional devices. A host of well-known cognitive errors at both the individual and the group level led the Bush decision-makers astray, but they failed to examine their own assumptions in any rigorous way. If we select some of the key insights from that literature, it does seem that George W. Bush and his colleagues fell prey to an exceptionally wide-ranging catalogue of cognitive and motivational errors. From the vantage point of Homo Psychologicus, at least six kinds of cognitive and/ or motivational error appear in especially prominent fashion during U.S. decision-making on Iraq: (1) decision-making on impulse, (2) the drunkard's search, (3) misperception-induced failure to empathize, (4) the use of analogical reasoning, and (5) the motivational drive to maintain cognitive consistency and wishful thinking in the face of psychologically uncomfortable information. Equally,

Saddam Hussein seems to have fundamentally miscalculated U.S. intentions and resolve in a manner similar to Milosevic (see chap. 9).

Decision-Making by Impulse

Given what we now know about the peremptory nature of the policymaking process on Iraq within the Bush 43 administration, it is tempting to conclude that the decision to invade was essentially made *in George W. Bush's head,* probably at some point before he became president. This kind of explanation has been proposed by James Bamford, who suggests that the major motive behind the Iraq war was probably revenge. Bamford recalls that Bush once said of Saddam, "this is the guy who tried to kill my dad" (Bamford 2004, 255). In 1993, Iraqi intelligence had allegedly hatched a plot to kill President George H. W. Bush during a visit to Kuwait. Though Bamford casts doubt on the notion that the Iraqis were really behind it, he notes that the plan—had it succeeded—would also probably have killed W.'s mother, wife, and two brothers as well. For Bamford, the WMD issue provided the pretext for a war, which was fought in reality to settle a personal score. Another version of this account has a more psychoanalytic flavor. It may well be, for instance, that "on Iraq it was [George W.] Bush himself who seized the chance to cast off the Oedipal burden and prove that he was his own man, better able than his father to deal with an old enemy" (Packer 2005, 45). Bush 43 supposedly hung up the telephone on Papa Bush 41 after an angry exchange over Iraq, for example. Although George W. Bush has dismissed claims that there was any disagreement as "ridiculous," he nevertheless concedes that he seldom sought his father's advice on foreign policy issues (see Risen 2006, 1, Bush 2010, 228).

These kind of explanations—one conspiratorial, the other psychoanalytic—are well-nigh impossible to verify, but then again most of the explanations we are likely to generate also fit that category. Iraq seems at the very least to have been a very private and very presidential thing, something that owed more to rapid cognition and emotional impulse than a considered collective process or anything resembling a textbook account of how decisions are made in government. Malcolm Gladwell's best-selling book *Blink* offers a defense for snap decisions in which gut feelings and intuition replace extensive, considered analysis. "Decisions made very quickly can be every bit as good as decisions made cautiously and deliberatively," Gladwell argues (Gladwell 2005, 14). He explains how the instant intuition of art experts and students is often superior to lengthy analysis, for example. Its publication caused various commentators to describe George W. Bush as the 'blink president' and to note the similarities between Gladwell's theme and Bush's cognitive style. According to Jonathan Alter, Bush "sizes up people and situations from his gut, often with ample 'emotional intelligence.' Operating on instinct keeps everything simple and clear, without the confusion of facts. Clarity is important, as Bush keeps pointing out, and clarity works politically. The voters like it" (Alter 2004, 29).

There is some support in recent psychological research for the proposition that blink decisions do in fact work. According to Ap Dijksterhuis and his colleagues, "contrary to conventional wisdom, it is not always advantageous to engage in thorough conscious deliberation before choosing." Inspired in part by Gladwell and drawing on theoretical insights into the characteristics of conscious and unconscious thought, these researchers investigated the idea that "simple choices (such as between different towels or different sets of oven mitts) indeed produce better results after conscious thought, but that choices in complex matters (such as between different houses or different cars) should be left to unconscious thought." They dub this the "deliberation-without-attention" hypothesis, and find in both laboratory studies and case studies of real shoppers that "purchases of complex products were viewed more favorably when decisions had been made in the absence of attentive deliberation" (Dijksterhuis et al. 2006, 1005).

There is a difference, of course, between choosing oven mitts and sending soldiers into battle. On an intuitive level, there is a wide consensus that snap judgments about complex problems are likely to be poor judgments. We should note that this kind of instantaneous cognition does not mean no cognition, but there has long been a consensus in the literature on foreign policy decision-making (for instance) that when it comes to information search and the appraisal of options, more is better. Alexander George notes that effective decision-making ideally requires at least *five* things: (1) a sufficient information search and considered diagnosis of the situation faced; (2) "consideration of all the major values and interests affected by the policy issue at hand"; (3) the generation of a wide range of options and alternatives, and consideration of the likely consequences which each would involve; (4) careful consideration of the problems that might arise during implementation of the various problems; and (5) attention to the success or failure of existing policies, and a willingness to change course if necessary (George 1980, 11). George notes that these are ideal conditions, which never respond entirely to real-life cases, but it is difficult to imagine how many of these judgments and other activities can be conducted in the blink of an eye, using rapid intuition alone. Interestingly, none of the examples that Gladwell offers us in *Blink* involve high-stakes political decisions, and it has to be said that the outcome in the Iraq case—if, indeed, this is how the president actually arrived at the view that Saddam had to go—offers a relatively poor advertisement for this kind of rapid, intuitive decision-making as applied to issues where the national interest, human lives, and other core values are at stake.

The Drunkard's Search

As Robert Jervis has shown, many of the theories which suggest that decision-makers are cognitive misers can be subsumed under the well-known principle of the drunkard's search (Jervis 1993; Kaplan 1964). This (apocryphal) story tells the tale of a drunkard searching for his lost house keys under a street light. A passerby offers to help and asks where drunk lost the keys. He replies that the keys were lost in a dark alley nearby. This puzzles the passerby, who not unnaturally then asks the man why he is not searching where he dropped the keys, and the drunkard replies, "because the light is better here." The lesson is that decision-makers may look for evidence in psychologically *convenient* places rather than in the *most likely* places or where common sense would dictate, even in the face of critics questioning what they are doing. This tendency is also evident in the study of social science, with its evident concentration of what appears to be quantifiable, rather than what is unclear or uncertain (Betts 1983, 142).

The Iraq decision-making process may well provide a classic illustration of this psychological phenomenon. The CIA's intelligence suggested that Saddam Hussein had little or nothing to do with 9/11, and as is now well known the trail of evidence pointed rather more clearly toward Afghanistan and Saudi Arabia. For various reasons, an attack on Saudi Arabia was deemed out of the question; moreover, both Donald Rumsfeld and Paul Wolfowitz felt that Iraq offered "better targets" than Afghanistan (Clarke 2004, 31). Bob Woodward notes that Wolfowitz "worried about 100,000 American troops bogged down in the notoriously treacherous mountains six months from then. In contrast, Iraq was a brittle oppressive regime that might break easily with an opposition yearning to topple Saddam" (Woodward 2004, 26). As Richard Clarke relates, at one of the first meetings on the afternoon of September 12, 2001:

> Rumsfeld was saying that we needed to bomb Iraq. And we all said … no, no. Al-Qaeda is in Afghanistan. We need to bomb Afghanistan. And Rumsfeld said there aren't any good targets in Afghanistan. And there are lots of good targets in Iraq. I said, "Well, there are lots of good targets in lots of places, but Iraq had nothing to do with it." Initially, I thought when he said, "There aren't enough targets in—in Afghanistan," I thought he was joking. I think they wanted to believe that there was a connection, but the CIA was sitting there, the FBI was sitting there, I was sitting there saying we've looked at this issue for years. For years we've looked and there's just no connection.[4]

This seems like an almost textbook case of the drunkard's search. Perhaps Rumsfeld, Cheney, and others latched onto the idea of invading Iraq because they thought it was more achievable or *doable*, i.e., they were looking where the light was better. Paul O'Neill recalled another meeting at which Paul Wolfowitz made a similar argument:

> I thought what Wolfowitz was asserting about Iraq was a reach, and I think others in the room did, too. It was like changing the subject. Iraq is not where Bin Laden is and not where there's trouble. I was mystified. It's like a bookbinder accidentally dropping a chapter from one book into the middle of another one. The chapter is coherent, in its way, but it doesn't seem to fit in this book (Suskind 2004, 188).

Although neither Clarke nor O'Neill uses the metaphor of the drunkard stumbling around for his keys, both make a startlingly similar point.

Misperception and a Failure to Empathize

We suggested in chapter 5 that what got the United States out of the Cuban missile crisis may in part have been Kennedy's ability to empathize with Khrushchev. Prompted by U.S. Ambassador to the Soviet Union Llewellyn "Tommy" Thompson,

JFK was able to place himself in the shoes of his adversary. As the great theorist of empathy and misperception Ralph White often explains, empathy is very different from sympathy, or at least each represents an opposite point along a continuum. The latter implies active approval, while the former simply entails putting oneself in the shoes of another in order to better understand his or her motives:

> Although the two words are often used interchangeably, "empathy" will be defined as a realistic understanding of the thoughts and feelings of others, while "sympathy" will be defined in accordance with its Greek derivation, as *feeling with* others—being happy because they are or unhappy because they are—which often implies doing what one can to help them. Empathy is cognitive, in the language of psychology; sympathy is affective (White 1986, 82).

Empathy is important because it is, in White's phrase, "the *great* corrective for all forms of war-promoting misperception" (White 1984, 160). White's work helped pioneer a rich tradition of work in the study of international relations on empathy, perception, and misperception that continues today (see Blight and Lang 2004; Brewster Smith 2004; Jervis 1968; Levy 1983; Stein 1982; Vertzberger 1990;Wagner 2004; Wessells et al. 2004; White 1968; and White 2004).

Empathy is difficult to achieve under some circumstances. It is patently easier to achieve in retrospect than it is at the time, for instance, and another example we discussed earlier—America's escalation of the Vietnam War—illustrates a further significant problem: one has to know the adversary sufficiently well to put oneself in their shoes. By McNamara's own admission, this was not the case with Vietnam. Lyndon Johnson and the principals in the Tuesday Lunch Group had little familiarity with the history of Vietnamese-Chinese relations; if they had, McNamara notes, they would have been far less likely to see the North Vietnamese as a mere satellite of China. Greater familiarity with the nationalist aspects of Ho Chi Minh's thinking—as opposed to his Communist beliefs, which were fairly well understood—might equally well have discouraged a tendency to see North Vietnam as a mere puppet of the Soviets. Sadly, those who did have the capacity to empathize with Ho were largely marginalized and regarded, in Thomson's phrase, as "troublemakers" (McNamara and Blight 2001, 64–73; Blight and Lang 2005, 27–57).

As is well known, Bush 43's inner circle expected that the invading U.S. forces would be greeted as "liberators." On March 16, 2003, for example, Cheney told Tim Russert on *Meet the Press*:

> I really do believe that we will be greeted as liberators. I've talked with a lot of Iraqis in the last several months myself, had them to the White House. The president and I have met with them, various groups and individuals, people who have devoted their lives from the outside to trying to change things inside Iraq. And like Kanan Makiya who's a professor at Brandeis, but an Iraqi, he's written great books about the subject, knows the country intimately, and is a part of the democratic opposition and resistance. The read we get on the people of Iraq is there is no question but what they want to the get rid of Saddam Hussein and they will welcome as liberators the United States when we come to do that.

On a visit to the Oval Office, Kanan Makiya had promised Bush that U.S. soldiers would be greeted with "sweets and flowers" by a grateful population (Packer 2005, 96–97). By and large of course this did not happen, and the reason was relatively simple: the Bush decision-makers failed to recognize the psychological impact that U.S. actions in 1991 had had upon the general population. After the Persian Gulf War, Bush 41 had famously urged the Kurds and Shia to rise up against Saddam Hussein. Both had responded enthusiastically to this call, but U.S. forces were under strict orders not to come to their aid as Saddam cracked down ruthlessly on the uprising. As noted earlier, Bush 41 was motivated principally by the realist's desire for stability and a restoration of the status quo in the region. Banned from using his warplanes under the terms of the postwar cease-fire, Hussein simply mowed down thousands of rebels using helicopter gunships instead. Understandably, many Shiites and Kurds felt bewildered and betrayed.

This is a classic example of the failure to exercise realistic empathy. It was ironic, moreover, that it was Makiya himself who made the "sweets and flowers" comment, since he almost certainly knew much better; indeed, he had written movingly in books like *Cruelty and Silence* of the events of 1991. "That's the bullshit he and Chalabi put out, but no one else believed that," Jay Garner recalls in no-nonsense fashion. "The military believed they would have a long, tough time of it." He maintains that the group he was with "didn't believe any of that kind of stuff" (Garner 2007). In truth, both Makiya and Chalabi were too far removed from ordinary Iraqis to appreciate that they were hardly likely to dance in the streets this time. Makiya's comments about sweets and flowers caused Feisal Istrabadi, a fellow Iraqi exile and Chicago lawyer, some consternation as well. "I knew nobody who spent four decades in exile knew what was going on in Iraq. I didn't and Kanan didn't. The only difference was I was a hell of a lot more cautious. He always made promises he knew he could not keep" (Packer 2005, 98). Neither the exiles nor the enthusiasts for war in the White House or the Pentagon seem to have placed themselves in the shoes of ordinary Iraqis or truly considered how they would be likely to react to the arrival of American troops. A scholar who studies analogical reasoning, however, could have predicted that U.S. troops would for the most part be viewed with a certain wariness. Psychological research has shown that people draw on events which not only resemble the situation being faced (the representativeness heuristic) but are vivid and personally significant to them (the availability heuristic) (Kahneman, Slovic, and Tversky 1982).

With this in mind, it is hardly surprising that the forces of another George Bush, this time Bush 43, were not entirely trusted when the United States returned in 2003, not much more than a decade later. U.S. military personnel who talked with ordinary Iraqis in their homes repeatedly confirm that Iraqis did not trust the Americans this time because of what had happened in 1991. One of the best accounts of what was on the minds of ordinary Iraqis in 2003 is provided by Jay Garner and his staff. Garner and his colleagues spent much time going from house to house across Iraq, asking ordinary Iraqis what they wanted from the United States, and in the process got an excellent sense of their hopes and fears. Asked whether Iraqis distrusted us as a result of the events of 1991, Garner's former assistant in Iraq Colonel Kim Olson said "absolutely, and they told us so." In her memoir *Iraq and Back*, she tells the story of one typical Shiite household. There was a mark on the wall where a portrait of Saddam had obviously been: the occupants were waiting to see whether the Americans would stay this time before deciding whether to retrieve the portrait from its hiding place behind the sofa (Olson 2006). "There was a huge reluctance to help us in any way because of what happened in 1991. According to some of the records, 1 to 1.2 million people were killed. ... They do not forget those kinds of things. If I were a Shiite, I would be very reluctant to trust us again. And they told us that. They told us time and time again ... everyone that we met had the same types of thoughts." The Shiites repeatedly told Garner and Olson that they would wait a year or two to see whether the United States stayed this time (Olson 2006).

The Kurds, Olson notes, "were much more accommodating to us, but they had a completely different outlook." As Garner recalls, "it depended on what part of Iraq you were in. If you were up North, the Kurds were ecstatic that we were there. They greeted you with flowers and cheers, and would do anything you asked them to do. If you were in the South, you had the Sunni and the Shia, and they were all sitting on the fence because they didn't trust us, because in 1991 the first George Bush incited them to a war against Saddam Hussein." After the United States signed a peace accord with Saddam, "the army rounded them all up and killed them by the hundreds of thousands." The Shia worried that we were going to "stab them in the back" again, Garner says. The Sunnis, on the other hand, "were in shock and wanted us to leave" (Garner 2007). Colonel Larry West, who served in Iraq in 2003 as Chief of the Civil-Military Operations Planning Team, First Marine Expeditionary Force (IMEF), had a similar experience, especially with regard to the Shia he met. "If I were an Iraqi, I would have a hard time trusting the Americans to be there for me," he states. "We could have left at any time" (West 2006).

In mid-2003, ORHA was replaced by the CPA, and a bewildered Garner was called home, replaced by the Kissinger protégé Paul Bremer. Bremer's instruction to dismantle the Ba'ath Party and then get rid of the Iraqi army—known respectively as CPA Orders No. 1 and No. 2, and announced in May 2003 during his first days in the job, rank as two of the most questionable American foreign policy decisions in living memory and among the most egregious examples of a basic failure to empathize. As the former Senior Adviser to the State Department David Phillips put it, "the Bush administration had committed one of the greatest errors in the history of U.S. warfare: it unnecessarily increased the ranks of its enemies. Embittered Arab Sunnis, who had dominated the military establishment, would reemerge to lead the insurgency against U.S. troops in the Sunni triangle." These mistakes "would have lasting and far-reaching ramifications" (Phillips 2005, 153). These decisions were made in spite of warnings from the late UN representative Sergio de Mello, from many ordinary Iraqis, and from our own advisers in the CIA, the military, and the State Department that they would almost certainly produce a violent backlash (Diamond 2005, 56; Phillips 2005, 151–52; Ricks 2006, 159). Jay Garner had favored de-Ba'athification as well, but he proposed skimming only the top layer off the state apparatus, not a root-and-branch purge. He had explained this policy to Rumsfeld before he left for Iraq, and he recalls that Rumsfeld told him at the time that this seemed like a "reasonable" policy to him (Garner 2007).

There was also a general failure to understand the kind of government and society that the war had dismantled. As Kim Olson explains, if you wanted a significant job in Iraq, you had to be a member of the Ba'ath party, whether you liked the party or not. As in Communist Russia—upon which the Iraqi system was deliberately modeled—if you wanted to teach in a university you had to join the party, whether you were sympathetic to its aims or not. The same was true of doctors, grade school teachers, and members of a whole host of other professions. In truth, little familiarity was needed with anything but the most basic elements of human nature in order to predict that throwing hundreds of thousands of army personnel and civil servants out of work on the grounds that they had once been nominal "members" of the Ba'ath party would create enormous discontent, laying the groundwork for the insurgency which soon appeared and would eventually morph into something even more deadly. "It pretty much was the catalyst for the insurgency," Olson says. "I really think the choice to disband the army was absolutely devastating, and they would not listen to Jay, they would not listen to the CIA chief who had worked with the army generals. And then [came] the firing of all the civil service workers that we'd just brought back to work" (Olson 2006).

After his failure at the Bay of Pigs became public, John F. Kennedy noted the old adage that "victory has a thousand fathers and failure is an orphan." If this is true, then the Bush 43's administration's policy of deep de-Ba'athification is the most abandoned orphan of our time. To this day, no one has been able to trace the line of responsibility back to the policy's author. Paul Bremer himself suggests that the decision to pursue root-and-branch de-Ba'athification was made at "very high policy levels" (Phillips 2005, 153). Jay Garner doubts that Bremer came up with the idea himself, which represented a total reversal of ORHA's approach. Garner had been working to bring back the civil servants to work in the ministries and had also tried with some success to regroup the Iraqi army. "When Garner protested to Bremer that the process went "far too deep," Bremer replied that he had his orders. "I have my instructions, and I am going to issue this," he insisted (Garner 2007).

"I don't think he had any flexibility," Jay Garner recalls. The retired general has never been able to find out exactly who gave the disastrous orders to create more than 400,000 enemies overnight, but he suggests that Chalabi and his sponsors in the Pentagon were behind the decision. Lt. General Joseph Kellogg—at that time serving on the staff of the Joint Chiefs—agrees. Kellogg recalls that Chalabi was continually urging the Pentagon to eradicate all traces of the Ba'ath party from Iraqi society. "He was calling for total de-Ba'athification, which is extreme," he remembers (Ricks 2006, 160). The actual author of the de-Ba'athification orders seems to have been Douglas Feith, or at least someone in his now notorious Office of Special Plans. "The document was shown to a Pentagon lawyer and to Wolfowitz and Rumsfeld but not to Rice or Powell, who believed the policy drafted in Feith's office did not represent the compromise forged at the March 10 war cabinet meeting. The final draft was printed in the Pentagon and carried to Baghdad by one of Bremer's aides," as Rajiv Chandrasekaran has discovered (Gordon and Trainor 2006, 476, Chandrasekaran 2006, 70).

Equally devastating was Bremer's dismissal of the Council of Seven, Garner's early attempt to involve Iraqis in running their own state. Kurdish leaders like Jalal Talabani had impressed upon Garner the necessity to "put an Iraqi face on the government of Iraq," Olson recalls. "It cannot be run by a white guy from Florida," the Kurds insisted. "The devastating thing that Bremer did at the end of five days in May, in which he made several mistakes, was to fire that Council of Seven," she says. Olson estimates that those seven individuals together represented about 15 million Iraqis. But when Bremer dismissed them, it seemed as if he was saying "you're not the government of Iraq, I am. So there was, I think, a fundamental misunderstanding of not only the people, but of what was required to run the population." She believes that the administration was "sold a bill of goods" by Chalabi, since he managed to convince a number of influential people within the administration that he could personally handle the entire situation and that little or nothing would be required from the U.S. government in the postwar stage (Olson 2006).

The greatest empathetic failure of all in the story of the U.S. invasion of Iraq may one day turn out to be larger and more profound than any of the examples so far given. It is puzzling indeed that Saddam Hussein apparently failed to take any steps to privately reassure the Bush administration that he did not in fact possess large stockpiles of nuclear, biological, or chemical weapons. If he did not have these, why keep up the pretense? It is reasonable to assume that Saddam took the threat of a U.S. invasion fairly seriously, since he had previously misinterpreted U.S. intentions before the first Persian Gulf War and was unlikely to repeat the same error. He also had everything to lose by continuing by deny UN inspectors access to some sites in Iraq (such as his presidential palaces), since this gave the whole world the impression that he had something to hide. From what Graham Allison and Philip Zelikow (1999) term a Model I perspective, at least, this is indeed a genuine puzzle. This is the approach that George W. Bush took at the time as well. As he relates in his memoirs, "if Saddam doesn't actually have WMD, I asked myself, why on earth would he subject himself to a war he will almost certainly lose?" (Bush 2010, 231).

Approaching the question from that perspective, it has been widely speculated that a weakened Saddam felt threatened by Iran and/or Israel and so wished to maintain the pretense of possessing these weapons in order to deter attacks by his regional adversaries. As Gordon and Trainor put it, "Saddam viewed Iran as his principal external enemy. The Iraqi leader had initially calculated that he could maintain the ambiguity over his WMD program to deter Iran, his opponents at home, and other adversaries even as he complied with the letter of the UN inspection demands" (Gordon and Trainor 2006, 504). Weakened by years of sanctions and dogged by UN supervision, the Iraqi leader may have developed a siege mentality from which he came to believe the only escape was to maintain a dangerous game of cat and mouse with the United States on the one hand and his Shiite regional rival on the other. If this is so, then decision-makers in Washington may have misinterpreted a signal which was designed for another audience entirely.

Until recently, it was difficult to assess the accuracy of claims such as these, not least because we lack access to information obtained from interviews with captured high-ranking Ba'athist officials. While the argument that the Bush administration fundamentally misread Saddam Hussein by failing to imagine the world *the way he saw it* was at least a rather plausible hypothesis, there was not much concrete evidence for it. However, in 2010 Bush conceded in his memoirs that this was probably the case. Although he maintains that Hussein's real intentions could not have been foreseen, to his credit the former president has admitted—in the kind of candor rare in presidential memoirs—that he miscalculated on this. As Bush notes, after his capture Saddam "told [FBI] agents that he was more worried about looking weak to Iran than being removed by the coalition. He never thought the United States would follow through on our promises to disarm him by force" (Bush 2010, 257).

Attribution theorists stress the ways in which leaders often fall victim to the *fundamental attribution error*. As Fiske and Taylor suggest, people are not always very careful when they make attributions. "On an everyday basis, people often make attributions in a relatively thoughtless fashion. The cognitive system is limited in capacity, so people take short cuts," they point out (Fiske and Taylor 1984, 11). When we are explaining our own actions, we very often use situational attributions, overestimating the extent to which our actions are the result of the situation. On the other hand, when asked to explain why someone else acted as they did, we often make the opposite kind of mistake: we underestimate the extent to which the situation mattered (and hence overestimate the importance of that person's dispositions). Larson notes that during the Cold War "Washington officials were too willing to impute ideological, expansionist motives to Soviet actions that could just as plausibly reflect security calculations similar to those that prompted analogous policies pursued by the United States" (Larson 1985, 38). Equally, it is possible that many high Bush officials failed to appreciate the highly insecure circumstances Saddam faced in 2003—perhaps because they had last held office at a time when he faced far fewer situational constraints—and therefore overestimated his ability to reconstitute his various weapons programs. Empathy can be a potent antidote to the use of such misplaced attributions, but it was clearly lacking in this case in a number of ways (Vertzberger 1990, 162–63).

Reliance on Faulty Analogies
As we have seen, a now substantial literature exists within cognitive science and political psychology on the ways in which decision-makers resort to (often facile) historical analogies when faced with highly uncertain and ambiguous situations (see Dyson and Preston 2006; Hemmer 2000; Houghton 2001; Hybel 1990; Jervis 1976; Khong 1992; and Neustadt and May 1986). Apart from comparisons with Vietnam—which appear to have exerted little influence on Bush's inner circle—at

least two historical analogies are mentioned recurrently in the write-ups on Iraq: the comparison with the denazification process in postwar Germany, and (to a lesser extent) the analogy to the first Persian Gulf War of 1991.

The first comparison was often used by Iraqi exile Ahmed Chalabi as a justification for removing all Ba'athists from the Iraqi government, a decision he stood to benefit from personally if (as some in the Pentagon clearly intended) Chalabi was installed as the new Iraqi leader and managed to form a government. He would claim that allowing the Ba'athists to remain in power was "like allowing Nazis into the German government after World War II" (Phillips 2005, 147). Though he seems to have possessed only a shallow understanding of post–World War II planning, Chalabi had certainly read books on this topic; indeed, he happened to be reading one when he and Kanan Makiya first met on an airline flight. "They were seatmates on a flight once in 1994, and when Chalabi got up to use the lavatory, Makiya glanced at the book he'd been reading: a thick tome on the reconstruction of Germany after World War II. It was the beginning of a long mutual attraction," George Packer relates (Packer 2005, 76). Paul Bremer's use of the denazification analogy, meanwhile, seems to have been more sophisticated. He compares the de-Ba'athification order he issued in 2003 in some ways to the rooting out of Nazis in post–World War II Germany. That order, he notes, "prohibited the 'image or likeness of Saddam Hussein' or other identifiable members of the former regime from public display. In this regard, de-Ba'athification was similar in its intent and scope to denazification in postwar Germany, which banned the swastika and portraits of Hitler, and MacArthur's decrees in occupied Japan that removed the trappings of the militarist regime" (Bremer 2006, 42).

But Bremer concedes in his memoirs that there were important differences between the two situations. He realized that the United States had "defeated a hated regime, not a country," and Iraqis seemed unlikely to tolerate a lengthy occupation as the Germans and Japanese had; moreover, Germany had been created as a result of the efforts of Germans themselves and Germans shared a common culture, while Iraq had been artificially created by the British out of mutually antagonistic ethnic factions (ibid. 37–38). "You know with denazification, we waited a while on that," Garner says. "We were very gentle with that, to begin with." Perhaps even more importantly, planning for postwar Europe began in 1942, several years before it was actually implemented. Both Garner and Bremer, on the other hand, were effectively being asked to make up a plan on the back of an envelope during the flight to Iraq (Garner 2007).

The true believers in the World War II analogy, on the other hand, seem to have been Paul Wolfowitz and Douglas Feith, though the comparison was cast in broader terms. Wolfowitz openly stated that the events of World War II and the Holocaust in particular "shaped a lot of my views," and he frequently compared Saddam's Iraq to Hitler's Germany (Ricks, 2006, 16). As Tom Ricks suggests:

> For Feith, as for Wolfowitz, the Holocaust—and the mistakes the West made in appeasing Hitler in the 1930s, rather than stopping him—became a keystone in thinking about policy. Like Wolfowitz, Feith came from a family devastated

by the Holocaust. His father lost both parents, three brothers, and four sisters to the Nazis. "My family got wiped out by Hitler, and. ... All this stuff about working things out—well, talking to Hitler to resolve the problem didn't make any sense to me," Feith later told Jeffrey Goldberg of the *New Yorker* in discussing how World War II had shaped his views. "The kind of people who put bumper stickers on their car that declare that 'War is not the answer,' are they making a serious comment? What's the answer to Pearl Harbor? What's the answer to the Holocaust?" (Ricks 2006, 77).

The second analogy is less discussed, but it may also have had a damaging effect on the already hasty planning for postwar Iraq. As Daalder and Lindsay put it, "Pentagon planners assumed that the most immediate postwar need would be to provide humanitarian assistance, deal with large numbers of refugees, and limit and clean up any environmental damage from burning oil well fires—all disasters that occurred during the Gulf War" (Daalder and Lindsay 2003, 151). As Jay Garner explains, none of these materialized in the event because the invasion forces moved swiftly to preempt these kind of problems, and he denies that he focused overly on the same problems he had faced in 1991 (Garner 2007). "Certainly there were some similarities, but I didn't think they would be two identical scenarios or even two related scenarios," Garner says. According to Daalder and Lindsay, on the other hand, "Garner's small staff spent a disproportionate time planning for these contingencies, while ignoring other, equally important aspects of postwar operations. ... Like generals everywhere, postwar planners apparently assumed the next war would be like the last" (Daalder and Lindsay 2003, 151–52). This is perhaps unfair, for in truth Garner had very little time to influence the reconstruction process before he was replaced by the more strident Bremer; nevertheless, it comports with what we know about the way in which decision-makers draw on experiences that are most familiar and hence cognitively available to them (Kahneman, Slovic and Tversky 1982).

Of course, some of the coping strategies that led the Bush decision-makers astray may not have been inadvisable in and of themselves. The use of analogical reasoning, for instance, may not be inherently wrongheaded; the real trick comes in using the correct analogies, and the Bush administration seems to have used the wrong ones. A far better analogy would have been with Russia after the end of the Cold War, Kim Olson argues, since this was the obvious case in which a dependent culture had been fashioned by the state and individual initiative stifled. "We probably should have looked to Russia when the [Berlin] Wall fell, and seen how those countries reacted and not thought it'll be just like Germany or Japan," she argues (Olson, 2006). While Cheney favorites like Bernard Lewis are fond of pointing out the similarities between the Iraqi Ba'ath party and the German Nazi party, an even stronger influence on Saddam was his hero and role model Joseph Stalin.

Wishful Thinking, Denial, and Cognitive Consistency
As we have seen, another body of theory within *Homo Psychologicus* deals with cognitive consistency or dissonance (Festinger 1957; Heider 1958; Aronson 1969).

As Yaacov Vertzberger notes, a considerable body of literature exists which suggests that "individuals have a strong need to maintain a consistent cognitive system that produces stable and simplified cognitive structures" (Vertzberger 1990,137). Cognitive consistency theory can potentially explain both the formation of the initial belief that Saddam was harboring WMDs and the resistance of this belief to negation by the weak or ambiguous evidence that he actually did have such weapons. First of all, various organizations within the administration may have come to believe that Iraq had WMDs purely because this was consistent with their "diabolical image" of Saddam Hussein. If we take the Bush administration's belief in an Iraqi WMD threat at face value, for instance, or the belief that Saddam Hussein was somehow behind 9/11, it becomes possible to understand the cherry-picking of intelligence within the Pentagon's Office of Special Plans as no more than the natural human striving for consistency between one's beliefs.

Cognitive consistency theory also suggests that beliefs often prove resistant to uncomfortable facts. As Deborah Welch Larson puts it, the approach "provides one possible explanation of the imperviousness of preconceived opinions to rational disconfirmation" (Larson 1985, 29). While individuals naturally use different strategies to cope with inconsistencies that emerge between beliefs, one common approach is of course to ignore or manipulate information, which might lead to cognitive inconsistency. The mind-set that most of Bush's advisers brought back to office in 2001 was one in which *states* are the real threats, and it was simply assumed that non-state actors could not pose a real threat without state sponsorship. Paul Wolfowitz, for instance, believed that the 1993 attack on the World Trade Center could not have been orchestrated by Al-Qaeda alone, and that it "must have had help from Iraq" (Clarke 2004, 30). Although the president and many of his advisers were convinced that Saddam was a real threat, so this account goes, they fitted the intelligence to the theory—not out of a desire to deceive, perhaps but of a mistaken belief which proved resistant to the facts. As Simon and Garfunkel put it in their song *The Boxer*, "a man hears what to wants to hear and disregards the rest."

As Vertzberger notes, in order to maintain cognitive consistency decision-makers may even fabricate causal connections in their own minds which do not exist in reality. Richard Clarke describes a relentless effort by President Bush in the days after 9/11 to uncover a connection between Saddam and 9/11, an effort later pursued by the Vice President to such lengths that he apparently "visited CIA headquarters on ten different occasions to urge operatives at Langley to find evidence ... which he was *convinced* must be there somewhere" (Pincus and Priest 2003). When faced with two incompatible (or only partially compatible) beliefs—such as "we were attacked by Al-Qaeda" and "we are attacking Iraq"—decision-makers may restore balance by adding a third element or belief; in this case, that third belief might be "there is a secret alliance between Saddam and Al-Qaeda" (Larson 1985, 30). In this way, the apparent inconsistency is reduced or eliminated.

The much older psychoanalytic tradition in psychology posits the widespread existence of *denial* as a common defense mechanism. This is, broadly speaking, the inability or unwillingness to cope with external reality or to look facts squarely in the face. Rose McDermott argues that denial is a common coping mechanism among foreign policy decision-makers and that it "typically takes two forms in international relations: pretending that an event will not happen or avoiding the value trade-offs required in deciding between mutually exclusive options" (McDermott 2004, 172). Lyndon Johnson and his associates appear to have convinced themselves that they were prevailing in Vietnam, even in the face of quite unequivocal evidence that this was not the case. "I'm not sure that he didn't think he was telling the truth. He had a capacity for self-deception about facts that was ten times the capacity of anybody else I've ever met," former Undersecretary of State Nicholas Katzenbach later said of his boss's self-delusion over the war.[5]

Although obviously not a work of political psychology per se, Bob Woodward's *State of Denial* clearly suggests that the president and his colleagues were deluding themselves about events in Iraq (Woodward 2006). Like others who have written about the Iraqi case, Woodward shows that the administration's assessment of events on the ground consistently lagged behind the more sober judgments of less partial observers, and his choice of title suggests that the author is explicitly offering us a theory of the psychological state of mind not only of George W. Bush but of those around him. Bush, Rumsfeld, and others repeatedly made claims of progress in Iraq which downplayed the grave nature of the insurgency and the extent of sectarian violence, claims which are now hard to give much credence to. Woodward argues that Bush's "habit of denial" was especially pronounced on the issue of weapons of mass destruction. Pushed to explain why the rhetorical justification for the war had been unfounded, Bush repeatedly refused to concede in an interview with Woodward that an error had been made; indeed, "it had taken five minutes and eighteen seconds for Bush simply to acknowledge the *fact* that we hadn't found weapons of mass destruction" (Woodward 2006, 488–89). This habit was shared by both Rumsfeld and Cheney, both of whom showed a seeming inability to face up to the facts of what was happening in Iraq. In what Woodward calls "a total denial of reality and of the trend," Cheney went on CNN's *Larry King Live* as late as May 2005 and claimed, "I think they're in the last throes, if you will, of the insurgency" (Woodward 2006, 397).

Added to the denial was a fair measure of *wishful thinking* (McDermott 2004, 172–73). Of the pervasive influence of Ahmed Chalabi, Olson says "I think those in power really wanted to believe what he had to say. It would have been nice had it worked out that way." Chalabi convinced people like Feith and Wolfowitz in particular that he could provide the kind of leadership that would allow the new Iraq to hit the ground running. "But the fact of the matter is, that was just not the reality on the ground, and I think his view of Iraq was so dated and so unrealistic." Most significantly, Chalabi "did not realize how the psychology of the people as a whole had been damaged" (Olson 2006).

Pentagon officials also overlooked the fact that exiles who had been out of the country for thirty or forty years—having left the country as small children— were unlikely to be welcomed with open arms by those who had suffered through the years of Saddam. "Most of the expatriates who came in were Shia," Garner notes. "And the Sunnis sure as hell didn't like them. And the Shia didn't seem to wrap their arms around them either. The Shia were more like 'we stayed and lived through all this. You don't know what went on, you don't have any credibility … you left, you had it easy. We stayed here. We had it tough'" (Garner 2007). Donald Rumsfeld's famous claim that the widespread looting that followed the invasion was a sign of freedom on the march—as opposed to anger and frustration-fuelled criminal activity—offers another especially notable example of wishful imagination at work.

As former ORHA official Colonel Larry West relates, "there was a sense of sadness among Iraqis that is difficult to convey. It was as if the whole country was suffering from post-traumatic stress disorder" (West 2006). Moreover, the Bush administration was simply unprepared for what happens when you tear the heart and nervous system out of a state which had been deliberately run in a way that rendered the population entirely dependent upon its dictatorial leader. Ordinary Iraqis were initially bewildered, in large part because they were used to being entirely subservient to the state. "Iraq was a socialist society," Olson notes. "Everything was subsidized, from electricity to food. And if you want to control a population, you make them reliant on you. You're the great giver, you're the one who gives their children food. … The government apparatus that he had set up was quite brilliant for controlling 24 million people, with only 3 million Sunnis. And with that comes a dependency for everything." The idea that the people would simply rise up overnight, embrace democratic freedoms, and become a clone of the United States was pure wishful thinking, she contends (Olson 2006).

ASSESSING THE THREE PERSPECTIVES

The limitations of what has been attempted in this chapter should be emphasized. At this point our access to the administration's internal documents is highly restricted, and establishing the accuracy of various hypotheses is accordingly equally limited. Nevertheless, we are still able to amass reasonable evidence in favor of each of our approaches from the large number of secondary accounts that exist. First of all, for advocates of *Homo Bureaucraticus* there is strong evidence of pulling and hauling for control of Iraq policy. Many advocates seem to fit the most traditional version of the where-you-sit axiom, and the public justification for invading Iraq may also have been little more than the product of bureaucratic compromise. Second, from the vantage point of *Homo Sociologicus*, although the decision to invade the country and depose Saddam Hussein was made by individuals who—with the notable exception of George W. Bush himself—had collectively amassed some two hundred years of experience, this did not prevent them from falling into the trap of collective delusion, and there is evidence of mindguarding and a strong pressure to buckle under to the consensus that the war was necessary. From the perspective of *Homo Psychologicus*, finally, this case study illustrates the ways in which the human mind shorts out the decision-making process through a variety of common cognitive and emotional devices. George W. Bush and his colleagues appear to have committed an exceptionally wide-ranging catalogue of cognitive and motivational errors, engaging in decision-making on impulse and the use of cognitive shortcuts resembling the drunkard's search, as well as general misperceptions and the use of analogical reasoning, denial, and wishful thinking in the face of psychologically uncomfortable information.

On the other hand, one can fault the *Homo Bureaucraticus* account in this case study as well. As Todd Purdum notes, disputes between the State and Defense Departments are an old story, but there was more than bureaucratic politics to the chasm between Powell and Rumsfeld (Purdum 2003, 34). Both had developed their own personal rules and philosophies about the use of military force, and their disputes were as much about their respective doctrines as they were about vantage points. Arguably, both Rumsfeld and Powell would have adopted the positions they took regardless of the bureaucratic positions they occupied, as might Cheney (who had undergone an ideological transformation since his days in the Ford and Bush 41 administrations). Equally, when one reconsiders *Homo Sociologicus,* the doubts that State Department officials now express in interviews may reflect views that they expressed at the time but felt far less strongly. Psychologists have shown that it is difficult to divorce knowledge of outcomes from our contemporaneous views (the "I-Knew-It-All-Along" effect). It is easy to be wise after the event, and perhaps those who appear so now were not actually so prescient at the time (Fischoff and Beyth 1975). Since the war turned out badly in many ways, it is conceivable that State Department officials who have since spoken out forcefully against the war did not feel that strongly at the time. Equally, one can easily overstate the *Homo Psychologicus* approach here. George W. Bush has defended his psychological misperception of the WMD issue on the reasonable grounds that it was rational at the time. Based on the information that Western decision-makers possessed, it was *not* unreasonable to conclude that Saddam was replenishing his stockpile of weapons, and almost every Western intelligence agency seems to have concluded that he was doing so. The passage of time, of course, will surely only lead to more revelations, allowing us to better adjudicate between the vast array of suggestive hypotheses that our three perspectives can help us generate. We shall return to these and other issues in the concluding chapter, and will also consider whether out three perspectives are really as different or irreconcilable as we have portrayed them to be in this book.

CHAPTER 11

Conclusions: A Personal View

By now, you may be convinced that *Homo Bureaucraticus* offers us the best vantage point for understanding our six case studies, or that *Homo Sociologicus* does. Equally, you may have concluded that *Homo Psychologicus* has the most to tell us overall. Or you may have concluded that some combination of all three works best. I have so far tried to remain impartial between these three perspectives, making the best case I can for each. In that sense, this book is a conscious tribute to Graham Allison, whose original version of *Essence of Decision* in particular was a tour de force in viewing the same case from multiple perspectives and angles (Allison 1971). Although I am not necessarily advocating its theoretical conclusions—the Cuban missile crisis was always a problematic case for *Homo Bureaucraticus*—Allison's book is a model in a social scientific sense, and I have tried to follow a similar kind of approach here (albeit using different theoretical approaches from what Allison and Zelikow call Model I, Model II and Model III). This has often involved acting as a devil's advocate, amassing the best evidence for an approach which I did not necessarily think really fit the case study. Unlike former Undersecretary of State George Ball, I have often acted in this book as a *real* devil's advocate. As you may recall from chapter 7, Ball's colleagues in the Johnson administration often treated him as if he were a genuine devil's advocate (he was not), and as if he did not really believe in the arguments he was espousing (he actually did). "Don't listen to old George," they would say in the gentleman's-club language affected by U.S. foreign policy elites at the time. "He doesn't really believe the things that he's saying." Like Ball—or indeed like anyone who has ever believed in something, which is presumably most of us—I have my own biases, and you may have worked out already what these are based on my occasional self-citations. That does not mean, however, that I necessarily think that a single approach is always better than the others. Indeed, in this chapter I am going to depart from the neutral tone of the rest of the book and address you directly as a teacher would, making the argument that each of our three approaches has something valuable to tell us about foreign policy decision-making, and something significant to say about why leaders do the things that they do. I am also going to suggest a way of blending together the three perspectives in a way that mostly preserves the theoretical integrity of each.

It is certainly true to say that each of our three approaches is in some ways hard to reconcile, and we have been treating them thus far as rivals. The working assumption in this book up to this point has been that they are philosophically *incommensurate*, which is a fancy word in social science for "things which do not go together" or cannot be combined. The bureaucratic politics and groupthink approaches are often mistaken for one another or conflated in basic introductory textbooks in international relations, but as Steve Yetiv has noted, what we have been calling *Homo Bureaucraticus* and *Homo Sociologicus* in this book are really mirror images of one another. While *Sociologicus* is at its best when trying to explain decision-making situations where almost everyone is in agreement, *Bureaucraticus* is in its element when dealing with the opposite situation, where everyone pulls in different directions (Yetiv 2004, 198). The latter point is also true of *Psychologicus*; since individuals are exposed to different experiences and everyone is to some extent unique, decision-makers inevitably develop beliefs and outlooks that are to some extent idiosyncratic and peculiar to them. While *Psychologicus* deals with the psychology of difference, *Sociologicus* deals with the psychology of sameness. Equally, *Bureaucraticus* seems to work best when accounting for *policy implementation*, when decision-makers have already decided what they want and the bureaucracy in effect takes over, perhaps altering the original intent of the decision-makers in subtle ways. On the other hand, *Sociologicus* and *Psychologicus* are primarily theories of *policy formulation* alone, dealing with the process of choice itself rather than what happens to policies once they filter down into the bureaucratic process. This already suggests one way of reconciling the three approaches that you may wish to consider.

The reader may have noticed that some of the work I have cited in this book has been used to make arguments for two or three approaches simultaneously. In chapter 7, for example, I drew upon James Thomson's classic critique of Vietnam policy in making a case for a *Bureaucraticus* approach to Vietnam *and* a *Sociologicus* view. This is because Thomson offered such rich insights about the policy process on that issue that he can be used to make the case for either view or both. In courses on American foreign policy, Thomson's piece is often used to make a case for the bureaucratic politics approach (see, i.e., McCormick and Wittkopf 1997), but Janis also used many of Thomson's insights to construct his groupthink-based account of the Vietnam decision-making. Although I did not do so in the chapter on Vietnam, one might even use Thomson to illustrate a *Homo Psychologicus* approach:

> Of course, one force—a constant in the vortex of commitment—was that of *wishful thinking*. I partook of it myself at many times. I did so especially during Washington's struggle with [South Vietnamese leader Ngo Dinh] Diem in the autumn of 1963 when some of us at State believed that for once, in dealing with a difficult client state, the U.S. government could use the leverage of our economic

and military assistance to make good things happen. ... If we could prove that point, I thought, and move into a new day, with or without Diem, then Vietnam was well worth the effort. Later came the wishful thinking of the air-strike planners in the late autumn of 1964; there were those who actually thought that after six weeks of air strikes, the North Vietnamese would come crawling to us to ask for peace talks. And what, someone asked in one of the meetings of the time, if they don't? The answer was that we would bomb for another four weeks, and that would do the trick. And a few weeks later came one instance of wishful thinking that was symptomatic of good men misled: in January 1965, I encountered one of the very highest figures in the Administration at a dinner, drew him aside, and told him of my worries about the air-strike option. He told me that I really shouldn't worry; it was his conviction that before any such plans could be put into effect, a neutralist government would come to power in Saigon that would politely invite us out. And finally, there was the recurrent wishful thinking that sustained many of us through the trying months of 1965–1966 after the air strikes had begun: that surely, somehow, one way or another, we would "be in a conference in six months," and the escalatory spiral would be suspended. The basis of our hope: "It simply can't go on." (Thomson 1968)

One of the most interesting things one can note about the literature on the Iran hostage crisis—especially that which focuses exclusively on the rescue mission— is the tendency of the authors to blend elements of *Homo Bureaucraticus, Homo Sociologicus,* and *Homo Psychologicus* together. The reader may have noticed in chapter 8 that the British political scientist Steve Smith has authored articles arguing for the relevance of both the bureaucratic politics approach and the groupthink approach (Smith 1984, 1985). Similarly, Betty Glad blends together a *Homo Psychologicus* perspective with a groupthink approach, adding elements at higher levels of analysis as well. And the emphasis on domestic political factors is a recurring motif in the Iran hostage crisis literature. Smith stresses the role of domestic politics in shaping the preferences of the presidential supporters, while Rose McDermott stresses the same factor with reference to Carter's perception of the situation he faced in March and April 1980, and other scholars have stressed these aspects as well (Glad 1989; Smith 1985; McDermott 1992).

We should certainly beware of picking and choosing elements of different theories in a random fashion. Foreign policy decision-making theory is not like a supermarket, where we simply drop into our grocery basket the things we like. We must be careful in particular not to combine theories whose assumptions are simply incompatible with one another. Nevertheless, the case studies we have examined in this book do suggest that the various explanations that we have so far kept separate from one another may be at least partially complementary. With that caveat in mind, how might we better specify the conditions under which our three general perspectives seem to work best (and, corresponding, least well)?

Homo Sociologicus seems to work best when we examine general policy *processes*, rather than policy *content*; in other words, this approach can explain the "how" but not the "what." It can in general terms tell us *how* a decision was arrived at, but not *why* the particular option chosen seemed to be the best one available.

It can tell us a great deal about what happens (or can happen) to a decision once it is already made, but it has little to say about choice per se. In that respect, it is ironically rather similar to *Homo Economicus*, which is devoid of any information about policy preferences (why is X preferred rather than Y). But in the Bay of Pigs and Vietnam cases, for instance, a groupthink explanation can tell us why Lyndon Johnson hunkered down after the decision to escalate was made or why JFK ignored seemingly obvious defects in the Bay of Pigs invasion plan, and it can offer us extraordinary insights about how otherwise smart people do dumb things, decisions and actions that (in retrospect at least) everyone can see were wrong and misguided. The title *In Retrospect*, Robert McNamara's memoir of the Vietnam decision-making, is an apt one, for at the time he was part of a team whose members seem to have been absolutely convinced that they were getting it right (McNamara 1995). Group dynamics can tell us a great deal about why dissenters fail to speak out when they know the wrong decision is being made, and why they make so few inroads once the policy deck is stacked against them.

Homo Bureaucraticus seems especially useful under two conditions in particular: where presidential attention is low and consequently organizational involvement is high, and where we are concerned with issues of policy implementation rather than formulation (Rosati 1981; Allison and Zelikow 1999). With regard to the first condition, organizations like the State Department and the Pentagon really did have a great deal of influence during the 1999 Kosovo crisis, but they did so in large part because the President was distracted and still reeling from his impeachment trial at the time the air war began. This may be one reason, as we noted in chapter 9, why the Kosovo War was often referred to as Madeleine's War rather than Clinton's War. With the exception of Clinton's insistence on approving particular targets, his involvement in the decision-making was only sporadic, and consequently there were many centers of power in the decision-making, whose influence seemed to go up or down in response to events like the Racak massacre. In the Bay of Pigs case, President Kennedy does not seem to have closely monitored the organizations under his supposed control, deferring to the CIA and the Joint Chiefs because he initially thought they possessed some sort of magical knowledge he did not.

Correspondingly, the influence of bureaucratic bargaining and infighting seems to be least impressive when a president is focusing all of his energy and attention on the issue, as Kennedy did during the Cuban missile crisis or Johnson did during the 1965 escalation decisions. In selecting the missile crisis, Graham Allison selected a "hardest case to prove" for Models II and III (collectively, our *Homo Bureaucraticus* approach). The logic behind such case studies should be fairly apparent: if it works here in this difficult case, so the reasoning goes, it must apply generally to a whole range of cases as well. But the case may have been *too* hard to prove, given how focused Kennedy was on the decision-making. Ever since *Essence of Decision* was first published in 1971, generations of scholars and students have picked apart Allison's claims that the naval blockade represented some kind of bureaucratic compromise and that the key players "stood where they sat." But in my own view, the bureaucratic politics argument performs relatively poorly here not because it is inherently flawed but because presidential involvement was so high, and because Kennedy had deliberately shaped the bureaucratic environment himself, cutting the Joint Chiefs in particular out of the process. In the Vietnam case too, the evidence of bureaucratic infighting is mostly rather weak because presidential involvement was high. The main example of bureaucratic infighting, as we saw in chapter 7, came when the President and Defense Secretary essentially eliminated the Joint Chiefs from the decision-making process on Vietnam and left them to fight it out among themselves as to whose organization could best fight the war. On the other hand, *Homo Bureaucraticus* seems very strong in another condition, where we are focused on questions of policy implementation rather than explaining why a given decision was reached in the first place. In this part of the missile crisis case, the bureaucratic argument works quite well, and we see civilian leaders struggling to maintain control over how their decisions get put into effect on the ground. The famous confrontation between McNamara and the Joint Chiefs on how the blockade should be implemented provides just one illustration of the way in which organizations cling to established ways of doing things, as this may well explain (as we saw in chap. 6) why the Soviet military failed to camouflage the missile sites in Cuba.

The picture for *Homo Psychologicus* is more complicated, since it is really a rather substantial collection of theories all packaged under the same category. In general, the great strength of *Psychologicus* lies with its focus on choice. It can give us quite detailed information about why X was chosen rather than Y. The analogical reasoning approach in particular can specify rather precisely why one option seemed better than another within a given decision-maker's mind-set. During the Bay of Pigs episode, for example, the Guatemala analogy exerted a huge pull of the minds of individuals like Allen Dulles and Richard Bissell—both of whom should have known better, one would think—and many members of the Clinton administration were misled by the analogy drawn between Kosovo and the Bosnian conflict. The Pearl Harbor analogy had more benign effects in pulling the ExCom away from the option of an air strike, meanwhile, but in all of these cases the analogies in their heads helped directly shape the choices they made. Equally, prospect theory can tell us the conditions under which leaders are apt to become reckless, engaging in risk-taking behavior, as well as the circumstances when they are unlikely to do so. Nikita Khrushchev's decision to place missiles in Cuba, for instance, seems to fit this approach well. But it seems clear that some elements of *Psychologicus* function better than others across the cases. While personality obviously plays some role in decision-making, it is difficult to show how one moves from a particular personality type to a specific policy decision. Policy change is also hard to explain using an explanation focused on this factor, since personality is relatively fixed.

Overall, then, different approaches and theories may be suited to different tasks. The various hypotheses we have entertained in this book are not mutually exclusive or independent of one another. How might they be woven together to form a more encompassing explanation than we have so far proposed? As I have suggested, cognitive processes at the individual level may be at their strongest when explaining policy *content*, or which policies get chosen; on the other hand, group- and organization-based approaches give us a theory of *process*, examining what happens to policy once a given option has been arrived at, so one obvious solution might be to combine (say) groupthink with the analogical reasoning approach. Perhaps the pull of the Korean and Munich analogies explained LBJ's choices, but then groupthink kicked in as Johnson sealed himself off from dissent. In fact, there are numerous ways in which we might usefully combine elements of these approaches. Once one has decided that "X is Y" as cognitive consistency theories within *Psychologicus* suggest, we resist information that suggests that in reality "X is Z." Group processes may combine with individual-level motivational forces to create an unquestioned wall of agreement, insulating experienced decision-makers who should be engaging in critical thinking and the consideration of a wide array of options. Sadly, the idea of *not* invading Iraq seems to have become unthinkable within Bush 43's inner circle at a very early stage in his presidency. Equally, this kind of interaction effect may underlie the Bay of Pigs and Vietnam decision-making processes as well.

Our brains appear to be hardwired to accept only data which is consistent with existing beliefs. Using evidence gleaned from MRI-based studies, Drew Westen and his colleagues have shown that the reasoning parts of our brains virtually shut down when we are confronted with dissonant information (Westen 2007). When it became clear that Iraq possessed no weapons of mass destruction, for instance, many Americans continued to assert in opinion polls that weapons had in fact been found (a claim the administration did little to dispel). Unfounded but convenient rumors began to circulate that the imagined WMD had been moved to a neighboring country such as Syria. George W. Bush and Dick Cheney initially rationalized the failure away partly by doing what critics called "moving the goal posts." Members of the administration began to argue that the real reason for invading was not Saddam's WMD at all but the more noble objective of bringing democracy to Iraq. And Cheney himself has reasserted as recently as April 2007 that the invasion was justified by a supposed link between Saddam and Al-Qaeda. The widespread phenomenon of dissonance deflection—by no means limited to Cheney or to the Bush administration, as I have tried to suggest—represents perhaps the most formidable obstacle to learning in policy contexts. As long as our minds remain hardwired to reject information which does not fit, we will continue to see what we believe, as opposed to believing what we see.

Notes

NOTE TO CHAPTER 1

[1] This has been done to avoid confusion with the approach we examine in chap. 4, *Homo Psychologicus*. In general, social psychologists focus on the social environment and conditions that surround the individual and the ways in which these affect his or her behavior, while cognitive psychology and cognitive science more generally examine the ways in which individual characteristics shape that behavior.

[2] For an excellent and readable contrast between a structural theory of foreign policy and an individual-level psychological one, see Ripley (1993).

NOTES TO CHAPTER 2

[1] The author is grateful to Gregory Moore for suggesting this example.

[2] In the original version of *Essence of Decision,* first published in 1971, Allison separated out what he called Model II (Organizational Process) from Model III (Governmental Politics), and the more recent second edition, co-authored with Philip Zelikow, does so as well. During the early 1970s, however, Allison worked with Morton Halperin to blend together the former's original to form a single perspective (Allison and Halperin 1972). In what follows I have followed the second approach, which has become standard practice in many textbooks.

[3] Rumsfeld was both the oldest occupant of the role (2001–06) and its youngest (1975–77).

NOTES TO CHAPTER 3

[1] Ronald Reagan, testimony at the trial of Admiral John Poindexter.

[2] Sadly, this later proved to be the case as Buckley died at the hands of his captors.

[3] Ronald Reagan, testimony at the trial of Admiral John Poindexter.

[4] Minutes, National Security Planning Group on Central America, June 25, 1984. Reproduced in Kornbluh and Byrne 1993, 69–82.

[5] He was in this respect little different from Jimmy Carter, Bill Clinton, and George W. Bush.

[6] Quoted in the PBS *Frontline* documentary *High Crimes and Misdemeanors*, first broadcast November 27, 1990.

NOTES TO CHAPTER 4

[1] Pol Pot soon became notorious for masterminding a genocide in his country and for his bizarre anti-industrial and anti-Western views.

[2] In formal terms, Kissinger held the positions of both secretary of state *and* national security adviser at the time, the only person in U.S. history to have occupied both jobs simultaneously. As we saw in chapter 2, Kissinger had repeatedly clashed with then Secretary of State William Rogers over China and other issues, so appointing the former to both jobs must have seemed to President Ford like a good way of preventing bureaucratic infighting. Not surprisingly, this proved quite burdensome for Kissinger, and it meant in practice that his "deputy" Brent Scowcroft assumed many of his duties, serving as the de facto NSA.

[3] Memorandum from Earl Wheeler to the President, Records of the Joint Chiefs of Staff, "Korea (*Pueblo*)," January 23–February 7, 1968, vol. 1, Box 29, National Archives, College Park, MD.

NOTES TO CHAPTER 5

[1] As often happens during times of crisis, the president enjoyed a considerable boost in the opinion polls despite the failure of the operation as Americans rallied around the flag, but there was no disguising the fact that this had been a significant and embarrassing humiliation.

[2] The plan also contained a (still somewhat murky) assassination component intended to dispose of Castro altogether (see Hersh 1998, 202–21).

[3] Fulbright had narrowly missed out on the secretary of state job in 1961, a position he reportedly did not want, but was respected by Kennedy for his long foreign policy experience.

[4] This phrase is reminiscent of Colin Powell's view that Saddam Hussein was "a toothache" (see chap. 10).

[5] This story seems to have been obtained from a single source at second- or thirdhand, relating a story that Bissell is supposed to have told.

[6] Interestingly, under Eisenhower the State Department had also been concerned about "the importance of maintaining deniability," even though it had not opposed the invasion as such (Gleijeses 1995, 19).

[7] Stevenson had not been briefed about the Bay of Pigs operation and seemed to have believed Kennedy's public assurances that the United States would not interfere in Cuba's internal affairs.

NOTES TO CHAPTER 6

[1] Dana Perino, who served as George W. Bush's press secretary between 2007 and 2009.

[2] In the opinion of Blight and Welch, McCone simply "got lucky" and could not decisively prove his case (Blight and Welch 1998, 180). Robert Kennedy seems to have believed that the CIA Director was the source of leaks to members of Congress (Hersh 1998, 349–50).

[3] This is a somewhat controversial view, since the consensus among most scholars of the missile crisis is that Khrushchev acted out of a mixture of motives (1) and (3), and that

domestic political considerations may also have played a part. (See Lebow and Stein 1994, 51–93, and Fischer 1998, 158).

4 Predictably perhaps, Adm. Anderson was far less forthcoming about this exchange in a later interview for the PBS series *War and Peace in the Nuclear Age* (vol. 5). According to his account, his reply was simply "Mr. Secretary, the Navy will not let you down."

5 The October 19 tape was part of a batch of ExCom meetings declassified by the Kennedy Library between 1994 and 1997, and the transcript was first published in May and Zelikow 1997. The second edition of *Essence of Decision* appeared in 1999.

6 Robert Kennedy specifically used the term "Pearl Harbor in reverse," which appears in a large number of the firsthand accounts. Others recall his precise phrase as "the Tojo of the 1960s," so it is possible that he actually used both phrases (see, for example, Hilsman 1967, 203; O'Donnell and Powers 1970, 317; and Ball 1982, 291).

NOTES TO CHAPTER 7

1 The HBO film *The Path to War* re-creates this debate in dramatic fashion, using actors to portray Clifford (played by Donald Sutherland) and McNamara (Alec Baldwin). The film is highly accurate historically, and students may find it instructive to watch *The Path to War* in conjunction with this case study.

2 We can apply the same reasoning to the Cuban missile crisis discussed in chap. 6. What if it had been Adlai Stevenson who drew the comparison between the airstrike on Cuba and Pearl Harbor, instead of Robert Kennedy? Would the President have listened as intently as he did? In fact, it was George Ball who was again the first to pick up on that analogy, but would the President have turned dead-set against an air strike if Robert Kennedy had not thought of the analogy as well?

NOTES TO CHAPTER 8

1 Cottam had even interviewed Khomeini in Paris at one point.

2 This is one reason why Iran today is in large part an Islamic theocracy but at times still resembles a Western-style democracy, since the political system that emerged from this struggle was a product of compromise between radicals and moderates.

3 Two trucks came along the road a short time later, one of which escaped.

4 Perhaps not coincidentally, all four men were also members of the secret planning group.

5 This later became the long-running new show *Nightline*.

NOTES TO CHAPTER 9

1 A transcript is available at the Miller Center's website at the University of Virginia. See http://millercenter.org/scripps/archive/speeches/detail/3932.

2 Quoted in the PBS *Frontline* documentary *War in Europe,* first broadcast February 22, 2000. A transcript is available at http://www.pbs.org/wgbh/pages/frontline/shows/kosovo/etc/tapes.html.

3 Quoted in the PBS *Frontline* documentary *War in Europe.* Monica Lewinsky was a young White House intern with whom President Clinton had an affair.

⁴ Ironically, members of the White House press corps were watching this film on the day Clinton made his admission to the affair.

⁵ This claim was denied by then National Security Adviser Samuel Berger. More puzzlingly, Clark himself later claimed that he had not meant to suggest that Al Gore had behaved this way, so it is still unclear what actually occurred (see Smith 2004 and Wyatt 2004).

⁶ The secretary of defense had served as a Republican senator from Maine (1979–87).

⁷ Quoted in the PBS *Frontline* documentary *War in Europe*.

⁸ This a reference to the ethnic cleansing of over 30,000 innocent Bosnians in and around the town of Srebrenica in July. For the United States, this was the straw (or sizable stick) that broke the camel's back.

⁹ Quoted in the PBS *Frontline* documentary *War in Europe*.

¹⁰ Interview with Richard Holbrooke, PBS *Frontline, War in Europe* website, available at http://www.pbs.org/wgbh/pages/frontline/shows/kosovo/interviews/holbrooke.html.

NOTES TO CHAPTER 10

¹ Portions of this chapter draw upon the author's article, "Invading and Occupying Iraq: Some Insights From Political Psychology," *Peace and Conflict: A Journal of Peace Psychology* 14 (May 2008): 169–92. I especially wish to thank Lt. General Jay Garner, Col. Kim Olson, Col. Paul Hughes, Col. Lawrence Wilkerson, Col. Ann Wright, and Col. Larry West, all of whom agreed to be interviewed on the topic of Iraq and gave generously of their time.

² Quoted in CBS News, "Bush Sought 'Way' To Invade Iraq?" at http://www.cbsnews.com/stories/2004/01/09/60minutes/main592330.shtml.

³ Department of Defense News Briefing, February 12, 2002.

⁴ See CBS News, "Clarke's Take on Terror," March 21, 2004, at http://www.cbsnews.com/stories/2004/03/19/60minutes/main607356.shtml.

⁵ Quoted in the PBS *American Experience* episode, "LBJ." See http://www.pbs.org/wgbh/amex/presidents/36_l_johnson/filmmore/filmscript.html.

Bibliography

Abelson, Robert. "The Psychological Status of the Script Concept." *American Psychologist* 36:715–29, 1981.

Acheson, Dean. "Dean Acheson's Version of Robert Kennedy's Version of the Cuban Missile Affair: Homage to Plain Dumb Luck." *Esquire*, February 1969.

Albright, Madeleine. *Madam Secretary: A Memoir.* New York: Miramax Books, 2003.

Allison, Graham. *Essence of Decision: Explaining the Cuban Missile Crisis.* Boston, MA: Little, Brown, 1971.

Allison, Graham, and Morton Halperin. "Bureaucratic Politics: A Paradigm and Some Policy Implications." *World Politics* 24 (1972): 40–79.

Allison, Graham, and Philip Zelikow. *Essence of Decision: Explaining the Cuban Missile Crisis*, 2nd. ed. New York: Longman, 1999.

Alter, Jonathan. "Your Gut Only Gets You So Far." *Newsweek*, October 11, 2004.

Aronson, Elliot. "The Theory of Cognitive Dissonance: A Current Perspective." In *Advances in Experimental Social Psychology*, vol. 4, edited by Leon Berkowitz. New York: Academic Press, 1969.

Art, Robert. "Bureaucratic Politics and American Foreign Policy: A Critique." *Policy Sciences* 4 (1972): 467–90.

Axelrod, Robert. "Argumentation in Foreign Policy Settings: Britain in 1918, Munich in 1938 and Japan in 1970." *Journal of Conflict Resolution* 21, no. 727 (December 1977): 56.

Baker, Peter, David Johnston, and Mark Mazzetti. "Abuse Issue Puts the CIA and Justice Department at Odds." *New York Times*, August 27, 2009.

Ball, George. *The Past Has Another Pattern: Memoirs.* New York: W.W. Norton, 1982.

Bamford, James, *The Puzzle Palace: Inside the National Security Agency, America's Most Secret Intelligence Organization.* New York: Penguin Books, 1983.

Bamford, James. *A Pretext for War: 9/11, Iraq and the Abuse of America's Intelligence Agencies.* New York: Doubleday, 2004.

Barber, James David, *The Presidential Character: Predicting Performance in the White House.* 3rd ed. Englewood Cliffs, NJ: Prentice-Hall, 1992.

Barrett, David. "The Mythology Surrounding Lyndon Johnson, His Advisers, and the 1965 Decision to Escalate the Vietnam War." *Political Science Quarterly* 103 (1988): 637–63.

Barrett, David. *Uncertain Warriors: Lyndon Johnson and His Vietnam Advisers.* Lawrence, : University Press of Kansas, 1993.

Bendor, Jonathan, and Thomas Hammond. "Rethinking Allison's Models." *American Political Science Review* 86 (1992): 301–22.

Berman, Larry. *Planning a Tragedy: The Americanization of the War in Vietnam.* New York: W. W. Norton, 1982.

Berman, Larry, and Emily Goldman. "Clinton's Foreign Policy at Midterm." In *The Clinton Presidency: First Appraisals,* edited by Colin Campbell and Bert Rockman. Chatham, NJ: Chatham House, 1996.

Beschloss, Michael, ed. *Reaching For Glory: Lyndon Johnson's Secret White House Tapes, 1964–1965.* New York: Simon and Schuster, 2001.

———. *Taking Charge: The Johnson White House tapes, 1963–1964.* New York: Simon and Schuster, 1997.

Betts, Richard. "Conventional Strategy: New Critics, Old Choices." *International Security* 7 (1983): 140–62.

Bill, James. *The Eagle and the Lion: The Tragedy of American-Iranian Relations.* New Haven, CT: Yale University Press, 1988.

Bissell, Richard. *Reflections of a Cold Warrior: From Yalta to the Bay of Pigs.* New Haven, CT: Yale University Press, 1996.

———. "Transcript of Oral Interview of Mr. Richard M. Bissell Jr. by Jack B. Pfeiffer on the Bay of Pigs Operation." Farmington, CT, October 17. 1975. Available online at http://www.gwu.edu/~nsarchiv/bayofpigs/bissellinterv.pdf.

Blight, James. *The Shattered Crystal Ball: Fear and Learning in the Cuban Missile Crisis.* Savage, MD: Rowman and Littlefield, 1990.

Blight, James, and David Welch. *Cuba on the Brink: Castro, the Missile Crisis, and the Soviet Collapse.* Rev. ed. for the Fortieth Anniversary. Lanham, MD; Rowman and Littlefield, 2002.

———. *On The Brink: Americans and Soviets Reexamine the Cuban Missile Crisis.* New York: Noonday Press, 1989.

Blight, James, and Peter Kornbluh, eds. *Politics of Illusion: The Bay of Pigs Invasion Reexamined.* Boulder, CO: Lynne Rienner, 1998.

Blight, James. and Janet Lang. *The Fog of War: Lessons From the Life of Robert S. McNamara.* New York: Rowman and Littlefield, 2005.

———. "Lesson Number One: '"Empathize with your Enemy."'" *Peace and Conflict* 10 (2004): 349–68.

Blight, James, Janet Lang, and David Welch, *Virtual JFK: Vietnam If Kennedy Had Lived.* New York: Rowman and Littlefield, 2009.

Bowden, Mark. *Black Hawk Down: A Story of Modern War.* New York: Atlantic Monthly Press, 1999.

———. *Guests of the Ayatollah: The First Battle in America's War with Militant Islam.* New York: Atlantic Monthly Press, 2006.

Bowles, Chester. "Memorandum from the Under Secretary of State (Bowles) to Secretary of State Rusk, March 31, 1961 (Arguing Against an invasion of Cuba)." U.S. Department of State, Foreign Relations of the United States, 1961–1963. Vol. 10, Cuba, 1961–1962, Washington, DC.

Bremer, Paul. *My Year in Iraq: The Struggle to Build a Future of Hope.* New York: Threshold Editions, 2006.

Brewster Smith, Michael. "Realistic Empathy: A Key to Sensible International Relations." *Peace and Conflict* 10 (2004): 335–39.

Brulé, David. "Explaining and Forecasting Leaders' Decisions: A Poliheuristic Analysis of the Iran Hostage Rescue Decision." *International Studies Perspectives* **6 (2005)**: 99–113.

Brzezinski, Zbigniew. "The Failed Rescue Mission: The Inside Account of the Attempt to Free the Hostages in Iran." *New York Times Magazine*, April 18, 1982.

———. *Power and Principle: Memoirs of the National Security Adviser, 1977–1981.* New York: Farrar, Strauss and Giroux, 1983.

Burger, Timothy, and Matthew Cooper. "The Incredible Shrinking CIA." *Time,* May 5, 2006.

Burke, John, and Greenstein, Fred. *How Presidents Test Reality: Decisions on Vietnam, 1954 and 1965.* New York: Russell Sage Foundation, 1989.

Bush, George W. *Decision Points.* New York: Crown Publishers, 2010.

Cannon, Lou. *President Reagan: The Role of a Lifetime.* Rev. ed. New York: Public Affairs, 2000.

Carlsnaes, Walter. "The Agency-Structure Problem in Foreign Policy Analysis." *International Studies Quarterly* 36 (1992): 245–70.

Carter, Jimmy. *Keeping Faith: Memoirs of a President.* New York: Bantam Books, 1982. CBS News. "Bush Sought 'Way' to Invade Iraq?" at http://www.cbsnews.com/stories/2004/01/09/60minutes/main592330.shtml.

CBS News. "Clarke's Take on Terror". March 21, 2004, at http://www.cbsnews.com/stories/2004/03/19/60minutes/main607356.shtml.

Chandrasekaran, Rajiv. *Imperial Life in the Emerald City: Inside Iraq's Green Zone.* New York: Knopf, 2006.

Chang, Laurence, and Peter Kornbluh, eds. *The Cuban Missile Crisis, 1962: A National Security Archive Documents Reader.* Rev. ed. New York: New Press, 1998.

Chomsky, Noam. *Rethinking Camelot: JFK, the Vietnam War, and US Political Culture.* Cambridge, MA: South End Press, 1993.

Clark, Wesley. *A Time To Lead: For Duty, Honor and Country.* New York: Palgrave Macmillan, 2007.

———. *Waging Modern War: Bosnia, Kosovo, and the Future of Combat.* New York: Public Affairs, 2001.

Clarke, Richard. *Against All Enemies: Inside America's War on Terror.* New York: Free Press, 2004.

Clinton, Bill. *My Life.* New York: Knopf, 2004.

Clifford, Clark. *Counsel to the President.* New York,: Random House, 1991.

Clifford, Garry. "Bureaucratic Politics." *Journal of American History* 77 (1990): 161–68.

Cohen, Eliot. "Why We Should Stop Studying the Cuban Missile Crisis." *National Interest* 6 (1985/86): 3–13.

Cohen, William, and George Mitchell. *Men of Zeal: A Candid Inside Story of the Iran-Contra Hearings.* New York: Viking Press, 1988.

Cottam, Richard. *Foreign Policy Motivation: A General Theory and a Case Study.* Pittsburgh: University of Pittsburgh Press, 1977.

Daalder, Ivo, and Michael O'Hanlon. *Winning Ugly: NATO's War to Save Kosovo.* Washington DC: Brookings Institution Press, 2000.

Dallek, Robert. *Flawed Giant: Lyndon Johnson and His Times, 1961–1973.* New York: Oxford University Press, 1999.

Dallek, Robert. *An Unfinished Life: John F. Kennedy, 1917–1963.* Boston, MA: Little, Brown, 2003.

Danner, Mark. *The Secret Way to War: The Downing Street Memo and the Iraq War's Buried History.* New York: New York Review of Books, 2006.

Damasio, Antonio. *Descartes' Error: Emotion, Reason and the Human Brain.* New York: Putnam, 1994.

Deal, Terry, and Allan Kennedy. *Corporate Cultures: The Rites and Rituals of Corporate Life.* New York: Perseus Books, 2000.

De Rivera, Joseph. *The Psychological Dimension of Foreign Policy.* Columbus, OH: C. E. Merrill, 1968.

Diamond, Larry. *Squandered Victory: The American Occupation and the Bungled Effort to Bring Democracy to Iraq.* New York: Times Books, 1995.

Dijksterhuis, Ap, Maarten Bos, Loran Nordgren, and Rick van Baaren. "On Making the Right Choice: The Deliberation-Without-Attention Effect." *Science* 311 (2006): 1005–7.

Dobbs, Michael. *Madeleine Albright: A Twentieth Century Odyssey.* New York: Henry Holt, 1999.

———. *One Minute to Midnight: Kennedy, Khrushchev and Castro on the Brink of Nuclear War.* New York: Knopf, 2008.

Draper, Theodore. *Castro's Revolution: Myths and Realities.* New York: Praeger, 1962.

———. *A Very Thin Line: The Iran-Contra Affairs.* New York: Hill and Wang, 1991.

Drew, Elizabeth. *On The Edge: The Clinton Presidency.* New York: Simon and Schuster, 1994.

Dyson, Stephen, and Thomas Preston. "Individual Characteristics of Political Leaders and the Use of Analogy in Foreign Policy Decision Making." *Political Psychology* 27 (2006): 265–88.

Emerson, Steven. *Secret Warriors: Inside the Covert Military Operations of the Reagan Era.* New York: Putnam, 1988.

Evans, Roland, and Robert Novak. *Nixon in the White House: The Frustration of Power.* New York: Random House, 1971.

Festinger, Leon. *Theory of Cognitive Dissonance.* Stanford, CA: Stanford University Press, 1957.

Festinger, Leon, Henry Riecken, and Stanley Schacter. *When Prophecy Fails: A Social and Psychological Study of a Modern Group that Predicted the Destruction of the World.* New York: Harper and Row, 1964.

Fischhoff, Baruch, and Ruth Beyth. "'I Knew It Would Happen': Remembered Probabilities of Once-Future Things." *Organizational Behavior and Human Performance* 13 (1975): 1–16.

Fischer, Beth. "Perception, Intelligence Errors, and the Cuban Missile Crisis." In *Intelligence and the Cuban Missile Crisis,* edited by James Blight and David Welch. London: Frank Cass, 1998.

Fiske, Susan. and Shelley Taylor. *Social Cognition.* Reading, MA: Addison-Wesley, 1984.

Ford, Gerald. *A Time to Heal.* New York: Harper and Row, 1979.

Fursenko, Aleksandr, and Timothy Naftali. *"One Hell of a Gamble": Khrushchev, Castro, and Kennedy, 1958–1964: The Secret History of the Cuban Missile Crisis.* New York: W. W. Norton, 1997.

Gabriel, Richard. *Military Incompetence: Why the American Military Doesn't Win.* New York: Hill and Wang, 1985.

Gaenslen, Fritz. "Decision-Making Groups." In *Political Psychology and Foreign Policy*, edited by Eric Singer and Valerie Hudson. Boulder, CO: Westview Press, 1992.

Galbraith, Peter. *The End of Iraq: How American Incompetence Created a War without End.* New York: Simon and Schuster, 2006.

Galbraith, Peter. *Unintended Consequences: How the War in Iraq Strengthened America's Enemies.* New York: Simon and Schuster, 2008.

Garner, Jay. interview with the author. Orlando, FL, February 19, 2007.

Garthoff, Raymond. "U.S. Intelligence in the Cuban Missile Crisis." In Blight and Welch, *Intelligence and the Cuban Missile Crisis.*

Gartner, Scott. "Predicting the Timing of Carter's Decision to Initiate a Hostage Rescue Attempt: Modeling a Dynamic Information Environment." *International Interactions* 18 (1993): 365–86.

Gelb, Leslie, and Richard Betts. *The Irony of Vietnam: The System Worked.* Washington, DC: Brookings Institution, 1979.

George, Alexander. *Bridging the Gap: Theory and Practice in Foreign Policy.* Washington, DC: United States Institute of Peace, 1993.

———. "The Causal Nexus between Cognitive Beliefs and Decision Making Behavior: The 'Operational Code' Belief System." In *Psychological Models in International Politics*, edited by Lawrence Falkowski. Boulder, CO: Westview Press, 1979.

———. "The 'Operational Code': A Neglected Approach to the Study of Political Leaders and Decision Making." *International Studies Quarterly* 13 (1969): 190–222.

———. *Presidential Decisionmaking in Foreign Policy: The Effective Use of Information and Advice.* Boulder, CO: Westview Press, 1980.

George, Alexander, and Juliette George. *Woodrow Wilson and Colonel House: A Personality Study.* New York: Dover, 1964.

Glad, Betty. "Personality, Political and Group Process Variables in Foreign Policy Decision-Making: Jimmy Carter's Handling of the Iranian Hostage Crisis." *International Political Science Review* 10 (1989): 35–61.

Gladwell, Malcolm. *Blink: The Power of Thinking without Thinking.* New York: Little, Brown, 2005.

Gleijeses, Piero. "Ships in the Night: The CIA, the White House and the Bay of Pigs." *Journal of Latin American Studies* 27 (1995): 1–42.

Glenny, Misha. *The Fall of Yugoslavia: The Third Balkan War.* 3rd ed. New York: Penguin, 1996.

Goodwin, Doris Kearns. *Lyndon Johnson and the American Dream.* New York: St. Martin's Press, 1976.

Goodwin, Richard. *Remembering America: A Voice from the Sixties.* New York: HarperCollins, 1989.

Gordon, Michael, and Eric Schmitt. "Pentagon Withholds Copters from Battlefields in Kosovo." *New York Times*, A1, May 16, 1999.

Gordon, Michael, and Bernard Trainor. *Cobra II: The Inside Story of the Invasion and Occupation of Iraq.* New York: Pantheon Books, 2006.

Greenberg, Daniel. "Mission Improbable." *Washington Post*, April 29, 1980.

Greenstein, Fred. "The Impact of Personality on the End of the Cold War." *Political Psychology* 19 (1998): 1–16.

Guilmartin, John. *A Very Short War: The Mayaguez and the Battle of Koh Tang.* College Station: Texas A&M University Press, 1995.

Haas, Mark. "Prospect Theory and the Cuban Missile Crisis." *International Studies Quarterly* 45 (2001): 241–70.

Halberstam, David. *The Best and the Brightest.* New York: Random House, 1969.

———. *War in a Time of Peace: Bush, Clinton and the Generals.* New York: Touchstone Books, 2002.

Halperin, Morton. *Bureaucratic Politics and Foreign Policy.* Washington, DC: Brookings Institution, 1974.

Hargrove, Erwin. *Jimmy Carter as President: Leadership and the Politics of the Public Good.* Baton Rouge: Louisiana State University Press, 1988.

Hawkins, Jack. "Memorandum From the Chief of WH/4/PM, Central Intelligence Agency (Hawkins) to the Chief of WH/4 of the Directorate for Plans (Esterline)." January 4, 1961, U.S. Department of State, *Foreign Relations of the United States*, 1961–1963, vol. 9, Cuba, 1961–1962, Washington, DC.

Head, Richard, Frisco Short, and Robert McFarlane. *Crisis Resolution: Presidential Decision Making in the Mayaguez and Korean Confrontations.* Boulder, CO: Westview Press, 1978.

Hehir, Aidan. "The Impact of Analogical Reasoning on US Foreign Policy Towards Kosovo." *Journal of Peace Research* 43 (2006): 67–81.

Heider, Fritz. *The Psychology of Interpersonal Relations.* New York: Wiley, 1958.

Hemmer, Christopher. *Which Lessons Matter? American Foreign Policy Decision Making in the Middle East, 1979–1987.* New York: SUNY Press, 2000.

Hersh, Seymour. *The Dark Side of Camelot.* New York: Back Bay Books, 1998.

Higgins, Trumbull. *The Perfect Failure: Kennedy, Eisenhower, and the CIA at the Bay of Pigs.* New York: W. W. Norton, 1987.

Hilsman, Roger. *To Move a Nation: The Politics of Foreign Policy in the Administration of John F. Kennedy.* New York: Doubleday, 1967.

Hirsch, Michael. "At War With Ourselves." *Harper's Magazine* 299:60–69, July 1999.

Holder, Eric. Interview with CNN's Paula Zahn, January 28, 2002. Available at http://premium.edition.cnn.com/TRANSCRIPTS/0201/28/ltm.03.html.

Hollis, Martin, and Steve Smith. *Explaining and Understanding International Relations.* Oxford: Clarendon Press, 1991.

———. "Roles and Reasons in Foreign Policy Decision Making." *British Journal of Political Science* 16 (1986): 269–86.

Holsti, Ole. "The Belief System and National Images: A Case Study." In *International Politics and Foreign Policy*, edited by James Rosenau. 2nd ed. New York: Free Press, 1969.

Holt, Pat. Interview with Donald Ritchie. Interview #5, "Fulbright and the Bay of Pigs Monday." October 27, 1980, available at http://www.senate.gov/artandhistory/history/resources/pdf/Holt_interview_5.pdf.

Hosmer, Stephen. *The Conflict Over Kosovo: Why Milosevic Decided To Settle When He Did.* Santa Monica, CA: Rand Corporation, 2001.

Houghton, David Patrick. "Essence of Excision: A Critique of the New Version of *Essence of Decision.*" *Security Studies* 10 (Autumn 2000): 162–91.

———. *Political Psychology: Situations, Individuals and Cases.* New York: Routledge, 2009.

———. *U.S. Foreign Policy and the Iran Hostage Crisis.* New York: Cambridge University Press, 2001.

Hudson, Valerie. *Foreign Policy Analysis: Classic and Contemporary Theory.* Lanham, MD: Rowman and Littlefield, 2007.

Hunt, Michael. *Lyndon Johnson's War: America's Cold War Crusade in Vietnam.* New York: Farrar, Strauss and Giroux, 1996.

Hybel, Alex. *How Leaders Reason: U.S. Intervention in the Caribbean Basin and Latin America.* Cambridge, MA: Basil Blackwell, 1990.

Inman, Bobby, Telephone interview with the author, February 7, 2007.

Isaacson, Walter. "Madeleine's War." *Time,* May 17, 1999.

Isaacson, Walter. *Kissinger: A Biography.* New York: Simon and Schuster, 1992.

Isikoff, Michael. *Hubris: The Inside Story of Spin, Scandal and the Selling of the Iraq War.* New York: Crown Publishers, 2006.

Janis, Irving. *Groupthink: Psychological Studies of Policy Decisions and Fiascoes.* Boston: Houghton Mifflin, 1982.

———. "In Rescue Planning, How Did Carter Handle Stress?" *New York Times,* May 18, 1980, E21.

Janis, Irving, and Leon Mann. *Decision Making: A Psychological Analysis of Conflict, Choice and Commitment.* New York: Free Press, 1977.

Jervis, Robert. "The Drunkard's Search." In *Explorations in Political Psychology,* edited by Shanto Iyengar and William McGuire. Durham, NC: Duke University Press, 1993.

———. "Hypotheses on Misperception." *World Politics* 20 (1968): 454–79.

———. *Perception and Misperception in International Politics.* Princeton, NJ: Princeton University Press, 1976.

Johnson, Tom. Interview with the author. Athens, Georgia, January 19, 2007.

Jordan, Hamilton. Miller Center interview, Carter Presidency Project, vol. 6. Jimmy Carter Library, Atlanta, GA, November 6, 1981.

Jordan, Hamilton. *Crisis: The Last Year of the Carter Presidency.* New York: Berkley, 1983.

Judah, Tim. *Kosovo: War and Revenge.* New Haven, CT: Yale University Press, 2000.

Kahneman, Daniel, and Amos Tversky. "Prospect Theory: An Analysis of Decision under Risk." *Econometrica* 47 (1979): 263–91.

Kahneman, Daniel, Paul Slovic, and Amos Tversky, eds. *Judgment Under Uncertainty: Heuristics and Biases.* Cambridge: Cambridge University Press, 1982.

Kaplan, Abraham. *The Conduct of Enquiry.* San Francisco: Chandler, 1964.

Kaplan, Robert. *Balkan Ghosts: A Journey through History.* New York: Vintage Books, 1994.

Karnow, Stanley. Interview for the PBS American Experience documentary *Nixon's China Game,* first aired in 2000. Available at http://www.pbs.org/wgbh/amex/china/filmmore/transcript/index.html.

Katzenbach, Nicholas. Interview with the author, November 8, 2006. Princeton, NJ.

Keisling, Philip. "Desert One: The Wrong Man and the Wrong Plan." *Washington Monthly,* December 1983.

Kennedy, Robert. *Thirteen Days: A Memoir of the Cuban Missile Crisis.* New York: W. W. Norton, 1968.

Khong, Yuen Foong. *Analogies at War: Korea, Munich, Dien Bien Phu, and the Vietnam Decisions of 1965.* Princeton, NJ: Princeton University Press, 1992.

Kissinger, Henry. *Diplomacy.* New York: Simon and Schuster, 1994.

———. Interview for the PBS American Experience documentary Nixon's *China Game,* first aired in 2000. Available at http://www.pbs.org/wgbh/amex/china/filmmore/transcript/index.html.

———. *White House Years.* Boston: Little, Brown, 1979.

Kornbluh, Peter, ed. *Bay of Pigs Declassified: The Secret CIA Report on the Invasion of Cuba.* New York: New Press, 1998.

Kornbluh, Peter, and Malcolm Byrne. *The Iran-Contra Scandal: The Declassified History.* New York: New Press, 1993.

Kowert, Paul. *Groupthink Versus Deadlock: When Do Leaders Learn From their Advisors?* Albany: SUNY Press, 2002.

——. "Leadership and Learning in Political Groups: The Management of Advice in the Iran-Contra Affair." *Governance* 14 (2001): 201–32.

Kramer, Roderick. "Revisiting the Bay of Pigs and Vietnam Decisions 25 Years Later: How Well Has the Groupthink Hypothesis Stood the Test of Time?" *Organizational Behavior* 73 (1998): 236–71.

Krasner, Stephen. "Are Bureaucracies Important? Or Allison Wonderland." *Foreign Policy* 7 (1972): 159–79.

Kunda, Ziva. "The Case for Motivated Reasoning.'" *Psychological Bulletin* 108 (1990): 480–98.

Lakshmanan, Indira. "Some See Double Standard in China Flap." *Boston Globe*, April 18, 2001.

Lamb, Christopher. "Belief Systems and Decision Making in the *Mayaguez* Crisis." *Political Science Quarterly* 99 (Winter 1984/85): 681–702.

Larson, Deborah Welch. *Origins of Containment: A Psychological Explanation.* Princeton, NJ: Princeton University Press, 1985.

Latané, Bibb, and John Darley. *The Unresponsive Bystander: Why Doesn't He Help?* Englewood Cliffs, NJ: Prentice-Hall, 1970.

Lebow, Richard Ned. *Between Peace and War: The Nature of International Crisis.* Baltimore, MD: Johns Hopkins University Press, 1981.

——. "Psychological Dimensions of Post-Cold War Foreign Policy." In *The Clinton Presidency: Campaigning, Governing, and the Psychology of Leadership,* edited by Stanley Renshon. Boulder, CO: Westview Press, 1995.

——. "What's So Different about a Counterfactual?" *World Politics* 52 (2000): 550–85.

Lebow, Richard Ned, and Janice Gross Stein. "Back to the Past: Counterfactuals and the Cuban Missile Crisis." In *Counterfactual Thought Experiments in World Politics,* edited by Philip Tetlock and Aaron Belkin. Princeton, NJ: Princeton University Press, 1996.

——. *We All Lost The Cold War.* Princeton, NJ: Princeton University Press, 1994.

Leonard, James. Interview with the author, November 1, 2006, Washington, DC.

Lerner, Mitchell. *The Pueblo Incident: A Spy Ship and the Failure of American Foreign Policy.* Lawrence: University Press of Kansas, 2002.

Levine, John. "Reaction to Opinion Deviance in Small Groups." In *Psychology of Group Influence*, edited by Paul Paulus. 2nd ed. Hillsdale, NJ: Lawrence Erlbaum, 1989.

Levine, David. "The Wheels of Washington: Groupthink and Iraq." *San Francisco Chronicle*, February 5, 2004.

Levy, Jack. "The Diversionary Theory of War: A Critique." In *Handbook of War Studies,* edited by Manus Midlarsky, London: Unwin-Hyman, 1989.

——. "Misperception and the Causes of War: Theoretical Linkages and Analytical Problems." *World Politics* 36 (1983): 76–99.

——. "'Prospect Theory and International Relations: Theoretical Applications and Analytical Problems." *Political Psychology* 13 (1992): 283–310.

Lippman, Thomas. "'Albright Misjudged Milosevic on Kosovo." *Washington Post*, A1, April 7, 1999.

Longley, Jeanne, and Dean Pruitt. "Groupthink: A Critique of Janis's Theory." In *Review of Personality and Social Psychology,* edited by Ladd Wheeler. Beverly Hills, CA: Sage Publications, 1980.

Luttwak, Edward. *The Pentagon and the Art of War: The Question of Military Reform.* New York: Simon and Schuster, 1984.

Lynch, Grayston. *Decision for Disaster: Betrayal at the Bay of Pigs.* Washington. DC: Brassey's, 1998.

McCormick, James, and Eugene Wittkopf. *The Domestic Sources of American Foreign Policy: Insights and Evidence.* 5th ed. New York: Rowman and Littlefield, 1997.

McDermott, Rose. *Political Psychology in International Relations.* Ann Arbor: University of Michigan Press, 2004.

———. "Prospect Theory in International Relations: The Iranian Hostage Rescue Mission." *Political Psychology* 13 (1992): 237–63.

McGraw, Kathleen, and Thomas Dolan. "Personifying the State: Consequences for Attitude Formation." *Political Psychology* 28 (2007): 299–327.

McMaster, H. R. *Dereliction of Duty: Lyndon Johnson, Robert McNamara, the Joint Chiefs of Staff, and the Lies that Led to Vietnam.* New York: Harper Perennial, 1998.

McNamara, Robert. *In Retrospect: The Tragedy and Lessons of Vietnam.* New York: Random House, 1995.

———. Oral History Interview, April 14 1964. John F. Kennedy Library, Boston, MA.

McNamara, Robert, James Blight, and Robert Brigham. *Argument Without End: In Search of Answers to the Vietnam Tragedy.* New York: Public Affairs, 1999.

McNamara, Robert, and James Blight. *Wilson's Ghost: Reducing the Risk of Conflict, Killing and Catastrophe in the 21st Century.* New York: Public Affairs, 2001.

McQueen, Alison. "A Groupthink Perspective on the Invasion of Iraq." *International Affairs Review* 14 (2005): 53–79.

Malcolm, Noel. *Kosovo: A Short History.* New York: New York University Press, 1998.

Mandelbaum, Michael. "A Perfect Failure: NATO's War Against Yugoslavia." *Foreign Affairs* 78 (1999): 2–8.

Mann, James. *About Face: A History of America's Curious Relationship with China, from Nixon to Clinton.* New York: Alfred Knopf, 1999.

———. *Rise of the Vulcans: The History of Bush's War Cabinet.* New York: Penguin Books, 2004.

March, James, and Herbert Simon. *Organizations.* 2nd ed. Cambridge, MA: Blackwell, 1993.

May, Ernest, and Philip Zelikow, eds. *The Kennedy Tapes: Inside the White House During the Cuban Missile Crisis.* Cambridge, MA: Belknap Press, 1997.

Mazzetti, Mark. "Turf Battles on Intelligence Pose Test for Spy Chiefs." *New York Times,* June 9, 2009.

Mercer, Jonathan. "Rationality and Psychology in International Politics." *International Organization* 59 (2005): 77–106.

Mintz, Alex. "Applied Decision Analysis: Utilizing Poliheuristic Theory to Explain and Predict Foreign Policy and National Security Decisions." *International Studies Perspectives* **6 (2005):** 94–98.

Mintz, Alex, Nehemia Geva, Steven Redd, and Amy Carnes. "The Effect of Dynamic and Static Choice Sets on Political Decision Making: An Analysis Using the Decision Board Platform." *American Political Science Review* 91 (1997): 553–66.

Moens, Alexander. "President Carter's Advisers and the Fall of the Shah." *Political Science Quarterly* 106 (1991): 211–37.

Moin, Baqer. *Khomeini: Life of the Ayatollah.* London: I. B. Tauris, 1999.

Morgenthau, Hans, Kenneth Thompson, and David Clinton. *Politics Among Nations.* 7th ed. New York: McGraw-Hill, 2005.

Myers, Steven. "US Military Chiefs Firm: No Ground Force For Kosovo." *New York Times*, A16, June 3, 1999.

Myers, Steven, and Eric Schmitt. "War's Conduct Creates Tension Among Chiefs." *New York Times*, 1, May 30, 1999.

Naftali, Timothy, and Philip Zelikow, eds. *The Presidential Recordings of John F. Kennedy: The Great Crises.* Vol. 2. New York; W. W. Norton, 2001.

Neack, Laura, Jeanne Hey, and Patrick Haney. *Foreign Policy Analysis: Continuity and Change in Its Second Generation.* Englewood Cliffs, NJ: Prentice Hall, 1995.

Neustadt, Richard, and Ernest May. *Thinking in Time: The Uses of History For Decision-Makers.* New York: Free Press, 1986.

Nisbett, Richard, and Lee Ross. *Human Inference: Strategies and Shortcomings of Social Judgment.* Englewood Cliffs, NJ: Prentice-Hall, 1980.

Nitze, Paul. Oral History Interview 2, 1969, Lyndon Baines Johnson Library, Austin, TX.

O'Donnell, Kenneth, and Dave Powers. *"Johnny, We Hardly Knew Ye": Memories of John Fitzgerald Kennedy.* Boston, MA: Little, Brown, 1970.

Olson, Kim. Interview with the author, Orlando, FL, November 9. 2006.

———. *Iraq and Back: Inside the War to Win the Peace.* Annapolis, MD: Naval Institute Press, 2006.

Osborn, Shane. Interview for the PBS Frontline documentary, *Dangerous Straits*, first aired October 18. 2001. Available at http://www.pbs.org/wgbh/pages/frontline/shows/china/interviews/osborn.html.

Packer, George. *The Assassin's Gate: America in Iraq.* New York: Farrar, Straus and Giroux, 2005.

Panetta, Leon., "No More. No Torture. No Exceptions." *Washington Monthly*, January-March 2008.

Paris, Roland. "Kosovo and the Metaphor War." *Political Science Quarterly* 117 (2002): 423–50.

Perlez, Jane. "Clinton and the Joint Chiefs to Discuss Ground Invasion." *New York Times*, A14, June 2, 1999.

Phillips, David. *Losing Iraq: Inside the Postwar Reconstruction Fiasco.* New York: Basic Books, 2006.

Pincus, Walter, and Dana Priest. "Some Iraq Analysts Felt Pressure from Cheney Visits." *Washington Post*, A1, June 5, 2003.

Pollack, Kenneth. *The Persian Puzzle: The Conflict Between Iran and America.* New York: Random House, 2004.

Popkin, Samuel. "Decision Making in Presidential Primaries." In Iyengar and McGuire, *Explorations in Political Psychology*.

Posen, Barry. "The War For Kosovo: Serbia's Political-Military Strategy." *International Security* 24 (2000): 39–84.

Powell, Colin, with Joseph Persico. *My American Journey.* New York: Random House, 1995.

Priest, Dana. "A Decisive Battle That Never Was." *Washington Post*, A1, September 19, 1999a.

——. "The Battle Inside Headquarters: Tension Grew With Divide Over Strategy." *Washington Post*, A1, September 21, 1999b.

——. "Risks and Restraint: Why the Apaches Never Flew in Kosovo." *Washington Post*, A1, December 29, 1999c.

——. *The Mission.* New York: W. W. Norton, 2003.

Purdum, Todd. A Time of Our Choosing: America's War in Iraq. New York: Times Books, 2003.

Redd, Steven. "The Influence of Advisers and Decision Strategies on Foreign Policy Choices: President Clinton's Decision to Use Force in Kosovo." *International Studies Perspectives* 6 (2005): 129–50.

Reeves, Richard. *President Kennedy: Profile of Power.* New York: Simon and Schuster, 1993.

Rhodes, Edward. "Do Bureaucratic Politics Matter? Some Disconfirming Findings from the Case of the U.S. Navy." *World Politics* 47 (1994): 1–41.

Ricks, Thomas. *Fiasco: The American Military Adventure in Iraq.* New York: Penguin, 2006.

Ripley, Brian. 'Psychology, Foreign Policy, and International Relations Theory,' *Political Psychology*, 14 (1993): 403-416.

Risen, James. *State of War: The Secret History of the CIA and the Bush Administration.* New York: Free Press, 2004.

Rosati, Jerel. "Developing a Systematic Decision-Making Framework: Bureaucratic Politics in Perspective." *World Politics* 33 (1981): 234–51.

Rosenau, James. "Pre-Theories and Theories of Foreign Policy." In *Approaches in Comparative and International Politics,* edited by Barry Farrell. Evanston, IL: Northwestern University Press, 1966.

Rumsfeld, Donald. "Rumsfeld's Rules: Advice on Government, Business and Life." *Wall Street Journal*, January 29, 2001.

Rusk, Dean. Oral History Interview 3, 1969, Lyndon Baines Johnson Library, Austin. TX.

Salinger, Pierre. *America Held Hostage: The Secret Negotiations.* Garden City, NY: Doubleday, 1981.

Sanger, David. Interview for the PBS Frontline documentary, *Dangerous Straits*, first aired October 18, 2001. Available at http://www.pbs.org/wgbh/pages/frontline/shows/china/interviews/sanger.html.

Sanger, David, and Steven Myers. "How Bush Had to Calm Hawks in Devising a Response to China." *New York Times*, April 13, 2001.

Scarborough, Rowan. *Rumsfeld's War: The Untold Story of America's Anti-Terrorist Commander.* Washington, DC: Regnery Publishing, 2004.

Schafer, Mark, and Stephen Walker, eds. *Beliefs and Leadership in World Politics: Methods and Applications of Operational Code Analysis.* New York: Palgrave, 2006a.

——. "Democratic Leaders and the Democratic Peace: The Operational Codes of Tony Blair and Bill Clinton." *International Studies Quarterly* 50 (2006): 561–83.

Schafer, Mark, and Scott Crichlow. *Groupthink Vs. High-Quality Decision-Making in International Relations.* New York: Columbia University Press, 2010.

Schank, Roger, and Robert Abelson. *Scripts, Plans, Goals and Understanding: An Inquiry into Human Knowledge Structures.* Hillsdale, NJ: Lawrence Erlbaum, 1977.

Schein, Edgar. *Organizational Culture and Leadership.* San Francisco: Jossey-Bass, 1985.

Schlesinger, Arthur. "Memorandum for the President," February 11, 1961, reproduced in *Politics of Illusion: The Bay of Pigs Invasion Reexamined,* edited by James Blight and Peter Kornbluh. (Boulder, CO: Lynne Rienner, 1998, 218–19.

———. *Robert F. Kennedy and His Times*. New York: Ballantine Books, 1979.

———. A *Thousand Days: John F. Kennedy in the White House*. Boston: Houghton Mifflin, 1965.

Schultzinger, Robert. *A Time For War: The United States and Vietnam, 1941–1975*. New York: Oxford University Press, 1997.

Schwartz, Steven. *Kosovo: Background to a War*. London: Anthem Press, 2000.

Sciolino, Elaine, and Ethan Bronner. "How a President, Distracted by Scandal, Entered Balkan War." *New York Times*, A1, April 18, 2004.

Shapiro, Mark, and Matthew Bonham. "Cognitive Process and Foreign Policy Decision-Making." *International Studies Quarterly* 17 (1993): 147–74.

Shelton, Hugh. *Without Hesitation: The Odyssey of an American Warrior*. New York: St. Martin's Press, 2010.

Sick, Gary. *All Fall Down: America's Tragic Encounter With Iran*. New York: Random House, 1985.

Simon, Herbert. "A Behavioral Model of Rational Choice." *Quarterly Journal of Economics* 69: (1955): 99–118.

———. *Models of Man, Social and Rational: Mathematical Essays on Rational Human Behavior in a Social Setting*. New York: Wiley, 1957.

———. *Reason in Human Affairs*. Stanford, CA: Stanford University Press, 1983.

Singer, J. David. "The Level-of-Analysis Problem in International Relations." *World Politics*, 14 (1961): 77–92.

Smith, Jeffrey. "Clark Papers Talk Politics and War." *Washington Post*, February 7, 2004, 1.

Smith, Steve. "Allison and the Cuban Missile Crisis: A Review of the Bureaucratic Politics Model of Foreign Policy Decision-Making." *Millenium* 9 (1980): 21–40.

———. "Groupthink and the Hostage Rescue Mission." *British Journal of Political Science* 15 (1985): 117–23.

———. "Policy Preferences and Bureaucratic Position: The Case of the American Hostage Rescue Mission." *International Affairs* 61 (Winter 1984/1985): 9–25.

Snyder, Richard, H. W. Bruck, and Burton Sapin. *Foreign Policy Decision-Making: An Approach to the Study of International Politics*. Glencoe, IL: Free Press, 1962.

Sorensen, Theodore. *Kennedy*. New York: Harper and Row, 1965.

———. Oral History Interview, March 26, 1964. John F. Kennedy Library, Boston, MA.

Special Operations Review Group, "Rescue Mission Report." Jimmy Carter Library, Atlanta, GA, August 1980. A copy can be found online in the National Security Archive at George Washington University at http://www.gwu.edu/~nsarchiv/NSAEBB/NSAEBB63/doc8.pdf. Stein, Arthur. "When Misperception Matters/" *World Politics* 34 (1982): 505–26.

Steinberg, Blema. *Shame and Humiliation: Presidential Decision Making on Vietnam*. .(Pittsburgh, PA: University of Pittsburgh Press, 1996.

Stern, Eric. "Probing the Plausibility of Newgroup Syndrome: Kennedy and the Bay of Pigs." In *Beyond Groupthink: Political Group Dynamics and Foreign Policy-Making*, edited by Paul 't Hart, Eric Stern, and Bengt Sundelius. Ann Arbor: University of Michigan Press, 1997. Stern, Eric, and Bengt Sundelius. "The Essence of Groupthink." *Mershon International Studies Review* 1 (1994): 101–8.

Surowiecki, James. *The Wisdom of Crowds: Why the Many Are Smarter Than the Few and How Collective Wisdom Shapes Business, Economies, Societies and Nations*. Boston: Little, Brown, 2004.

Suskind, Ron. *The One Percent Doctrine: Deep Inside America's Pursuit of its Enemies since 9/11*. New York: Simon and Schuster, 2006.

Suskind, Ron. *The Price of Loyalty: George W. Bush, the White House, and the Education of Paul O'Neill*. New York: Simon and Schuster, 2004.

't Hart, Paul. *Groupthink in Government: A Study of Small Groups and Policy Failure*. Baltimore, MD: Johns Hopkins University Press, 1990.

't Hart, Paul, Eric Stern, and Bengt Sundelius, eds. *Beyond Groupthink: Political Group Dynamics and Foreign Policy-Making*. Ann Arbor: The University of Michigan Press, 1997.

Taheri, Amir. *Nest of Spies: America's Journey to Disaster in Iran*. London: Hutchison, 1988.

Taylor, Maxwell. "Analogies (II): Was Desert One Another Bay of Pigs?" *Washington Post*, May , 1980.

———. Oral History Interview, June 21, 1964. John F. Kennedy Library, Boston, MA.

Tavris, Carol, and Elliot Aronson. *Mistakes Were Made (But Not By Me): Why We Justify Foolish Beliefs, Bad Decisions, and Hurtful Acts*. New York: Harcourt, 2007.

Tenet, George. *At the Center of The Storm: My Years at the CIA*. New York: HarperCollins, 2007.

Tetlock, Philip, Randall Peterson, Charles McGuire, Shi-jie Chang, and Peter Feld. "Assessing Political Group Dynamics: A Test of the Groupthink Model." *Journal of Personality and Social Psychology* 63 (1992): 403–25.

Tetlock, Philip, and Aaron Belkin, eds. *Counterfactual Thought Experiments in World Politics*. Princeton, NJ: Princeton University Press, 1996.

Thagard, Paul, and Cameron Shelley., "Emotional Analogies and Analogical Inference." In *The Analogical Mind: Perspectives from Cognitive Science,* edited by Dedre Gentner, Keith Holyoak, and Boicho Kokinov, (335–62. Cambridge, MA: MIT Press, 2001.

Thompson, Robert Smith. *The Missiles of October: The Declassified Story of John F. Kennedy and the Cuban Missile Crisis*. New York: Simon and Schuster, 1992.

Thomson, James., "How Could Vietnam Happen? An Autopsy." *Atlantic Monthly*, April 1968.

New York Times. The Tower Commission Report: The Full Text of the President's Special Review Board. Bantam Books/Times Books, 1987.

Turner, Stansfield. *Burn Before Reading: Presidents, CIA Directors, and Secret Intelligence*. New York: Hyperion, 2005.

———. *Terrorism and Democracy*. Boston: Houghton Mifflin, 1991.

Tversky, Amos, and Daniel Kahneman. "Judgment Under Uncertainty: Heuristics and Biases. *Science* 185 (1974): 1124–31.

Vance, Cyrus. *Hard Choices: Four Critical Years in Managing America's Foreign Policy*. New York: Simon and Schuster, 1983.

Vandenbroucke, Lucien. "Anatomy of a Failure: The Decision to Land at the Bay of Pigs." *Political Science Quarterly* 99 (1984): 471–91.

———. *Perilous Options: Special Operations as an Instrument of U.S. Foreign Policy*. Oxford: Oxford University Press, 1993.

Vertzberger, Yaacov. *The World in Their Minds: Information Processing, Cognition and Perception in Foreign Policy Decisionmaking*. Stanford, CA; Stanford University Press, 1990.

Wagner, Richard. "The Earliest Pioneer: Ralph K. White." *Peace and Conflict* 10 (2004): 313–15.

Wallach, Michael, Nathan Kogan, and Daryl Bem. "Diffusion of Responsibility and Level of Risk Taking in Groups." *Journal of Abnormal and Social Psychology* 68 (1964): 263–74.

Walsh, Lawrence. *Firewall: The Iran-Contra Conspiracy and Cover-Up.* New York: W. W. Norton, 1997.

Wang, Chi. *George W. Bush and China: Policies, Problems, and Partnership.* New York: Lexington Books, 2009.

Welch, David. "The Organizational Process and Bureaucratic Politics Paradigms." *International Security* 17 (1992):112–46.

Wendt, Alexander. "The Agent/Structure Problem in International Relations Theory." *International Organization* 41 (1987): 335–70.

Wessells, Michael, Michael Roe, and Susan McKay. "Pioneers in Peace Psychology: Ralph K. White." *Peace and Conflict* 10 (2004): 317–34.

West, Larry. Interview with the author, Orlando, FL, November 15, 2006.

Westen, Drew. *The Political Brain: The Role of Emotion in Deciding the Fate of the Nation.* New York: Public Affairs, 2007.

White, Mark. *The Kennedys and Cuba: The Declassified Documentary History.* Chicago: Ivan Dee, 1999.

White, Ralph. "Empathizing with the Soviet Government." In *Psychology and the Prevention of Nuclear War: A Book of Readings.* New York: New York University Press, 1986.

———. *Fearful Warriors: A Psychological Profile of U.S.-Soviet Relations.* New York: Free Press, 1984.

———. "Misperception and War." *Peace and Conflict* 10 (2004): 399–409.

White, Ralph. *Nobody Wanted War: Misperception in Vietnam and Other Wars.* Garden City, NY: Doubleday, 1968.

Wilkerson, Lawrence. Interview with the author. Orlando, FL, November 8, 2007.

Wilson, Joseph. *The Politics of Truth: Inside the Lies that Led to War and Betrayed my Wife's CIA Identity.* New York: Carroll and Graf, 2004.

Woodward, Bob. *Bush at War.* New York: Simon and Schuster, 2002.

———. *Plan of Attack.* New York; Simon and Schuster, 2004.

———. *State of Denial: Bush at War,* Part 3. New York: Simon and Schuster, 2006.

———. *Veil: The Secret Wars of the CIA 1981-1987.* New York: Simon and Schuster, 1987.

———. *The War Within: A Secret White House History, 2006-200.* New York: Simon and Schuster, 2009.

Woodward, Susan. *Balkan Tragedy: Chaos and Dissolution after the Cold War.* Washington D.C.: The Brookings Institution, 1995.

Wyatt, Edward. "Clark Denies Being pressed to End Kosovo War Early." *New York Times,* February 8, 2004,N21.

Wyden, Peter. *Bay of Pigs: The Untold Story.* New York: Simon and Schuster, 1979.

Yetiv, Steve. *Explaining Foreign Policy: U.S. Decision-Making and the Persian Gulf War.* Baltimore, MD: Johns Hopkins University Press, 2004.

Index

CPSIA information can be obtained
at www.ICGtesting.com
Printed in the USA
BVHW040533150819
555913BV00004B/11/P